S·A
Special A

KEI & ALISA

6 YEARS OLD

Volume 13

Story & Art by

Maki Minami

STORY

★At the tender age of 6, carpenter's daughter Hikari Hanazono suffered her first loss to the wealthy Kei Takishima in a wrestling match. Now the hardworking Hikari has followed Kei to the most elite school for the rich just to beat him! I call this story "Overthrow Takishima! Rise Above Perpetual Second Place!!" It's the story of Hikari's sweat, tears and passion, with a little bit of love thrown in!

★ Hikari finally admitted her feelings to Kei, so now they're dating. ♥ Kei forges ahead with his plan to convince his grandfather to allow him to stay with Hikari. But just when Kei has everything practically wrapped up, his grandfather squashes his dreams and demands that Kei marry the daughter of an important client.

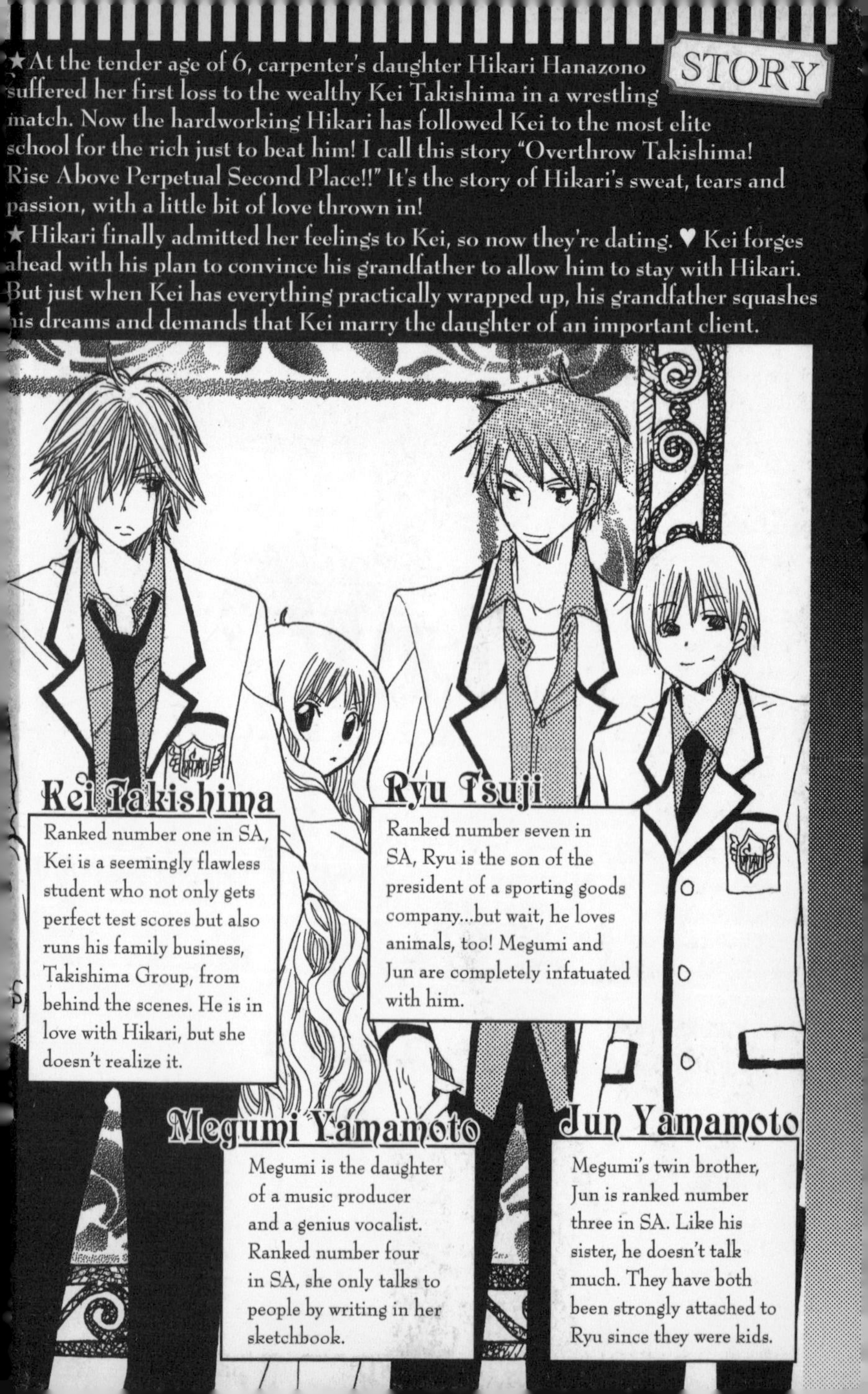

Kei Takishima

Ranked number one in SA, Kei is a seemingly flawless student who not only gets perfect test scores but also runs his family business, Takishima Group, from behind the scenes. He is in love with Hikari, but she doesn't realize it.

Ryu Tsuji

Ranked number seven in SA, Ryu is the son of the president of a sporting goods company...but wait, he loves animals, too! Megumi and Jun are completely infatuated with him.

Megumi Yamamoto

Megumi is the daughter of a music producer and a genius vocalist. Ranked number four in SA, she only talks to people by writing in her sketchbook.

Jun Yamamoto

Megumi's twin brother, Jun is ranked number three in SA. Like his sister, he doesn't talk much. They have both been strongly attached to Ryu since they were kids.

S·A CHARACTERS

Hikari goes to an elite school called Hakusenkan High School. This school divides each grade level into groups A through F, according to the students' test scores. Group A includes only the top seven students in each class. Then the top seven students from all grades' A groups are put into a group called Special A, which is considered much higher than all others. Known as SA, they are "the elite among the elite."

What is "Special A"?

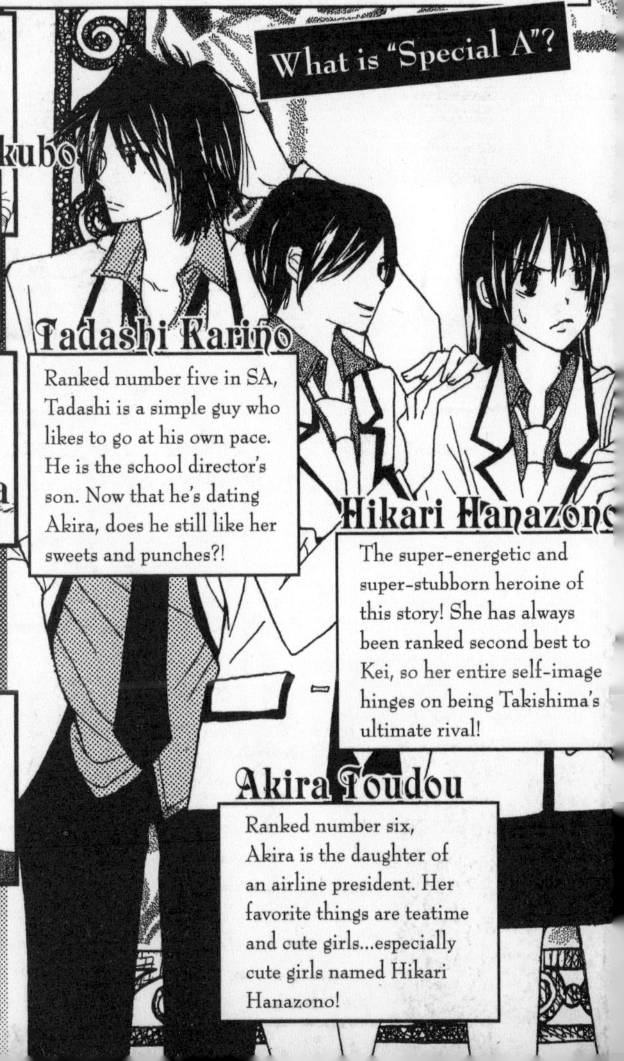

Sakura Ushikubo

Sakura's family set her up with Kei via a matchmaker. Right now she is head-over-heels for Jun.♥

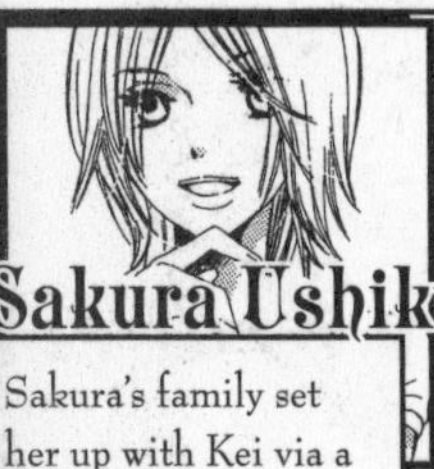

Yahiro Saiga

A childhood friend of Kei and Akira. His family is richer than the Takishima Group.

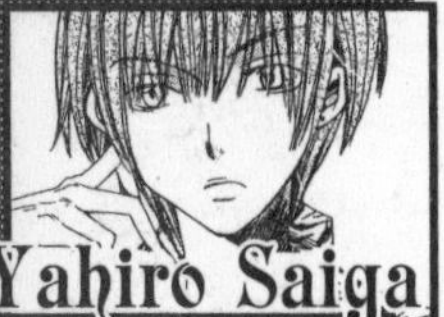

Aoi Ogata

Aoi is an apprentice to Kei's grandfather, but he completely lives for Kei.

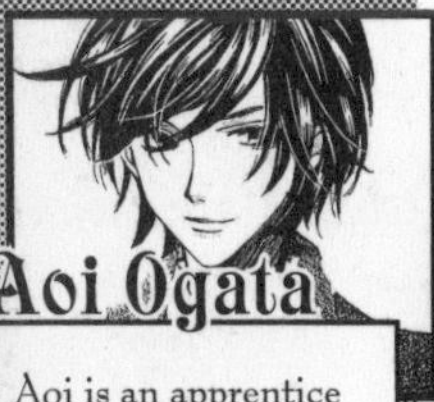

Tadashi Karino

Ranked number five in SA, Tadashi is a simple guy who likes to go at his own pace. He is the school director's son. Now that he's dating Akira, does he still like her sweets and punches?!

Hikari Hanazono

The super-energetic and super-stubborn heroine of this story! She has always been ranked second best to Kei, so her entire self-image hinges on being Takishima's ultimate rival!

Akira Toudou

Ranked number six, Akira is the daughter of an airline president. Her favorite things are teatime and cute girls...especially cute girls named Hikari Hanazono!

Contents

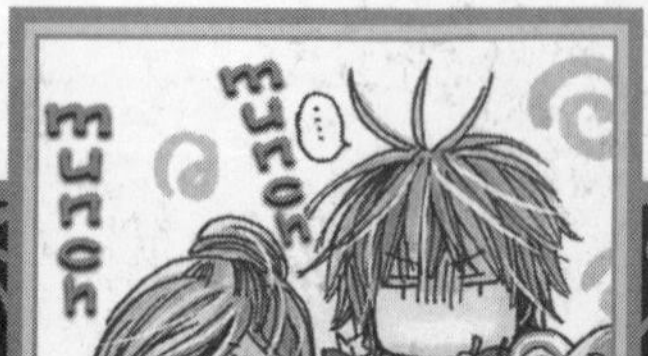

munch
...
munch
For Alisa
FOOD

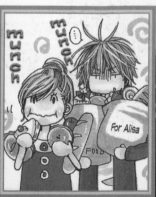

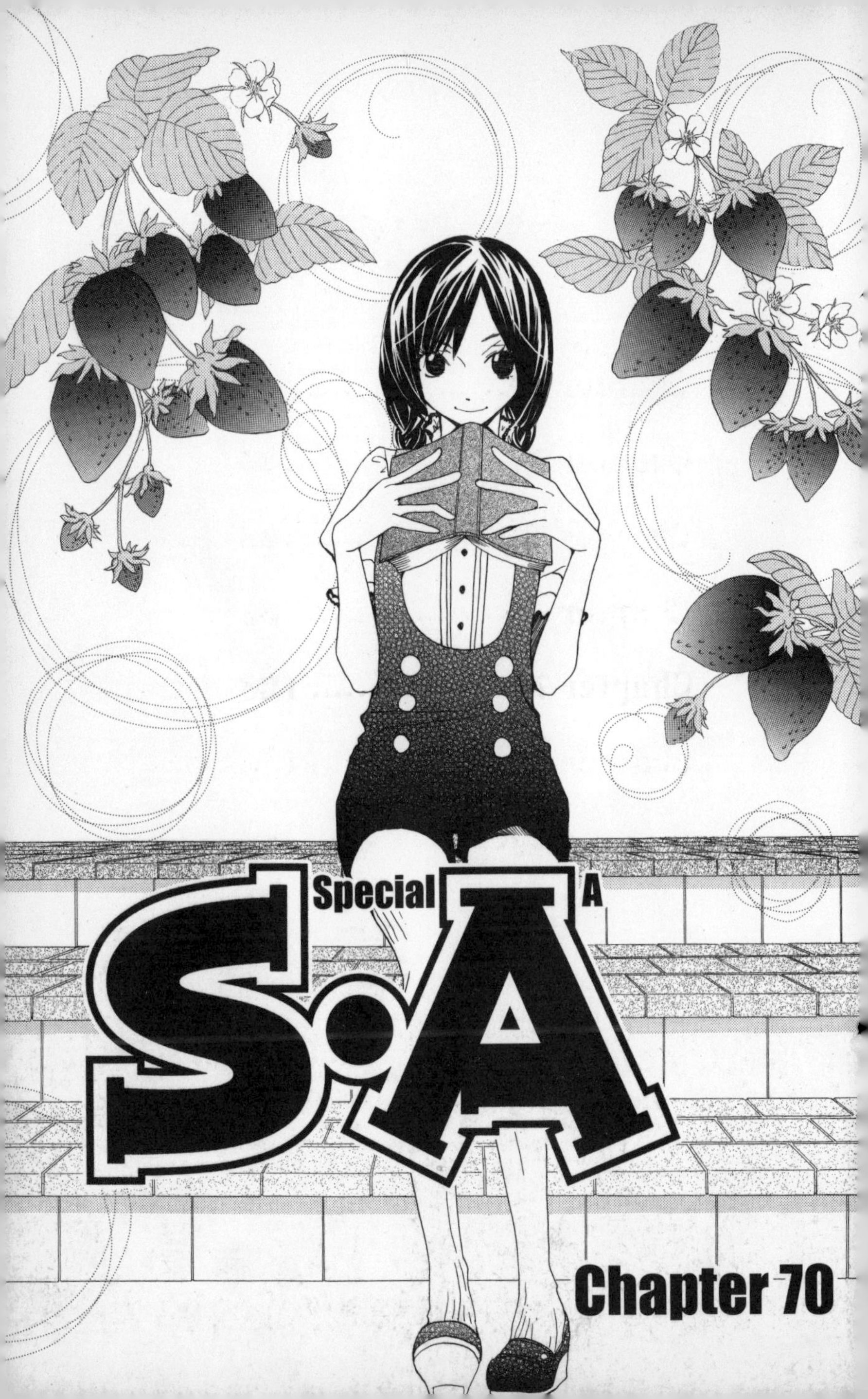
Special A
S.A
Chapter 70

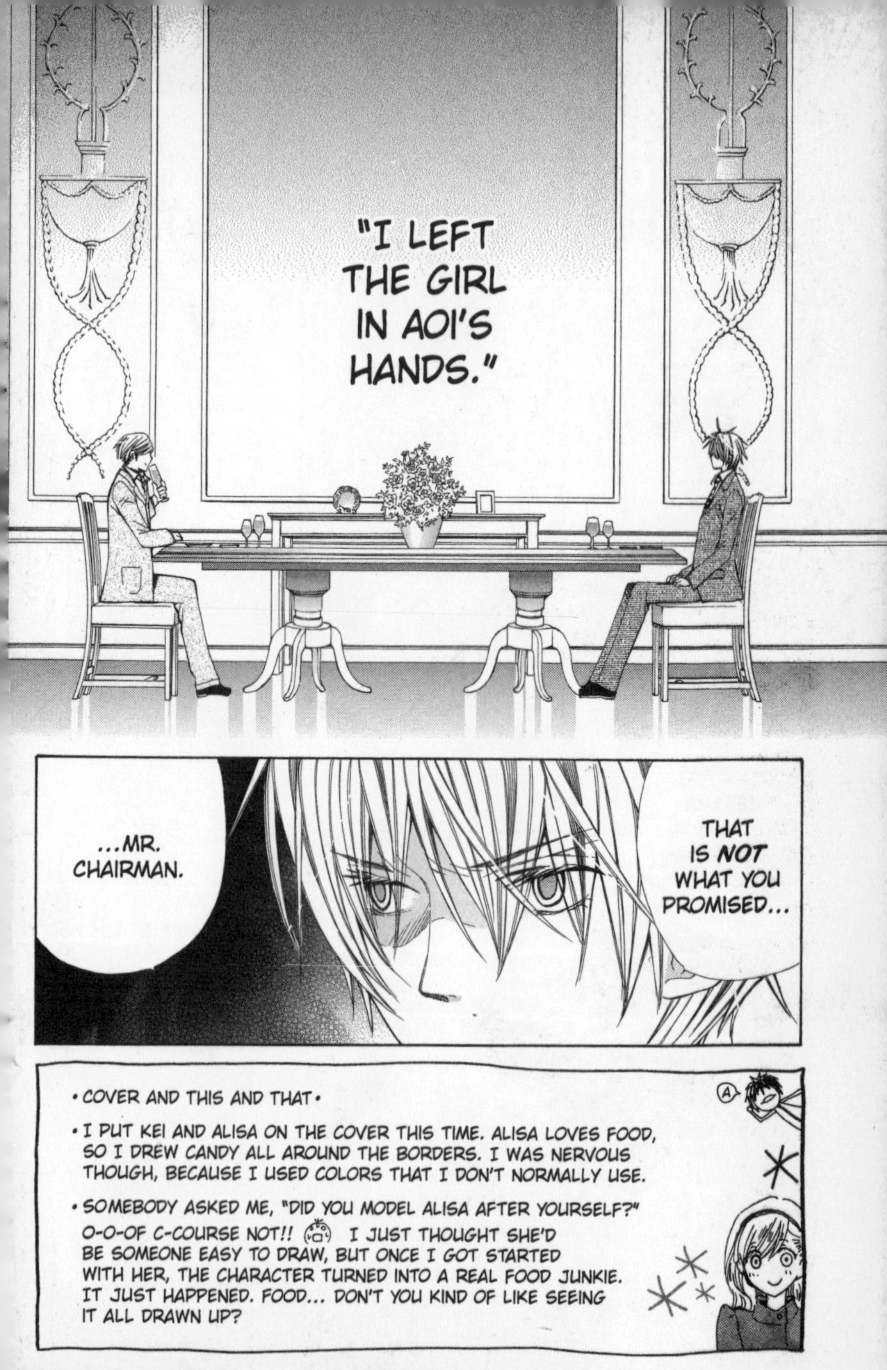
"I LEFT THE GIRL IN AOI'S HANDS."
THAT IS ***NOT*** WHAT YOU PROMISED...
...MR. CHAIRMAN.

• COVER AND THIS AND THAT •

• I PUT KEI AND ALISA ON THE COVER THIS TIME. ALISA LOVES FOOD, SO I DREW CANDY ALL AROUND THE BORDERS. I WAS NERVOUS THOUGH, BECAUSE I USED COLORS THAT I DON'T NORMALLY USE.

• SOMEBODY ASKED ME, "DID YOU MODEL ALISA AFTER YOURSELF?" O-O-OF C-COURSE NOT!! I JUST THOUGHT SHE'D BE SOMEONE EASY TO DRAW, BUT ONCE I GOT STARTED WITH HER, THE CHARACTER TURNED INTO A REAL FOOD JUNKIE. IT JUST HAPPENED. FOOD... DON'T YOU KIND OF LIKE SEEING IT ALL DRAWN UP?

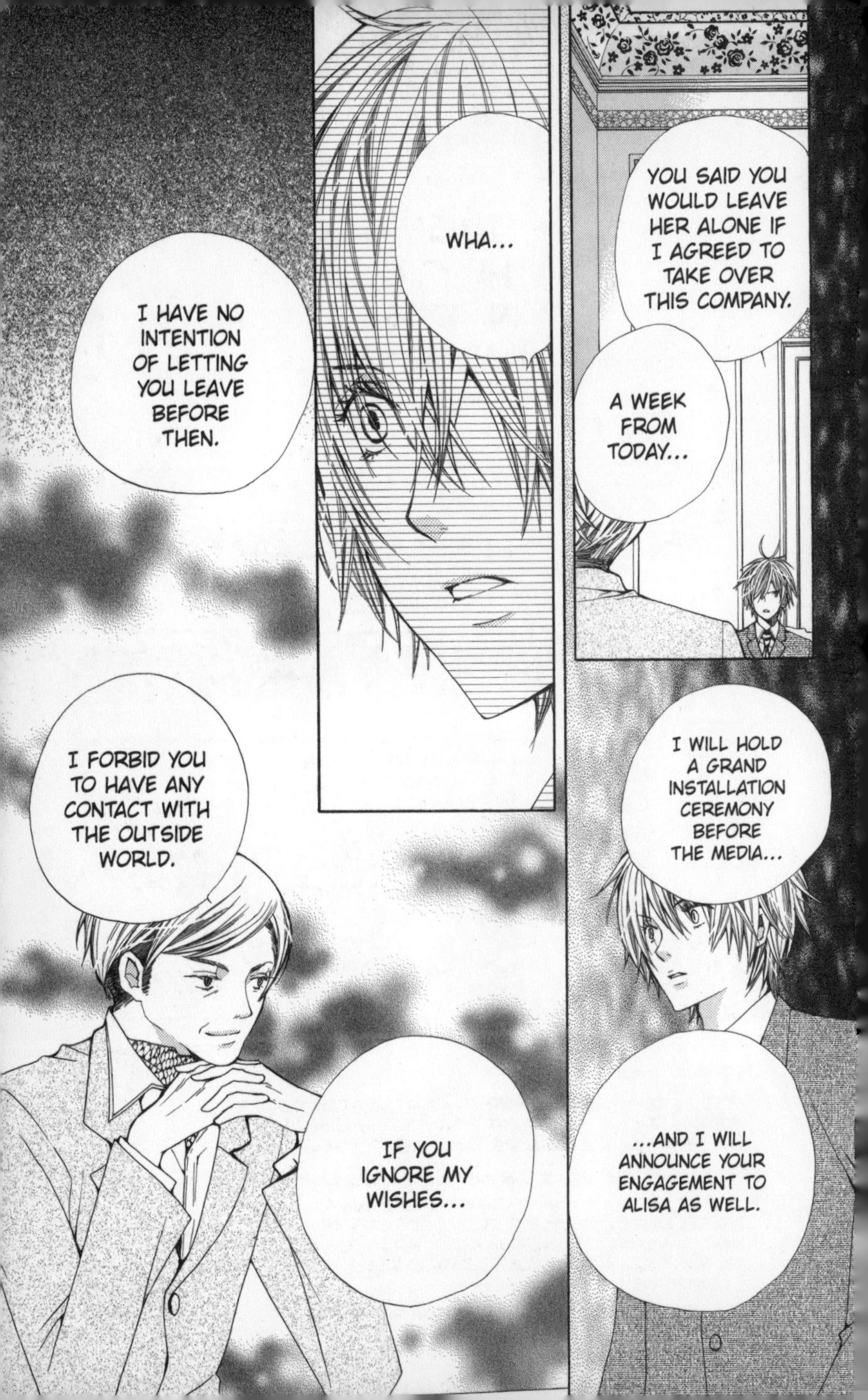
YOU SAID YOU WOULD LEAVE HER ALONE IF I AGREED TO TAKE OVER THIS COMPANY.
A WEEK FROM TODAY...
I WILL HOLD A GRAND INSTALLATION CEREMONY BEFORE THE MEDIA...
...AND I WILL ANNOUNCE YOUR ENGAGEMENT TO ALISA AS WELL.
WHA...
I HAVE NO INTENTION OF LETTING YOU LEAVE BEFORE THEN.
I FORBID YOU TO HAVE ANY CONTACT WITH THE OUTSIDE WORLD.
IF YOU IGNORE MY WISHES...

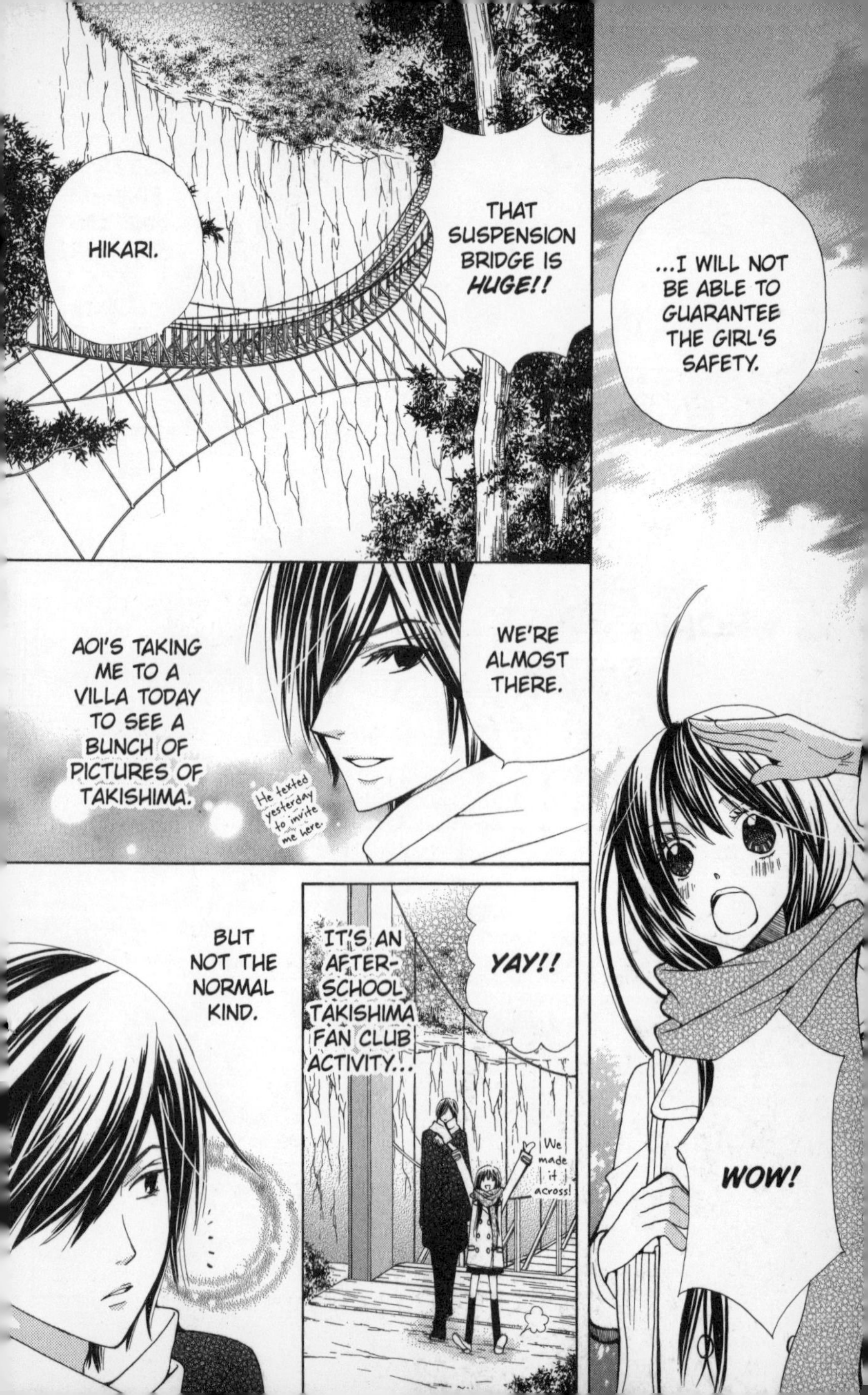
...I WILL NOT BE ABLE TO GUARANTEE THE GIRL'S SAFETY.
WOW!
THAT SUSPENSION BRIDGE IS *HUGE!!*
HIKARI.
WE'RE ALMOST THERE.
AOI'S TAKING ME TO A VILLA TODAY TO SEE A BUNCH OF PICTURES OF TAKISHIMA.
He texted yesterday to invite me here.
YAY!!
IT'S AN AFTER-SCHOOL TAKISHIMA FAN CLUB ACTIVITY...
We made it across!
BUT NOT THE NORMAL KIND.

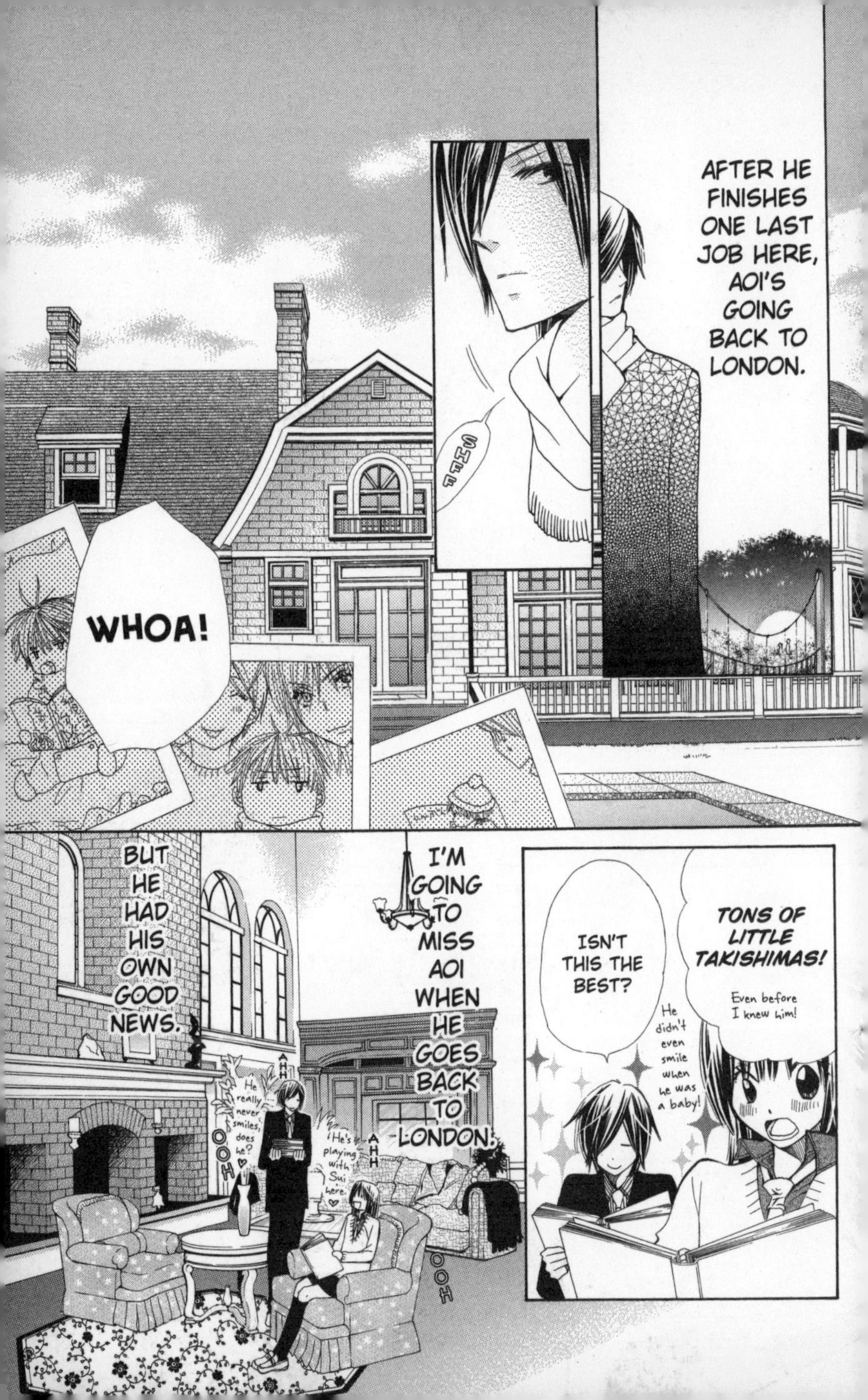
AFTER HE FINISHES ONE LAST JOB HERE, AOI'S GOING BACK TO LONDON.
SHFF
WHOA!
TONS OF LITTLE TAKISHIMAS!
Even before I knew him!
ISN'T THIS THE BEST?
He didn't even smile when he was a baby!
I'M GOING TO MISS AOI WHEN HE GOES BACK TO LONDON.
BUT HE HAD HIS OWN GOOD NEWS.
AHH
He really... never smiles, does he? ♥
OOH
He's playing with Sui here.
AHH
OOH

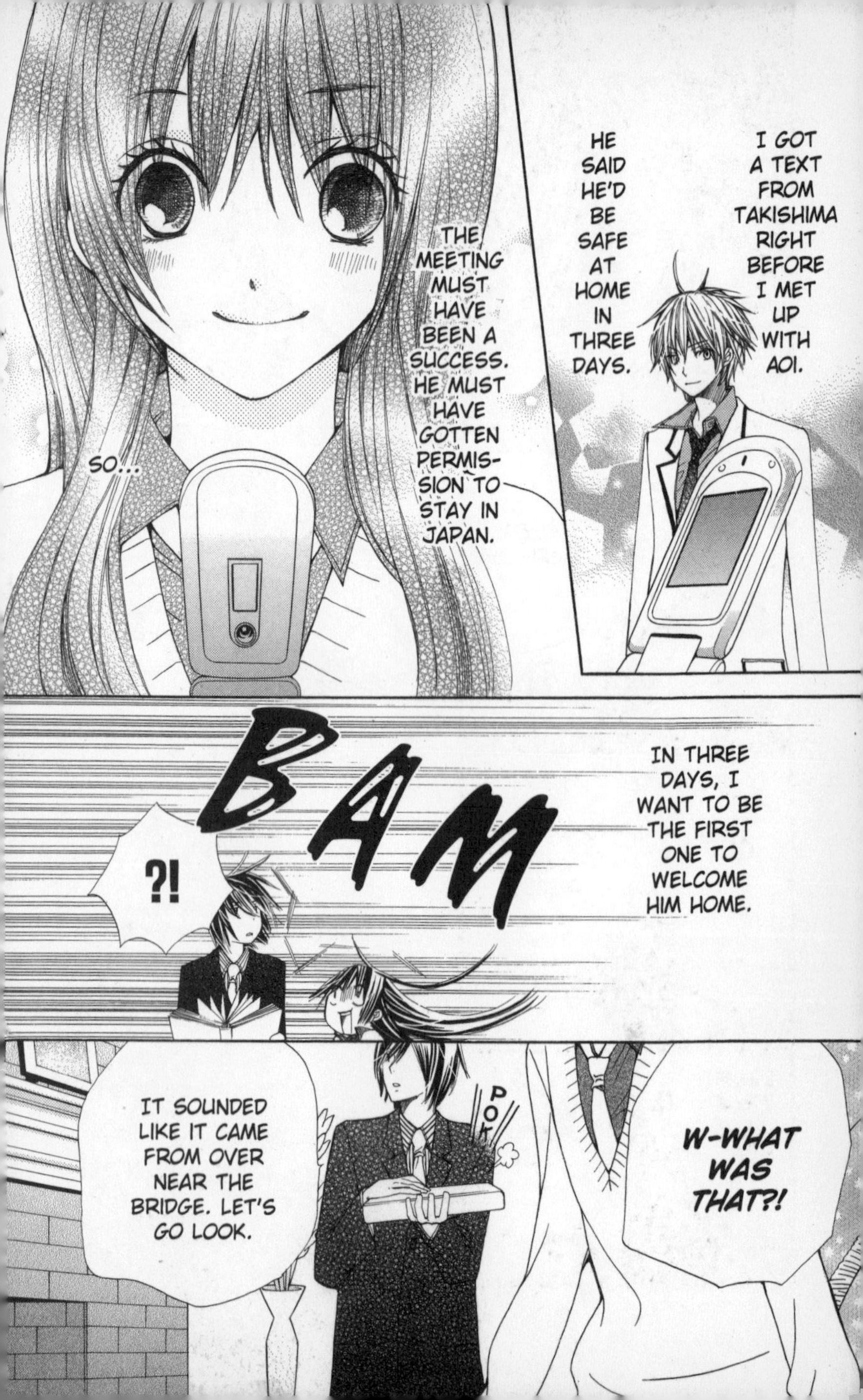
I GOT A TEXT FROM TAKISHIMA RIGHT BEFORE I MET UP WITH AOI.
HE SAID HE'D BE SAFE AT HOME IN THREE DAYS.
THE MEETING MUST HAVE BEEN A SUCCESS. HE MUST HAVE GOTTEN PERMISSION TO STAY IN JAPAN.
SO...
IN THREE DAYS, I WANT TO BE THE FIRST ONE TO WELCOME HIM HOME.
BAM
?!
W-WHAT WAS THAT?!
POK
IT SOUNDED LIKE IT CAME FROM OVER NEAR THE BRIDGE. LET'S GO LOOK.

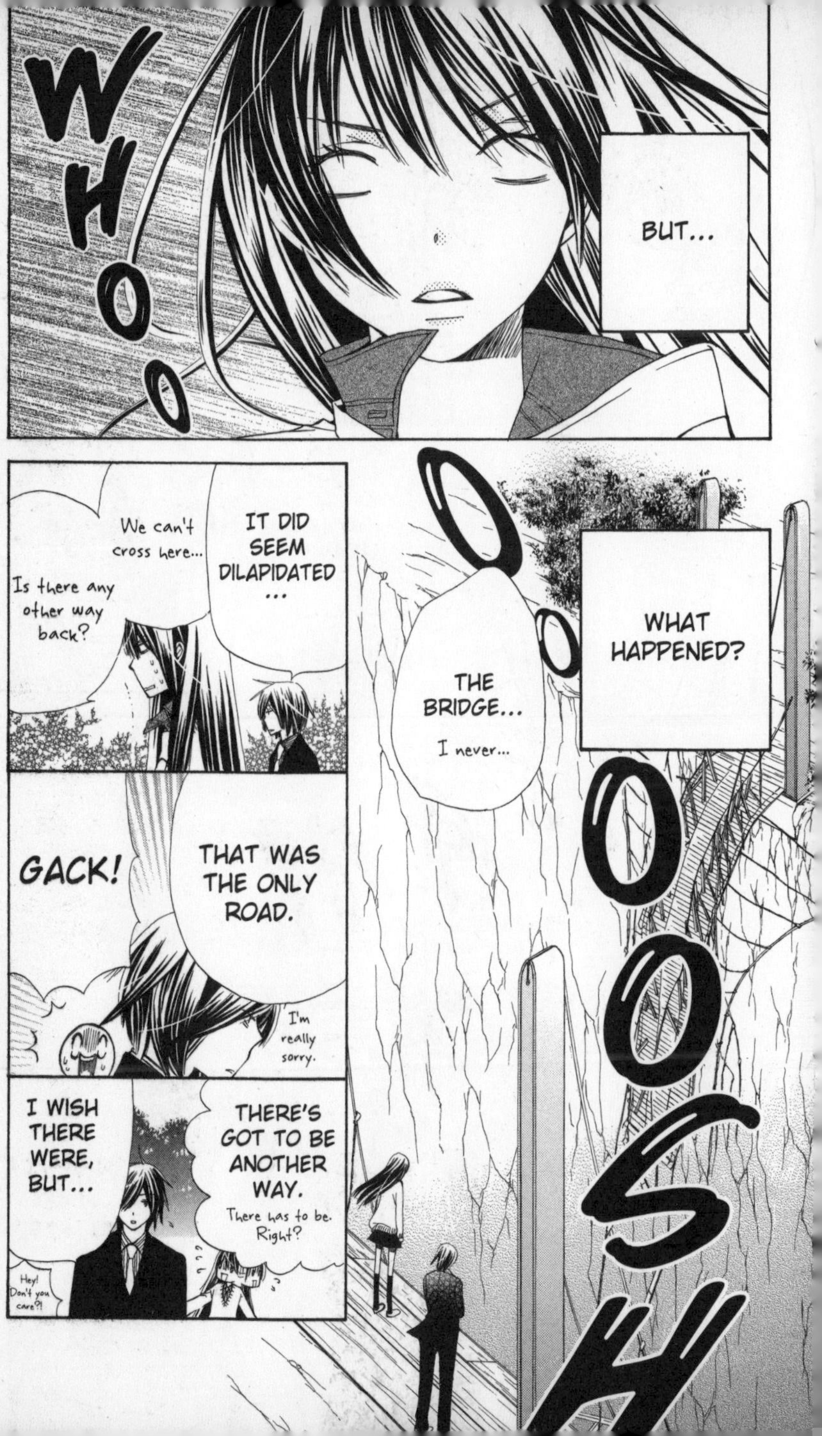
BUT...
WHOO
WHAT HAPPENED?
THE BRIDGE...
I never...
OOOOSH
IT DID SEEM DILAPIDATED...
We can't cross here...
Is there any other way back?
THAT WAS THE ONLY ROAD.
I'm really sorry.
GACK!
THERE'S GOT TO BE ANOTHER WAY.
There has to be. Right?
I WISH THERE WERE, BUT...
Hey! Don't you care?!

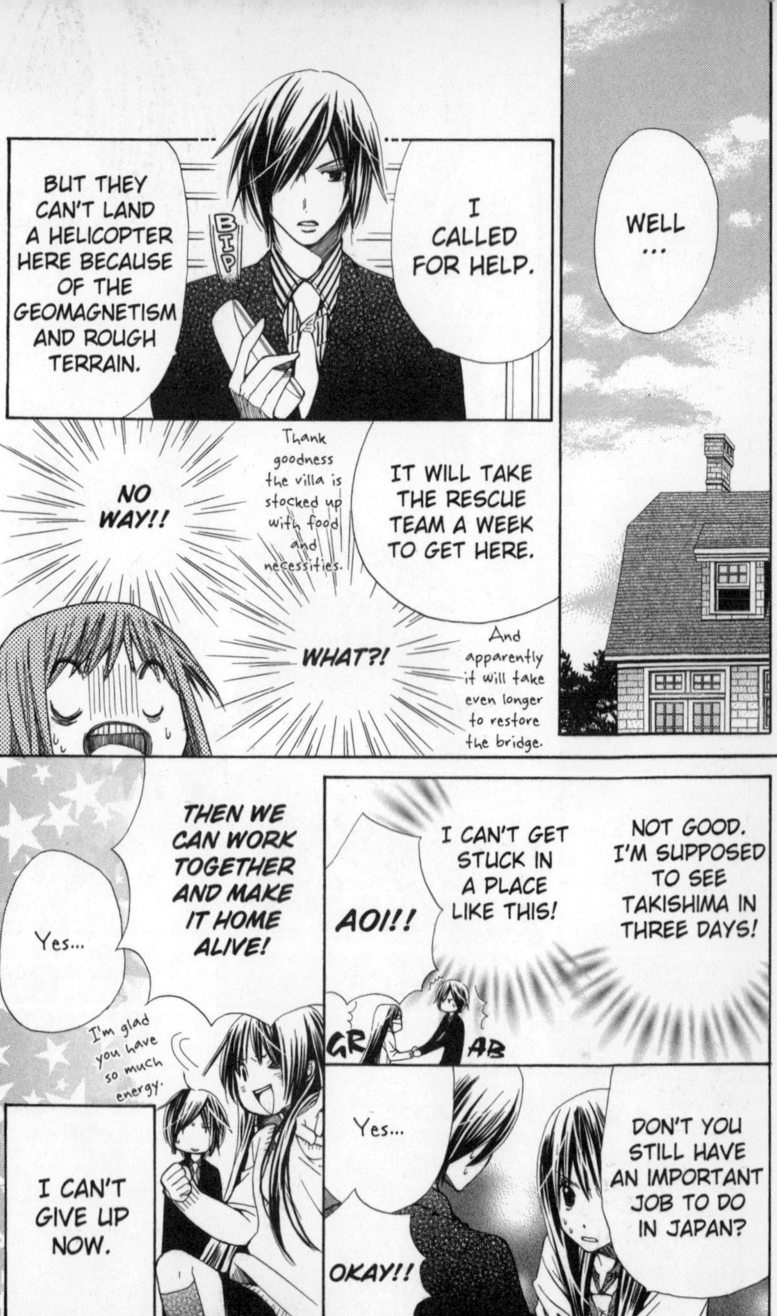
WELL ...
I CALLED FOR HELP.
BUT THEY CAN'T LAND A HELICOPTER HERE BECAUSE OF THE GEOMAGNETISM AND ROUGH TERRAIN.
BIP
IT WILL TAKE THE RESCUE TEAM A WEEK TO GET HERE.
Thank goodness the villa is stocked up with food and necessities.
And apparently it will take even longer to restore the bridge.
WHAT?!
NO WAY!!
NOT GOOD. I'M SUPPOSED TO SEE TAKISHIMA IN THREE DAYS!
I CAN'T GET STUCK IN A PLACE LIKE THIS!
AOI!!
GRAB
DON'T YOU STILL HAVE AN IMPORTANT JOB TO DO IN JAPAN?
Yes...
OKAY!!
THEN WE CAN WORK TOGETHER AND MAKE IT HOME ALIVE!
Yes...
I'm glad you have so much energy.
I CAN'T GIVE UP NOW.

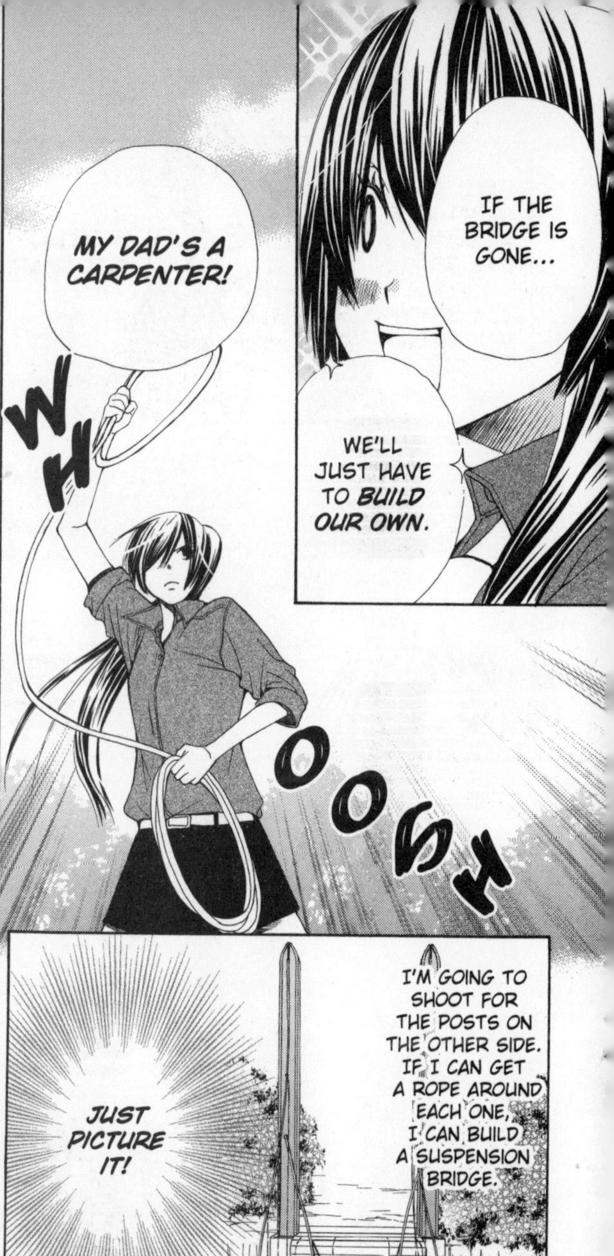
IF THE BRIDGE IS GONE...
WE'LL JUST HAVE TO BUILD OUR OWN.
MY DAD'S A CARPENTER!
WHOOOSH
I'M GOING TO SHOOT FOR THE POSTS ON THE OTHER SIDE. IF I CAN GET A ROPE AROUND EACH ONE, I CAN BUILD A SUSPENSION BRIDGE.
JUST PICTURE IT!

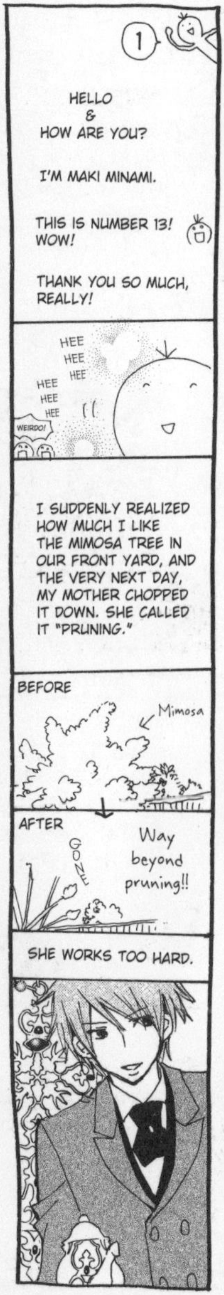
1
HELLO & HOW ARE YOU?
I'M MAKI MINAMI.
THIS IS NUMBER 13! WOW!
THANK YOU SO MUCH, REALLY!
HEE HEE HEE
HEE HEE HEE
WEIRDO!
I SUDDENLY REALIZED HOW MUCH I LIKE THE MIMOSA TREE IN OUR FRONT YARD, AND THE VERY NEXT DAY, MY MOTHER CHOPPED IT DOWN. SHE CALLED IT "PRUNING."
BEFORE
Mimosa
AFTER
GONE
Way beyond pruning!!
SHE WORKS TOO HARD.

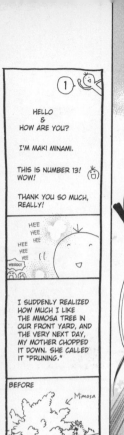

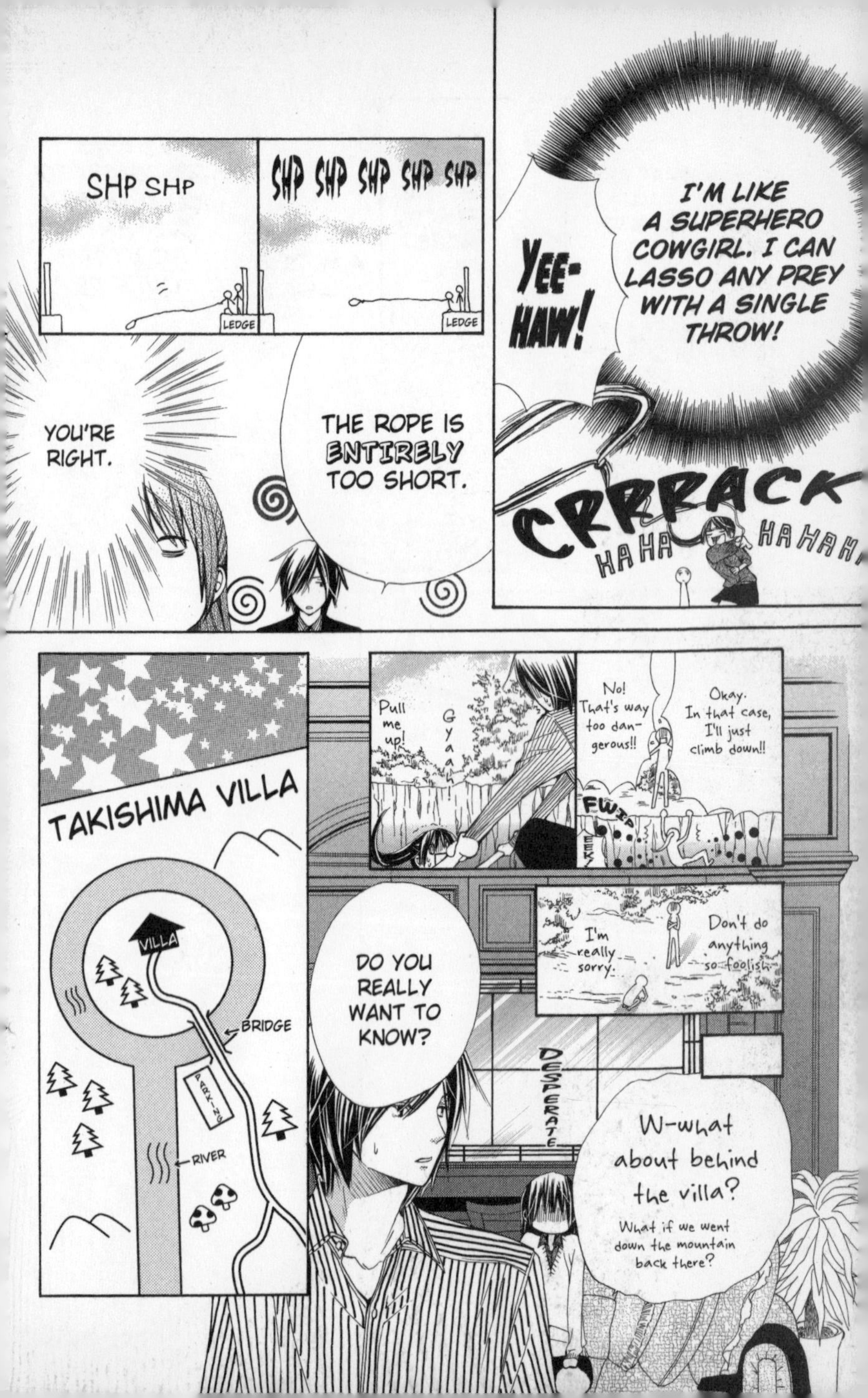
YEE-HAW!
I'M LIKE A SUPERHERO COWGIRL. I CAN LASSO ANY PREY WITH A SINGLE THROW!
CRRRACK
HA HA
HA HA HA
SHP SHP SHP SHP SHP
LEDGE
SHP SHP
LEDGE
THE ROPE IS ENTIRELY TOO SHORT.
YOU'RE RIGHT.
Okay. In that case, I'll just climb down!!
No! That's way too dangerous!!
FWIP
EEK
Pull me up!
Gyaaah
Don't do anything so foolish.
I'm really sorry.
W-what about behind the villa?
What if we went down the mountain back there?
DESPERATE
DO YOU REALLY WANT TO KNOW?
TAKISHIMA VILLA
VILLA
BRIDGE
PARKING
RIVER

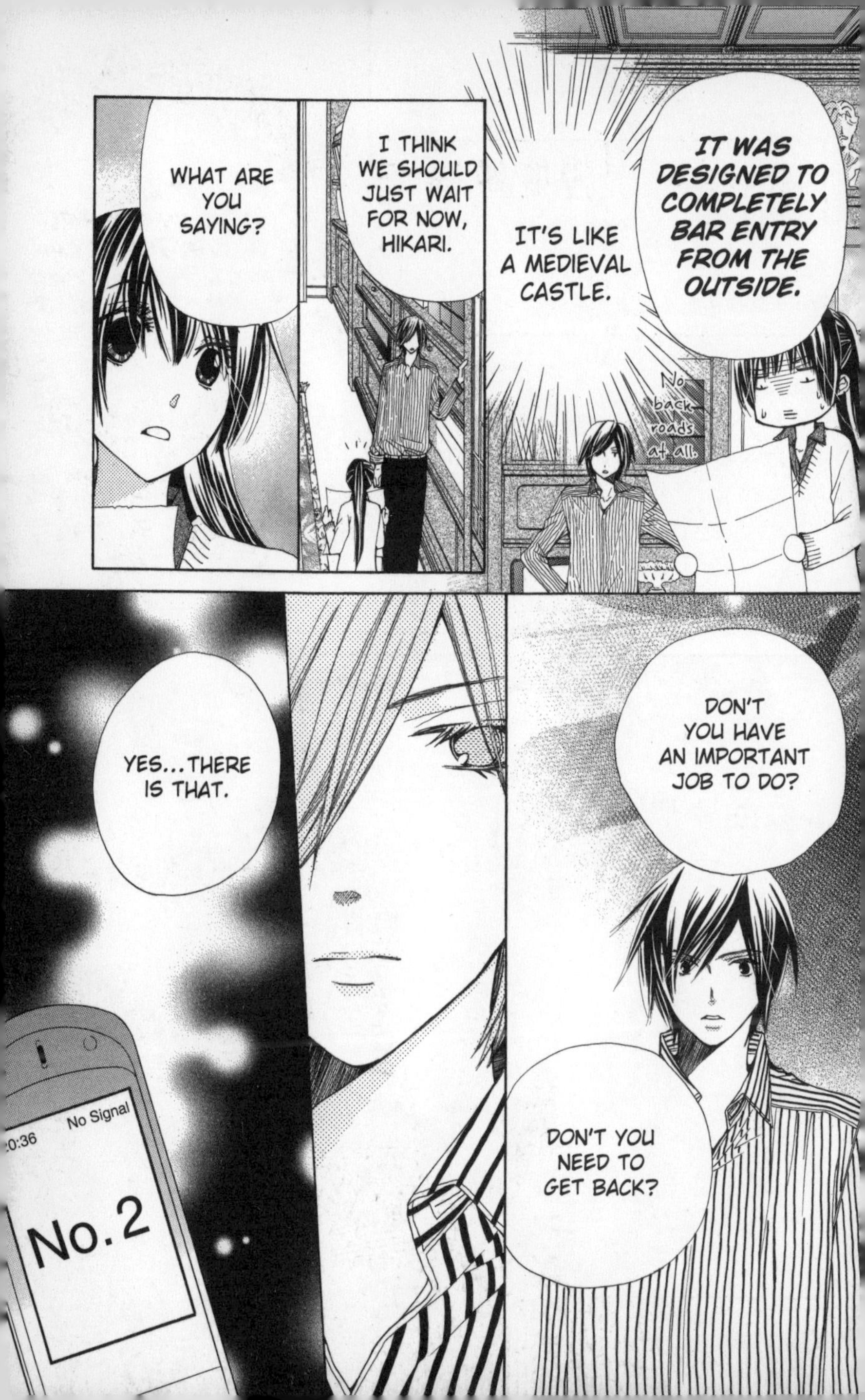
IT WAS DESIGNED TO COMPLETELY BAR ENTRY FROM THE OUTSIDE.
IT'S LIKE A MEDIEVAL CASTLE.
No back roads at all.
I THINK WE SHOULD JUST WAIT FOR NOW, HIKARI.
WHAT ARE YOU SAYING?
DON'T YOU HAVE AN IMPORTANT JOB TO DO?
DON'T YOU NEED TO GET BACK?
YES... THERE IS THAT.
No Signal
0:36
No.2

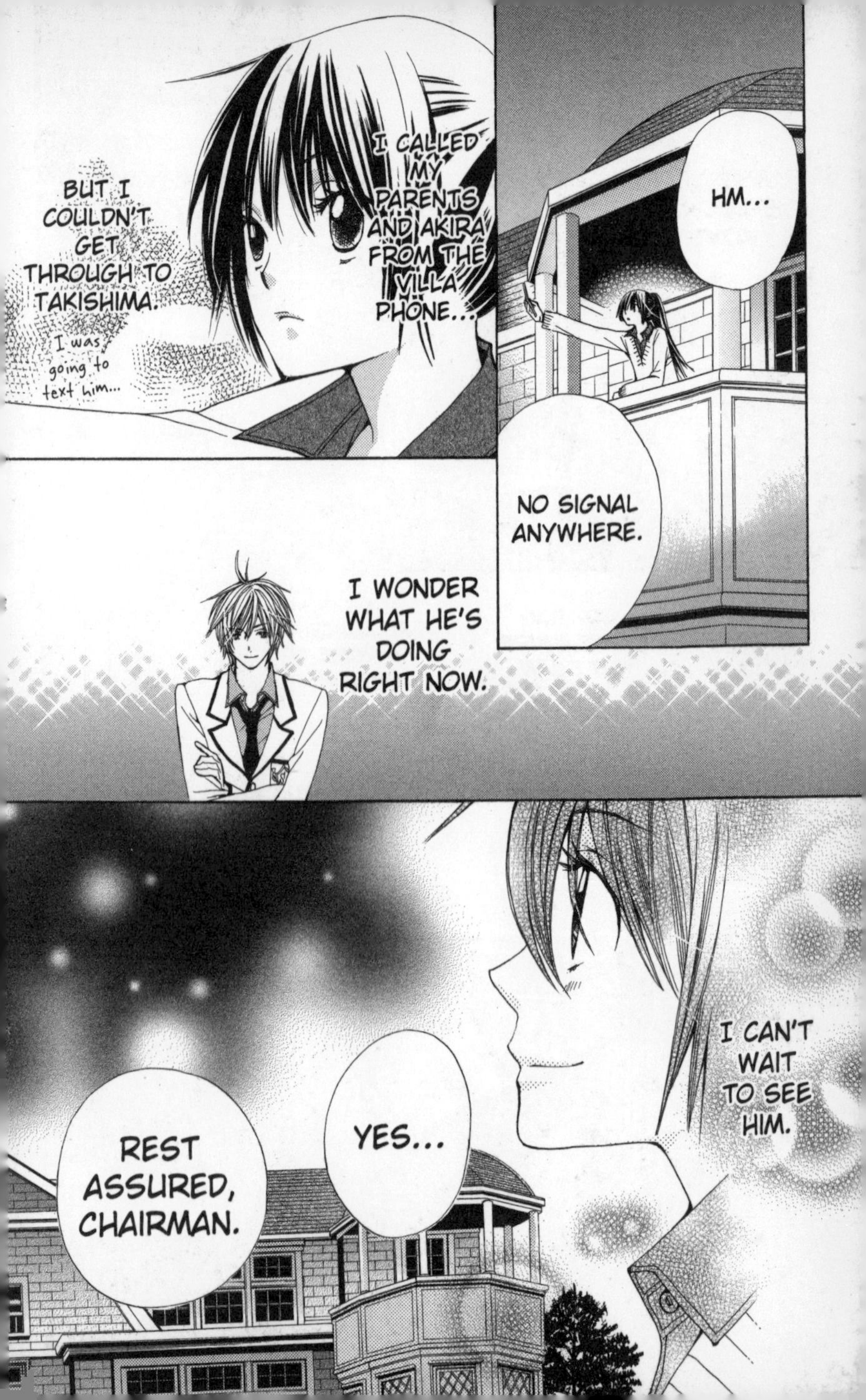
HM...
NO SIGNAL ANYWHERE.
I CALLED MY PARENTS AND AKIRA FROM THE VILLA PHONE...
BUT I COULDN'T GET THROUGH TO TAKISHIMA.
I was going to text him...
I WONDER WHAT HE'S DOING RIGHT NOW.
I CAN'T WAIT TO SEE HIM.
YES...
REST ASSURED, CHAIRMAN.

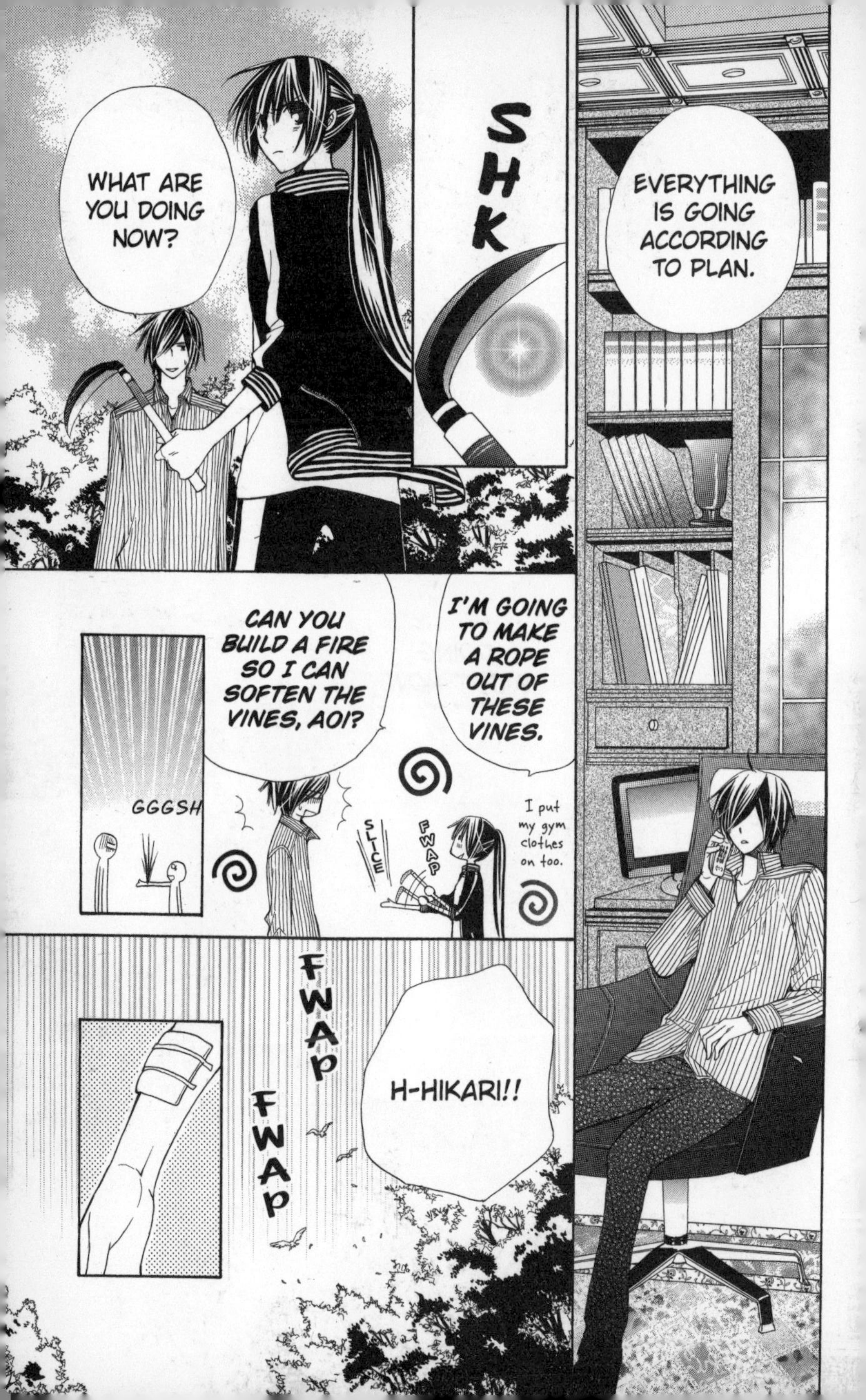
EVERYTHING IS GOING ACCORDING TO PLAN.
SHK
WHAT ARE YOU DOING NOW?
I'M GOING TO MAKE A ROPE OUT OF THESE VINES.
CAN YOU BUILD A FIRE SO I CAN SOFTEN THE VINES, AOI?
I put my gym clothes on too.
FWAP
SLICE
GGGSH
FWAP
FWAP
H-HIKARI!!

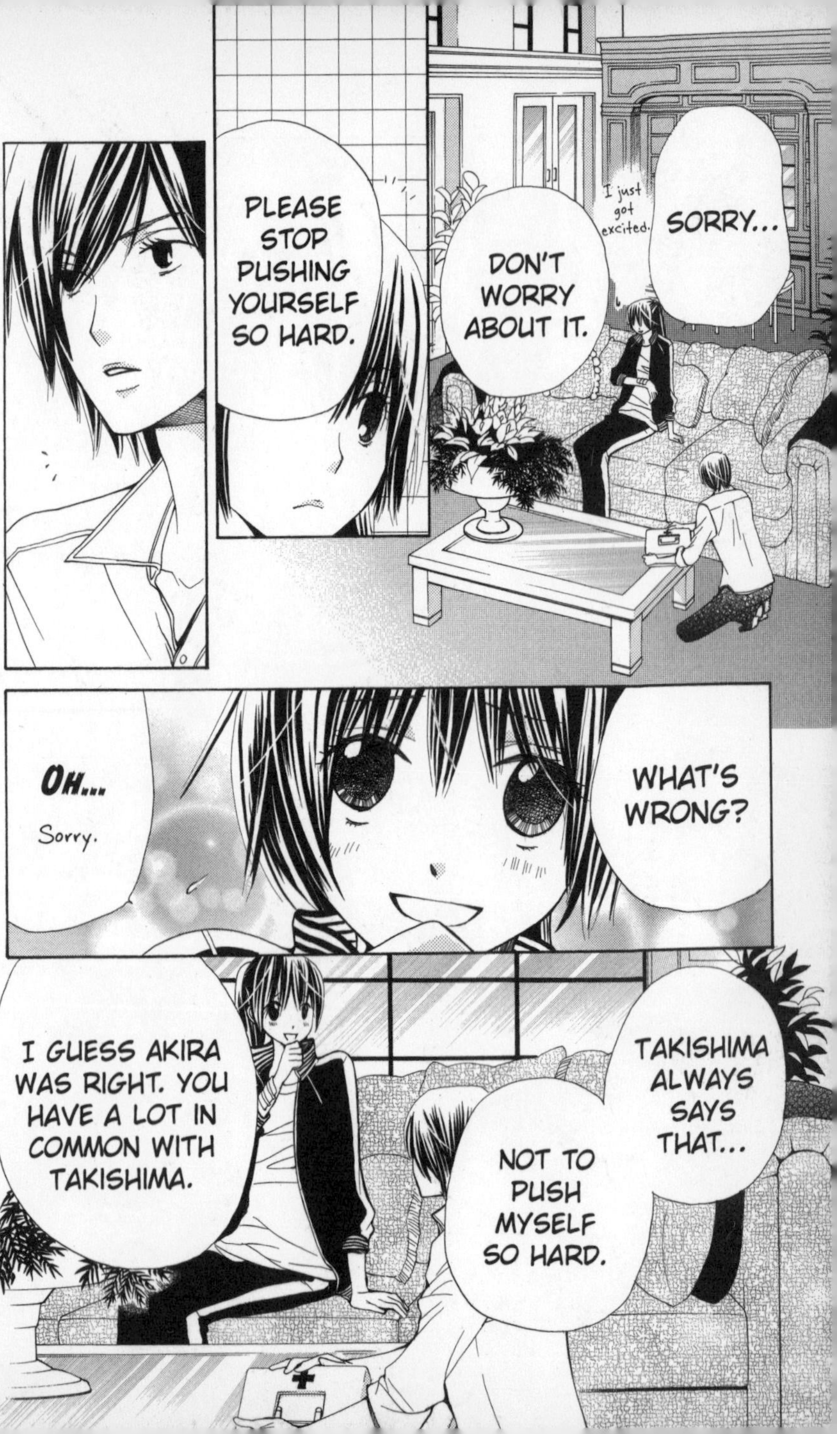
SORRY...
I just got excited.
DON'T WORRY ABOUT IT.
PLEASE STOP PUSHING YOURSELF SO HARD.
WHAT'S WRONG?
OH...
Sorry.
TAKISHIMA ALWAYS SAYS THAT...
NOT TO PUSH MYSELF SO HARD.
I GUESS AKIRA WAS RIGHT. YOU HAVE A LOT IN COMMON WITH TAKISHIMA.

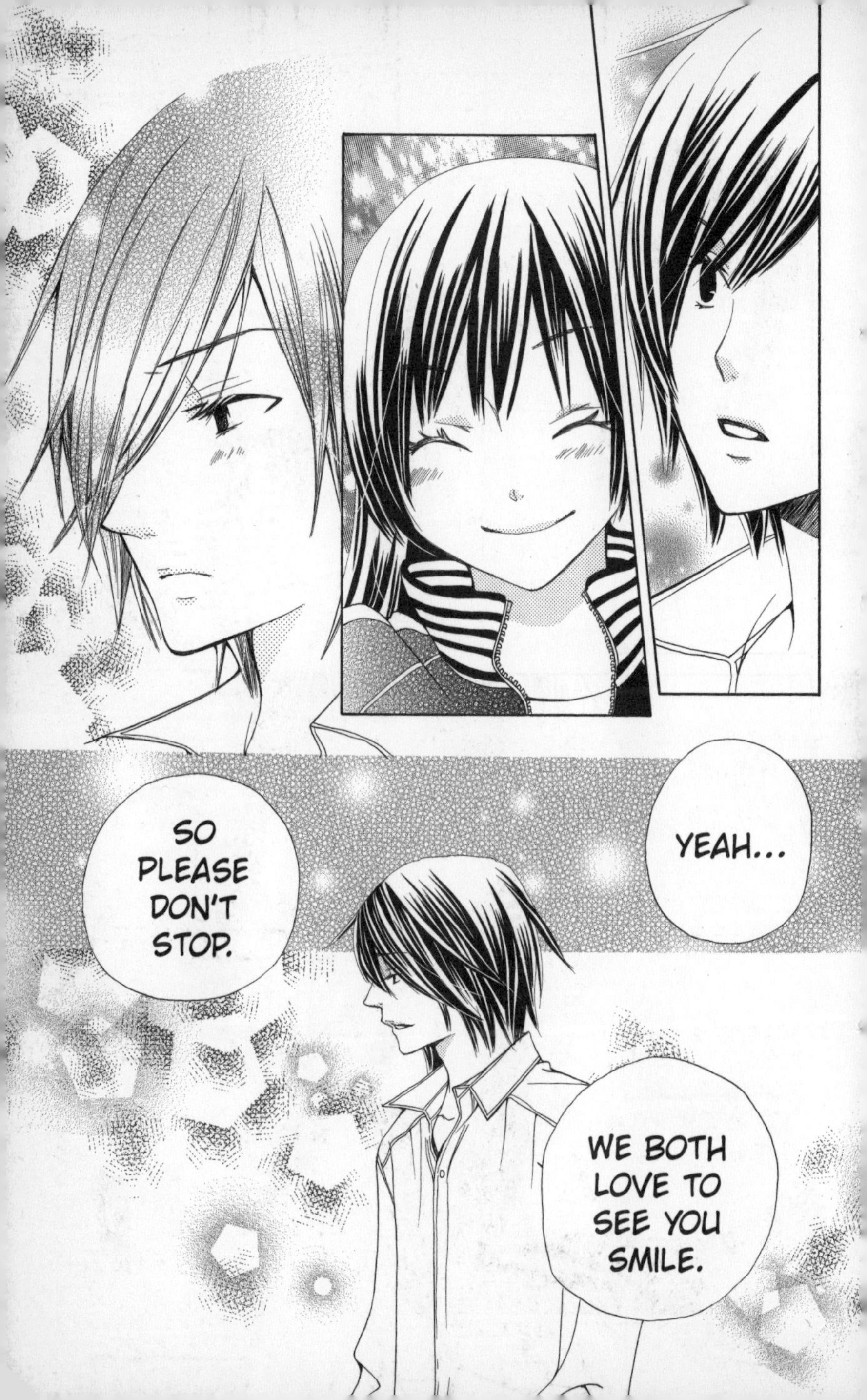
YEAH...
SO PLEASE DON'T STOP.
WE BOTH LOVE TO SEE YOU SMILE.

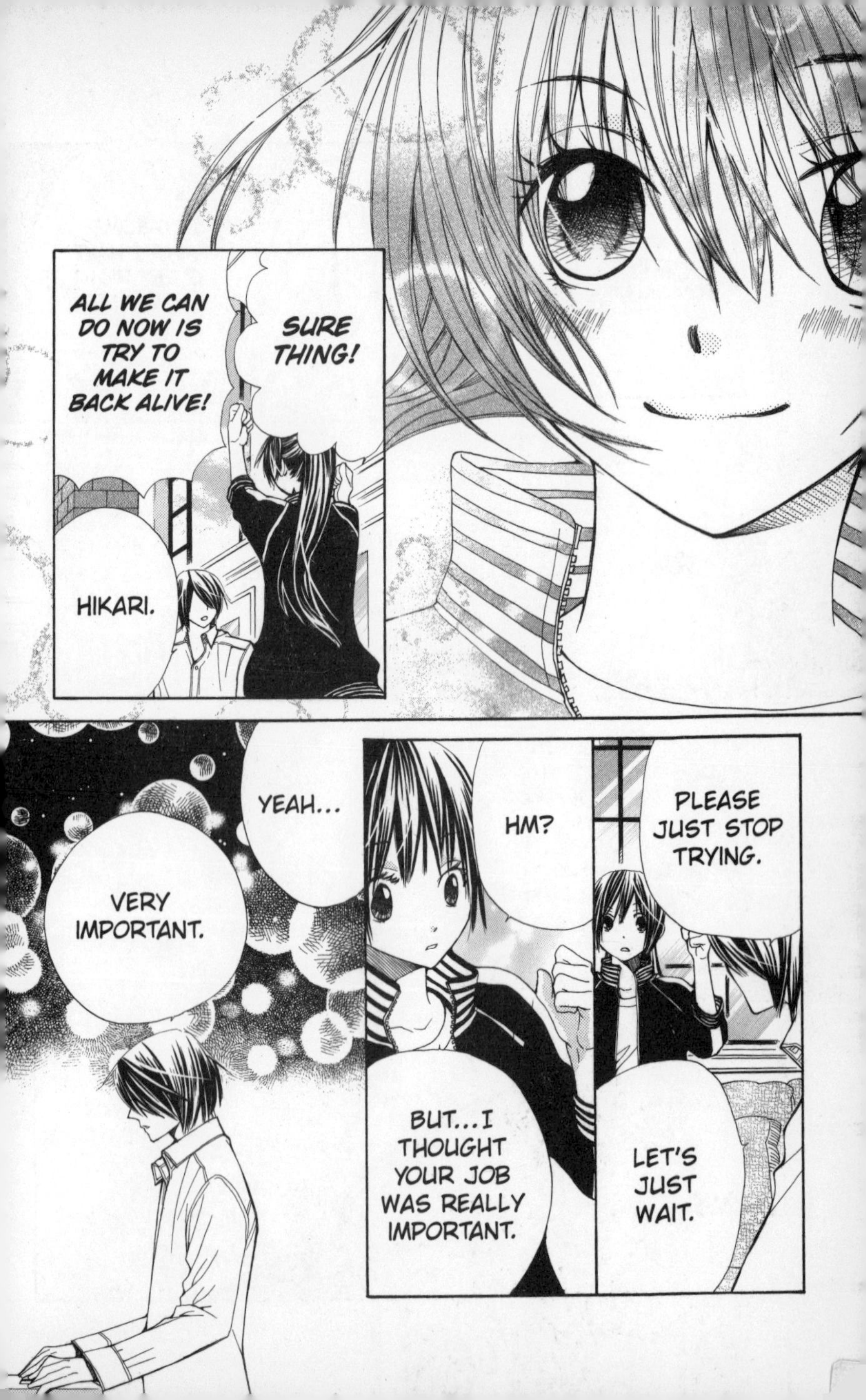
ALL WE CAN DO NOW IS TRY TO MAKE IT BACK ALIVE!
SURE THING!
HIKARI.
PLEASE JUST STOP TRYING.
LET'S JUST WAIT.
HM?
BUT...I THOUGHT YOUR JOB WAS REALLY IMPORTANT.
YEAH...
VERY IMPORTANT.

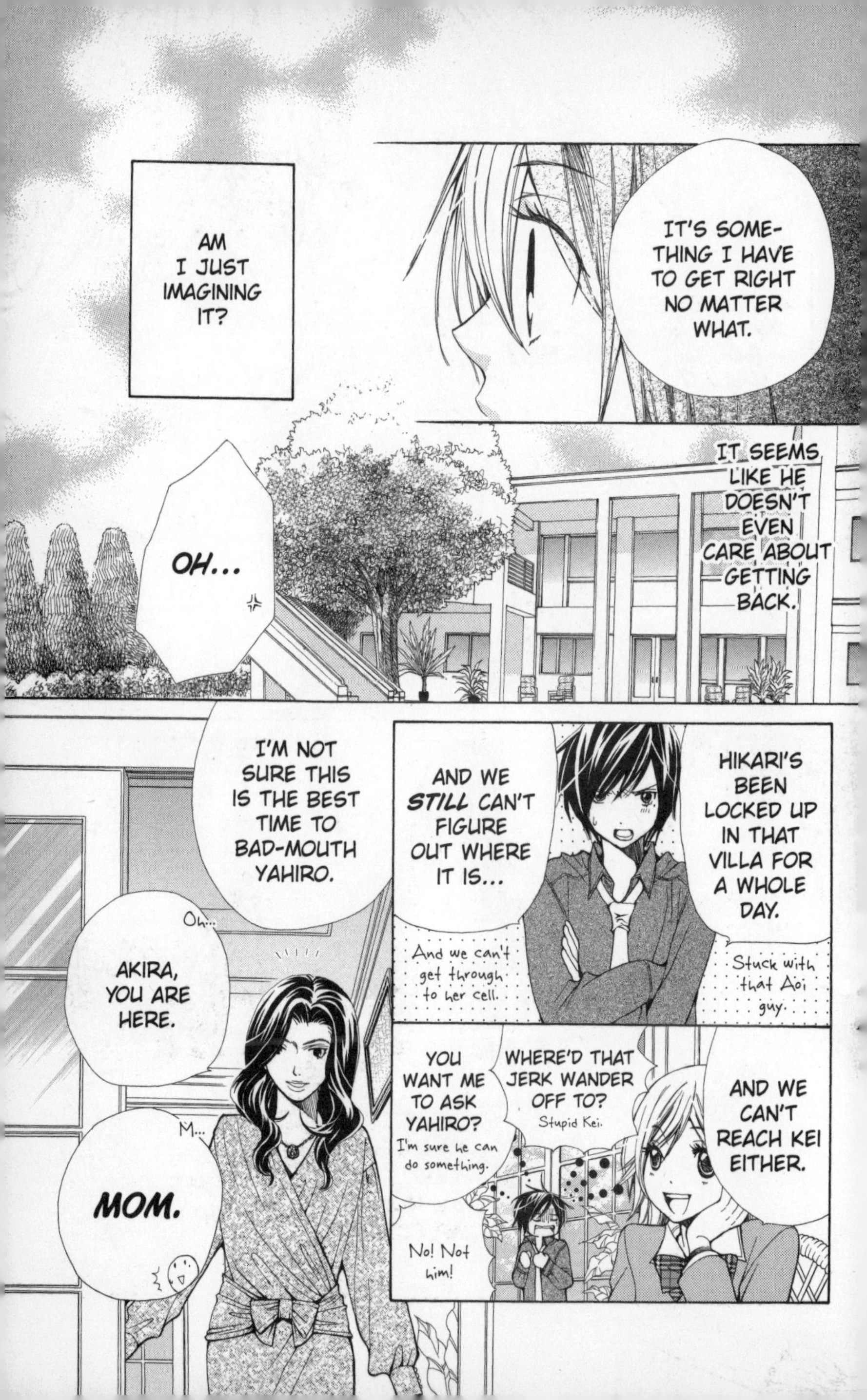
IT'S SOME-THING I HAVE TO GET RIGHT NO MATTER WHAT.
AM I JUST IMAGINING IT?
IT SEEMS LIKE HE DOESN'T EVEN CARE ABOUT GETTING BACK.
OH...
HIKARI'S BEEN LOCKED UP IN THAT VILLA FOR A WHOLE DAY.
Stuck with that Aoi guy.
AND WE STILL CAN'T FIGURE OUT WHERE IT IS...
And we can't get through to her cell.
AND WE CAN'T REACH KEI EITHER.
WHERE'D THAT JERK WANDER OFF TO?
Stupid Kei.
YOU WANT ME TO ASK YAHIRO?
I'm sure he can do something.
No! Not him!
I'M NOT SURE THIS IS THE BEST TIME TO BAD-MOUTH YAHIRO.
Oh...
AKIRA, YOU ARE HERE.
M...
MOM.

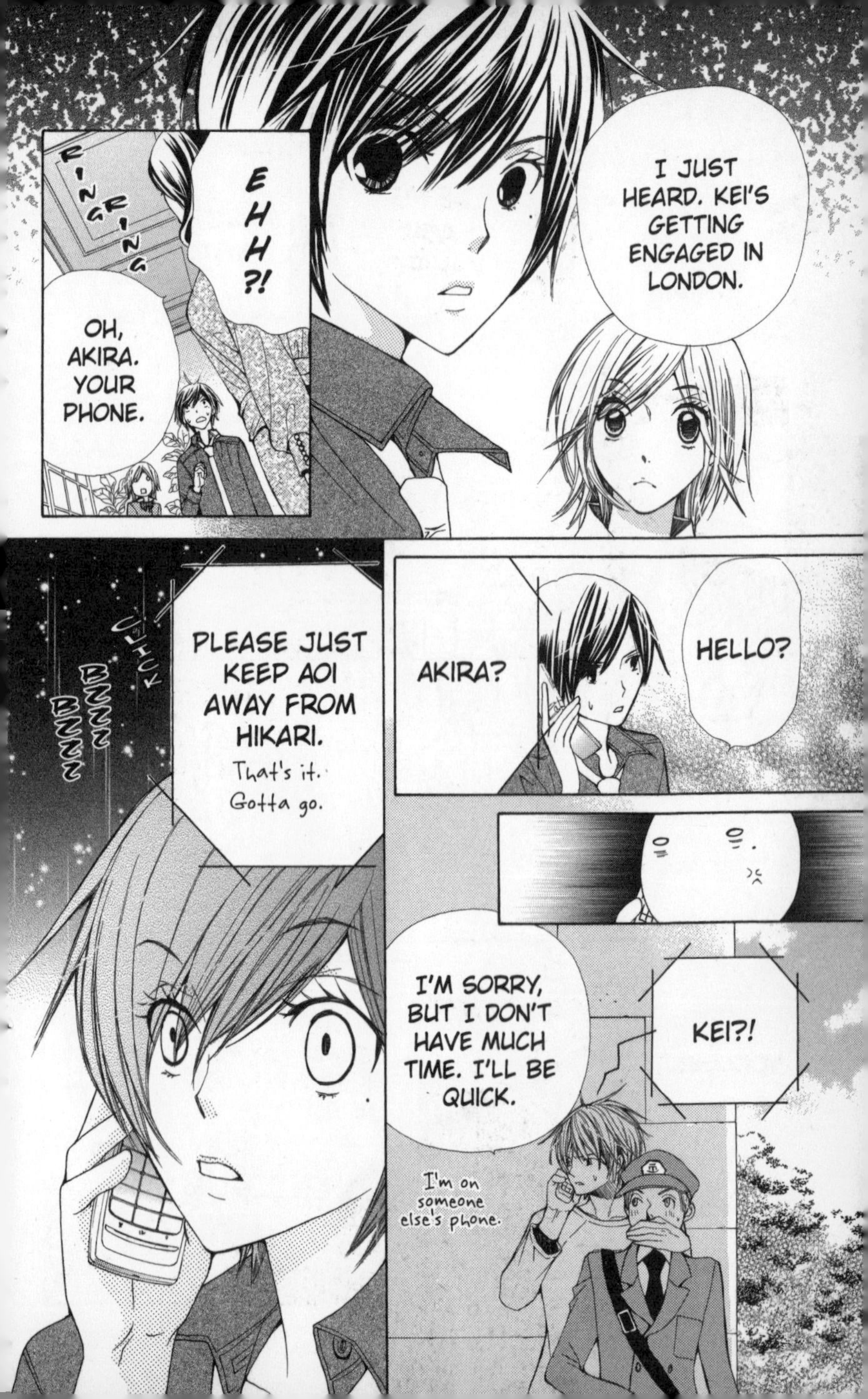
I JUST HEARD. KEI'S GETTING ENGAGED IN LONDON.
RING RING
EHHH?!
OH, AKIRA. YOUR PHONE.
HELLO?
AKIRA?
KEI?!
I'M SORRY, BUT I DON'T HAVE MUCH TIME. I'LL BE QUICK.
I'm on someone else's phone.
PLEASE JUST KEEP AOI AWAY FROM HIKARI.
That's it. Gotta go.
CLICK
BZZZ
BZZZ

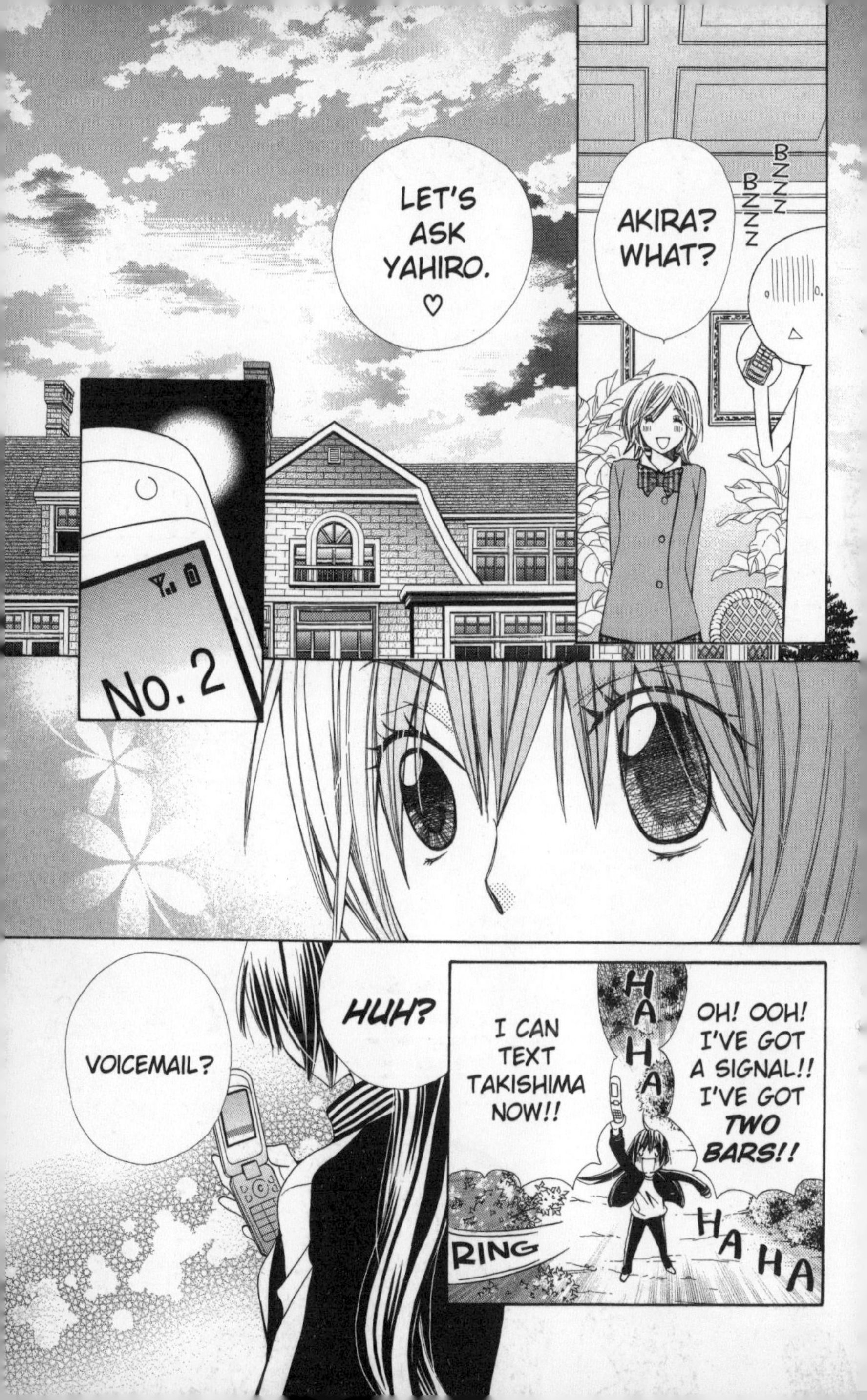
BZZZ BZZZ
AKIRA? WHAT?
LET'S ASK YAHIRO. ♡
No. 2
OH! OOH! I'VE GOT A SIGNAL!! I'VE GOT TWO BARS!!
HA HA HA
I CAN TEXT TAKISHIMA NOW!!
HA HA HA HA
RING
HUH?
VOICEMAIL?

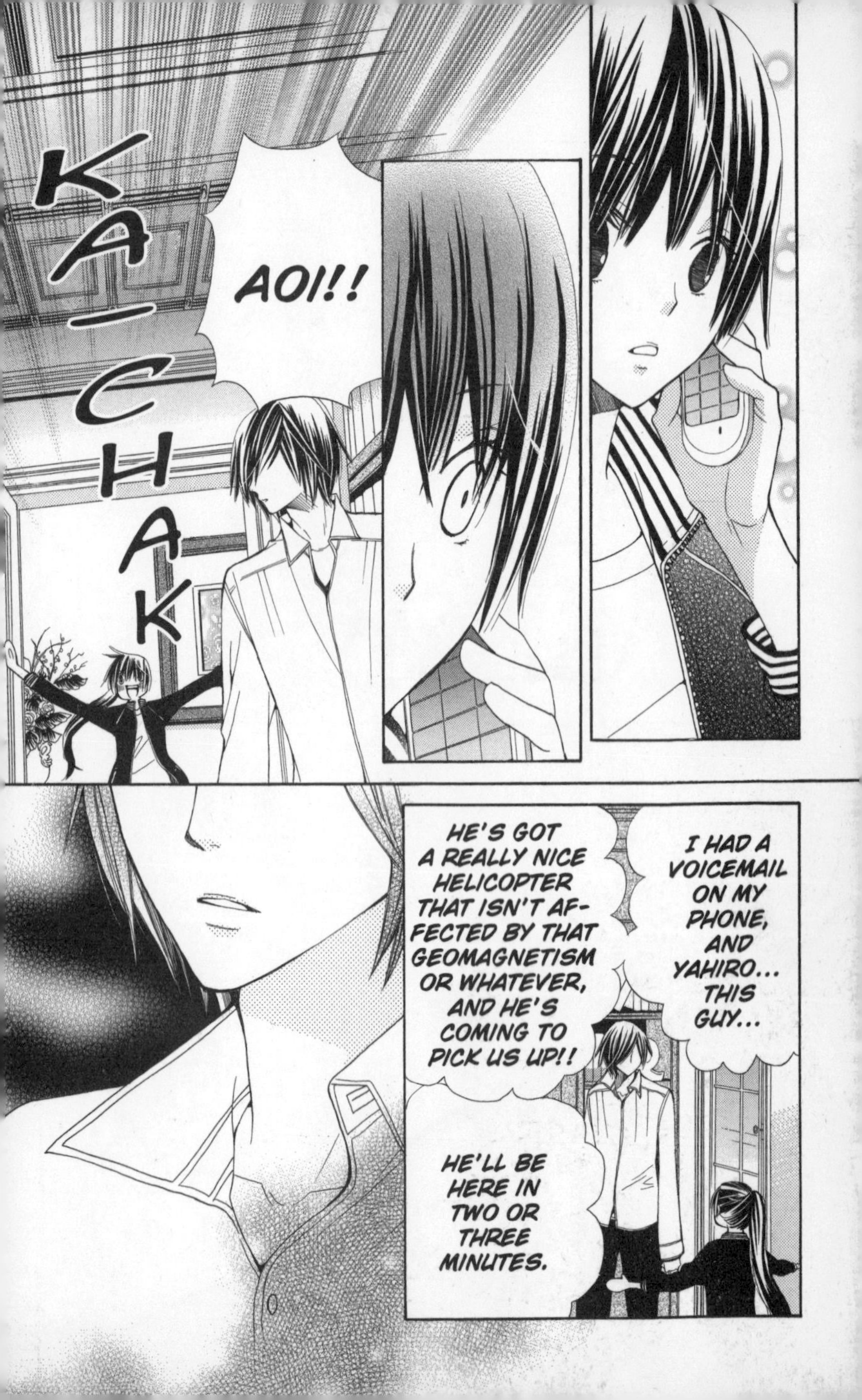
AOI!!
KA-CHAK
I HAD A VOICEMAIL ON MY PHONE, AND YAHIRO... THIS GUY...
HE'S GOT A REALLY NICE HELICOPTER THAT ISN'T AF-FECTED BY THAT GEOMAGNETISM OR WHATEVER, AND HE'S COMING TO PICK US UP!!
HE'LL BE HERE IN TWO OR THREE MINUTES.

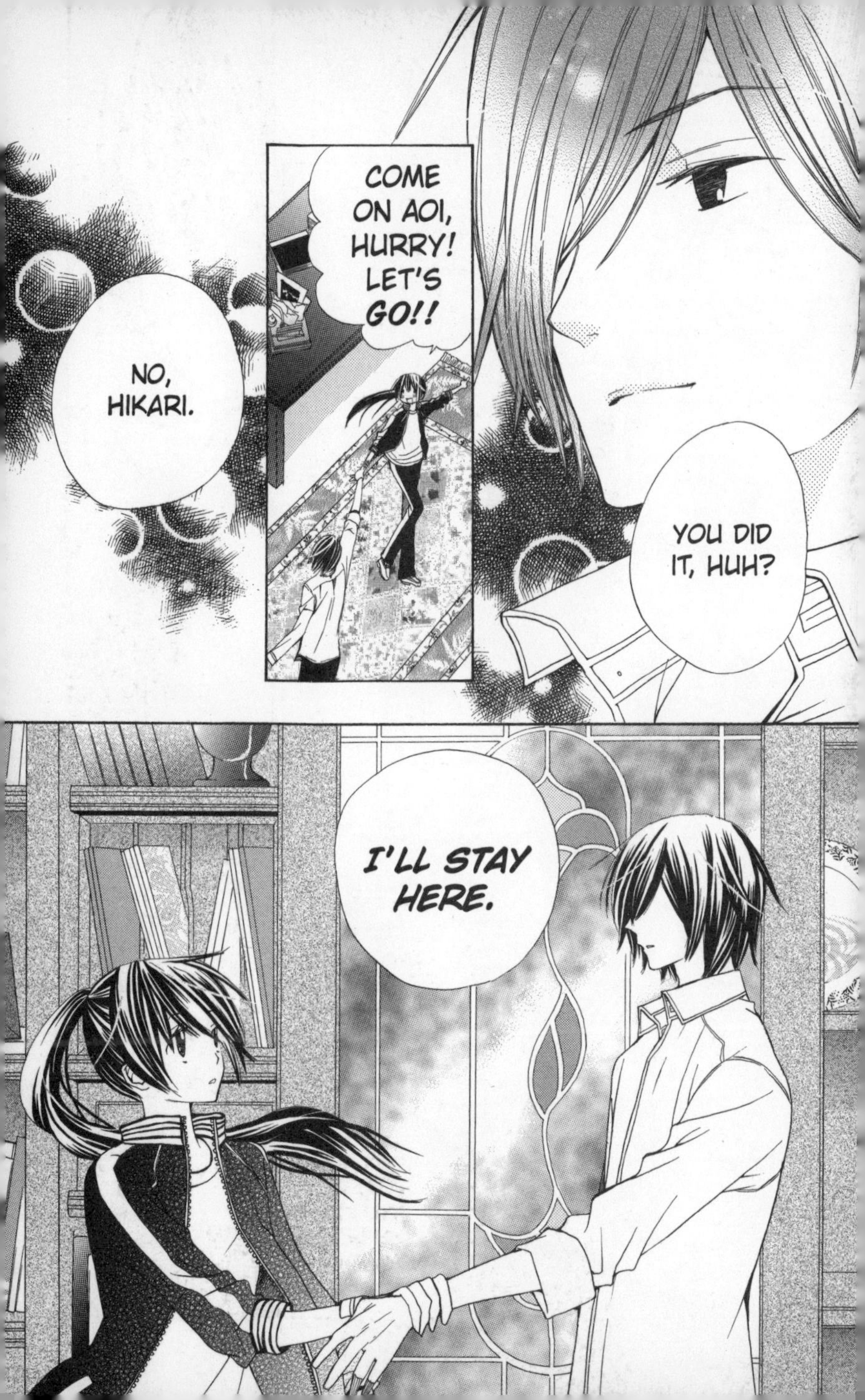
YOU DID IT, HUH?
COME ON AOI, HURRY! LET'S GO!!
NO, HIKARI.
I'LL STAY HERE.

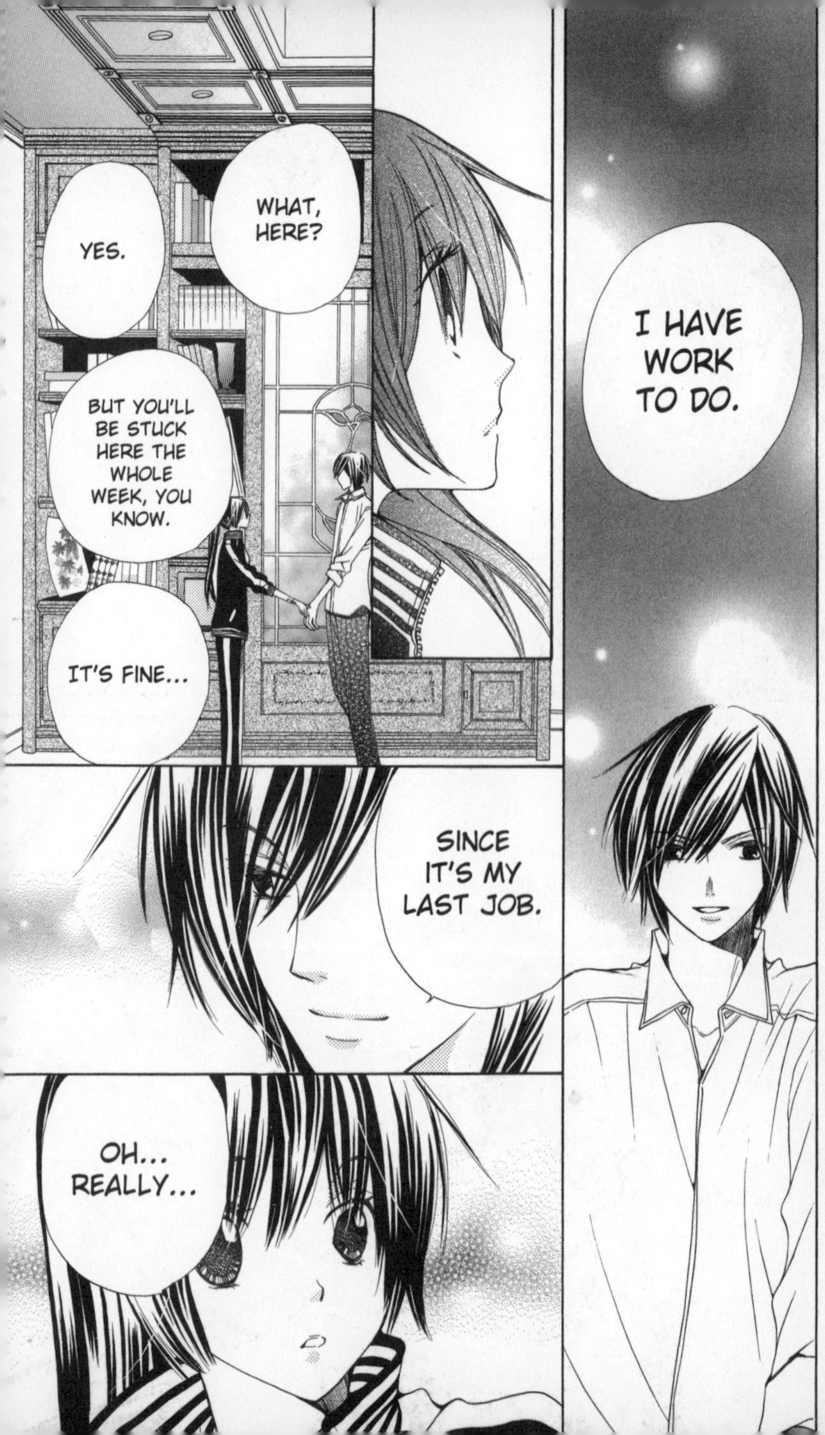
I HAVE WORK TO DO.
WHAT, HERE?
YES.
BUT YOU'LL BE STUCK HERE THE WHOLE WEEK, YOU KNOW.
IT'S FINE…
SINCE IT'S MY LAST JOB.
OH… REALLY…

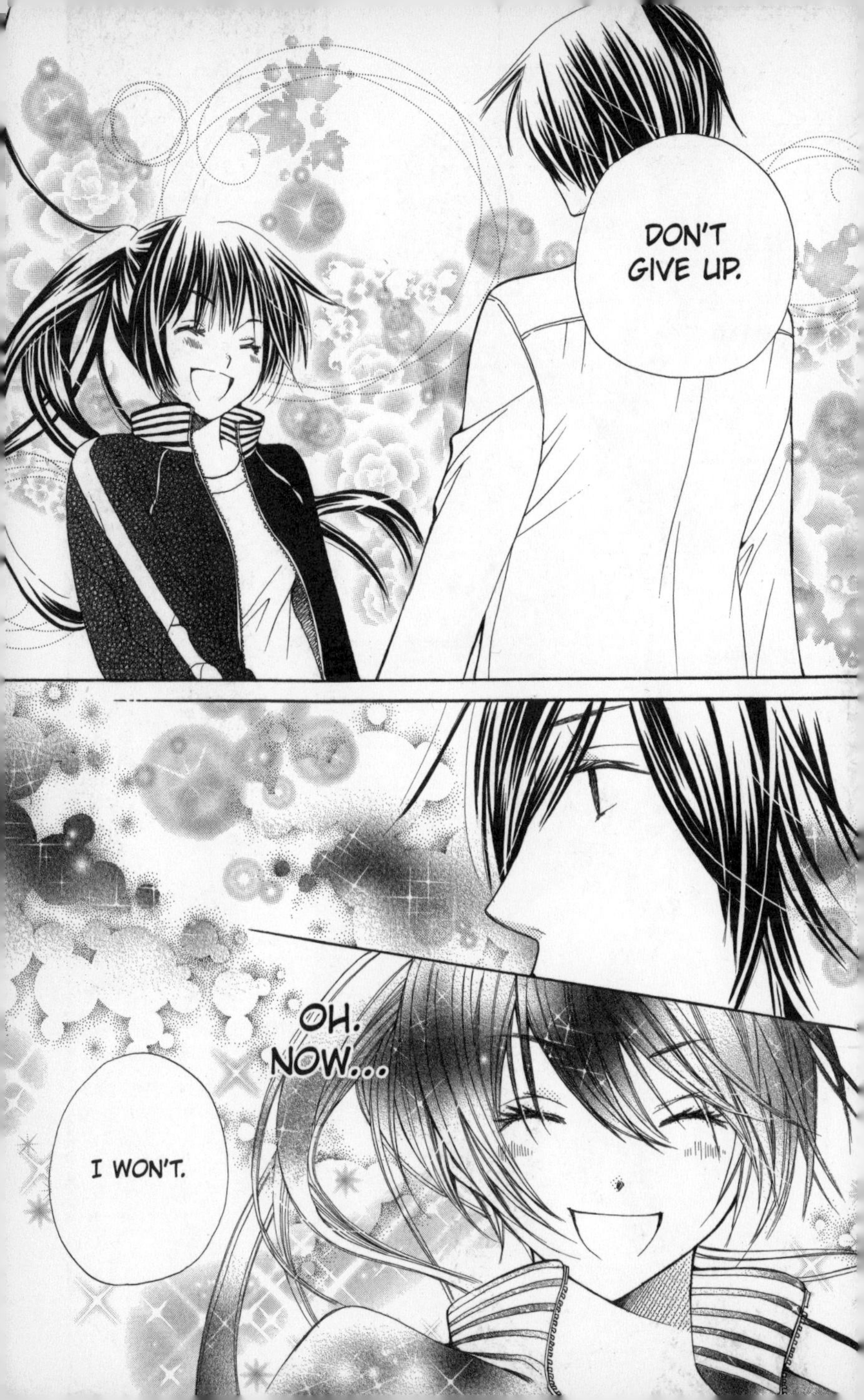
DON'T GIVE UP.
OH. NOW...
I WON'T.

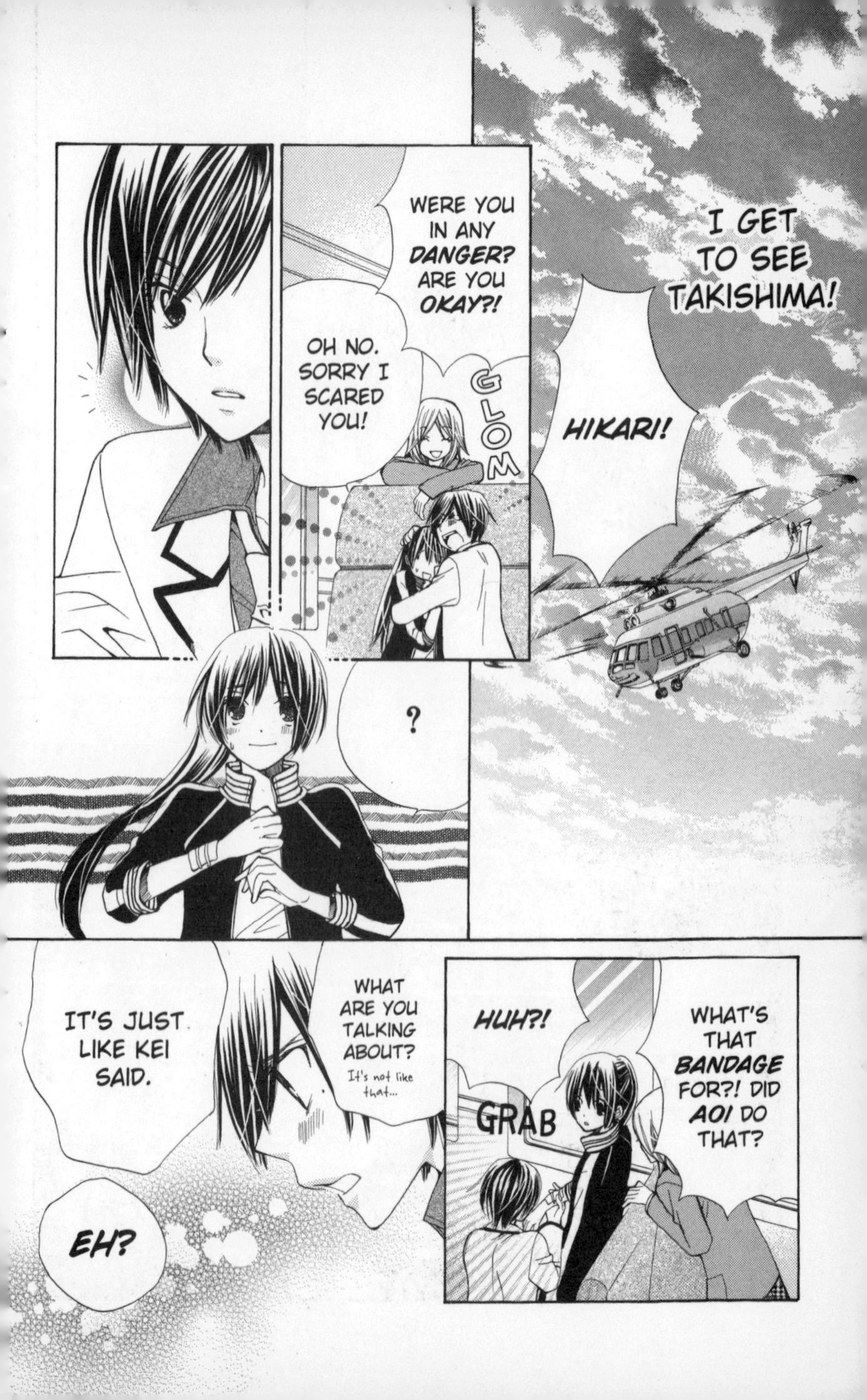
I GET TO SEE TAKISHIMA!
HIKARI!
WERE YOU IN ANY DANGER? ARE YOU OKAY?!
OH NO. SORRY I SCARED YOU!
GLOM
?
WHAT'S THAT BANDAGE FOR?! DID AOI DO THAT?
HUH?!
GRAB
WHAT ARE YOU TALKING ABOUT?
It's not like that...
IT'S JUST LIKE KEI SAID.
EH?

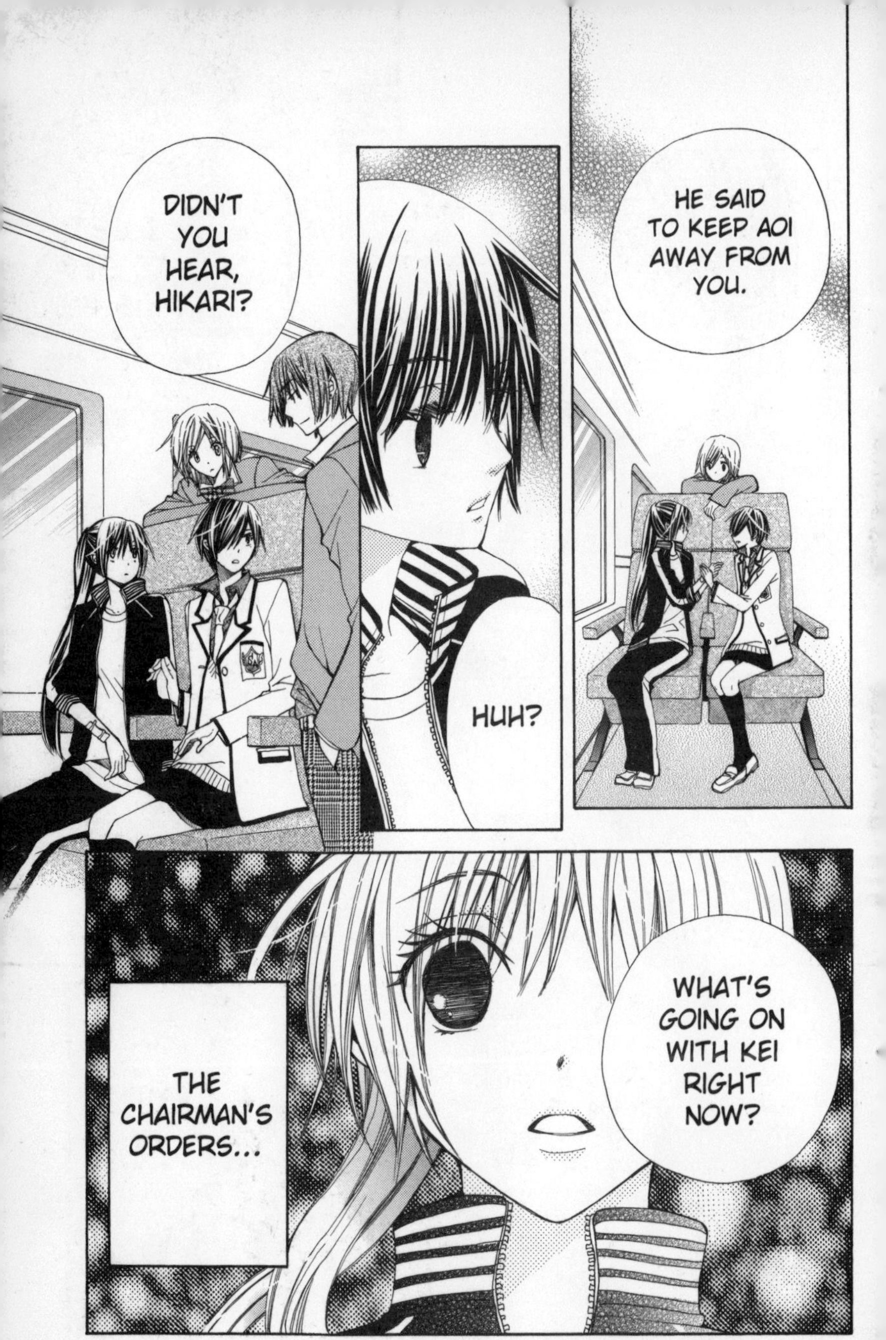
HE SAID TO KEEP AOI AWAY FROM YOU.
HUH?
DIDN'T YOU HEAR, HIKARI?
WHAT'S GOING ON WITH KEI RIGHT NOW?
THE CHAIRMAN'S ORDERS...

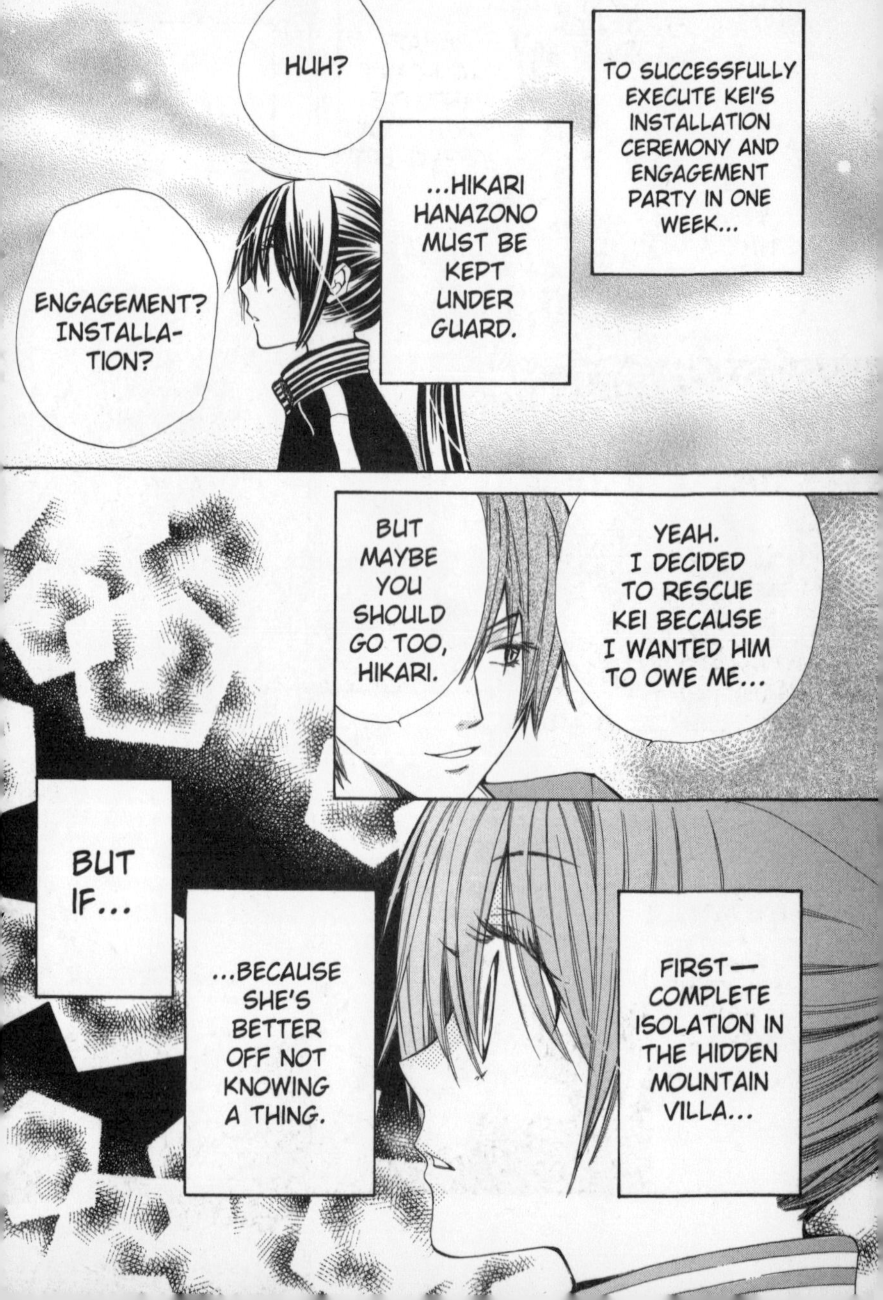
TO SUCCESSFULLY EXECUTE KEI'S INSTALLATION CEREMONY AND ENGAGEMENT PARTY IN ONE WEEK...
...HIKARI HANAZONO MUST BE KEPT UNDER GUARD.
HUH?
ENGAGEMENT? INSTALLA-TION?
YEAH. I DECIDED TO RESCUE KEI BECAUSE I WANTED HIM TO OWE ME...
BUT MAYBE YOU SHOULD GO TOO, HIKARI.
FIRST— COMPLETE ISOLATION IN THE HIDDEN MOUNTAIN VILLA...
...BECAUSE SHE'S BETTER OFF NOT KNOWING A THING.
BUT IF...

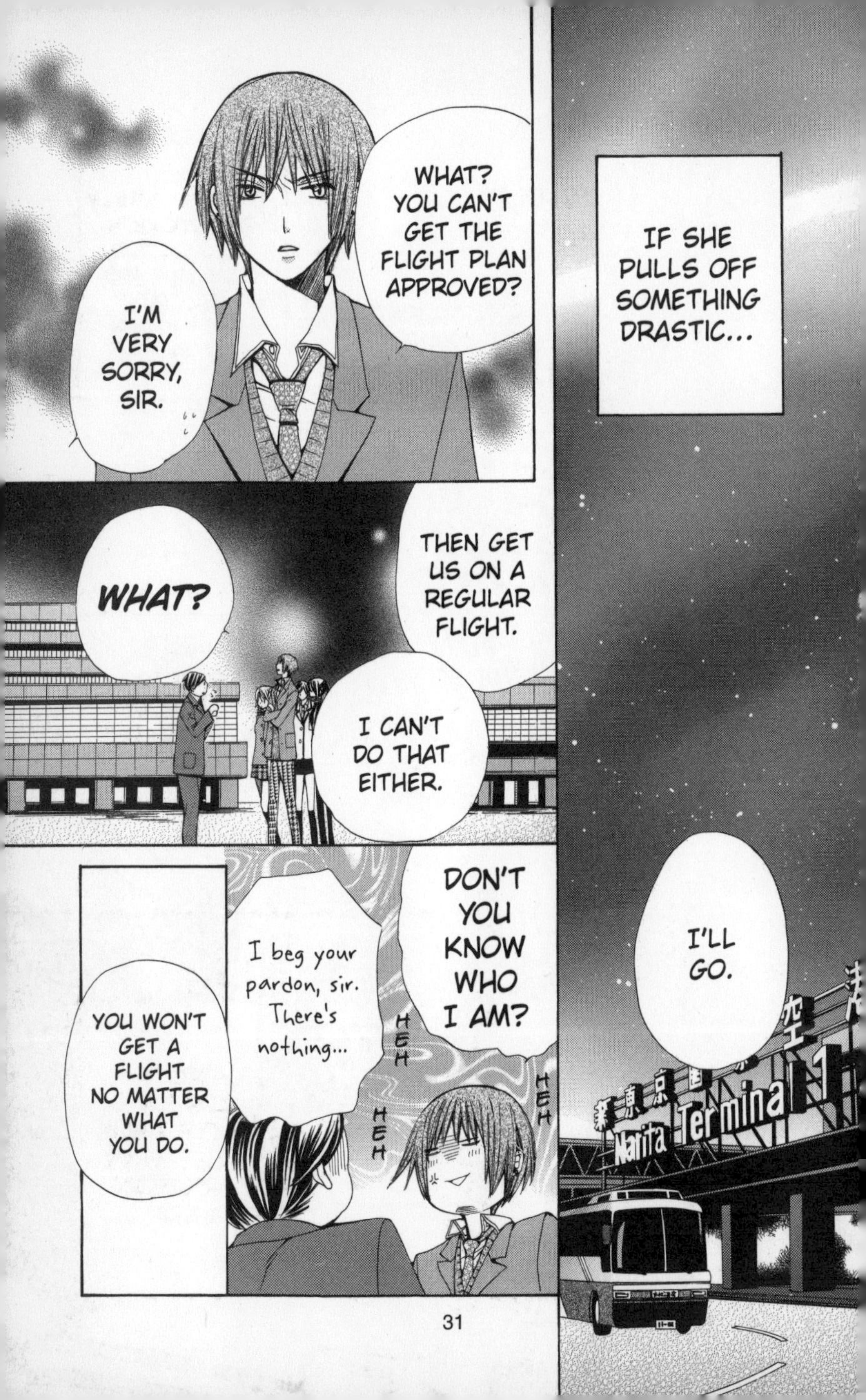
IF SHE PULLS OFF SOMETHING DRASTIC...
Narita Terminal 1
I'LL GO.
WHAT? YOU CAN'T GET THE FLIGHT PLAN APPROVED?
I'M VERY SORRY, SIR.
THEN GET US ON A REGULAR FLIGHT.
WHAT?
I CAN'T DO THAT EITHER.
DON'T YOU KNOW WHO I AM?
HEH HEH HEH
I beg your pardon, sir. There's nothing...
YOU WON'T GET A FLIGHT NO MATTER WHAT YOU DO.

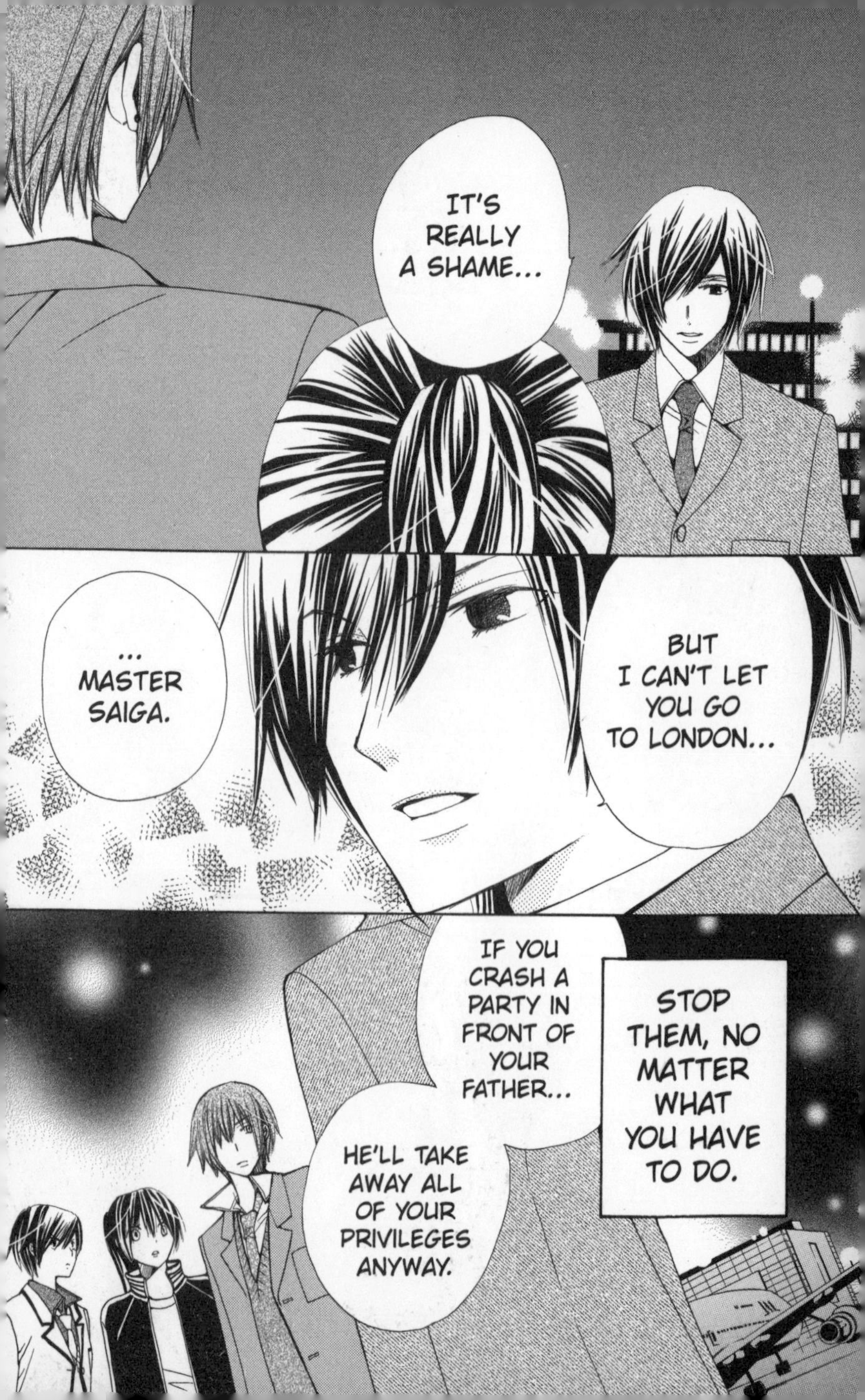
IT'S REALLY A SHAME...
BUT I CAN'T LET YOU GO TO LONDON...
... MASTER SAIGA.
STOP THEM, NO MATTER WHAT YOU HAVE TO DO.
IF YOU CRASH A PARTY IN FRONT OF YOUR FATHER...
HE'LL TAKE AWAY ALL OF YOUR PRIVILEGES ANYWAY.

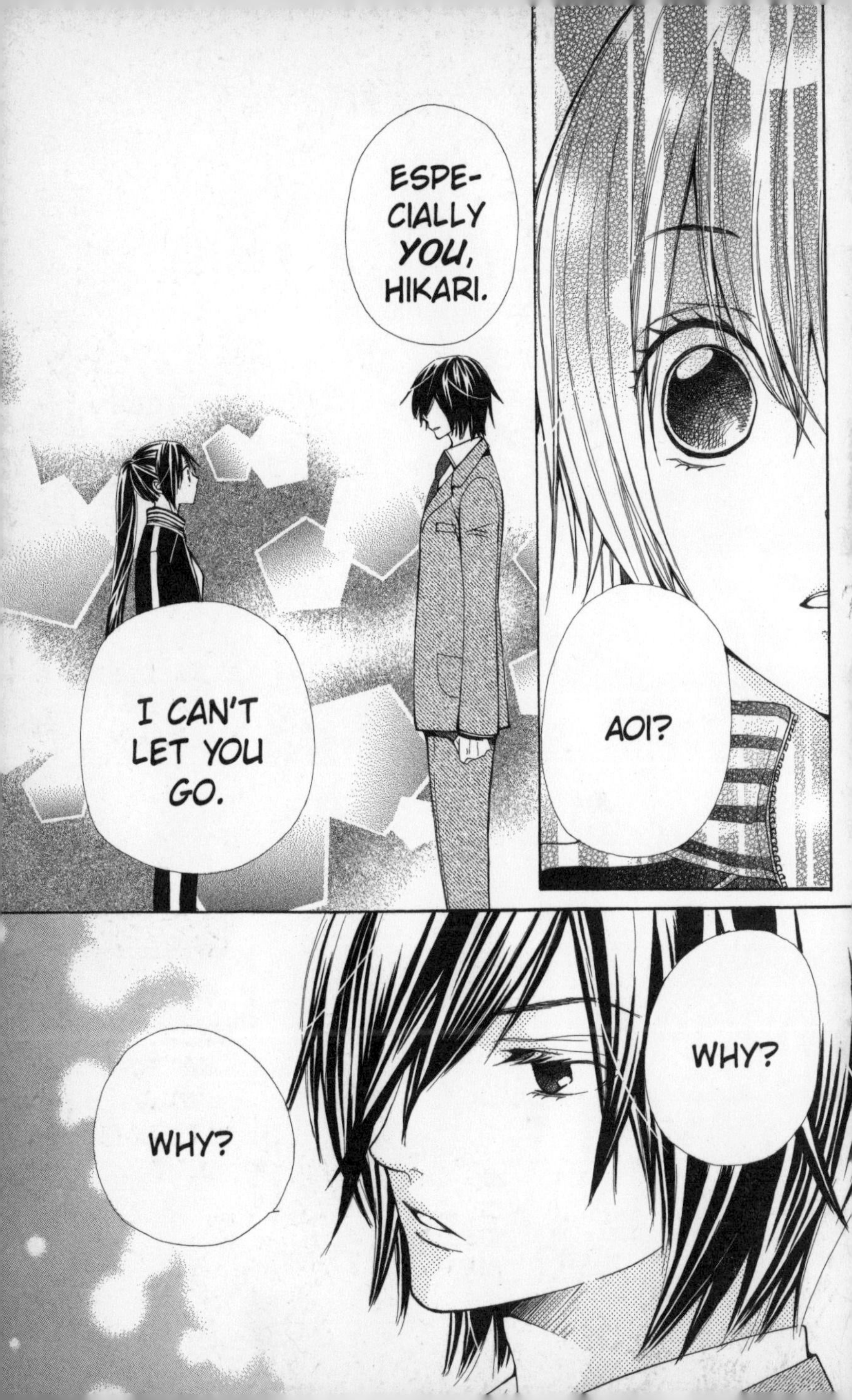
AOI?
ESPE-
CIALLY
YOU,
HIKARI.
I CAN'T
LET YOU
GO.
WHY?
WHY?

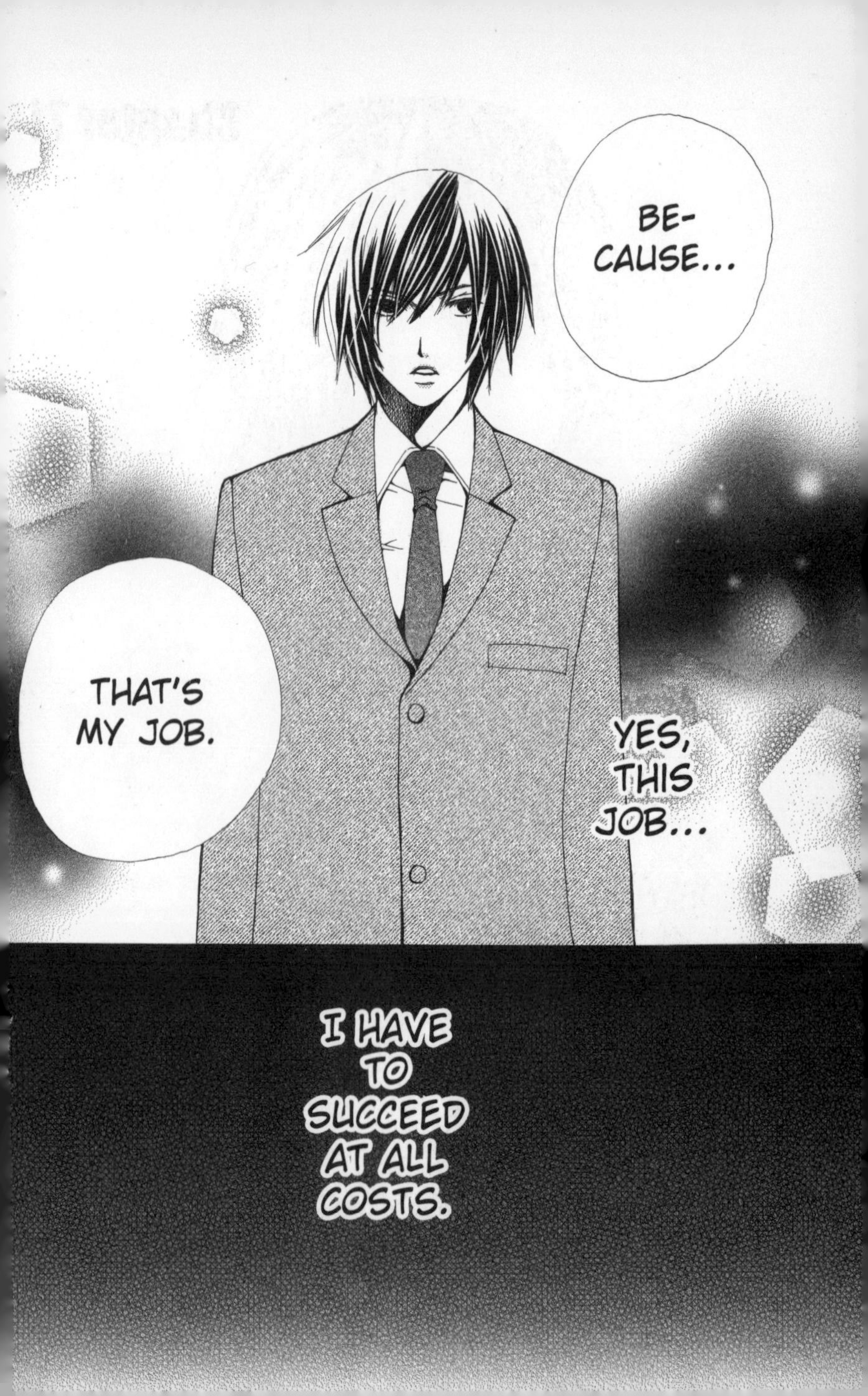
BE-CAUSE...
THAT'S MY JOB.
YES, THIS JOB...
I HAVE TO SUCCEED AT ALL COSTS.

Chapter 71

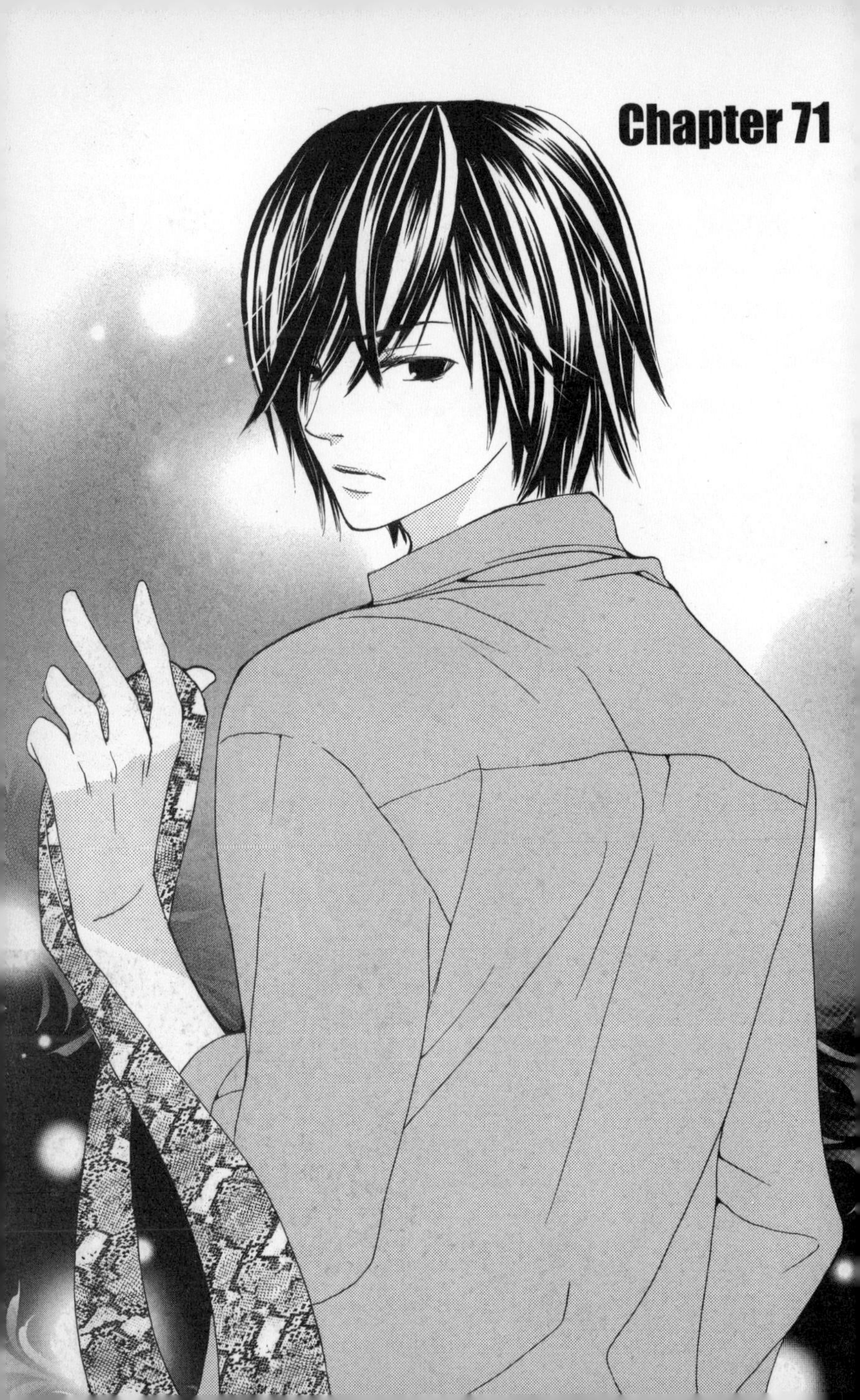

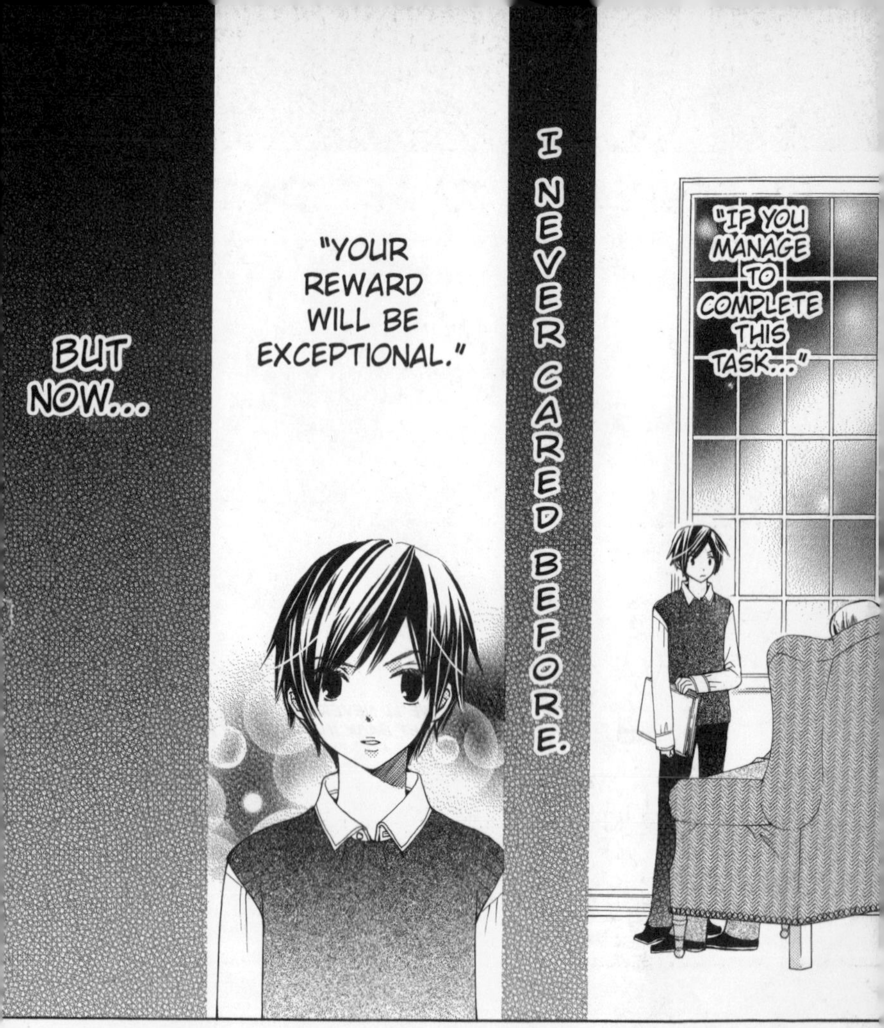
"IF YOU MANAGE TO COMPLETE THIS TASK..."
I NEVER CARED BEFORE.
"YOUR REWARD WILL BE EXCEPTIONAL."
BUT NOW...

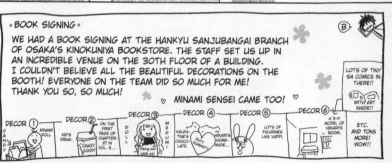

∘BOOK SIGNING∘

WE HAD A BOOK SIGNING AT THE HANKYU SANJUBANGAI BRANCH OF OSAKA'S KINOKUNIYA BOOKSTORE. THE STAFF SET US UP IN AN INCREDIBLE VENUE ON THE 30TH FLOOR OF A BUILDING. I COULDN'T BELIEVE ALL THE BEAUTIFUL DECORATIONS ON THE BOOTH! EVERYONE ON THE TEAM DID SO MUCH FOR ME! THANK YOU SO, SO MUCH!

♡ MINAMI SENSEI CAME TOO! ♡

B

LOTS OF TINY SA COMICS IN THERE!! WITH ART INSIDE!!

DECOR ① CANDY MINAMI DOLL

DECOR ② KEI'S DRINK. CRAZY GOOD! ON THE FIRST PAGE OF CHAPTER 27 IN VOL. 5...

DECOR ③ DOLL MEGUMI! Hang out with us!

DECOR ④ VALENTINE'S CHOCOLATE. DUTY HUMANITY HIKARI'S HOMEMADE...

DECOR ⑤ LOTS OF FIGURINES LIKE YAPPI.

DECOR ⑥ A 3-D MODEL OF HIKARI'S ROOM.

ETC. AND TONS MORE! WOW!!

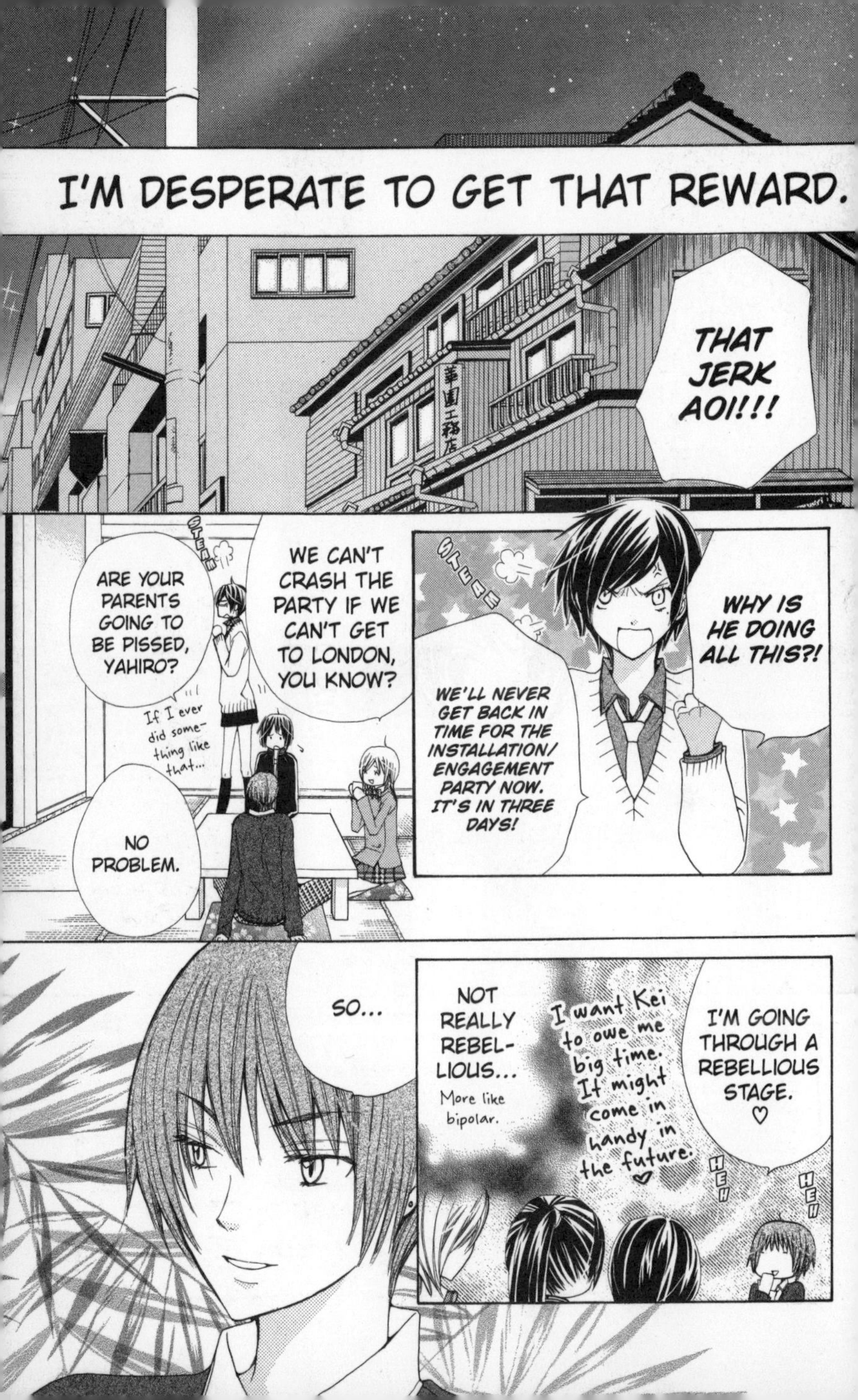
I'M DESPERATE TO GET THAT REWARD.
THAT JERK AOI!!!
STARE
WHY IS HE DOING ALL THIS?!
WE'LL NEVER GET BACK IN TIME FOR THE INSTALLATION/ ENGAGEMENT PARTY NOW. IT'S IN THREE DAYS!
WE CAN'T CRASH THE PARTY IF WE CAN'T GET TO LONDON, YOU KNOW?
STEAM
ARE YOUR PARENTS GOING TO BE PISSED, YAHIRO?
If I ever did some-thing like that...
NO PROBLEM.
I'M GOING THROUGH A REBELLIOUS STAGE. ♡
HEH
HEH
I want Kei to owe me big time. It might come in handy in the future. ♡
NOT REALLY REBEL-LIOUS...
More like bipolar.
SO...

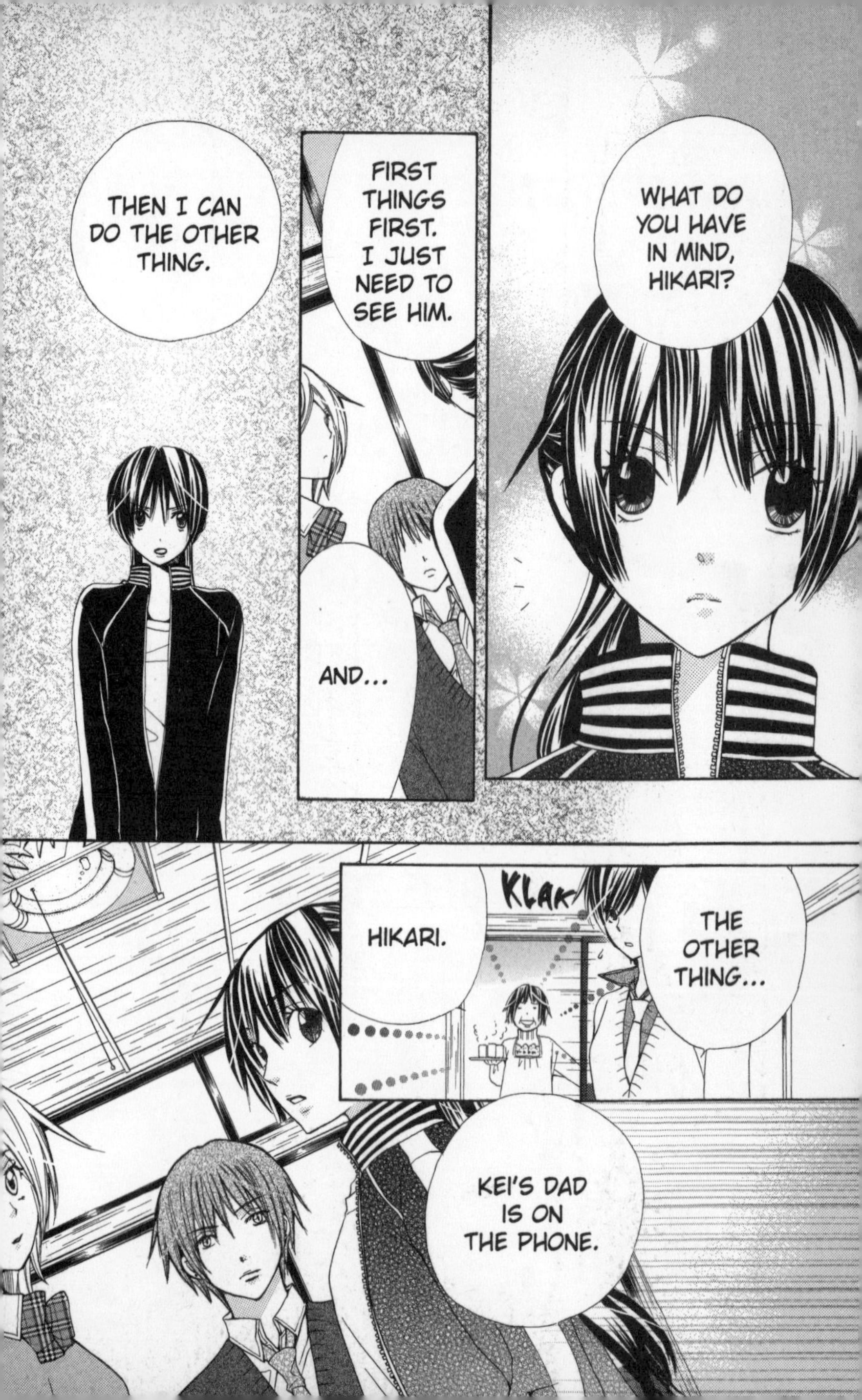
WHAT DO YOU HAVE IN MIND, HIKARI?
FIRST THINGS FIRST. I JUST NEED TO SEE HIM.
AND...
THEN I CAN DO THE OTHER THING.
THE OTHER THING...
KLAK
HIKARI.
KEI'S DAD IS ON THE PHONE.

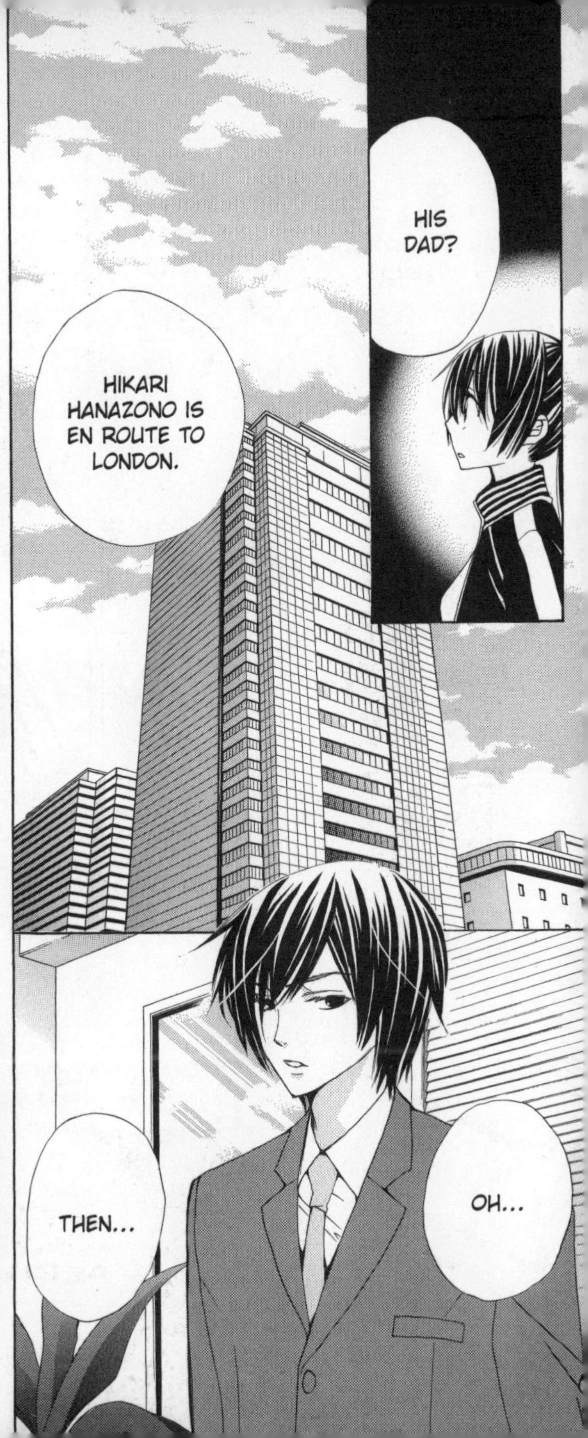
HIS DAD?
HIKARI HANAZONO IS EN ROUTE TO LONDON.
OH...
THEN...

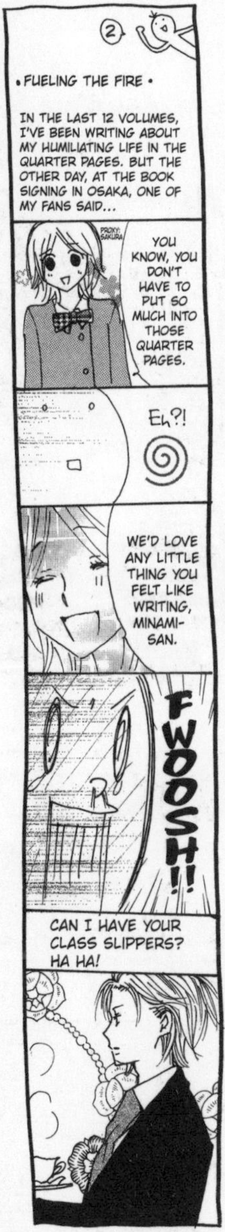
2
• FUELING THE FIRE •
IN THE LAST 12 VOLUMES, I'VE BEEN WRITING ABOUT MY HUMILIATING LIFE IN THE QUARTER PAGES. BUT THE OTHER DAY, AT THE BOOK SIGNING IN OSAKA, ONE OF MY FANS SAID...
PROXY: SAKURA
YOU KNOW, YOU DON'T HAVE TO PUT SO MUCH INTO THOSE QUARTER PAGES.
Eh?!
WE'D LOVE ANY LITTLE THING YOU FELT LIKE WRITING, MINAMI-SAN.
FWOOSH!!
CAN I HAVE YOUR CLASS SLIPPERS? HA HA!

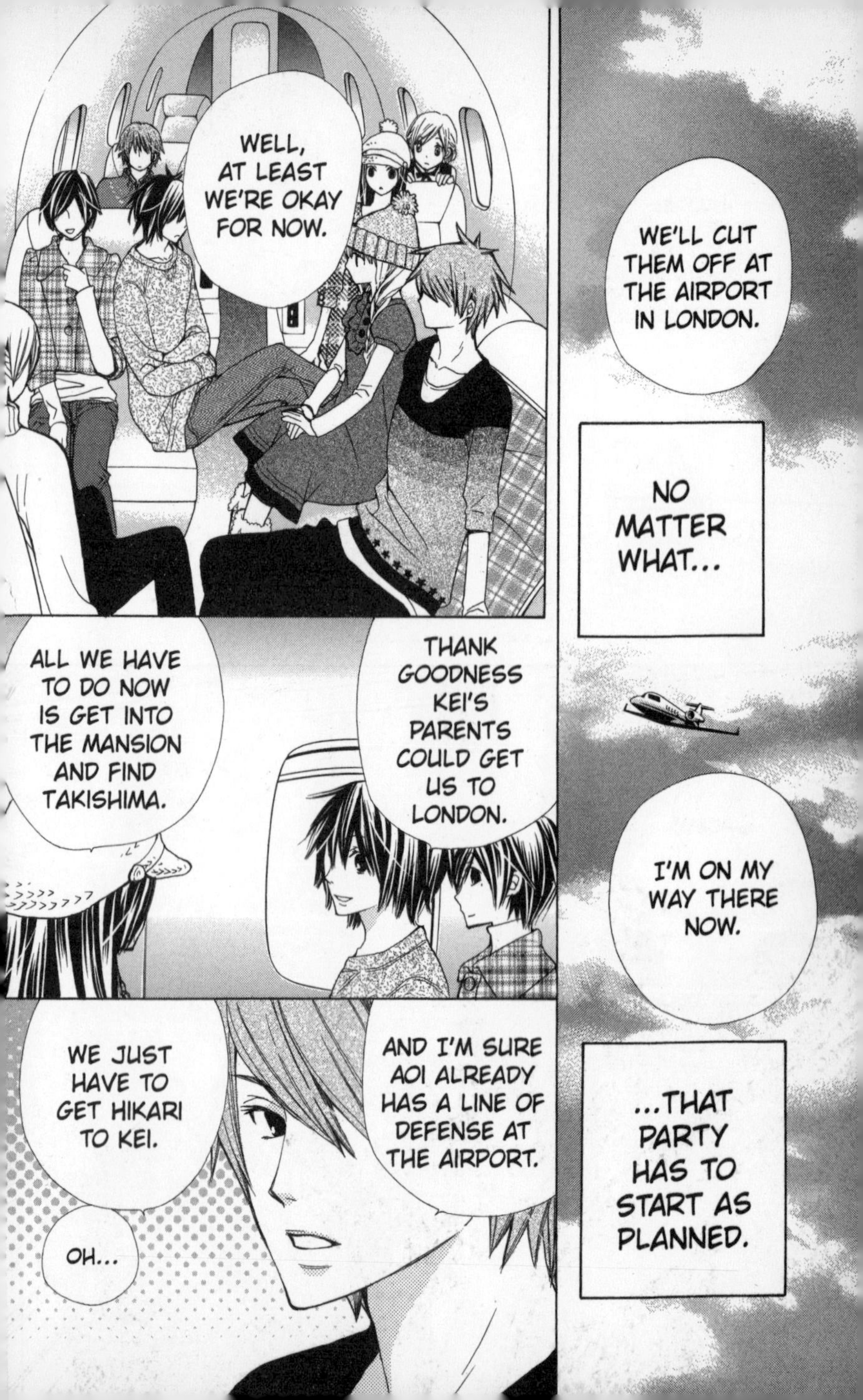
WE'LL CUT THEM OFF AT THE AIRPORT IN LONDON.
NO MATTER WHAT...
I'M ON MY WAY THERE NOW.
...THAT PARTY HAS TO START AS PLANNED.
WELL, AT LEAST WE'RE OKAY FOR NOW.
THANK GOODNESS KEI'S PARENTS COULD GET US TO LONDON.
ALL WE HAVE TO DO NOW IS GET INTO THE MANSION AND FIND TAKISHIMA.
AND I'M SURE AOI ALREADY HAS A LINE OF DEFENSE AT THE AIRPORT.
WE JUST HAVE TO GET HIKARI TO KEI.
OH...

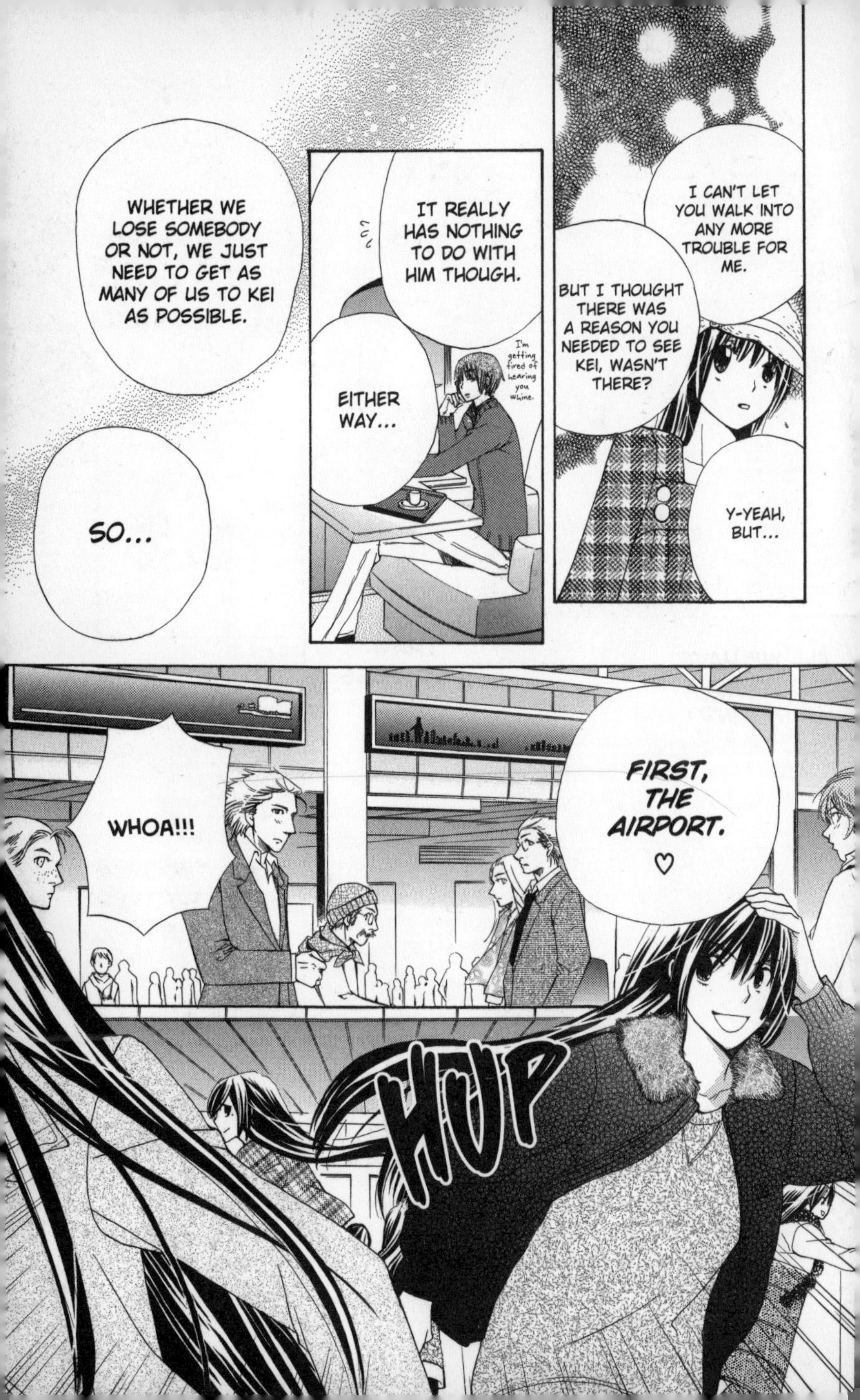
I CAN'T LET YOU WALK INTO ANY MORE TROUBLE FOR ME.
BUT I THOUGHT THERE WAS A REASON YOU NEEDED TO SEE KEI, WASN'T THERE?
Y-YEAH, BUT...
IT REALLY HAS NOTHING TO DO WITH HIM THOUGH.
I'm getting tired of hearing you whine.
EITHER WAY...
WHETHER WE LOSE SOMEBODY OR NOT, WE JUST NEED TO GET AS MANY OF US TO KEI AS POSSIBLE.
SO...
FIRST, THE AIRPORT. ♡
WHOA!!!
HUP

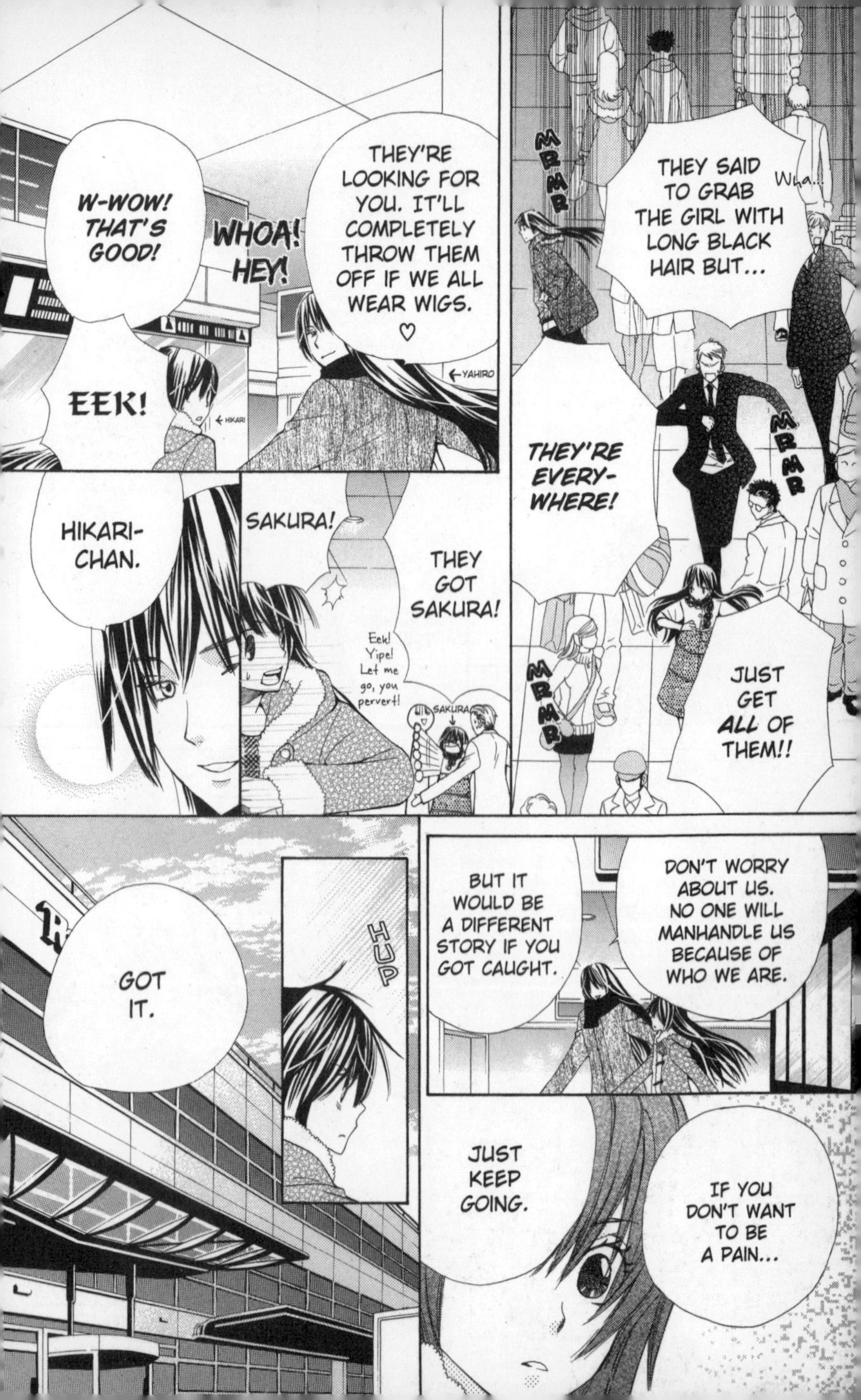
MRMR
THEY SAID TO GRAB THE GIRL WITH LONG BLACK HAIR BUT...
Wha...
MRMR
THEY'RE EVERY-WHERE!
MRMR
JUST GET ALL OF THEM!!
THEY'RE LOOKING FOR YOU. IT'LL COMPLETELY THROW THEM OFF IF WE ALL WEAR WIGS. ♡
YAHIRO
WHOA! HEY!
W-WOW! THAT'S GOOD!
EEK!
HIKARI
SAKURA!
THEY GOT SAKURA!
Eek! Yipe! Let me go, you pervert!
SAKURA
HIKARI-CHAN.
DON'T WORRY ABOUT US. NO ONE WILL MANHANDLE US BECAUSE OF WHO WE ARE.
BUT IT WOULD BE A DIFFERENT STORY IF YOU GOT CAUGHT.
IF YOU DON'T WANT TO BE A PAIN...
JUST KEEP GOING.
HUP
GOT IT.

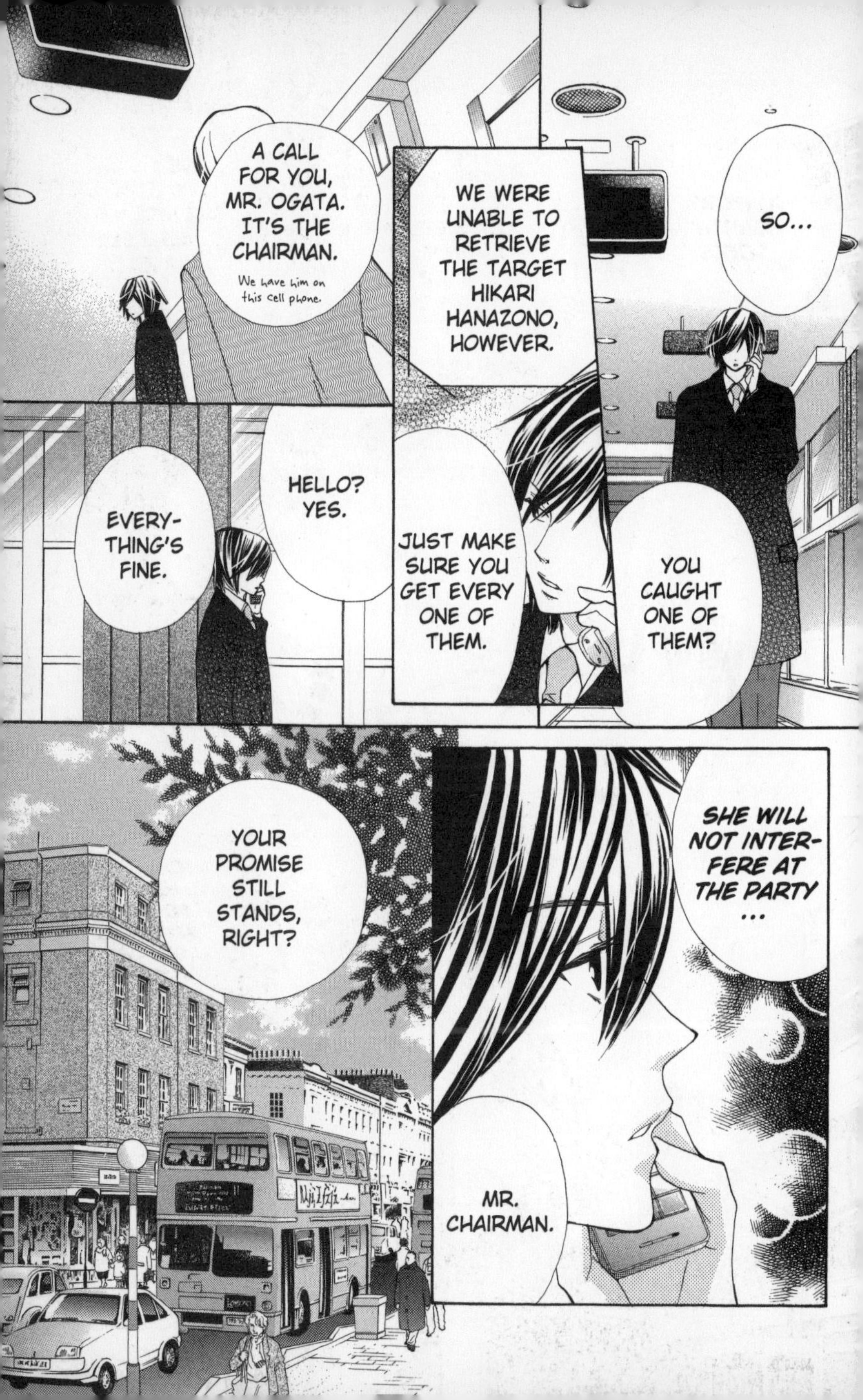
A CALL FOR YOU, MR. OGATA. IT'S THE CHAIRMAN.
We have him on this cell phone.
HELLO? YES.
EVERY-THING'S FINE.
SO...
YOU CAUGHT ONE OF THEM?
WE WERE UNABLE TO RETRIEVE THE TARGET HIKARI HANAZONO, HOWEVER.
JUST MAKE SURE YOU GET EVERY ONE OF THEM.
SHE WILL NOT INTER-FERE AT THE PARTY...
MR. CHAIRMAN.
YOUR PROMISE STILL STANDS, RIGHT?

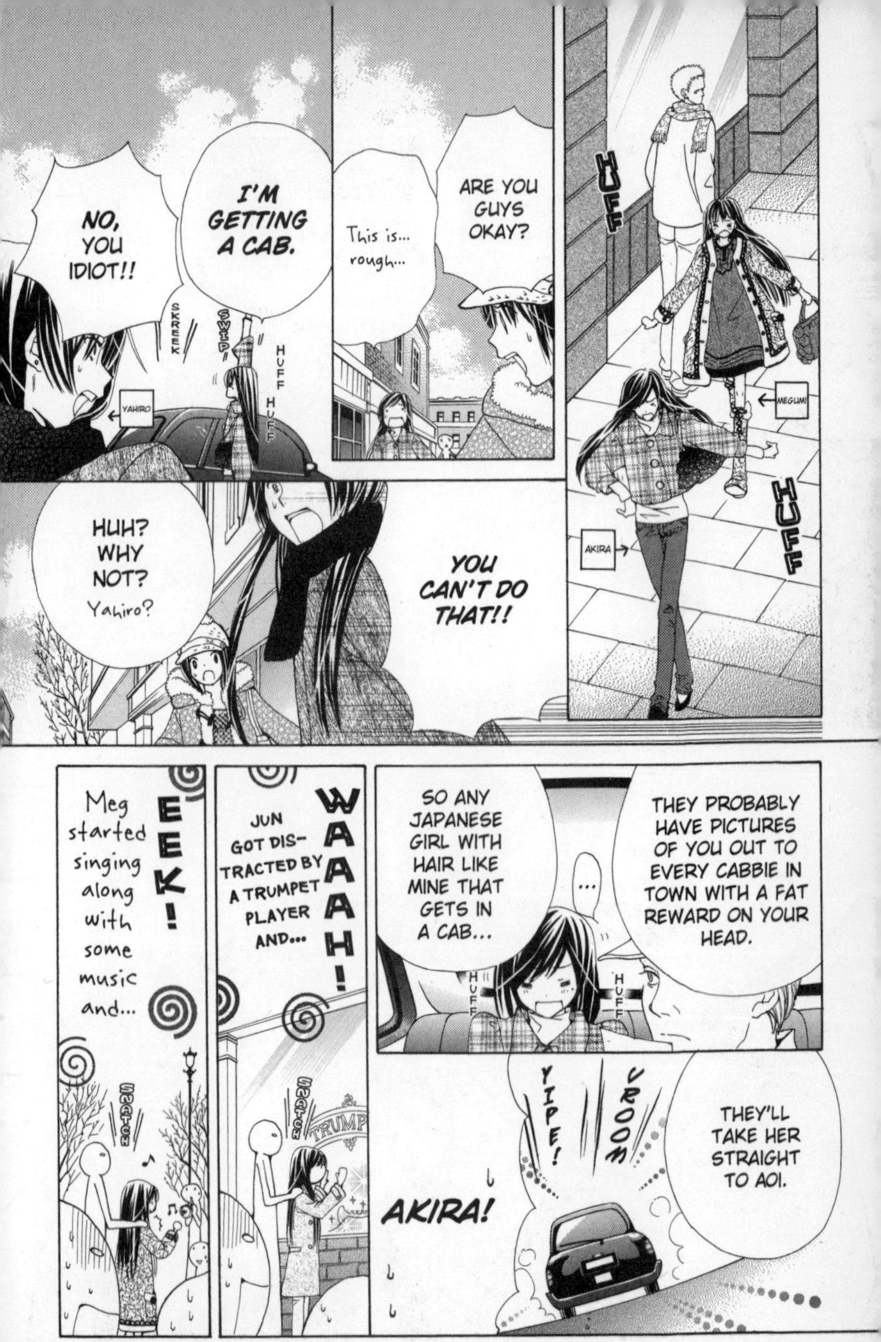
HUFF
MEGUMI
AKIRA
HUFF
ARE YOU GUYS OKAY?
This is... rough...
I'M GETTING A CAB.
NO, YOU IDIOT!!
SKREEK
SWIP
HUFF HUFF
YAHIRO
YOU CAN'T DO THAT!!
HUH? WHY NOT? Yahiro?
THEY PROBABLY HAVE PICTURES OF YOU OUT TO EVERY CABBIE IN TOWN WITH A FAT REWARD ON YOUR HEAD.
SO ANY JAPANESE GIRL WITH HAIR LIKE MINE THAT GETS IN A CAB...
...
HUFF
HUFF
THEY'LL TAKE HER STRAIGHT TO AOI.
VROOM
YIPE!
AKIRA!
WAAAAH!
JUN GOT DISTRACTED BY A TRUMPET PLAYER AND...
SNATCH
TRUMP
EEEK!
Meg started singing along with some music and...
SNATCH

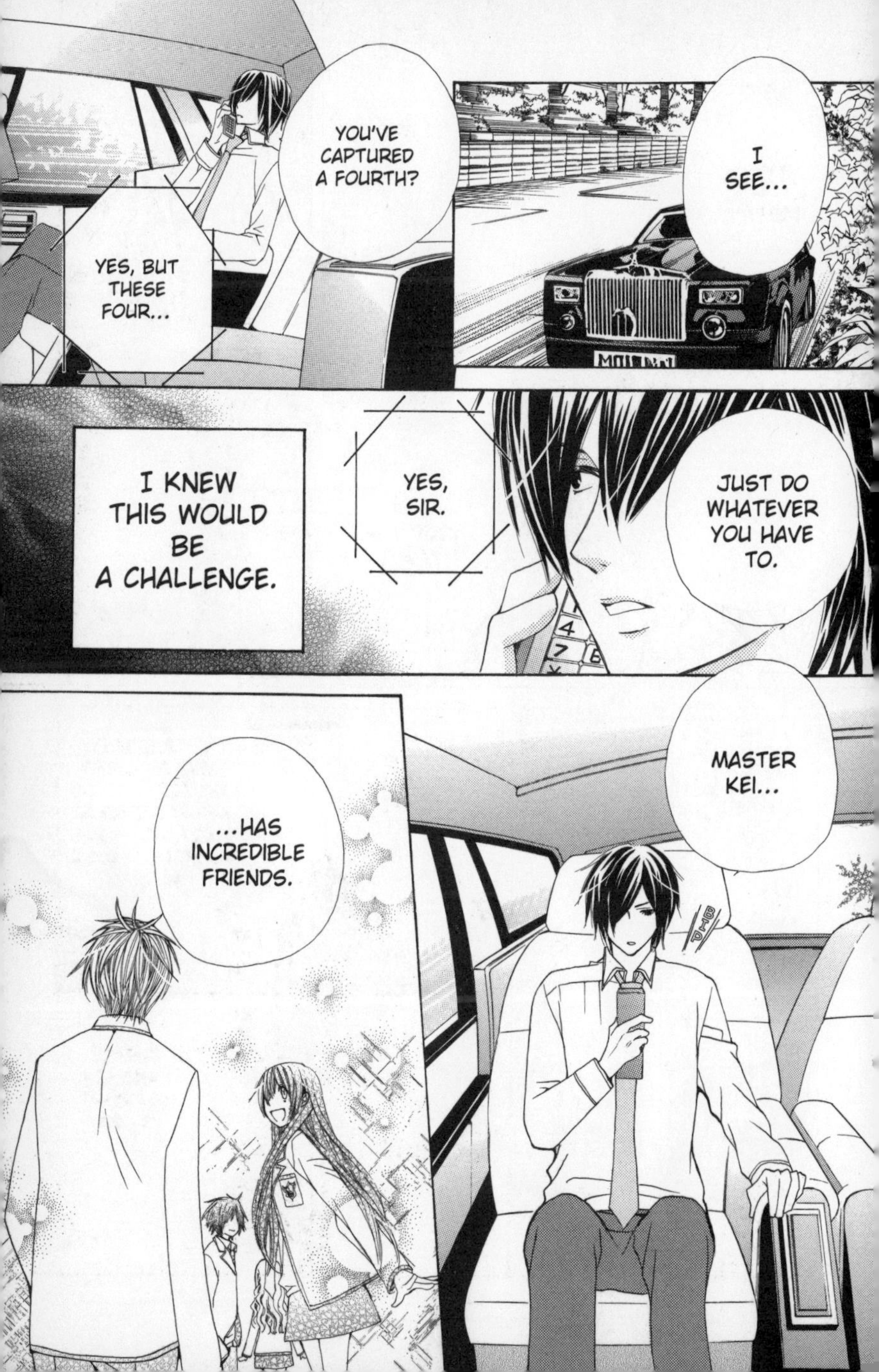
I SEE...
YOU'VE CAPTURED A FOURTH?
YES, BUT THESE FOUR...
JUST DO WHATEVER YOU HAVE TO.
YES, SIR.
I KNEW THIS WOULD BE A CHALLENGE.
MASTER KEI...
BIP
...HAS INCREDIBLE FRIENDS.

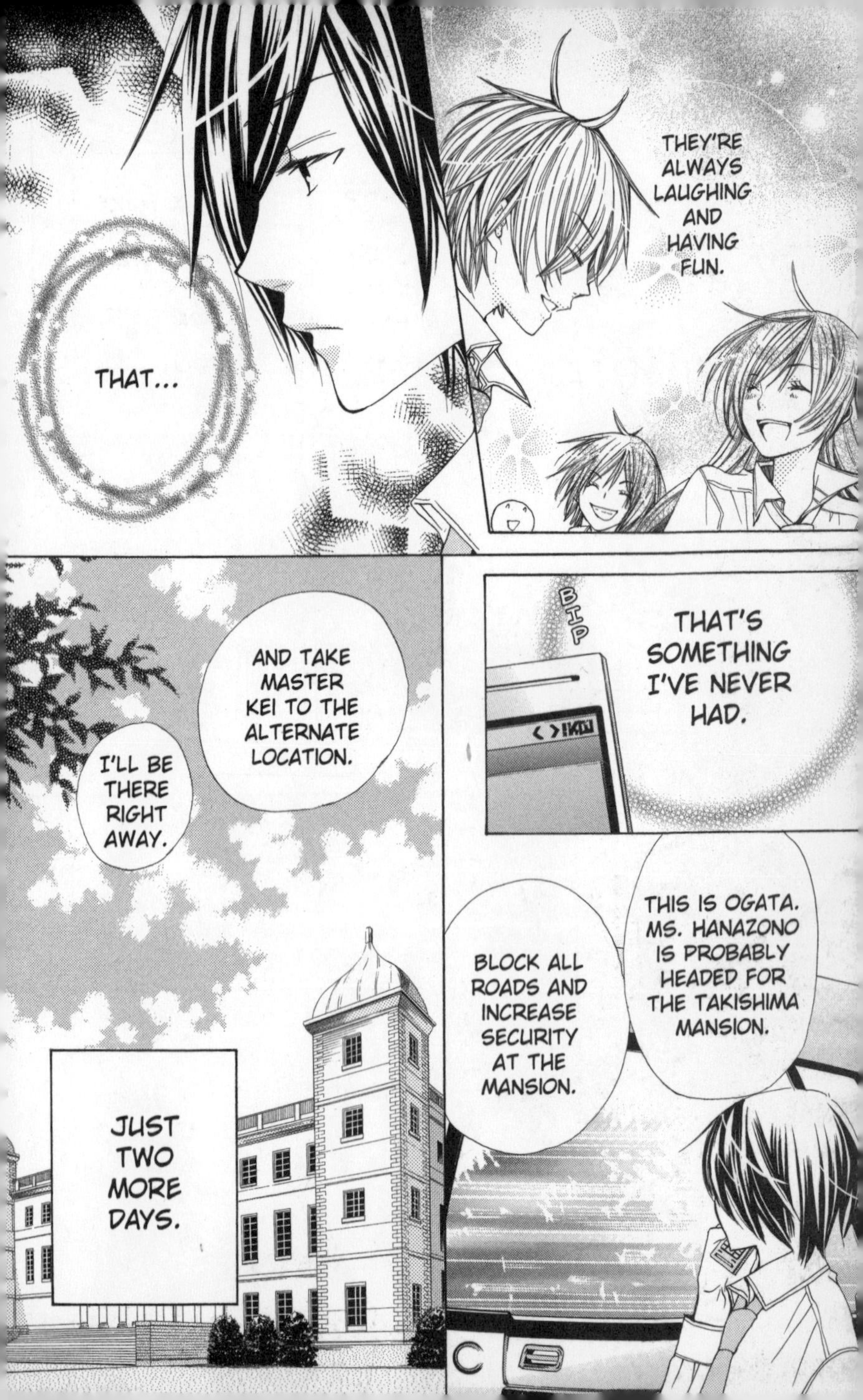
THEY'RE ALWAYS LAUGHING AND HAVING FUN.
THAT...
BIP
THAT'S SOMETHING I'VE NEVER HAD.
THIS IS OGATA. MS. HANAZONO IS PROBABLY HEADED FOR THE TAKISHIMA MANSION.
BLOCK ALL ROADS AND INCREASE SECURITY AT THE MANSION.
AND TAKE MASTER KEI TO THE ALTERNATE LOCATION.
I'LL BE THERE RIGHT AWAY.
JUST TWO MORE DAYS.

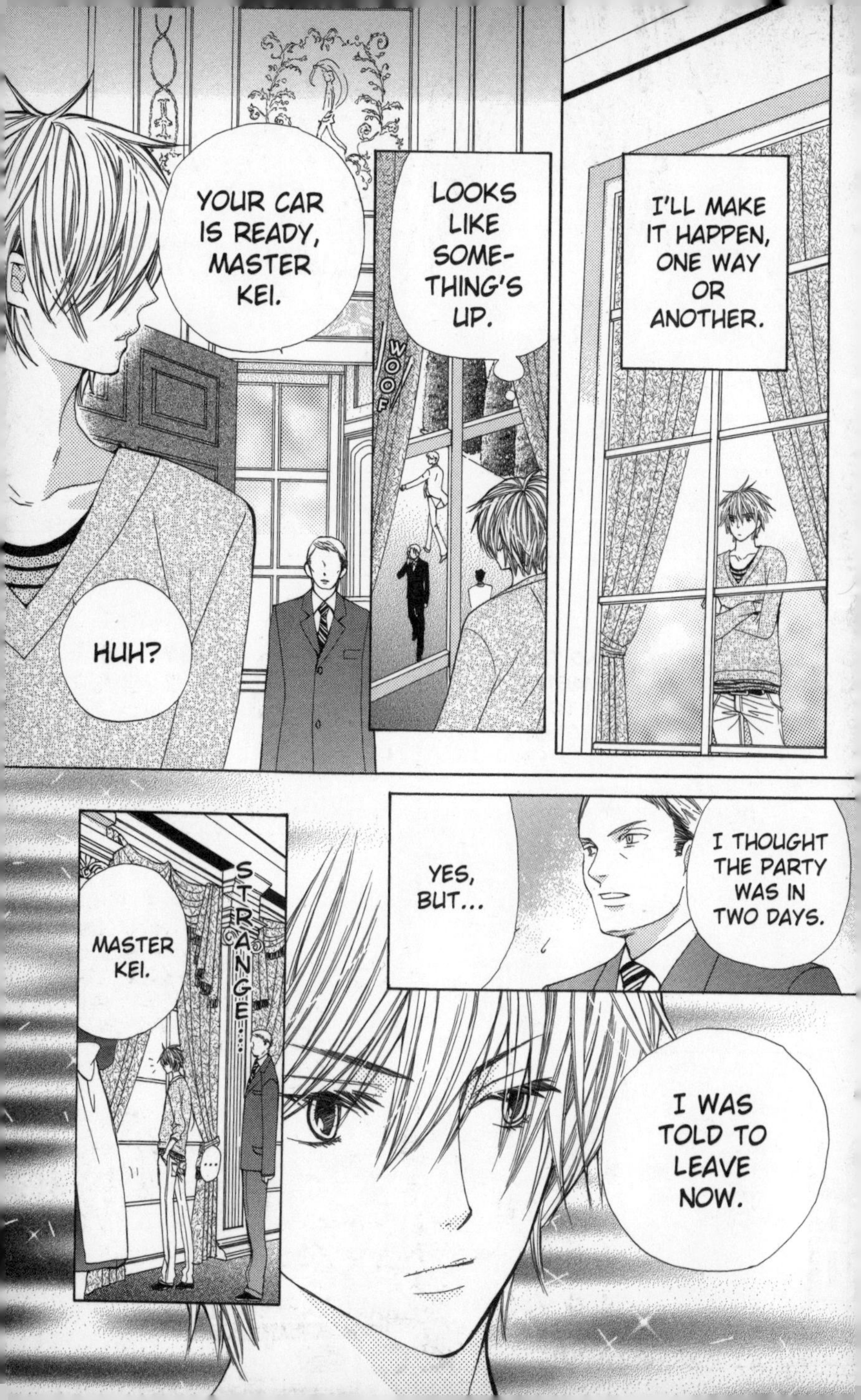
I'LL MAKE IT HAPPEN, ONE WAY OR ANOTHER.
WOOF
LOOKS LIKE SOME-THING'S UP.
YOUR CAR IS READY, MASTER KEI.
HUH?
I THOUGHT THE PARTY WAS IN TWO DAYS.
YES, BUT...
I WAS TOLD TO LEAVE NOW.
MASTER KEI.
STRANGE...
...

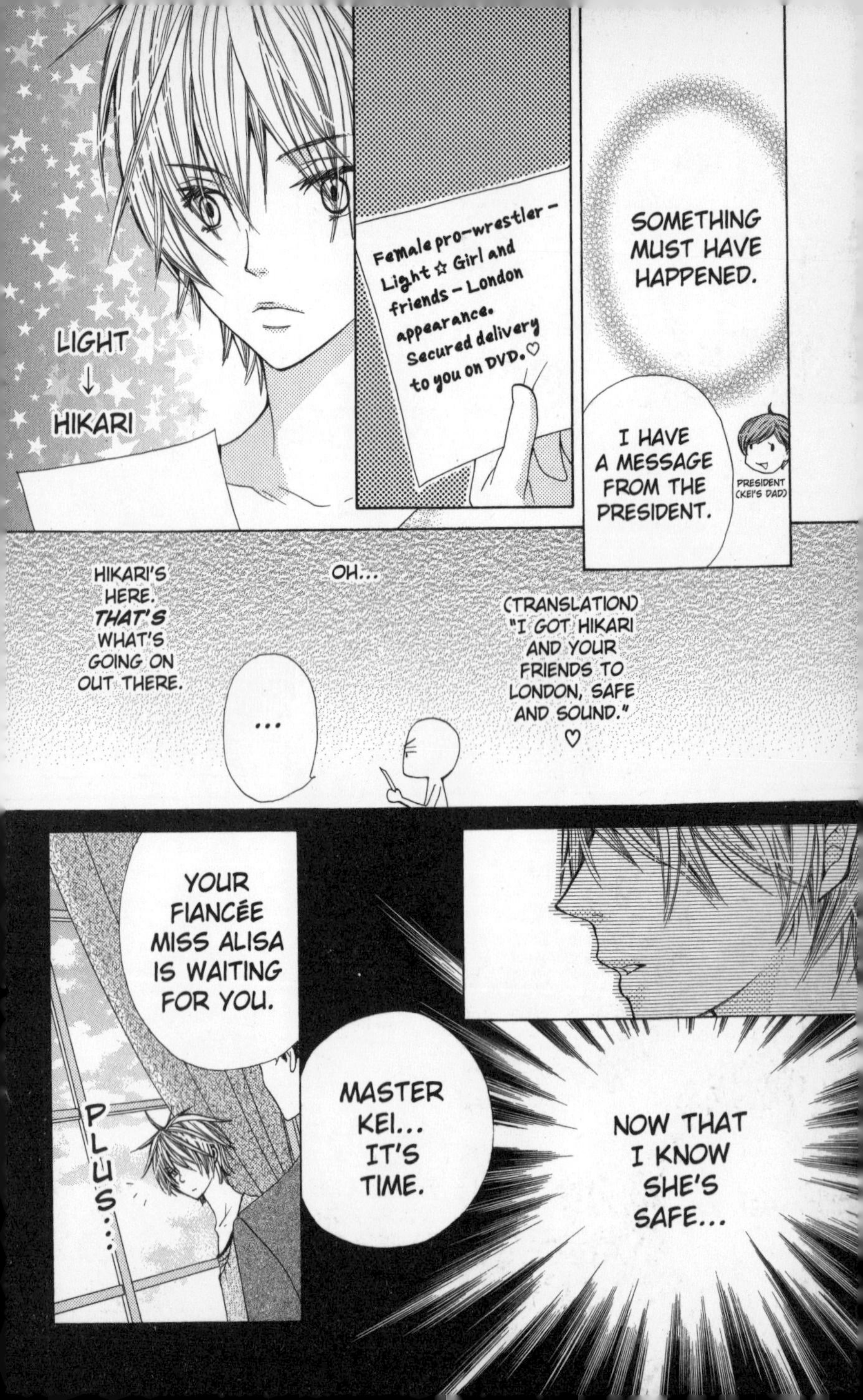
SOMETHING MUST HAVE HAPPENED.
I HAVE A MESSAGE FROM THE PRESIDENT.
PRESIDENT (KEI'S DAD)
Female pro-wrestler - Light ☆ Girl and friends - London appearance. Secured delivery to you on DVD. ♡
LIGHT ↓ HIKARI
(TRANSLATION) "I GOT HIKARI AND YOUR FRIENDS TO LONDON, SAFE AND SOUND." ♡
OH...
HIKARI'S HERE. *THAT'S* WHAT'S GOING ON OUT THERE.
...
NOW THAT I KNOW SHE'S SAFE...
MASTER KEI... IT'S TIME.
YOUR FIANCÉE MISS ALISA IS WAITING FOR YOU.
PLUS...

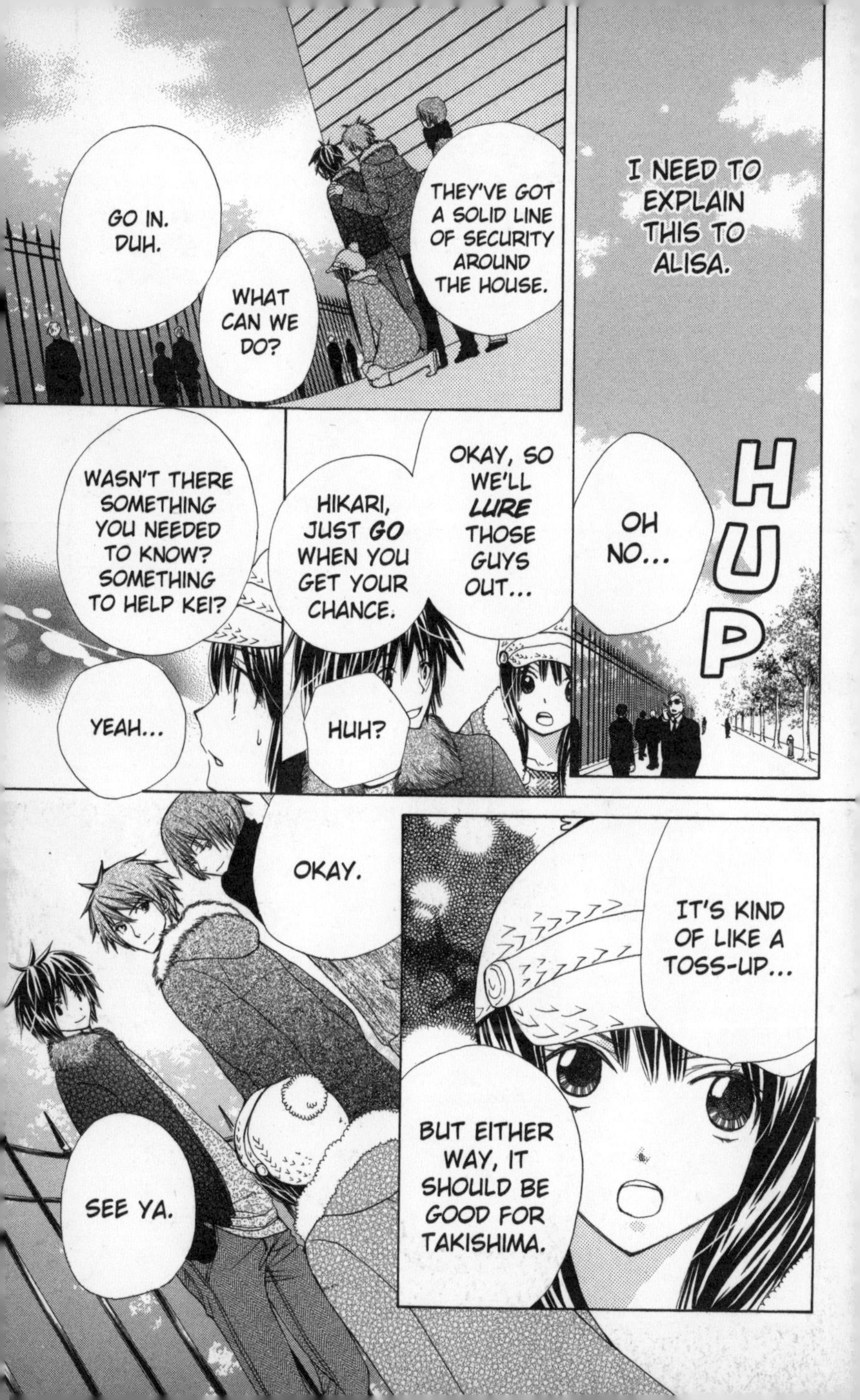
I NEED TO EXPLAIN THIS TO ALISA.
HUP
OH NO...
THEY'VE GOT A SOLID LINE OF SECURITY AROUND THE HOUSE.
WHAT CAN WE DO?
GO IN. DUH.
OKAY, SO WE'LL LURE THOSE GUYS OUT...
HIKARI, JUST GO WHEN YOU GET YOUR CHANCE.
HUH?
WASN'T THERE SOMETHING YOU NEEDED TO KNOW? SOMETHING TO HELP KEI?
YEAH...
IT'S KIND OF LIKE A TOSS-UP...
BUT EITHER WAY, IT SHOULD BE GOOD FOR TAKISHIMA.
OKAY.
SEE YA.

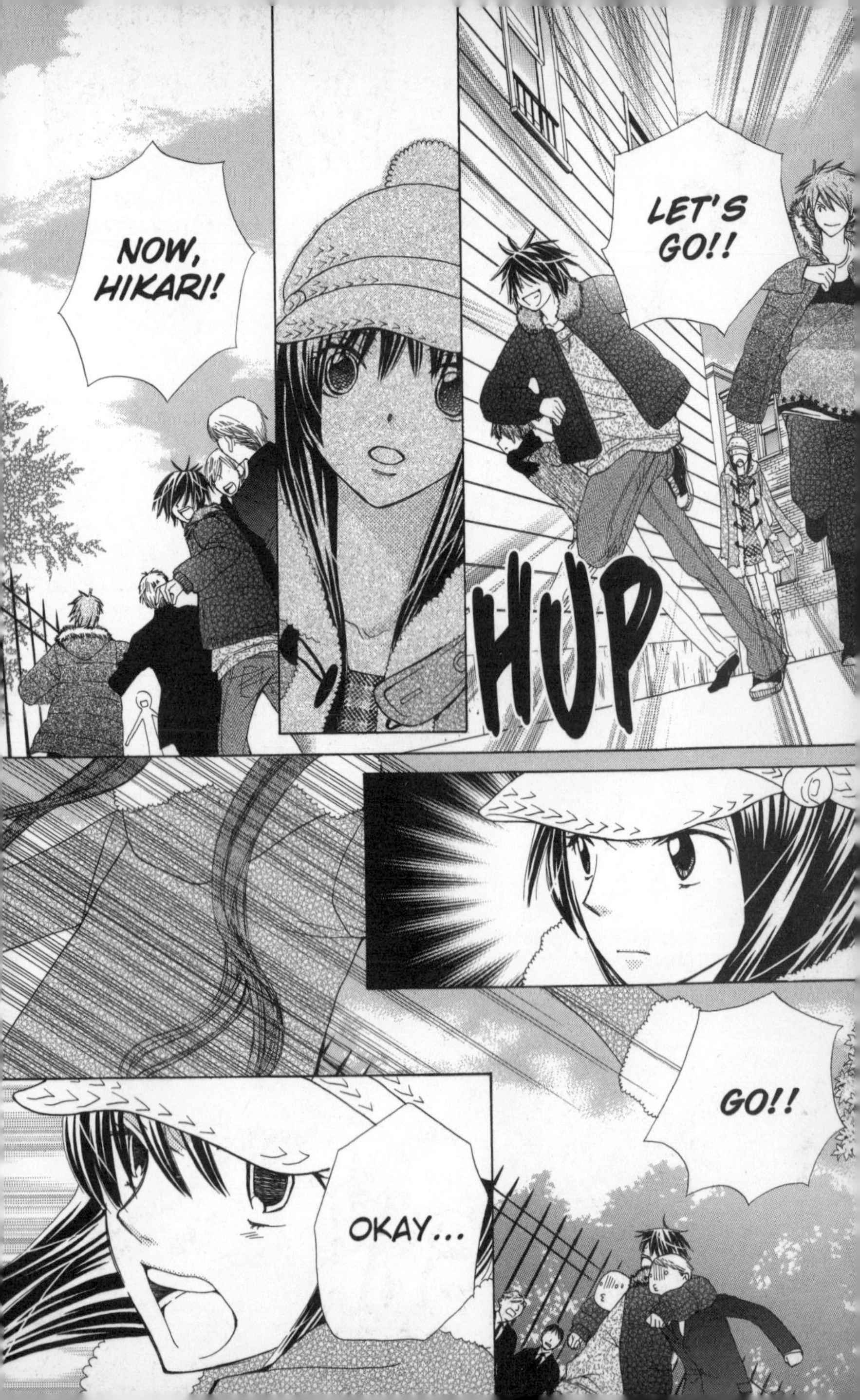
LET'S GO!!
HUP
NOW, HIKARI!
GO!!
OKAY...

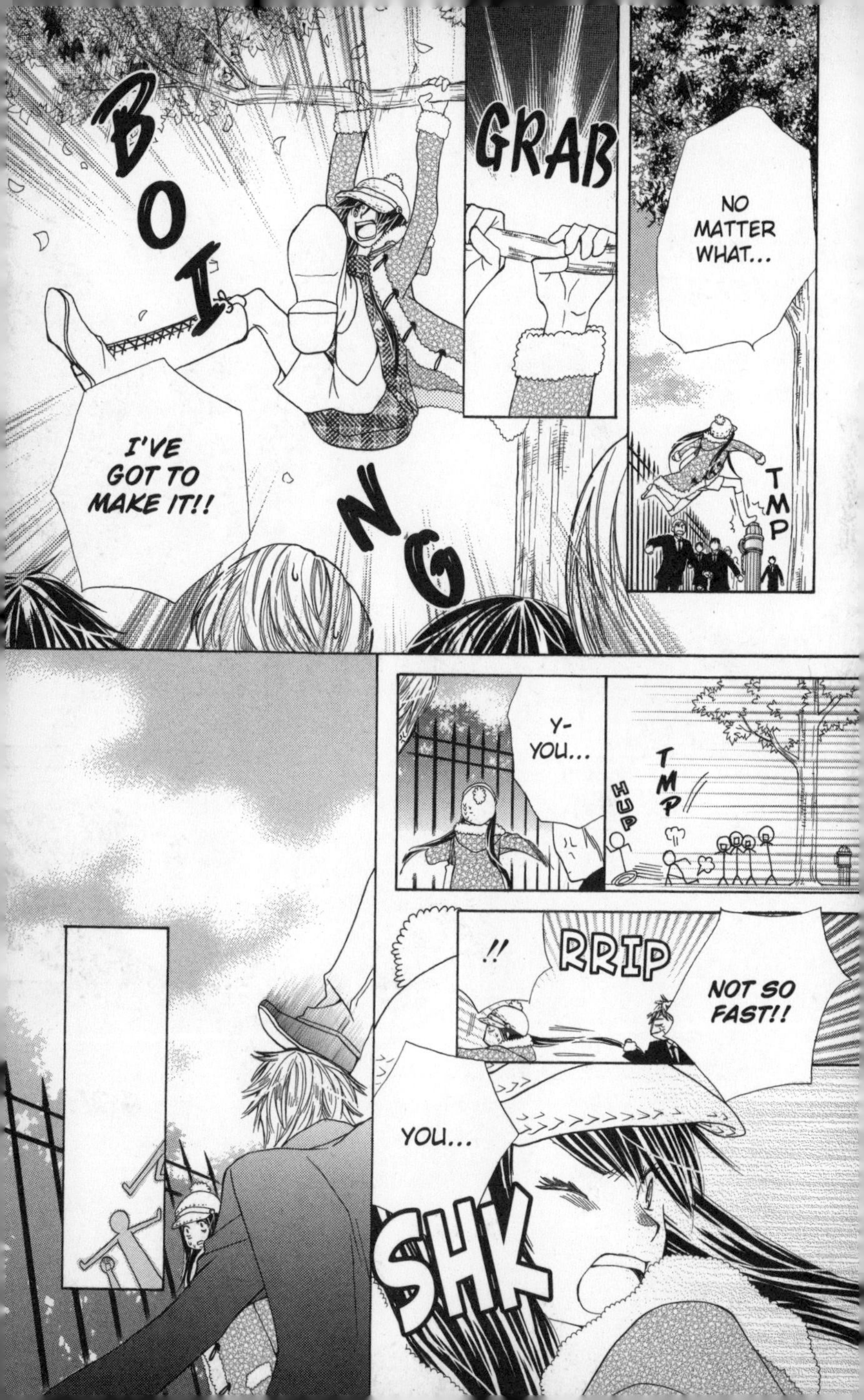
NO MATTER WHAT...
TMP
GRAB
BOING
I'VE GOT TO MAKE IT!!
TMP
HUP
Y- YOU...
NOT SO FAST!!
RRIP
!!
YOU...
SHK

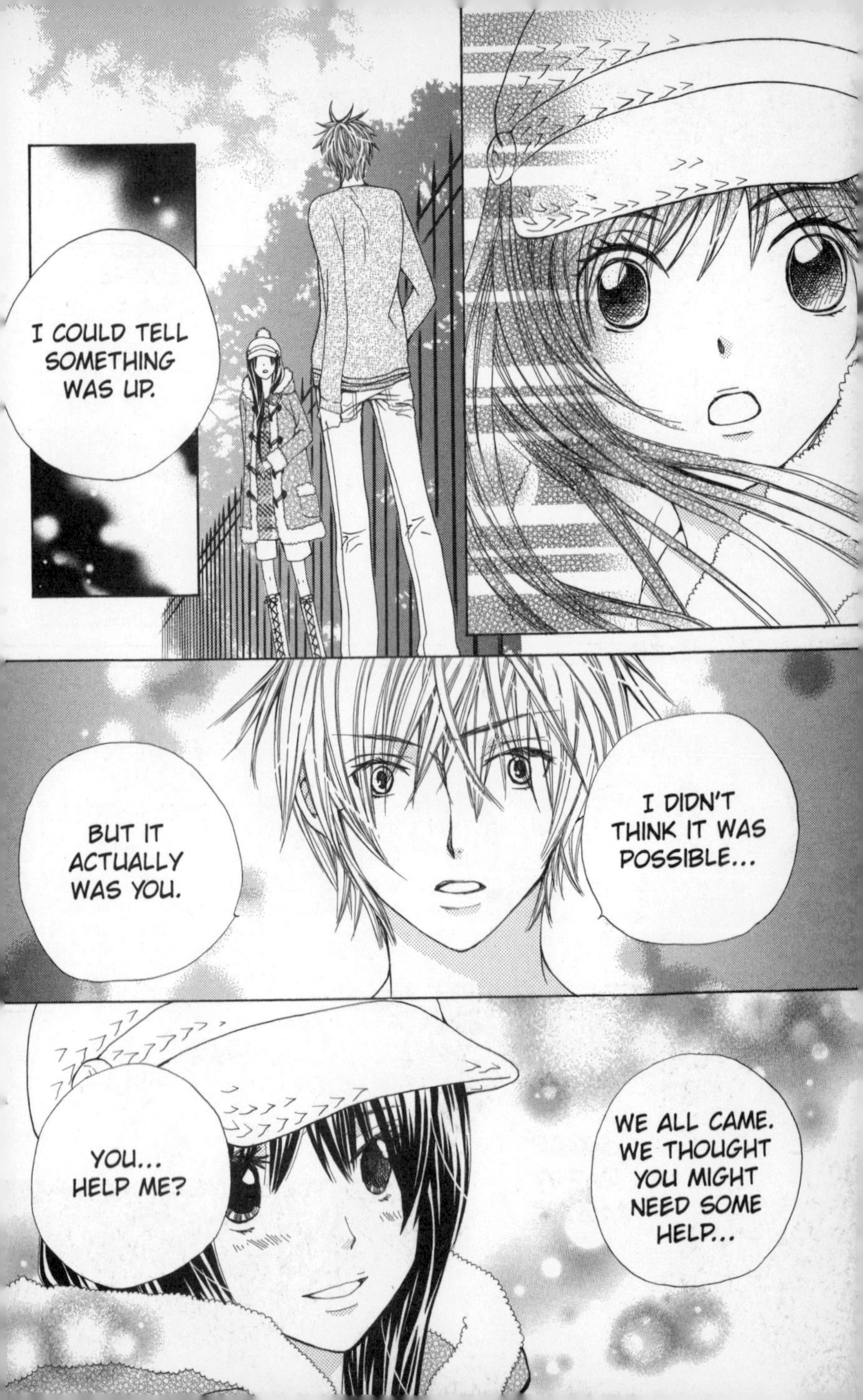
I COULD TELL SOMETHING WAS UP.
I DIDN'T THINK IT WAS POSSIBLE...
BUT IT ACTUALLY WAS YOU.
WE ALL CAME. WE THOUGHT YOU MIGHT NEED SOME HELP...
YOU... HELP ME?

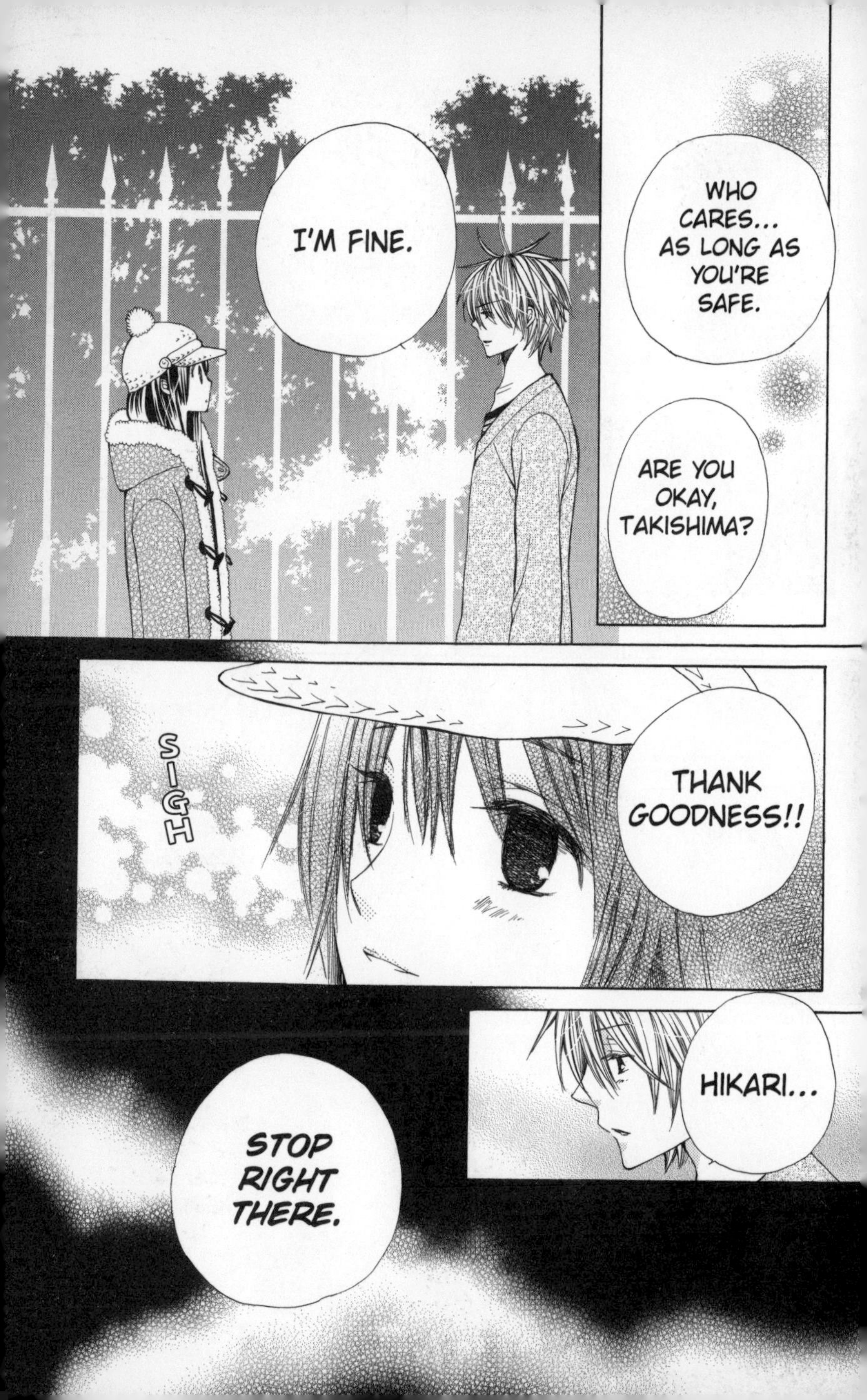
WHO CARES... AS LONG AS YOU'RE SAFE.
ARE YOU OKAY, TAKISHIMA?
I'M FINE.
THANK GOODNESS!!
SIGH
HIKARI...
STOP RIGHT THERE.

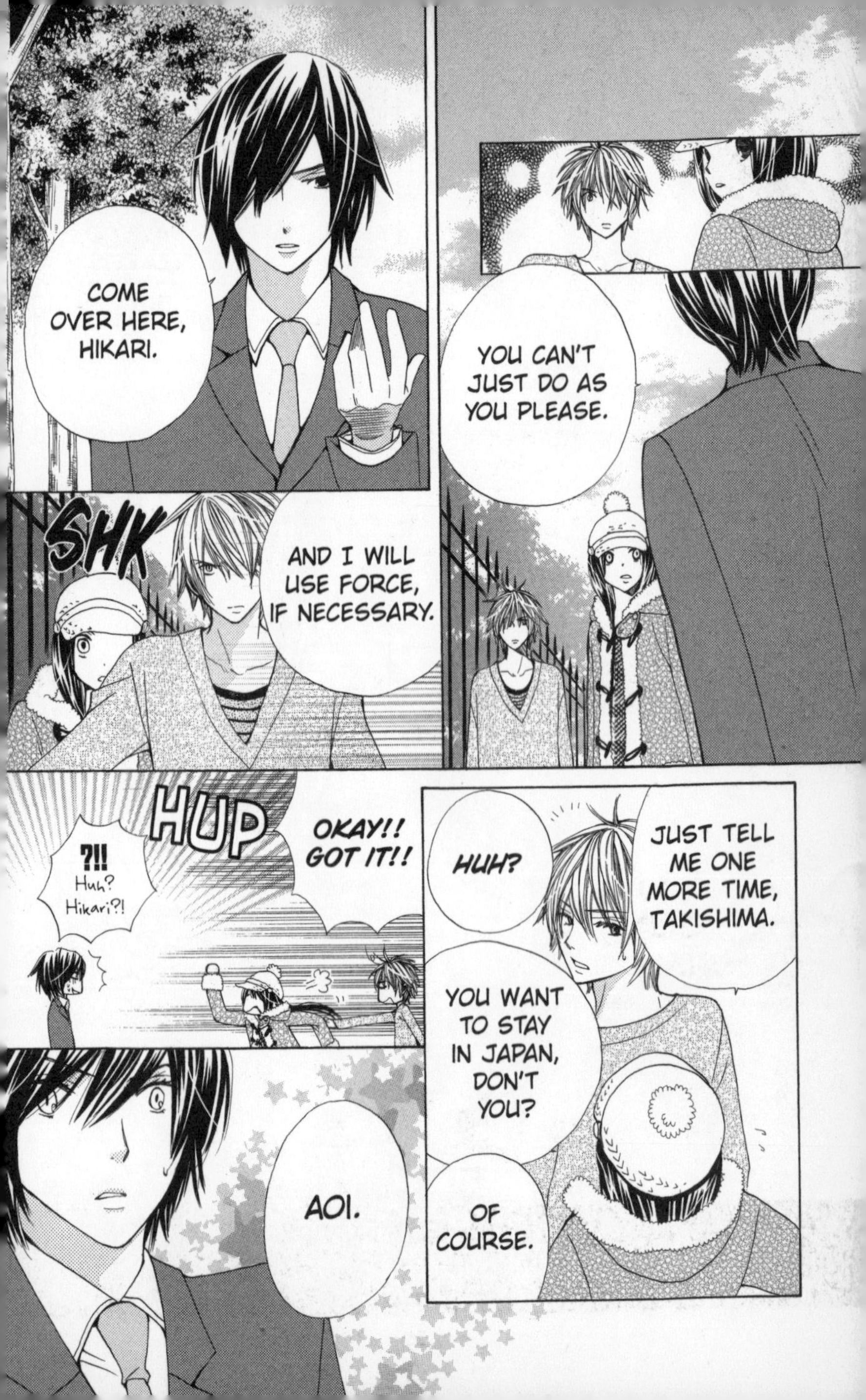
YOU CAN'T JUST DO AS YOU PLEASE.
COME OVER HERE, HIKARI.
SHK
AND I WILL USE FORCE, IF NECESSARY.
JUST TELL ME ONE MORE TIME, TAKISHIMA.
HUH?
YOU WANT TO STAY IN JAPAN, DON'T YOU?
OF COURSE.
OKAY!! GOT IT!!
HUP
?!! Huh? Hikari?!
AOI.

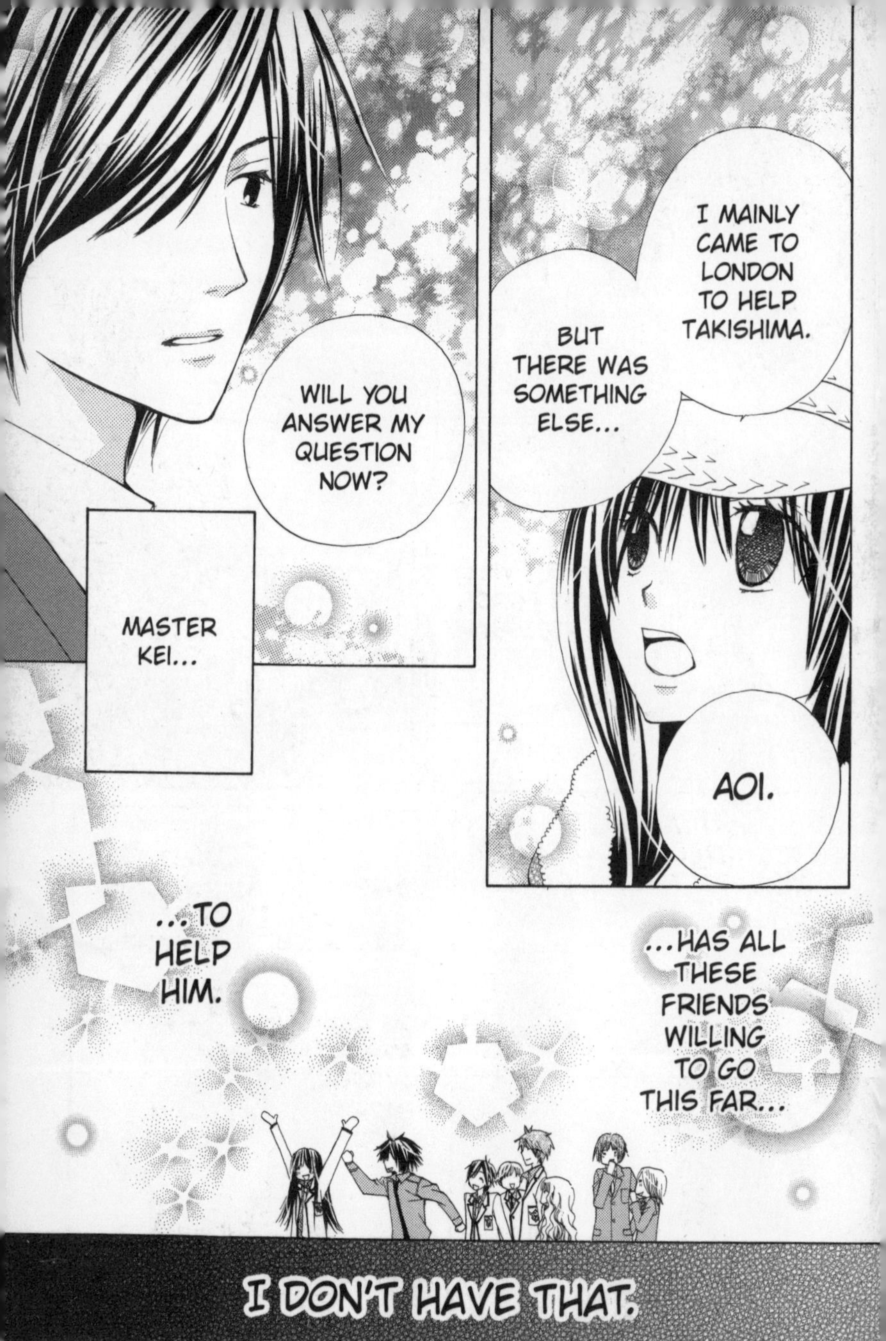
I MAINLY CAME TO LONDON TO HELP TAKISHIMA.
BUT THERE WAS SOMETHING ELSE...
AOI.
WILL YOU ANSWER MY QUESTION NOW?
MASTER KEI...
...HAS ALL THESE FRIENDS WILLING TO GO THIS FAR...
...TO HELP HIM.
I DON'T HAVE THAT.

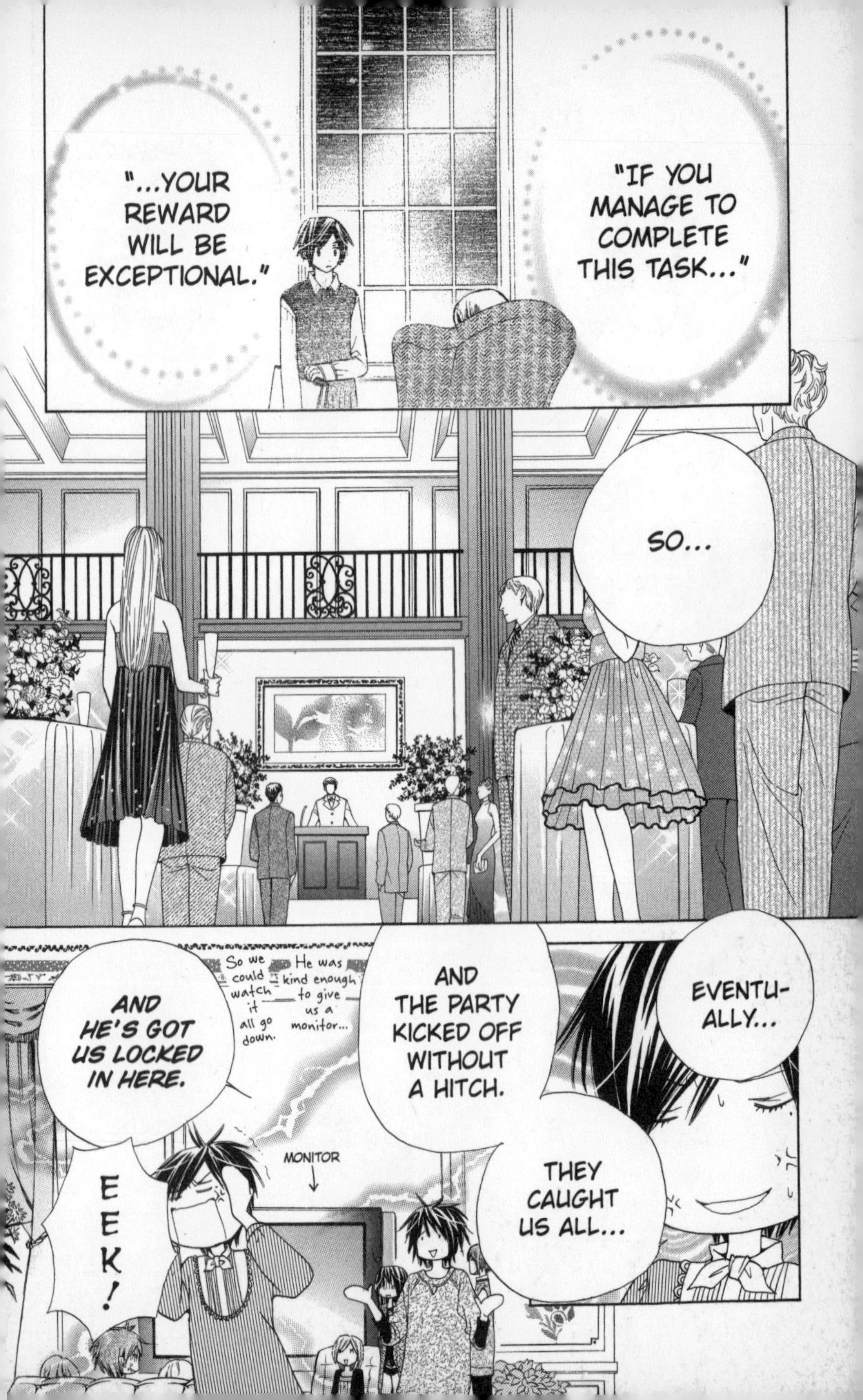
"IF YOU MANAGE TO COMPLETE THIS TASK..."
"...YOUR REWARD WILL BE EXCEPTIONAL."
SO...
EVENTU-ALLY...
THEY CAUGHT US ALL...
AND THE PARTY KICKED OFF WITHOUT A HITCH.
He was kind enough to give us a monitor...
So we could watch it all go down.
AND HE'S GOT US LOCKED IN HERE.
MONITOR
EEK!

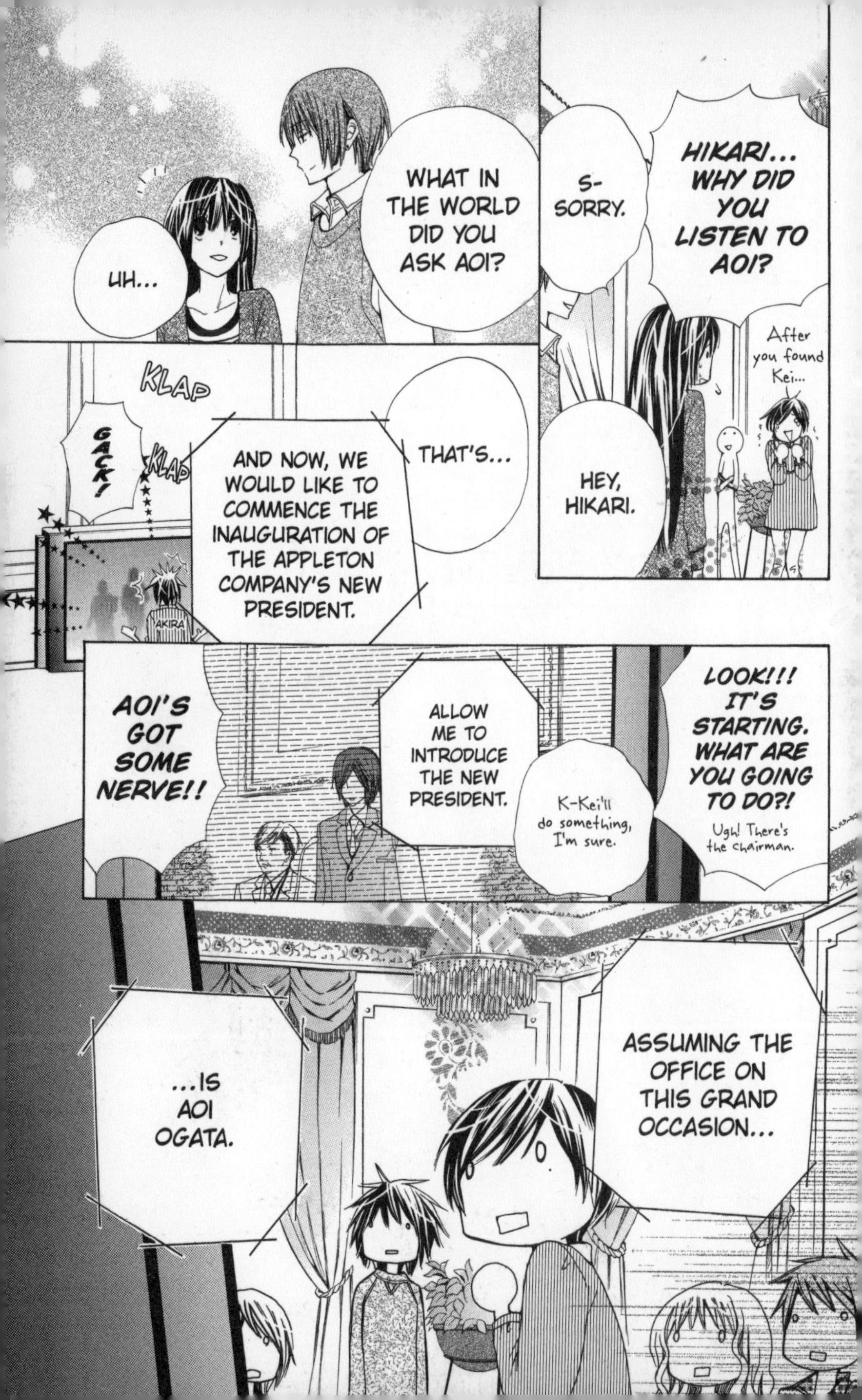
HIKARI... WHY DID YOU LISTEN TO AOI?
S-SORRY.
After you found Kei...
HEY, HIKARI.
WHAT IN THE WORLD DID YOU ASK AOI?
UH...
THAT'S...
AND NOW, WE WOULD LIKE TO COMMENCE THE INAUGURATION OF THE APPLETON COMPANY'S NEW PRESIDENT.
KLAP
GACK!
KLAP
AKIRA
LOOK!!! IT'S STARTING. WHAT ARE YOU GOING TO DO?!
Ugh! There's the chairman.
K-Kei'll do something, I'm sure.
ALLOW ME TO INTRODUCE THE NEW PRESIDENT.
AOI'S GOT SOME NERVE!!
ASSUMING THE OFFICE ON THIS GRAND OCCASION...
...IS AOI OGATA.

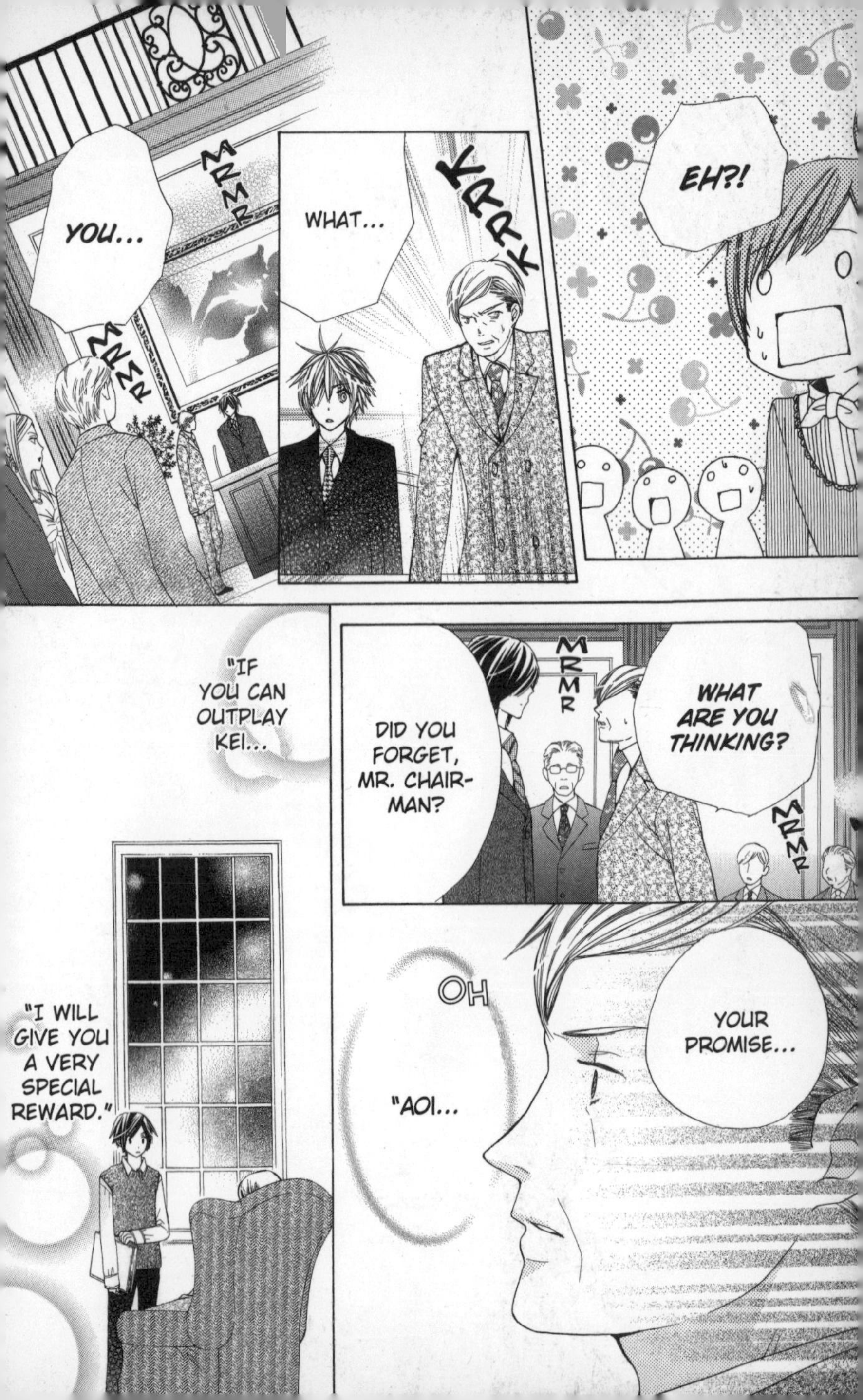
EH?!
KRRRK
WHAT...
MRMR
YOU...
MRMR
WHAT ARE YOU THINKING?
MRMR
MRMR
DID YOU FORGET, MR. CHAIR-MAN?
YOUR PROMISE...
OH
"AOI...
"IF YOU CAN OUTPLAY KEI...
"I WILL GIVE YOU A VERY SPECIAL REWARD."

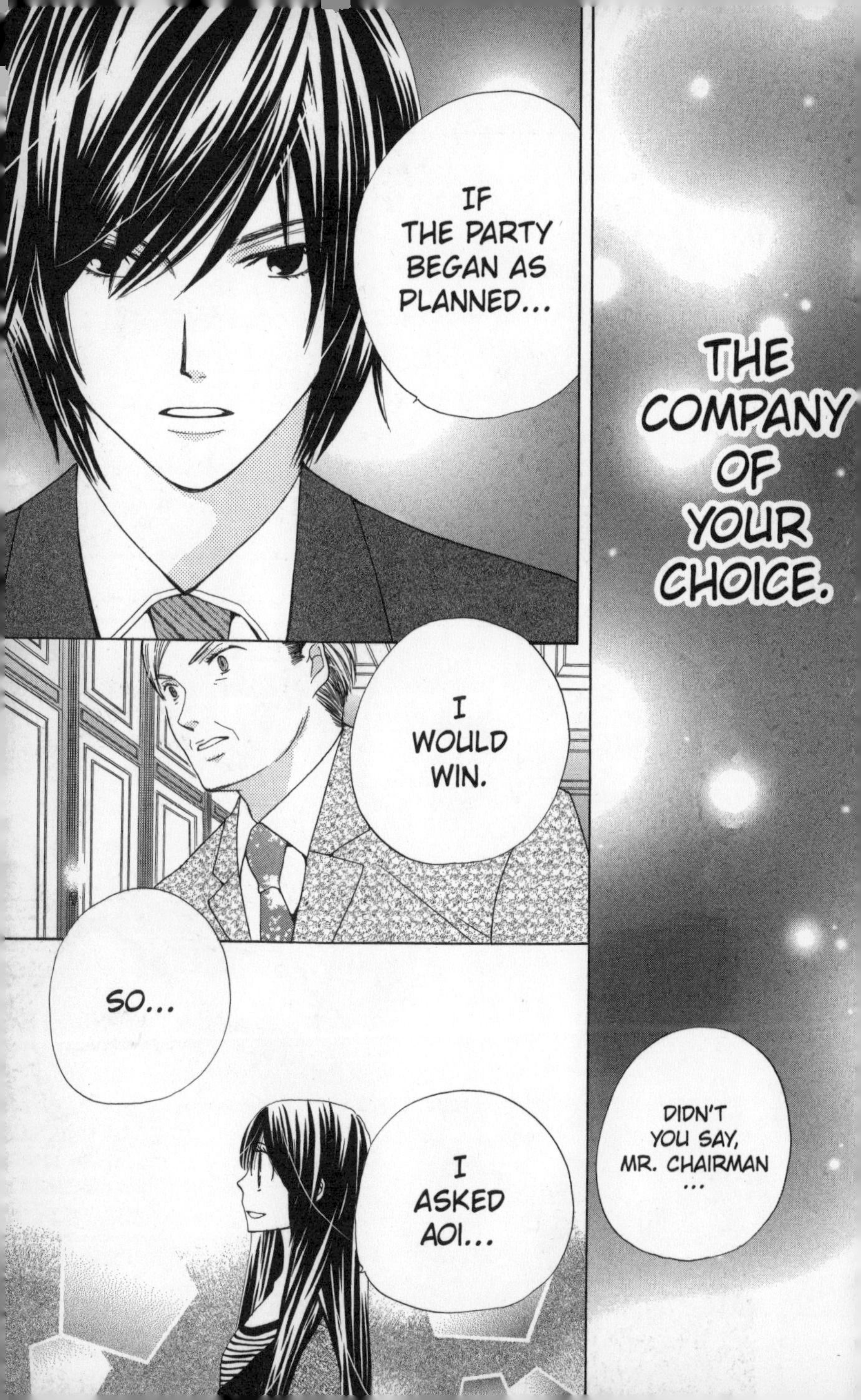
THE COMPANY OF YOUR CHOICE.
DIDN'T YOU SAY, MR. CHAIRMAN ...
IF THE PARTY BEGAN AS PLANNED...
I WOULD WIN.
SO...
I ASKED AOI...

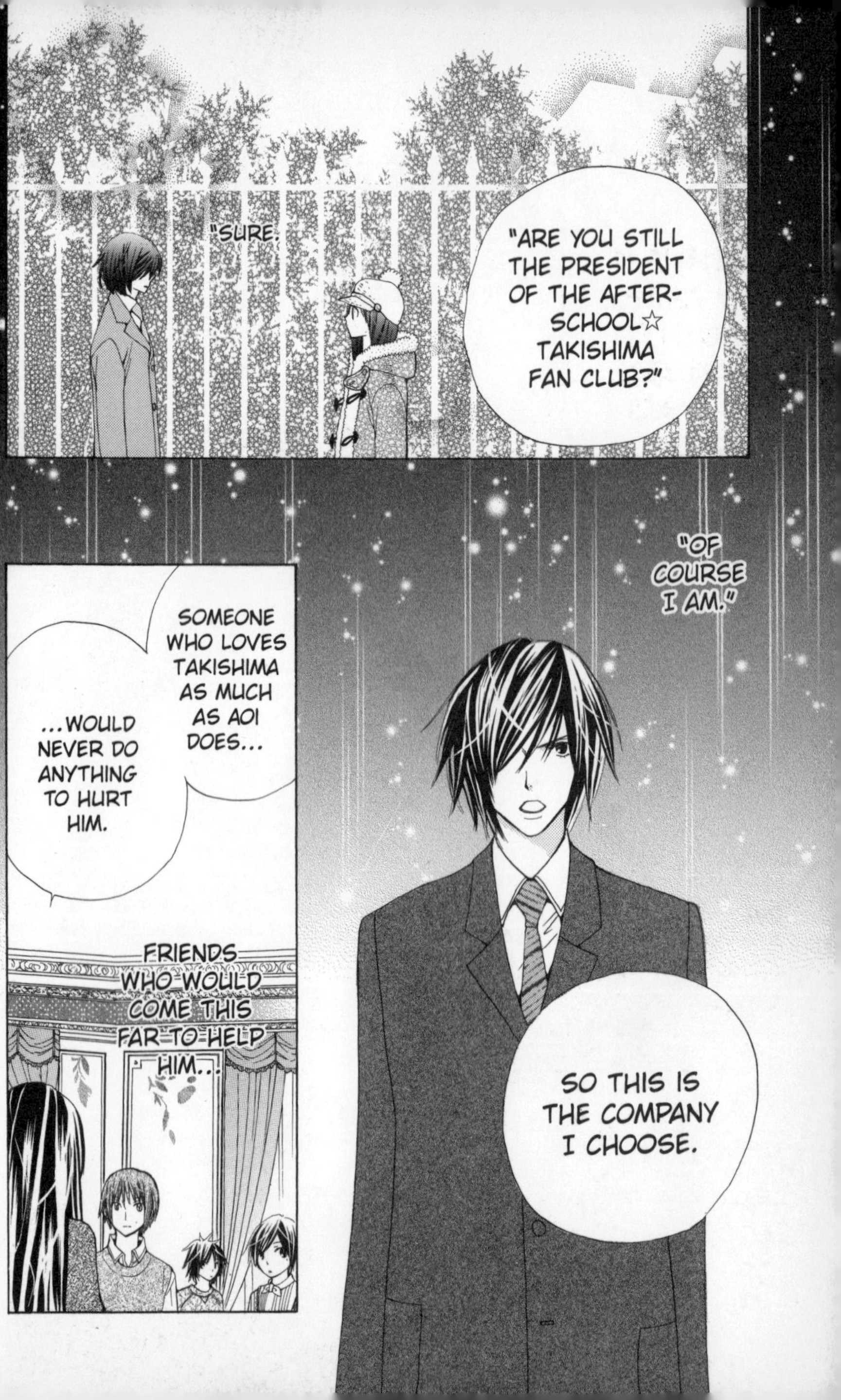
"ARE YOU STILL THE PRESIDENT OF THE AFTER-SCHOOL☆ TAKISHIMA FAN CLUB?"
"SURE.
"OF COURSE I AM."
SOMEONE WHO LOVES TAKISHIMA AS MUCH AS AOI DOES...
...WOULD NEVER DO ANYTHING TO HURT HIM.
FRIENDS WHO WOULD COME THIS FAR TO HELP HIM...
SO THIS IS THE COMPANY I CHOOSE.

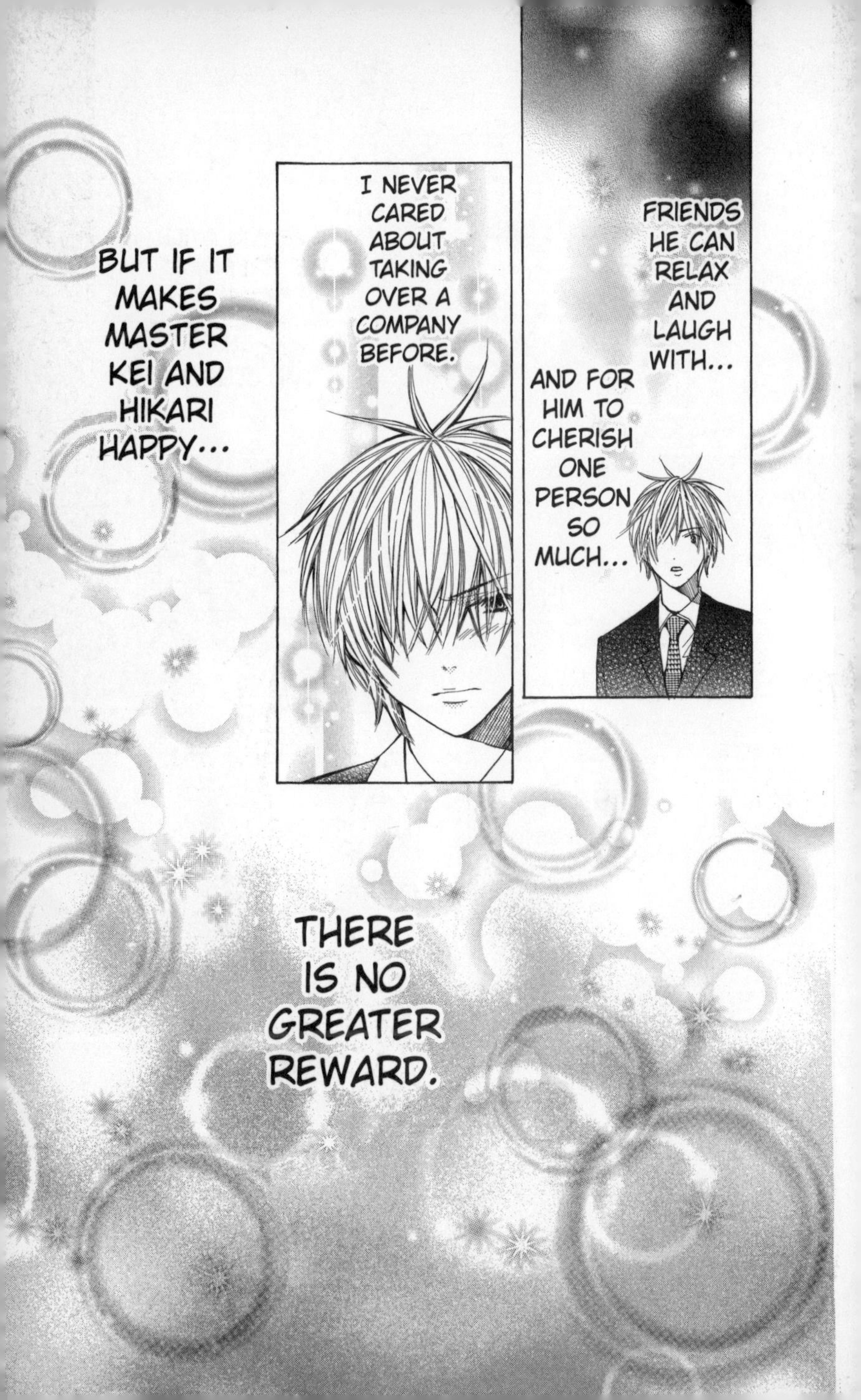
FRIENDS HE CAN RELAX AND LAUGH WITH...
AND FOR HIM TO CHERISH ONE PERSON SO MUCH...
I NEVER CARED ABOUT TAKING OVER A COMPANY BEFORE.
BUT IF IT MAKES MASTER KEI AND HIKARI HAPPY...
THERE IS NO GREATER REWARD.

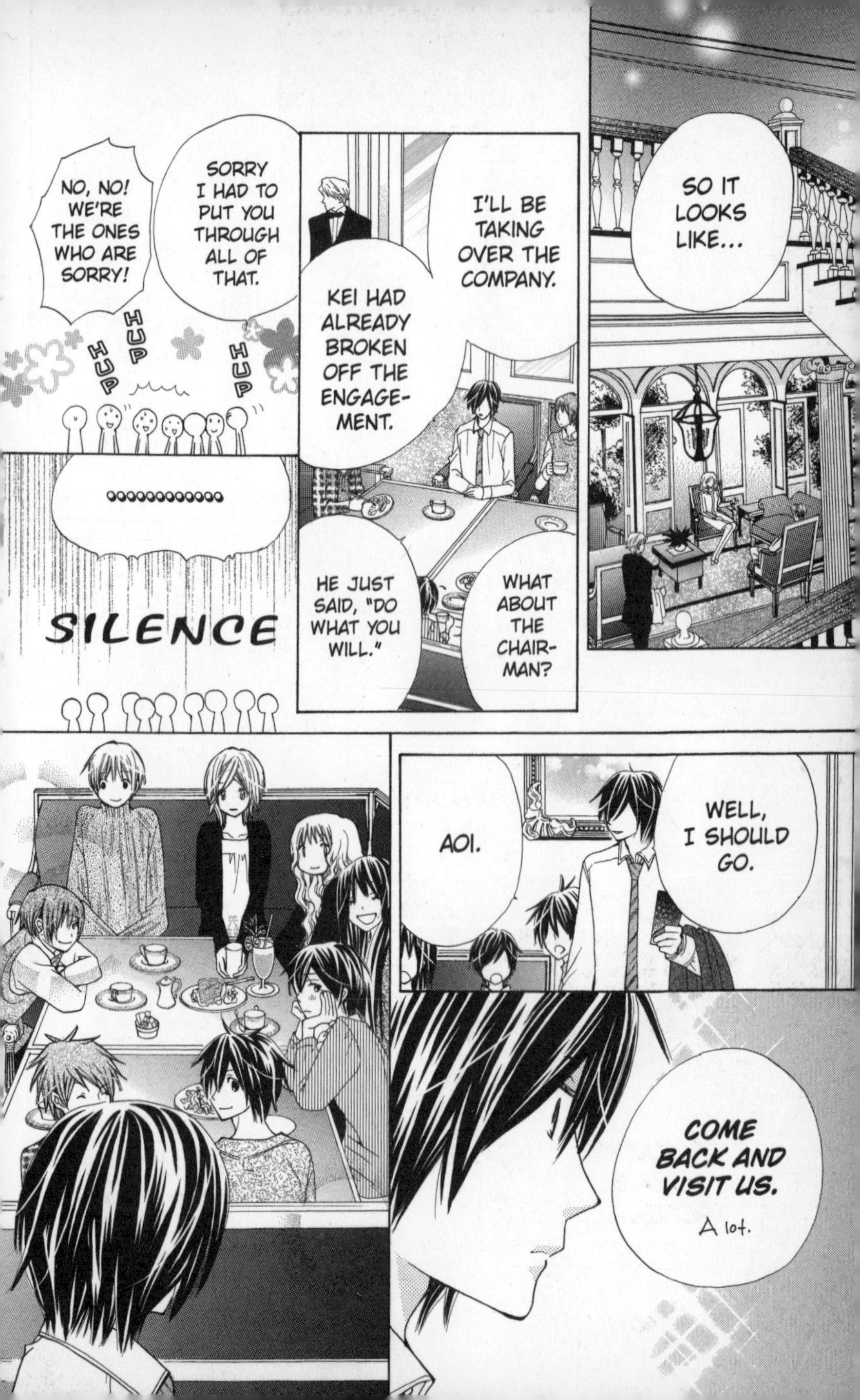
SO IT LOOKS LIKE...
I'LL BE TAKING OVER THE COMPANY.
KEI HAD ALREADY BROKEN OFF THE ENGAGE-MENT.
WHAT ABOUT THE CHAIR-MAN?
HE JUST SAID, "DO WHAT YOU WILL."
SORRY I HAD TO PUT YOU THROUGH ALL OF THAT.
NO, NO! WE'RE THE ONES WHO ARE SORRY!
HUP HUP HUP
....
SILENCE
WELL, I SHOULD GO.
AOI.
COME BACK AND VISIT US.
A lot.

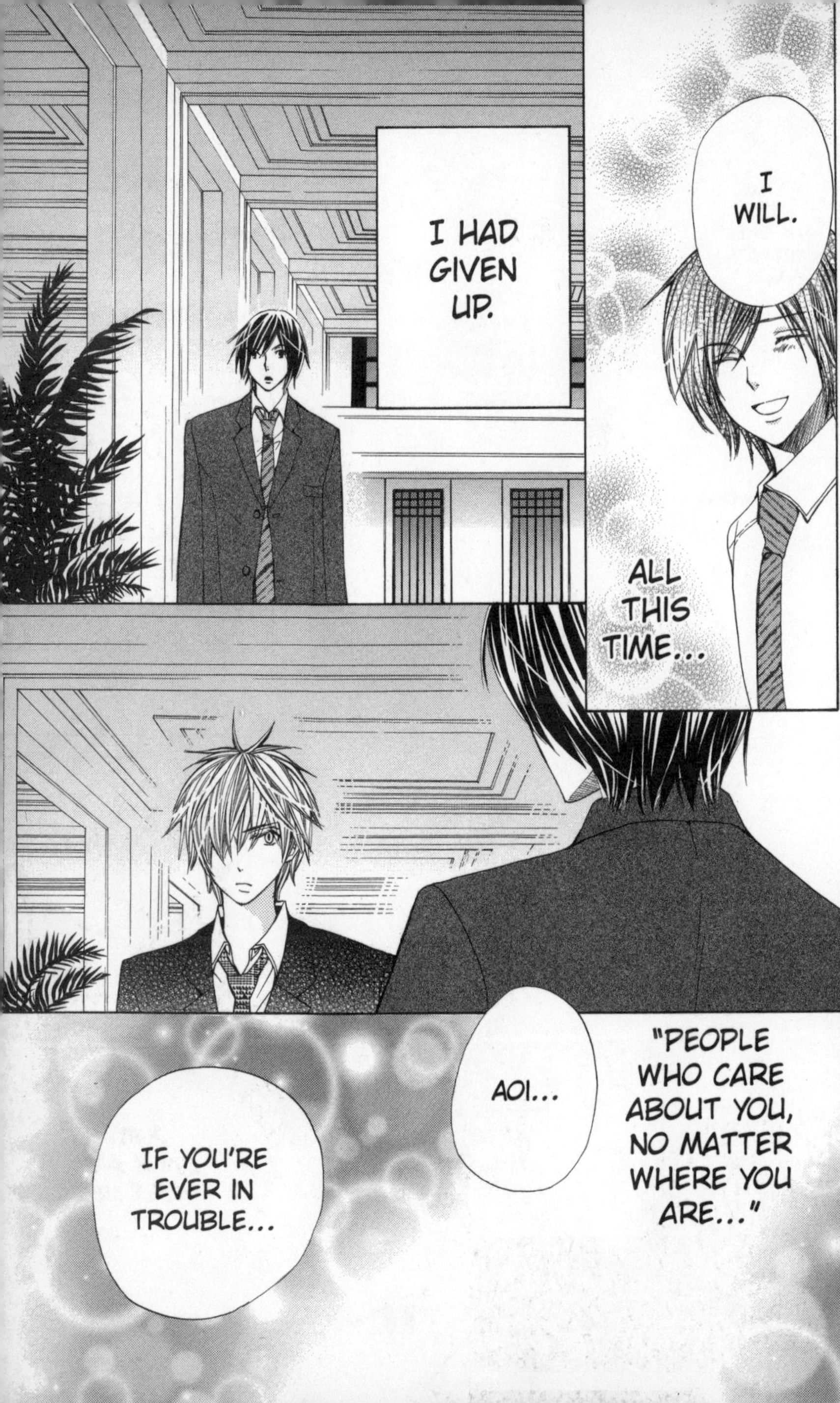
I WILL.
ALL THIS TIME...
I HAD GIVEN UP.
"PEOPLE WHO CARE ABOUT YOU, NO MATTER WHERE YOU ARE..."
AOI...
IF YOU'RE EVER IN TROUBLE...

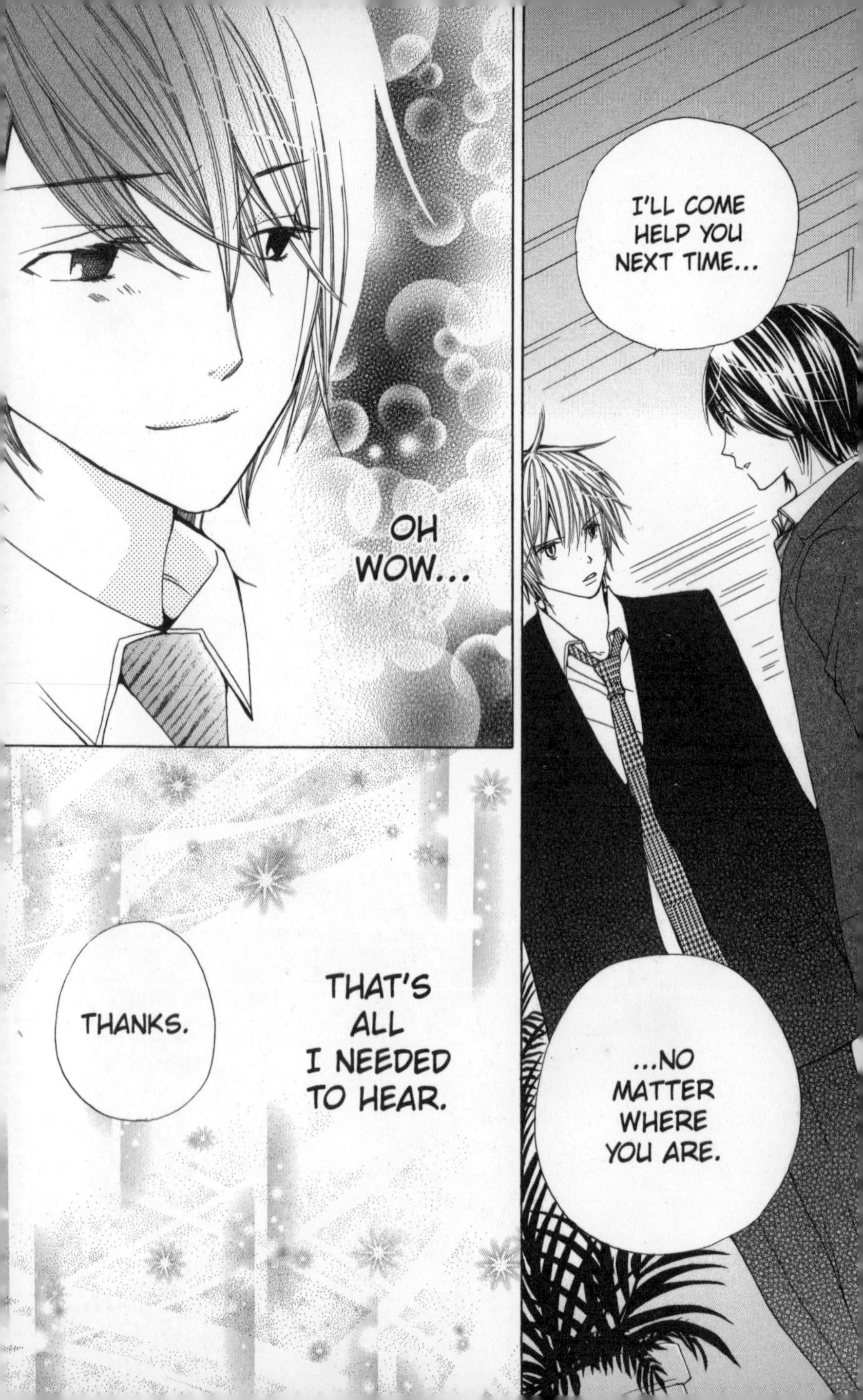
I'LL COME HELP YOU NEXT TIME...
...NO MATTER WHERE YOU ARE.
OH WOW...
THAT'S ALL I NEEDED TO HEAR.
THANKS.

Chapter 72

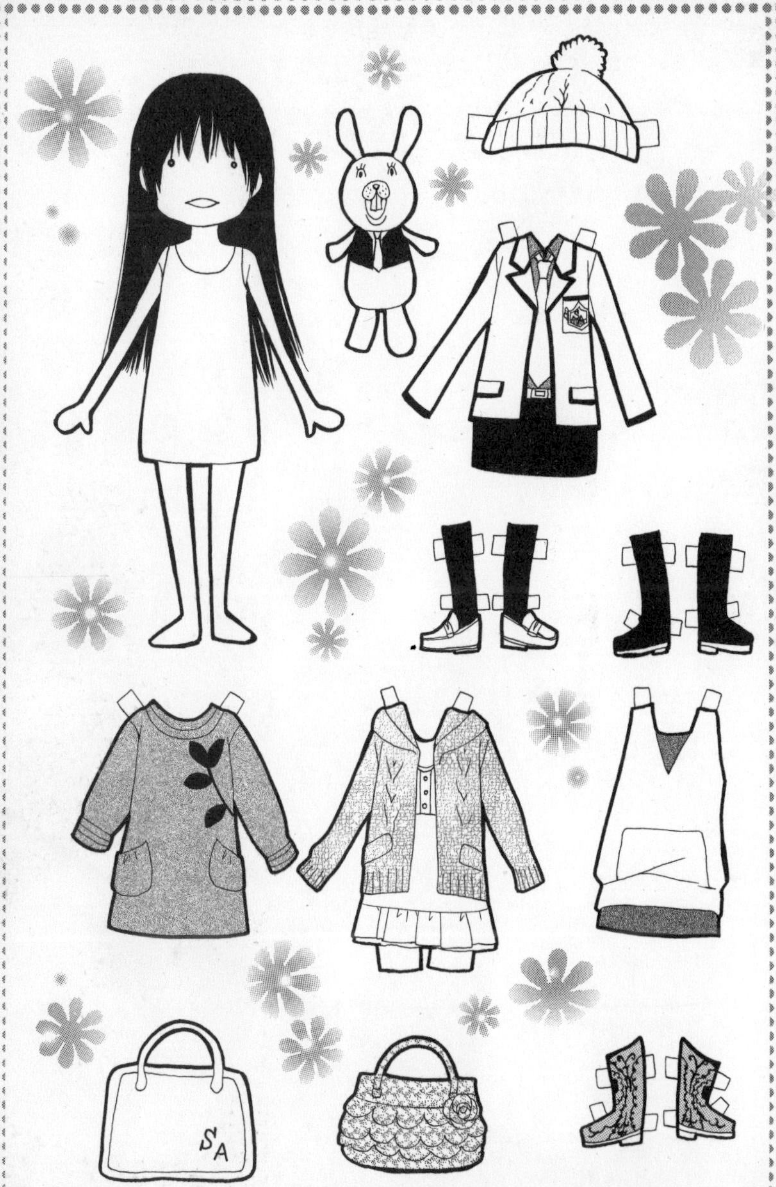
SA

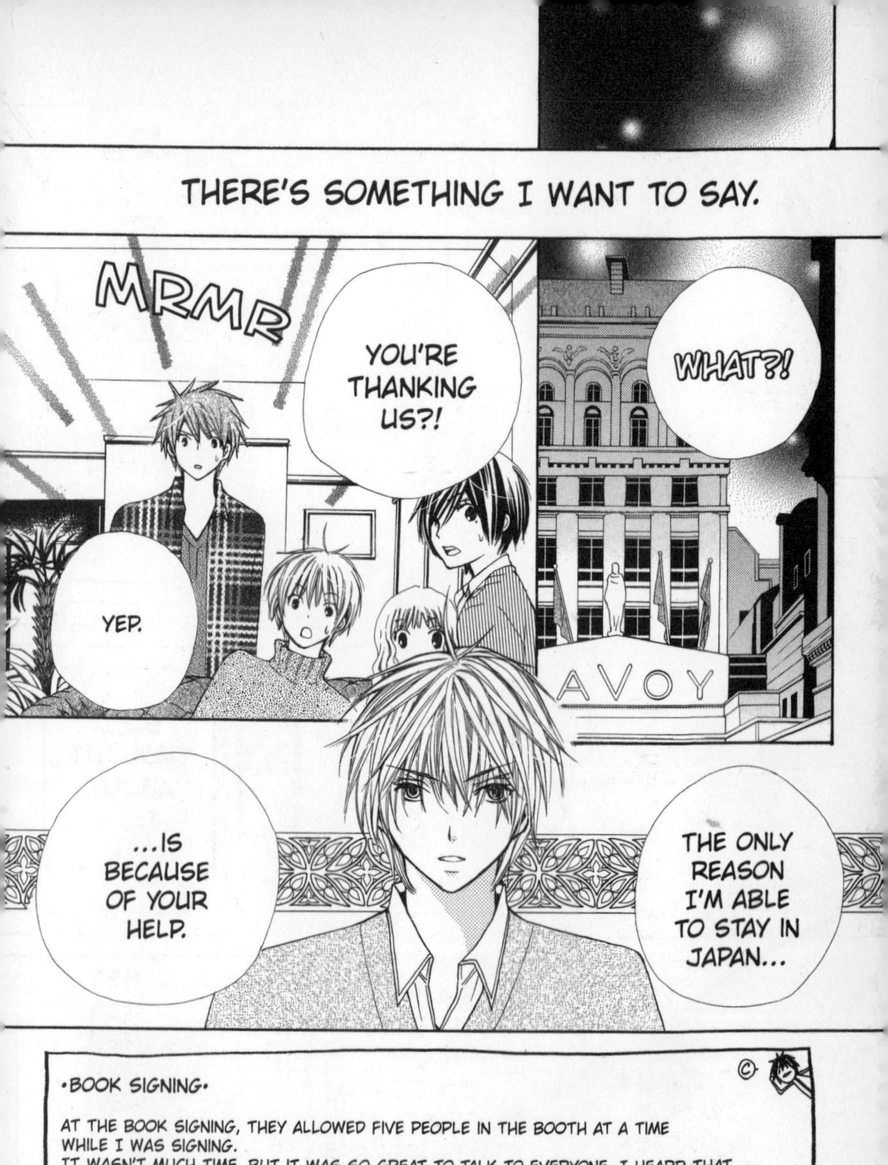
THERE'S SOMETHING I WANT TO SAY.
WHAT?!
YOU'RE THANKING US?!
MRMR
YEP.
THE ONLY REASON I'M ABLE TO STAY IN JAPAN...
...IS BECAUSE OF YOUR HELP.
AVOY

•BOOK SIGNING•

AT THE BOOK SIGNING, THEY ALLOWED FIVE PEOPLE IN THE BOOTH AT A TIME WHILE I WAS SIGNING.
IT WASN'T MUCH TIME, BUT IT WAS SO GREAT TO TALK TO EVERYONE. I HEARD THAT PEOPLE USUALLY BRING YOU FLOWERS AT BOOK SIGNINGS, BUT I GOT LOTS OF FOOD! ♡ YOU GUYS ARE SO GREAT! I SHARED IT ALL WITH MY ASSISTANTS AND MY FAMILY! THANK YOU SO MUCH! THE BEST PART WAS BEING ABLE TO MEET MY FANS. SOME PEOPLE BROUGHT THEIR PARENTS AND SOME PEOPLE CAME FROM YOKOHAMA. I GOT TO MEET SOME OF THE PEOPLE WHO WRITE ME LETTERS TOO. I'M THE LUCKIEST WRITER. IT WAS NICE TO BE ABLE TO TALK TO THE PEOPLE WHO WAITED UNTIL IT WAS ALL OVER. IT WAS REALLY SUCH A GREAT EVENT. THANK YOU, EVERYBODY!

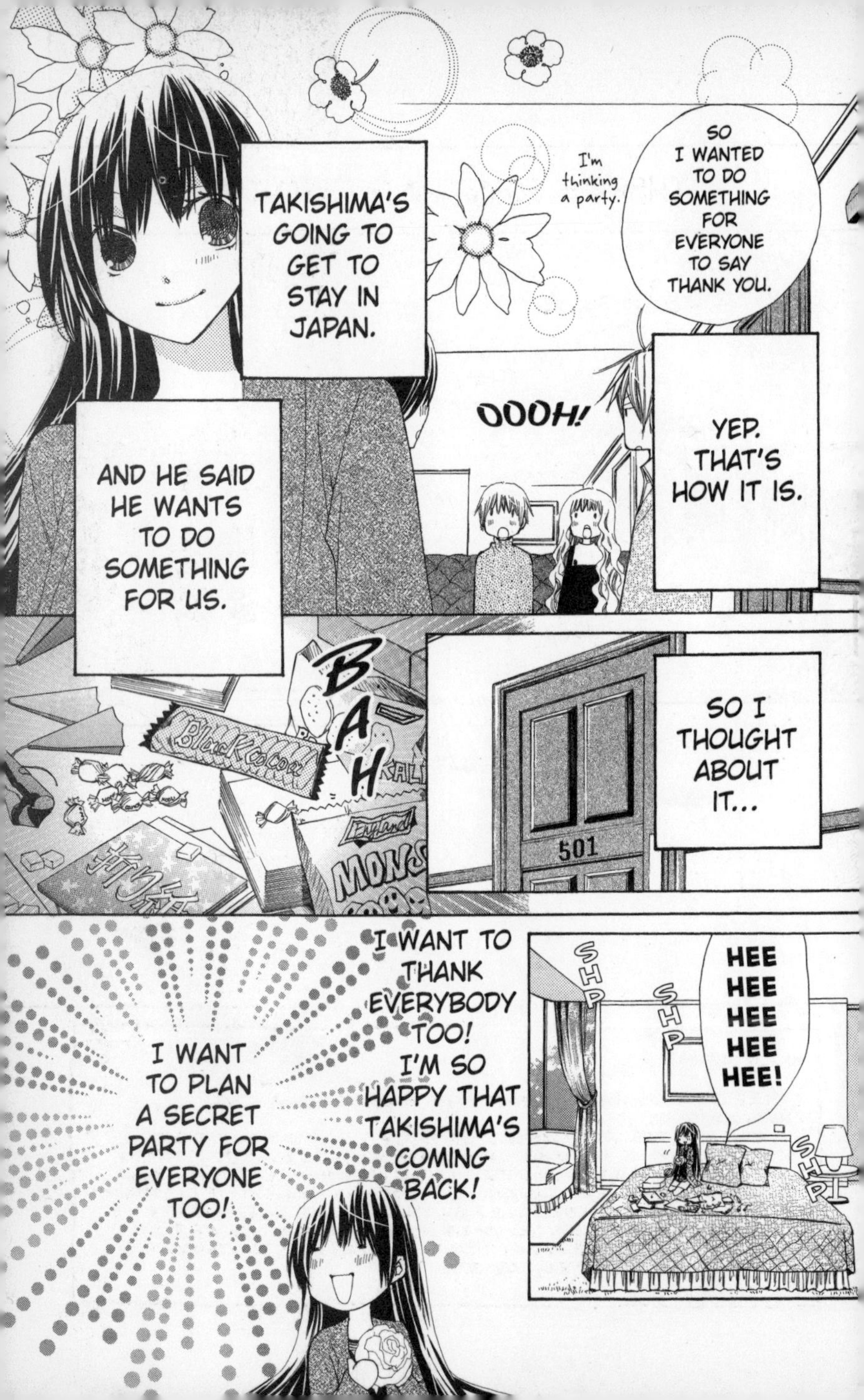
SO I WANTED TO DO SOMETHING FOR EVERYONE TO SAY THANK YOU.
I'm thinking a party.
YEP. THAT'S HOW IT IS.
OOOH!
TAKISHIMA'S GOING TO GET TO STAY IN JAPAN.
AND HE SAID HE WANTS TO DO SOMETHING FOR US.
SO I THOUGHT ABOUT IT...
501
BAH
Black Cocoa
England
MONS
SHP
SHP
HEE HEE HEE HEE HEE!
SHP
I WANT TO THANK EVERYBODY TOO! I'M SO HAPPY THAT TAKISHIMA'S COMING BACK!
I WANT TO PLAN A SECRET PARTY FOR EVERYONE TOO!

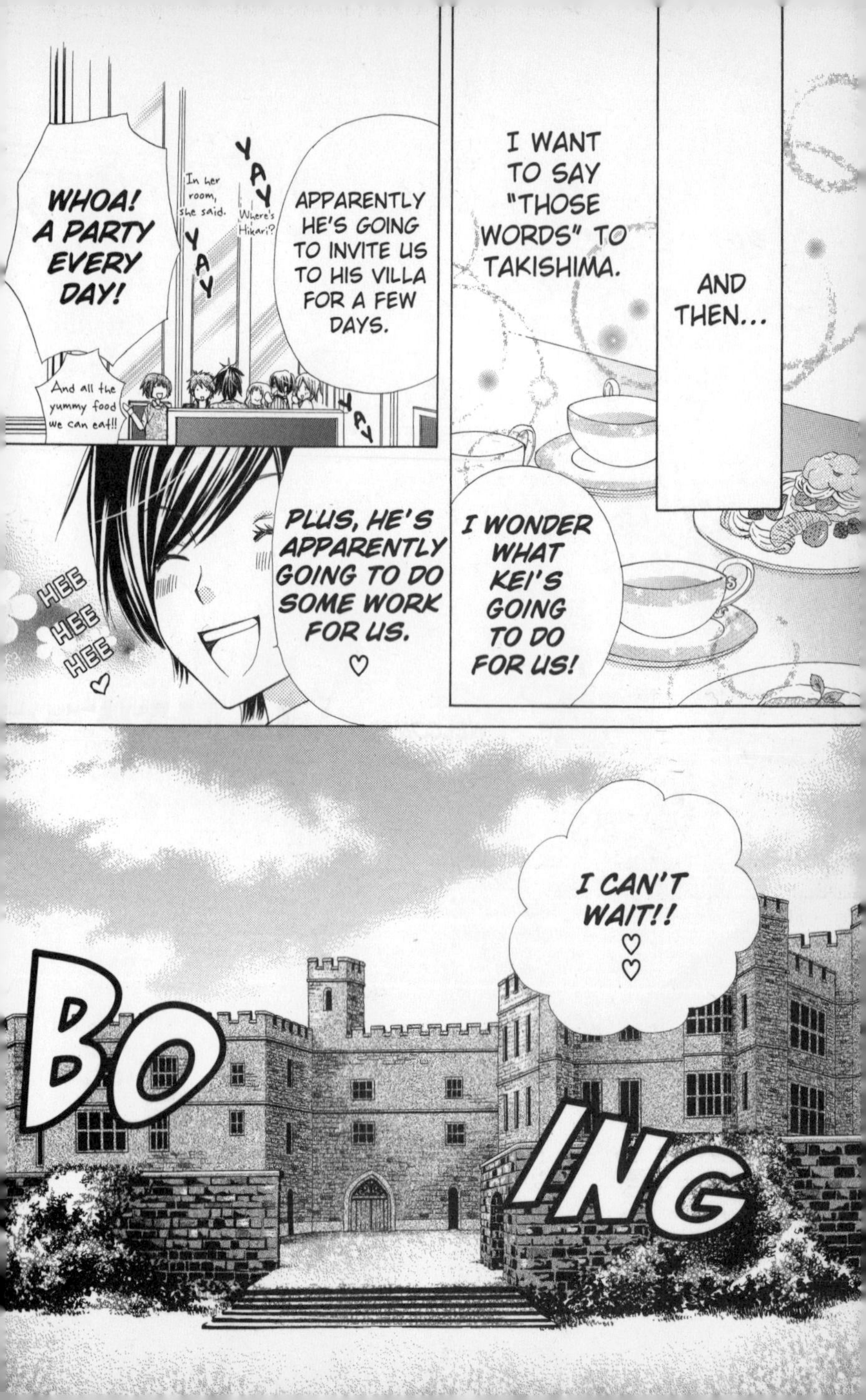
AND THEN...
I WANT TO SAY "THOSE WORDS" TO TAKISHIMA.
APPARENTLY HE'S GOING TO INVITE US TO HIS VILLA FOR A FEW DAYS.
YAY YAY YAY
Where's Hikari?
In her room, she said.
WHOA! A PARTY EVERY DAY!
And all the yummy food we can eat!!
I WONDER WHAT KEI'S GOING TO DO FOR US!
PLUS, HE'S APPARENTLY GOING TO DO SOME WORK FOR US. ♡
HEE HEE HEE ♡
I CAN'T WAIT!! ♡ ♡
BOING

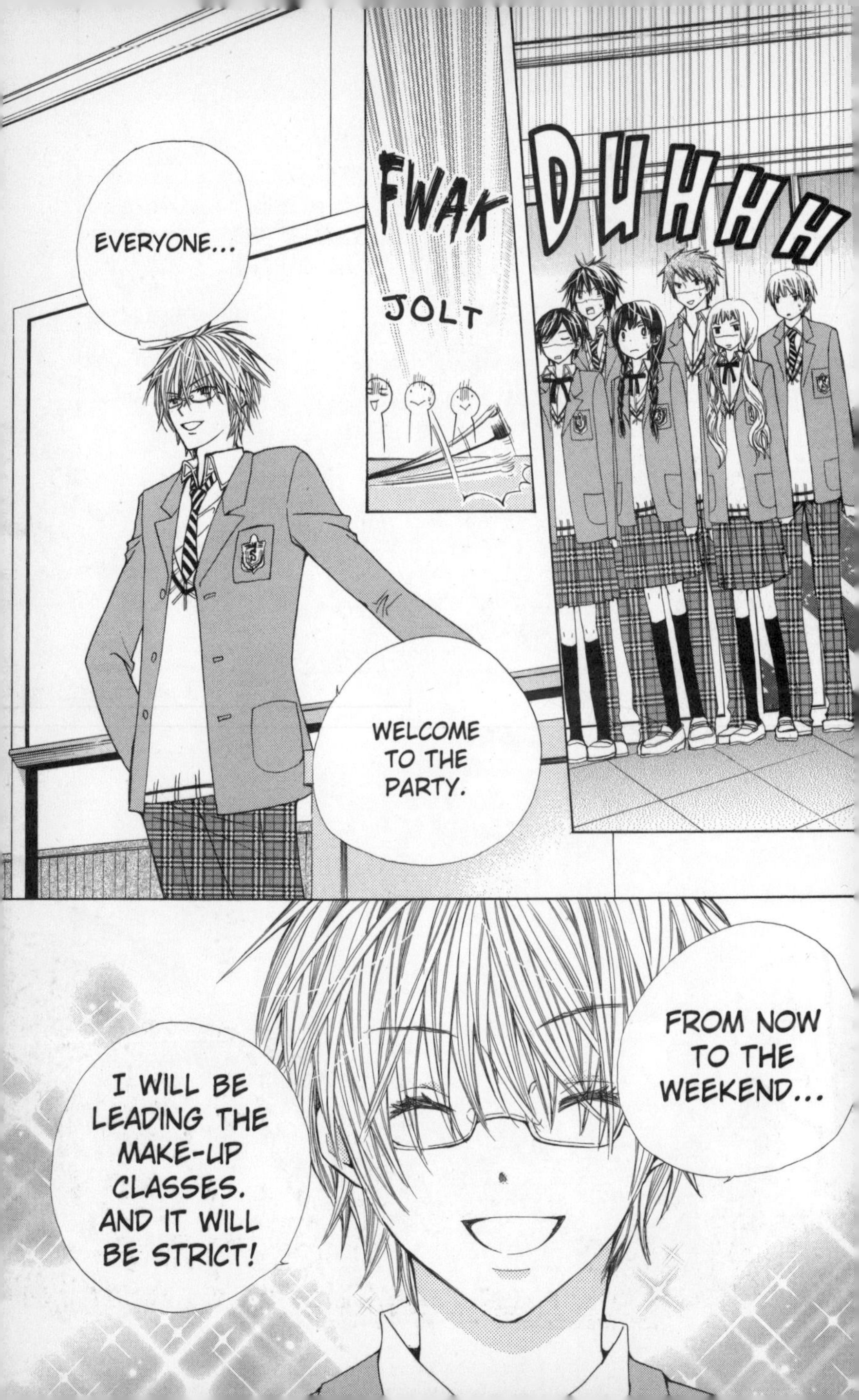
DUHHHH
FWAK
JOLT
EVERYONE...
WELCOME TO THE PARTY.
FROM NOW TO THE WEEKEND...
I WILL BE LEADING THE MAKE-UP CLASSES. AND IT WILL BE STRICT!

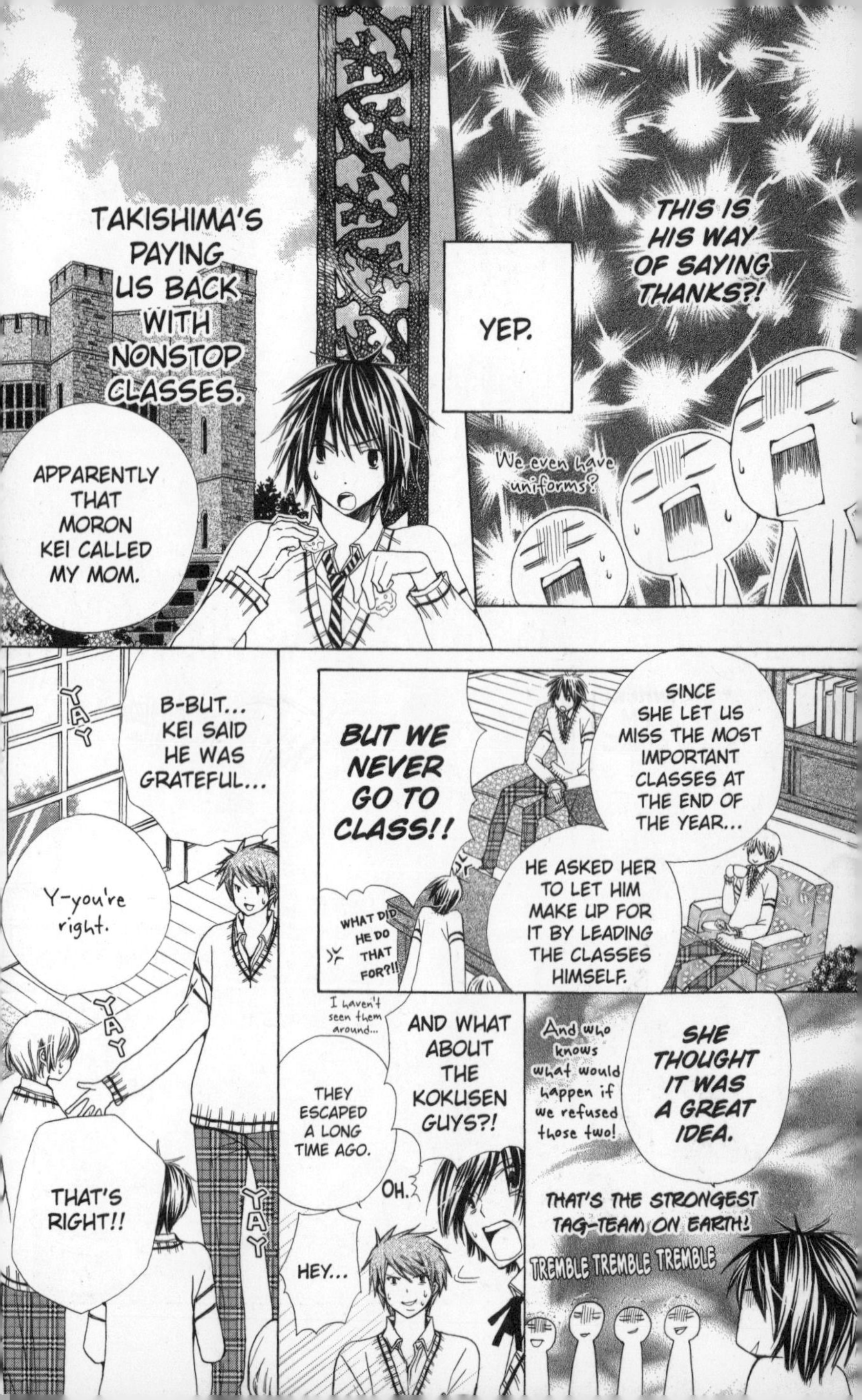
THIS IS HIS WAY OF SAYING THANKS?!
YEP.
We even have uniforms?
TAKISHIMA'S PAYING US BACK WITH NONSTOP CLASSES.
APPARENTLY THAT MORON KEI CALLED MY MOM.
SINCE SHE LET US MISS THE MOST IMPORTANT CLASSES AT THE END OF THE YEAR...
HE ASKED HER TO LET HIM MAKE UP FOR IT BY LEADING THE CLASSES HIMSELF.
BUT WE NEVER GO TO CLASS!!
WHAT DID HE DO THAT FOR?!!
SHE THOUGHT IT WAS A GREAT IDEA.
And who knows what would happen if we refused those two!
THAT'S THE STRONGEST TAG-TEAM ON EARTH!
TREMBLE TREMBLE TREMBLE
AND WHAT ABOUT THE KOKUSEN GUYS?!
I haven't seen them around...
THEY ESCAPED A LONG TIME AGO.
OH.
HEY...
B-BUT... KEI SAID HE WAS GRATEFUL...
YAY
Y-you're right.
YAY
THAT'S RIGHT!!
YAY

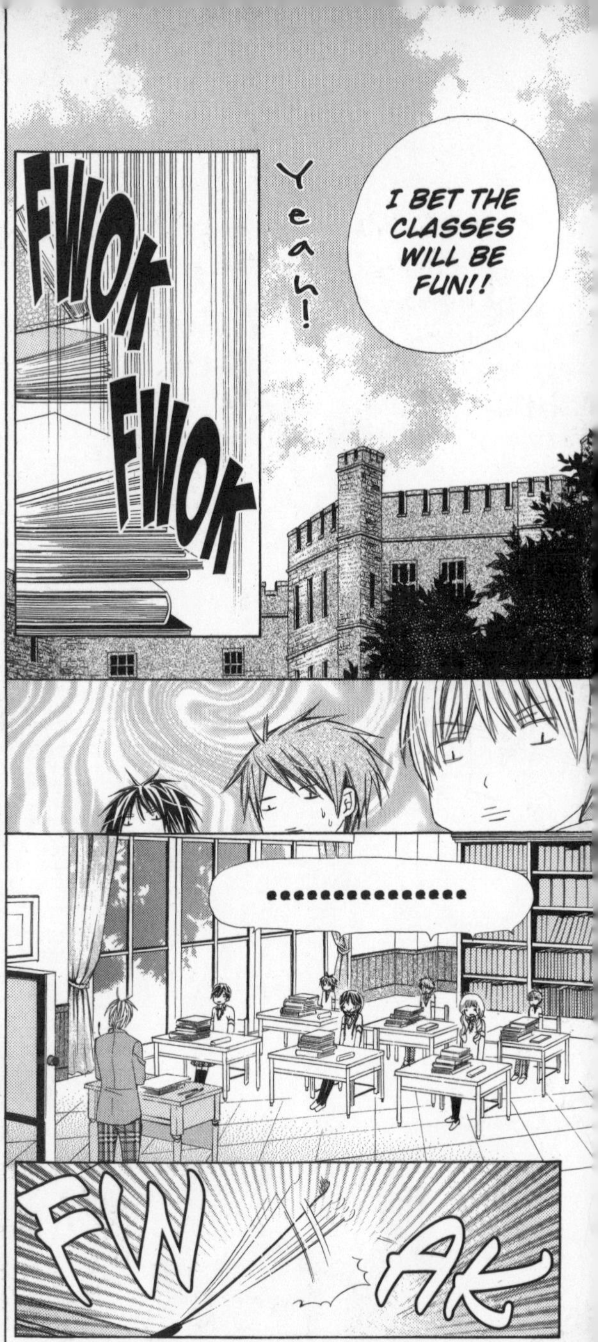
I BET THE CLASSES WILL BE FUN!!
Yeah!
FWOK
FWOK
....
FW AK

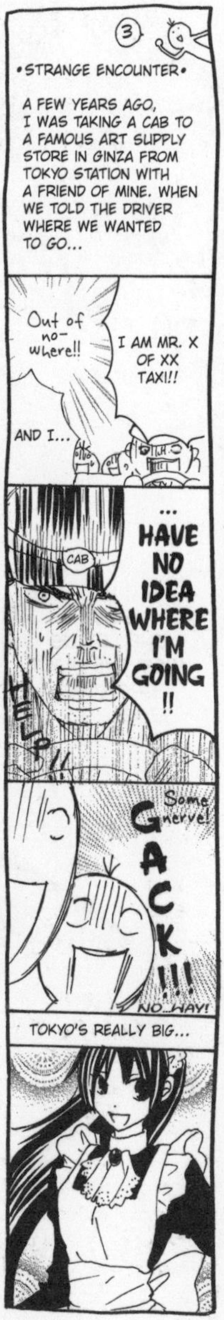
3
•STRANGE ENCOUNTER•
A FEW YEARS AGO, I WAS TAKING A CAB TO A FAMOUS ART SUPPLY STORE IN GINZA FROM TOKYO STATION WITH A FRIEND OF MINE. WHEN WE TOLD THE DRIVER WHERE WE WANTED TO GO...
Out of no-where!!
I AM MR. X OF XX TAXI!!
AND I...
CAB
... HAVE NO IDEA WHERE I'M GOING !!
HELP!!
Some nerve!
GACK!!!
NO...WAY!
TOKYO'S REALLY BIG...

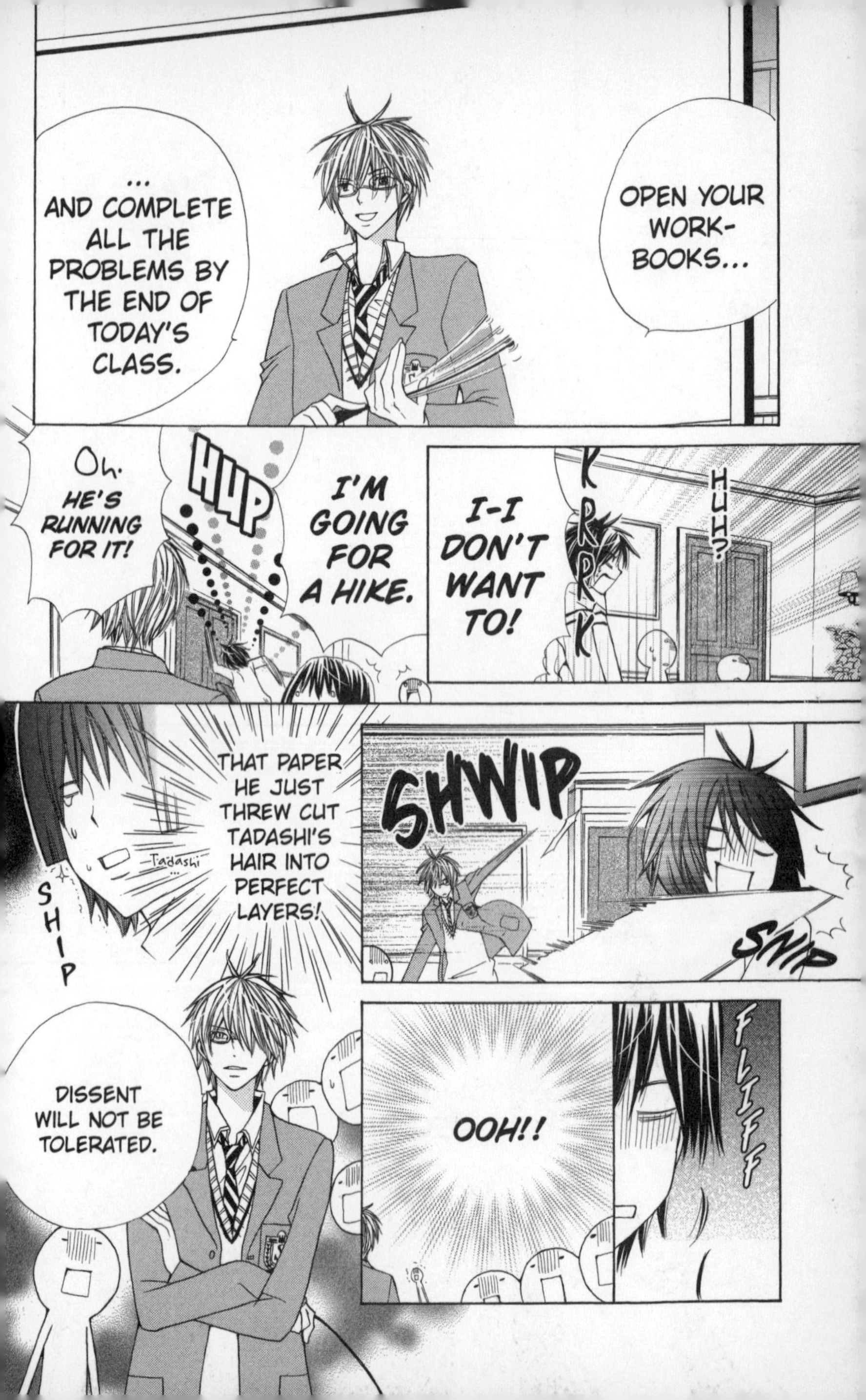
OPEN YOUR WORK-BOOKS...
... AND COMPLETE ALL THE PROBLEMS BY THE END OF TODAY'S CLASS.
HUH?
KRRK
I-I DON'T WANT TO!
I'M GOING FOR A HIKE.
HUP
Oh. HE'S RUNNING FOR IT!
SHWIP
SNIP
OOH!!
FLIFF
THAT PAPER HE JUST THREW CUT TADASHI'S HAIR INTO PERFECT LAYERS!
Tadashi...
SHIP
DISSENT WILL NOT BE TOLERATED.

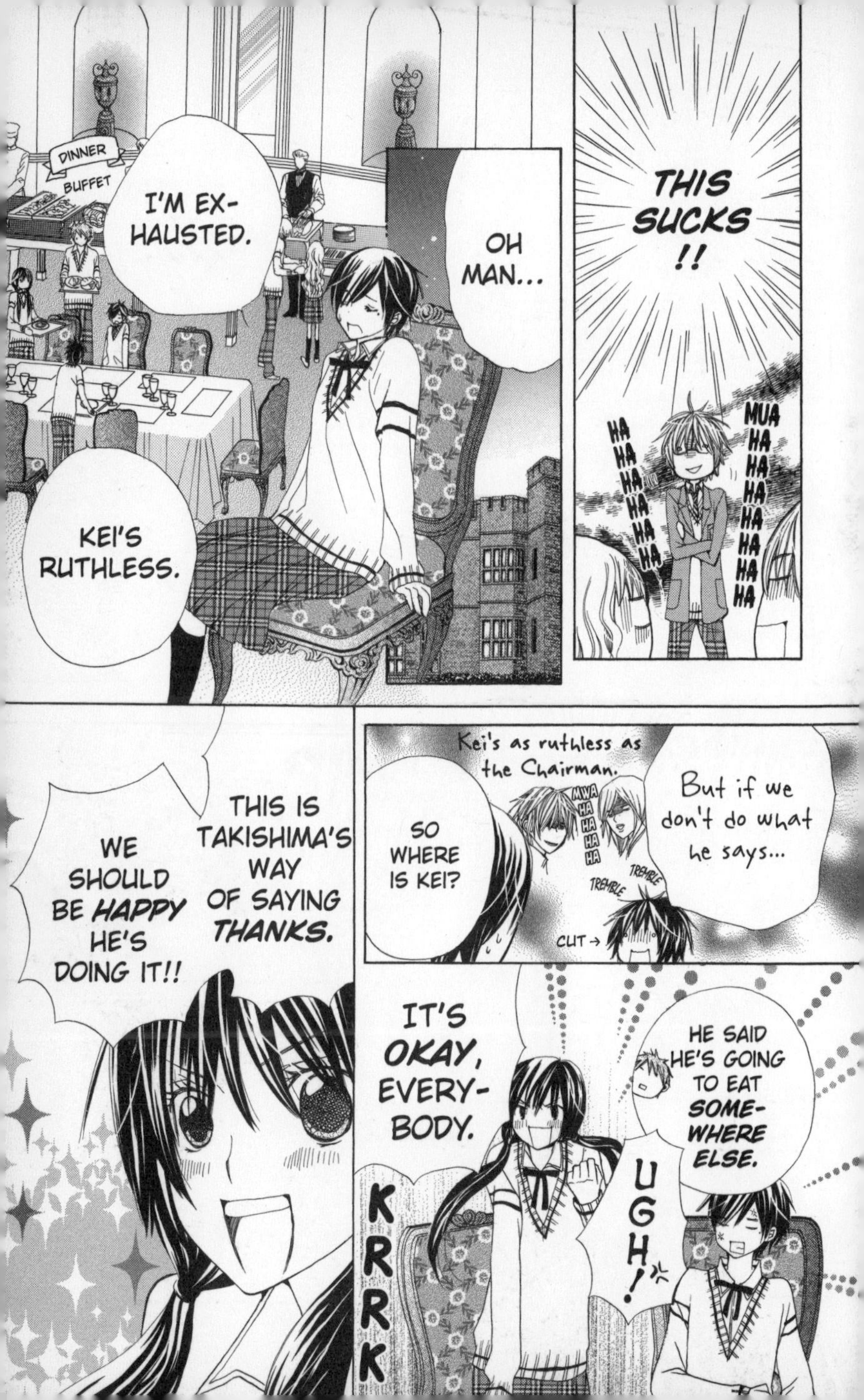
THIS SUCKS!!
MUA HA HA HA HA HA HA HA HA
HA HA HA HA HA HA HA
OH MAN...
I'M EX-HAUSTED.
DINNER
BUFFET
KEI'S RUTHLESS.
But if we don't do what he says...
Kei's as ruthless as the Chairman.
MWA HA HA HA HA HA
TREMBLE
TREMBLE
CUT →
SO WHERE IS KEI?
HE SAID HE'S GOING TO EAT SOME-WHERE ELSE.
UGH!
IT'S OKAY, EVERY-BODY.
KRRK
THIS IS TAKISHIMA'S WAY OF SAYING THANKS.
WE SHOULD BE HAPPY HE'S DOING IT!!

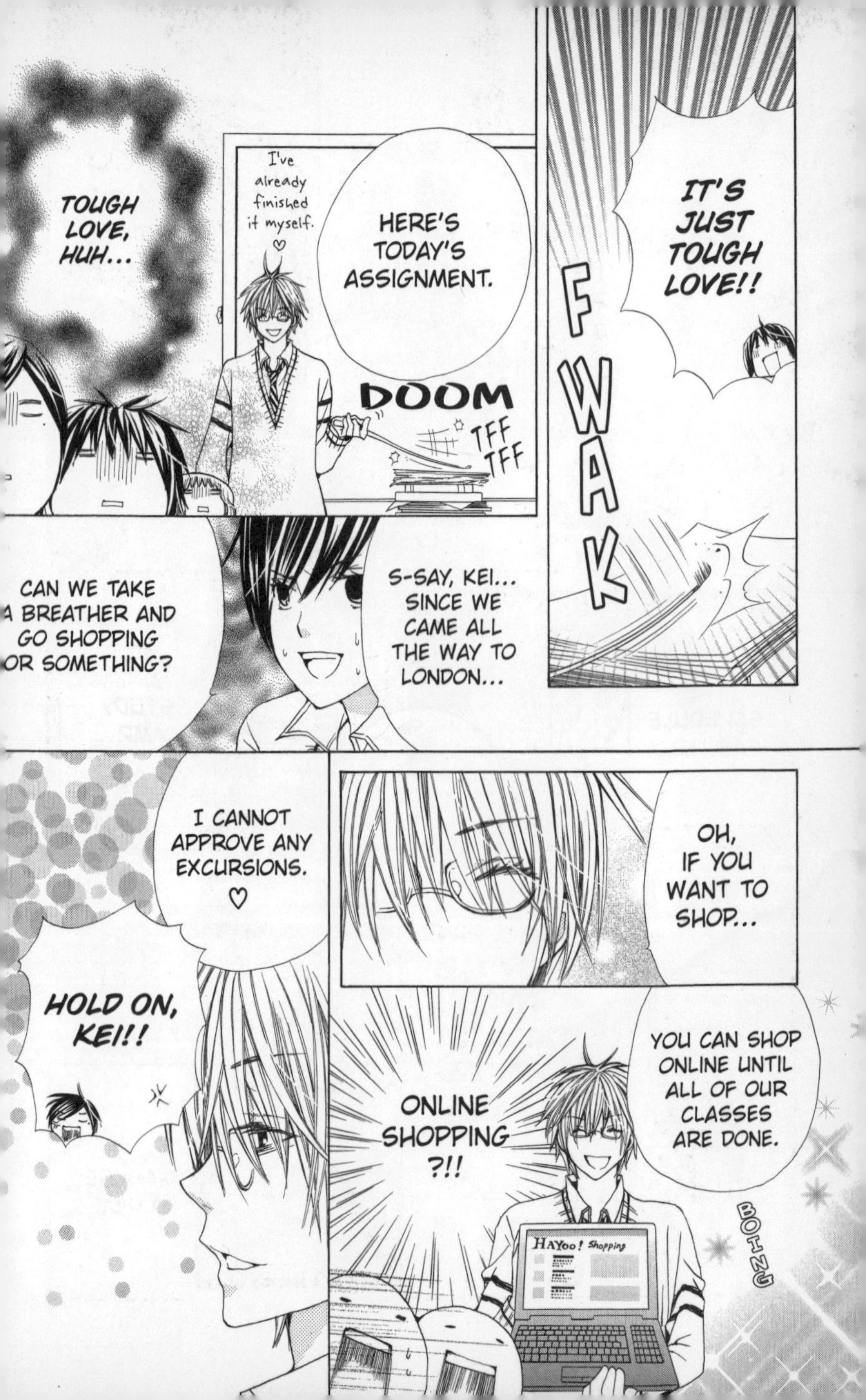

IT'S JUST TOUGH LOVE!!
FWAK
I've already finished it myself. ♡
HERE'S TODAY'S ASSIGNMENT.
DOOM
TFF TFF
TOUGH LOVE, HUH...
S-SAY, KEI... SINCE WE CAME ALL THE WAY TO LONDON...
CAN WE TAKE A BREATHER AND GO SHOPPING OR SOMETHING?
OH, IF YOU WANT TO SHOP...
YOU CAN SHOP ONLINE UNTIL ALL OF OUR CLASSES ARE DONE.
ONLINE SHOPPING ?!!
BOING
HAYoo! Shopping
I CANNOT APPROVE ANY EXCURSIONS. ♡
HOLD ON, KEI!!

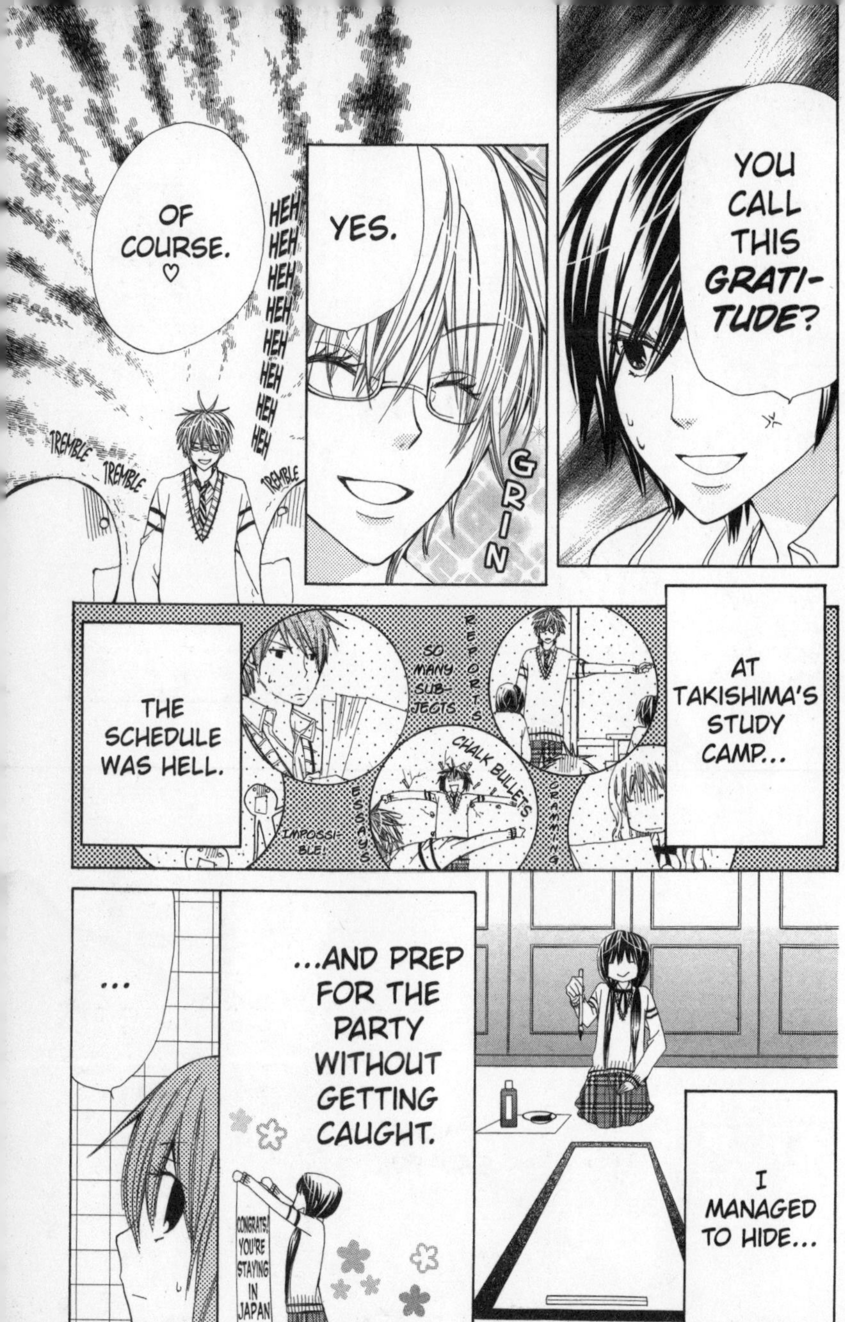
YOU CALL THIS GRATITUDE?
YES.
GRIN
HEH HEH HEH HEH HEH HEH HEH HEH
OF COURSE. ♡
TREMBLE
TREMBLE
TREMBLE
AT TAKISHIMA'S STUDY CAMP...
REPORTS
CRAMMING
CHALK BULLETS
SO MANY SUBJECTS
ESSAYS
IMPOSSIBLE!
THE SCHEDULE WAS HELL.
I MANAGED TO HIDE...
...AND PREP FOR THE PARTY WITHOUT GETTING CAUGHT.
CONGRATS! YOU'RE STAYING IN JAPAN
...

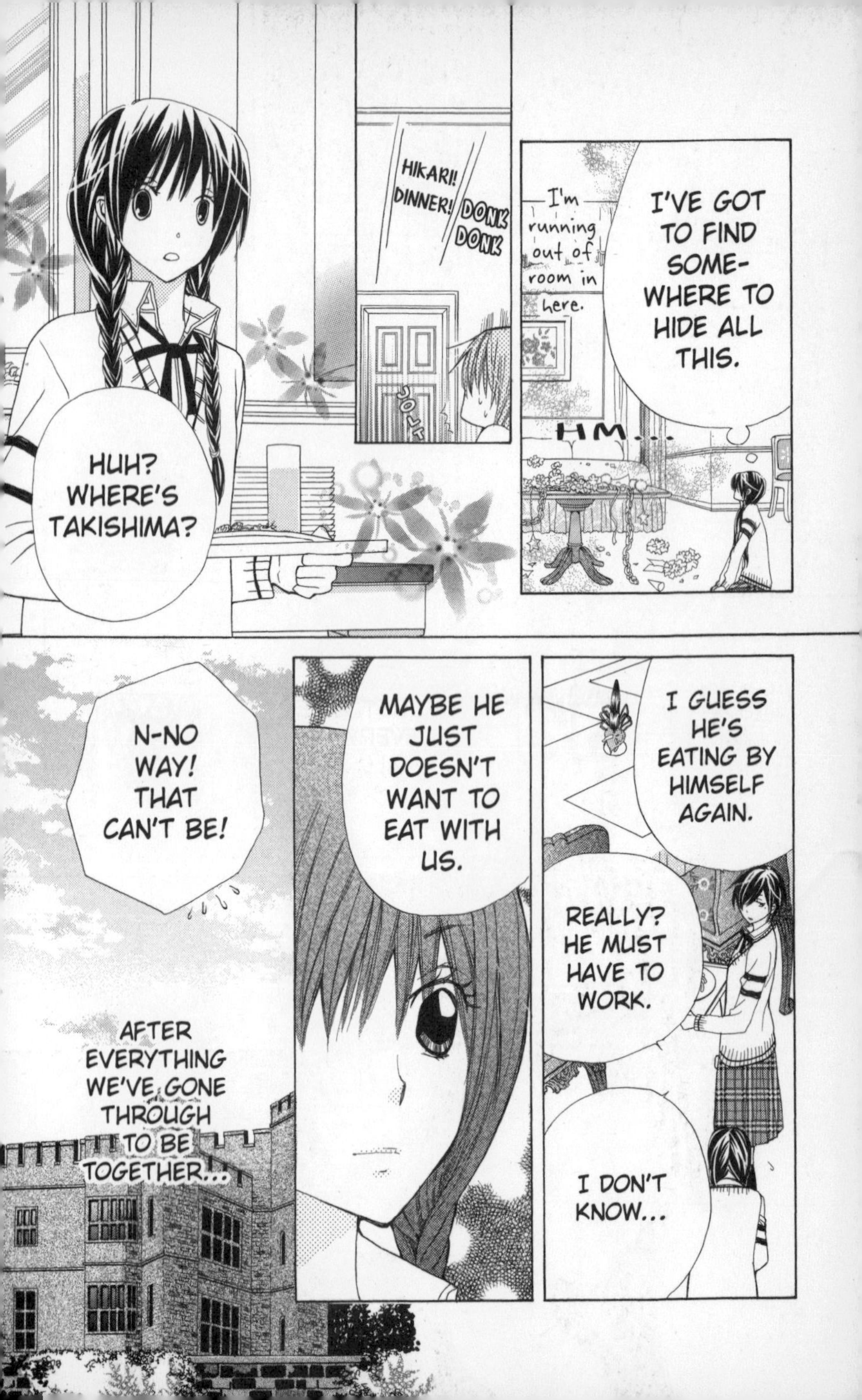
I'VE GOT TO FIND SOME-WHERE TO HIDE ALL THIS.
I'm running out of room in here.
HM...
HIKARI! DINNER!
DONK DONK
JOLT
HUH? WHERE'S TAKISHIMA?
I GUESS HE'S EATING BY HIMSELF AGAIN.
REALLY? HE MUST HAVE TO WORK.
I DON'T KNOW...
MAYBE HE JUST DOESN'T WANT TO EAT WITH US.
N-NO WAY! THAT CAN'T BE!
AFTER EVERYTHING WE'VE GONE THROUGH TO BE TOGETHER...

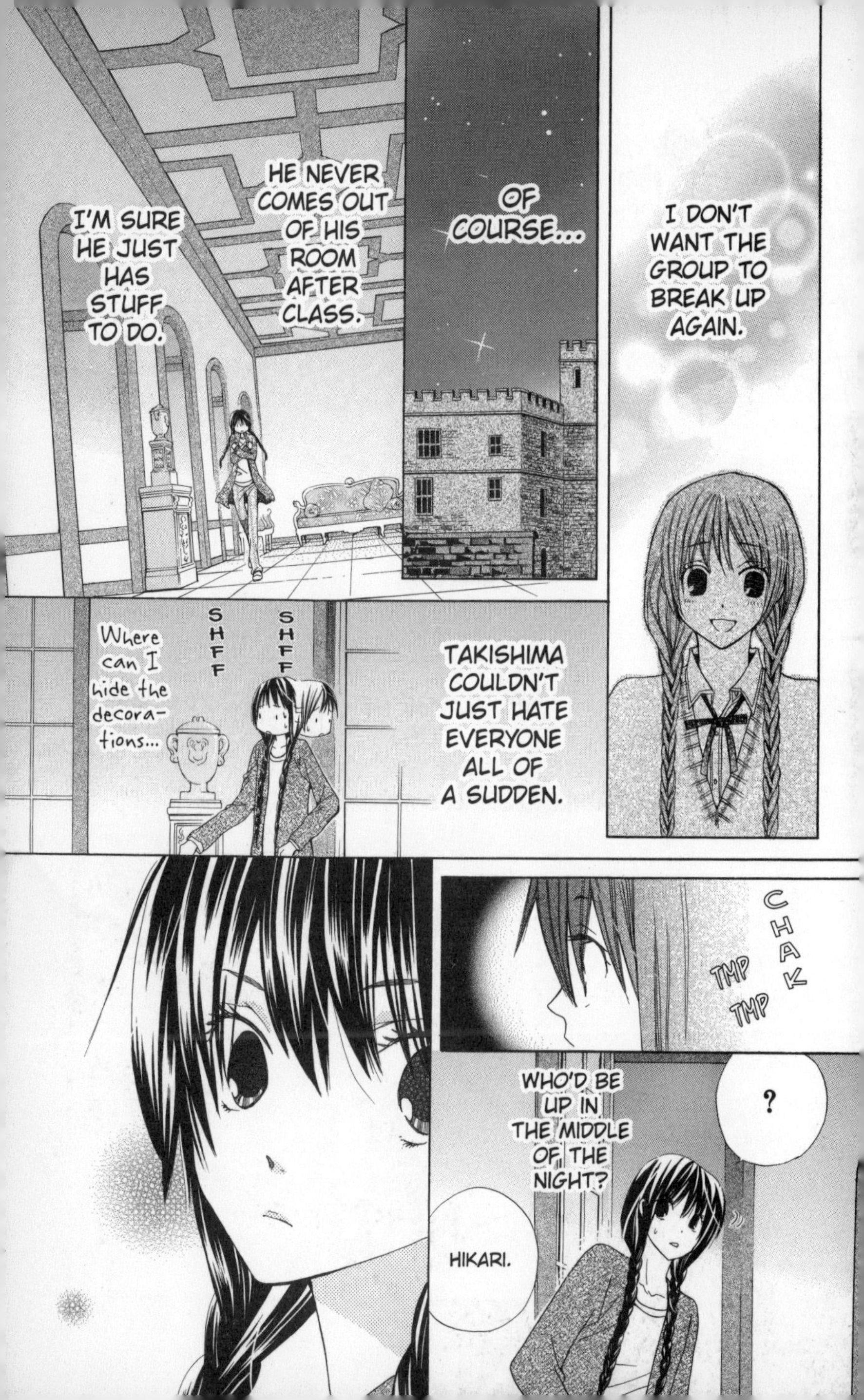
I DON'T WANT THE GROUP TO BREAK UP AGAIN.
OF COURSE...
HE NEVER COMES OUT OF HIS ROOM AFTER CLASS.
I'M SURE HE JUST HAS STUFF TO DO.
TAKISHIMA COULDN'T JUST HATE EVERYONE ALL OF A SUDDEN.
SHFF
SHFF
Where can I hide the decorations...
CHAK
TMP
TMP
?
WHO'D BE UP IN THE MIDDLE OF THE NIGHT?
HIKARI.

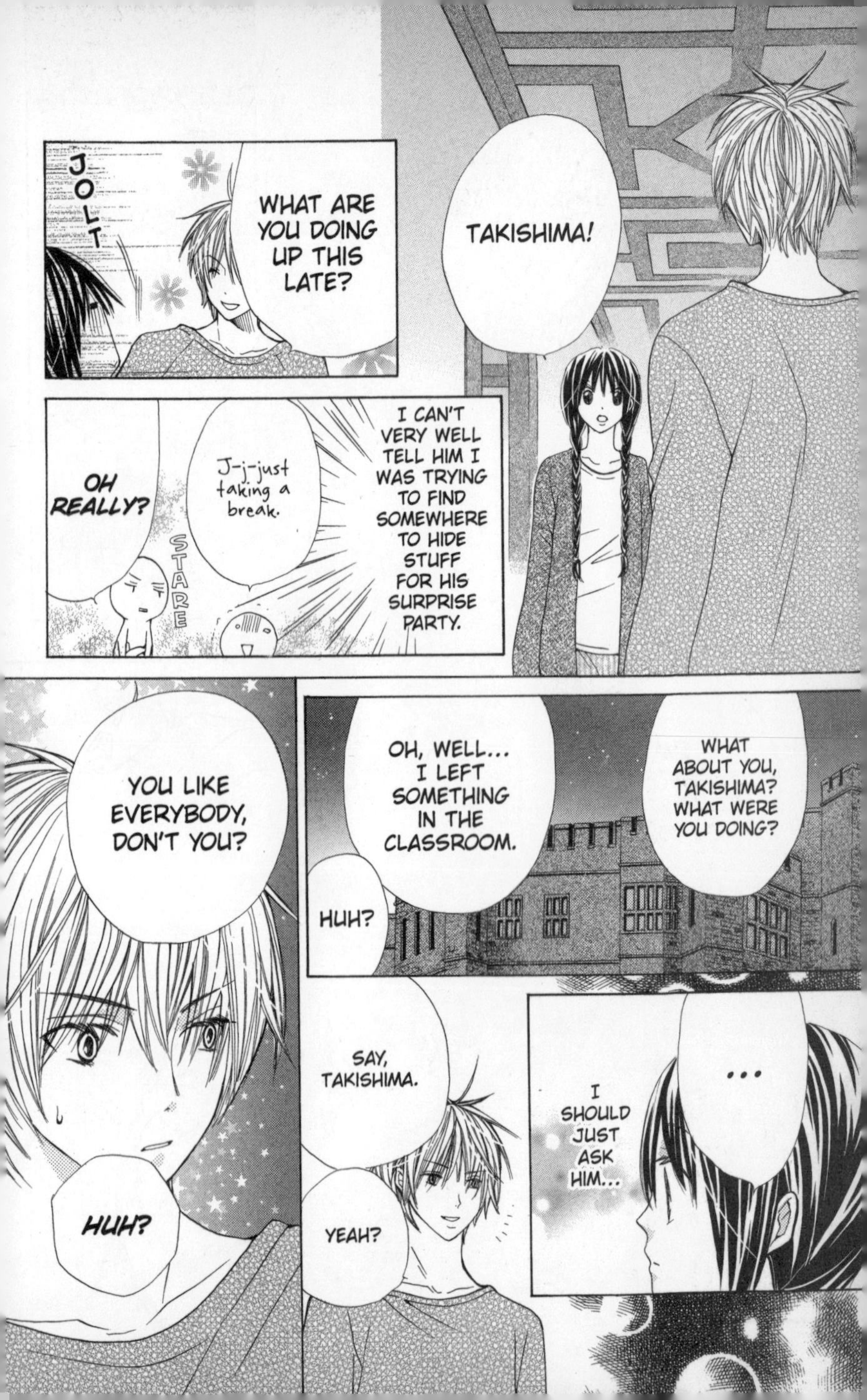
TAKISHIMA!
WHAT ARE YOU DOING UP THIS LATE?
JOLT
I CAN'T VERY WELL TELL HIM I WAS TRYING TO FIND SOMEWHERE TO HIDE STUFF FOR HIS SURPRISE PARTY.
J-j-just taking a break.
OH REALLY?
STARE
WHAT ABOUT YOU, TAKISHIMA? WHAT WERE YOU DOING?
OH, WELL... I LEFT SOMETHING IN THE CLASSROOM.
HUH?
...
I SHOULD JUST ASK HIM...
SAY, TAKISHIMA.
YEAH?
YOU LIKE EVERYBODY, DON'T YOU?
HUH?

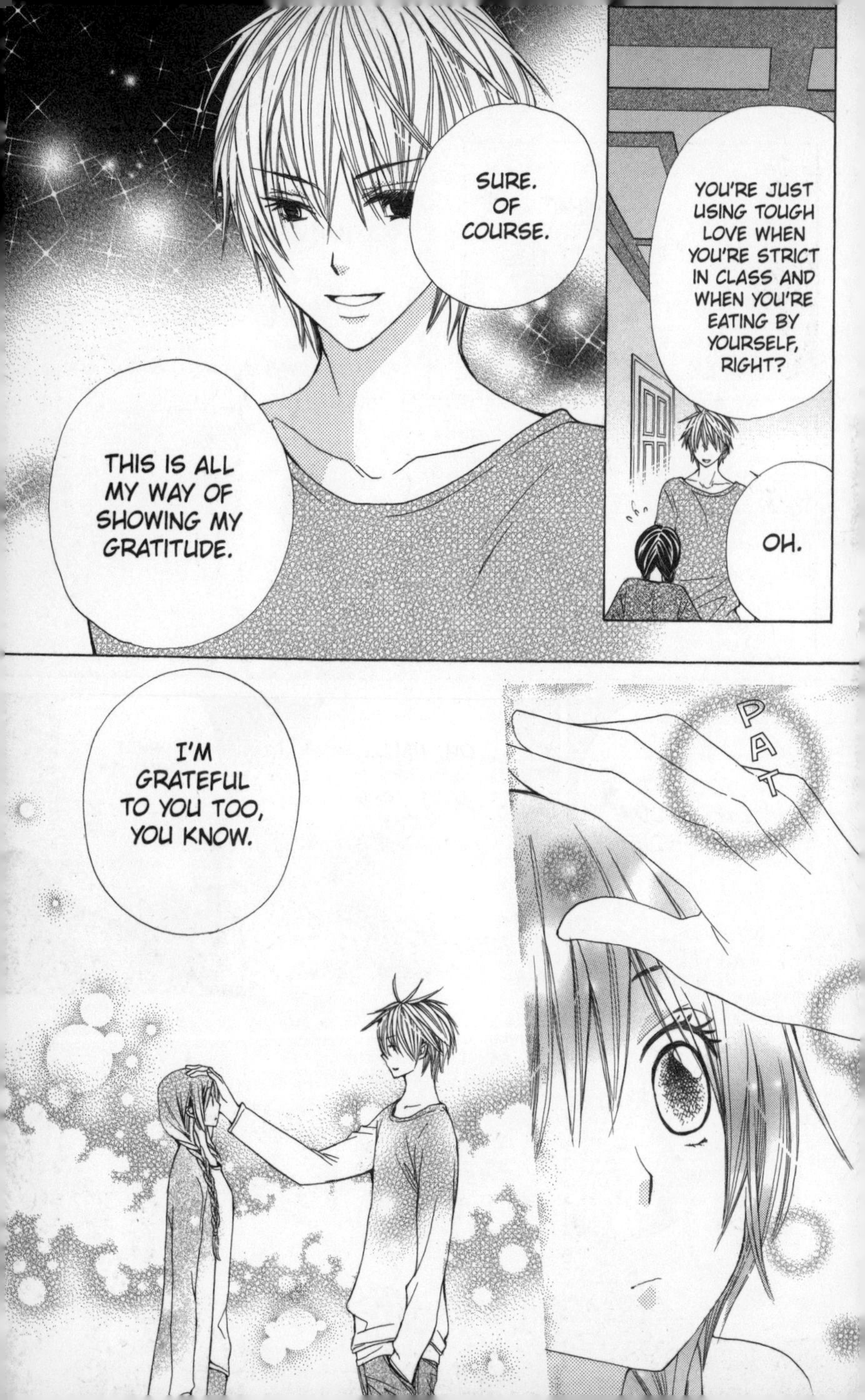
YOU'RE JUST USING TOUGH LOVE WHEN YOU'RE STRICT IN CLASS AND WHEN YOU'RE EATING BY YOURSELF, RIGHT?
OH.
SURE. OF COURSE.
THIS IS ALL MY WAY OF SHOWING MY GRATITUDE.
PAT
I'M GRATEFUL TO YOU TOO, YOU KNOW.

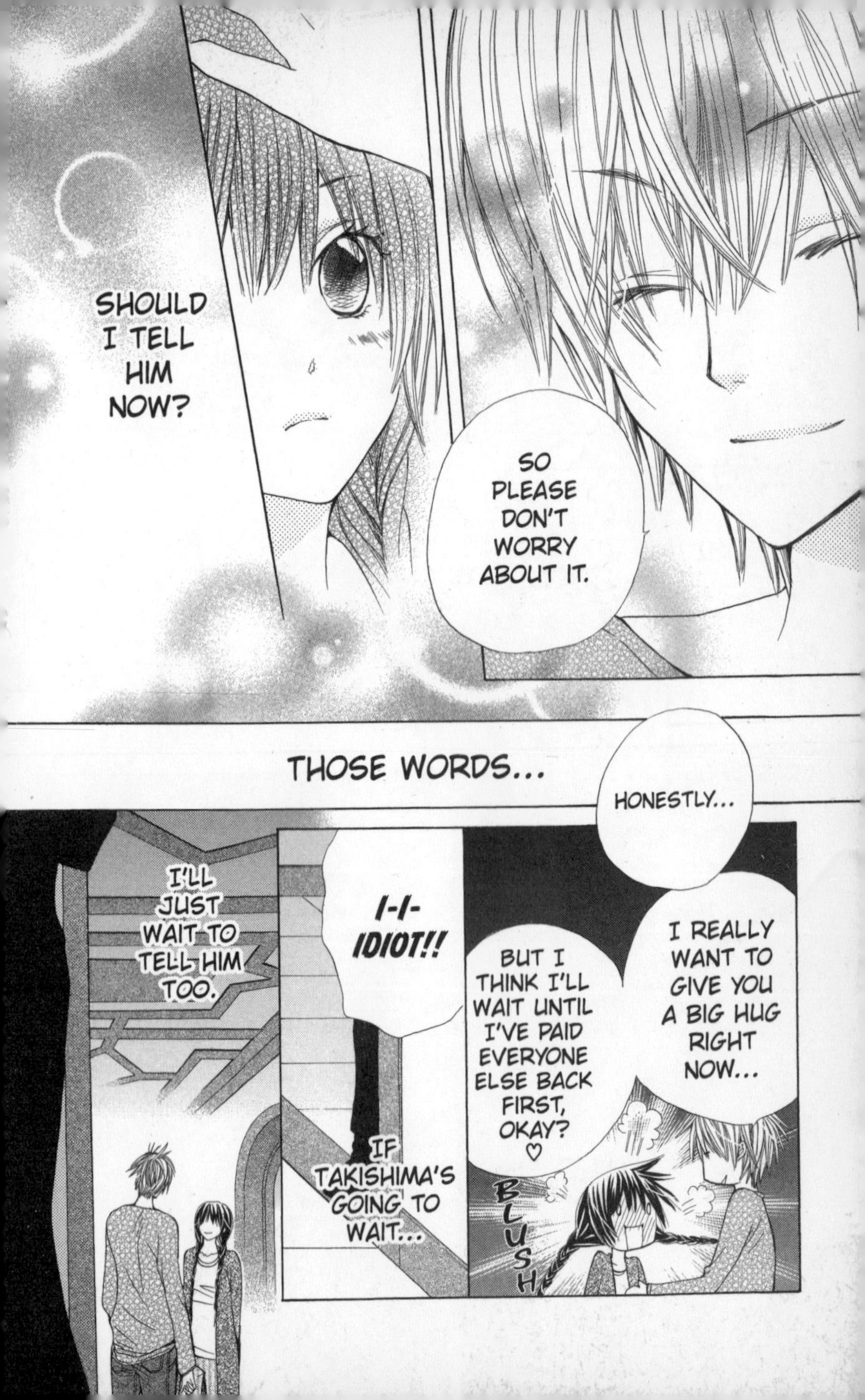
SO PLEASE DON'T WORRY ABOUT IT.
SHOULD I TELL HIM NOW?
THOSE WORDS...
HONESTLY...
I REALLY WANT TO GIVE YOU A BIG HUG RIGHT NOW...
BUT I THINK I'LL WAIT UNTIL I'VE PAID EVERYONE ELSE BACK FIRST, OKAY? ♡
BLUSH
I-I-IDIOT!!
IF TAKISHIMA'S GOING TO WAIT...
I'LL JUST WAIT TO TELL HIM TOO.

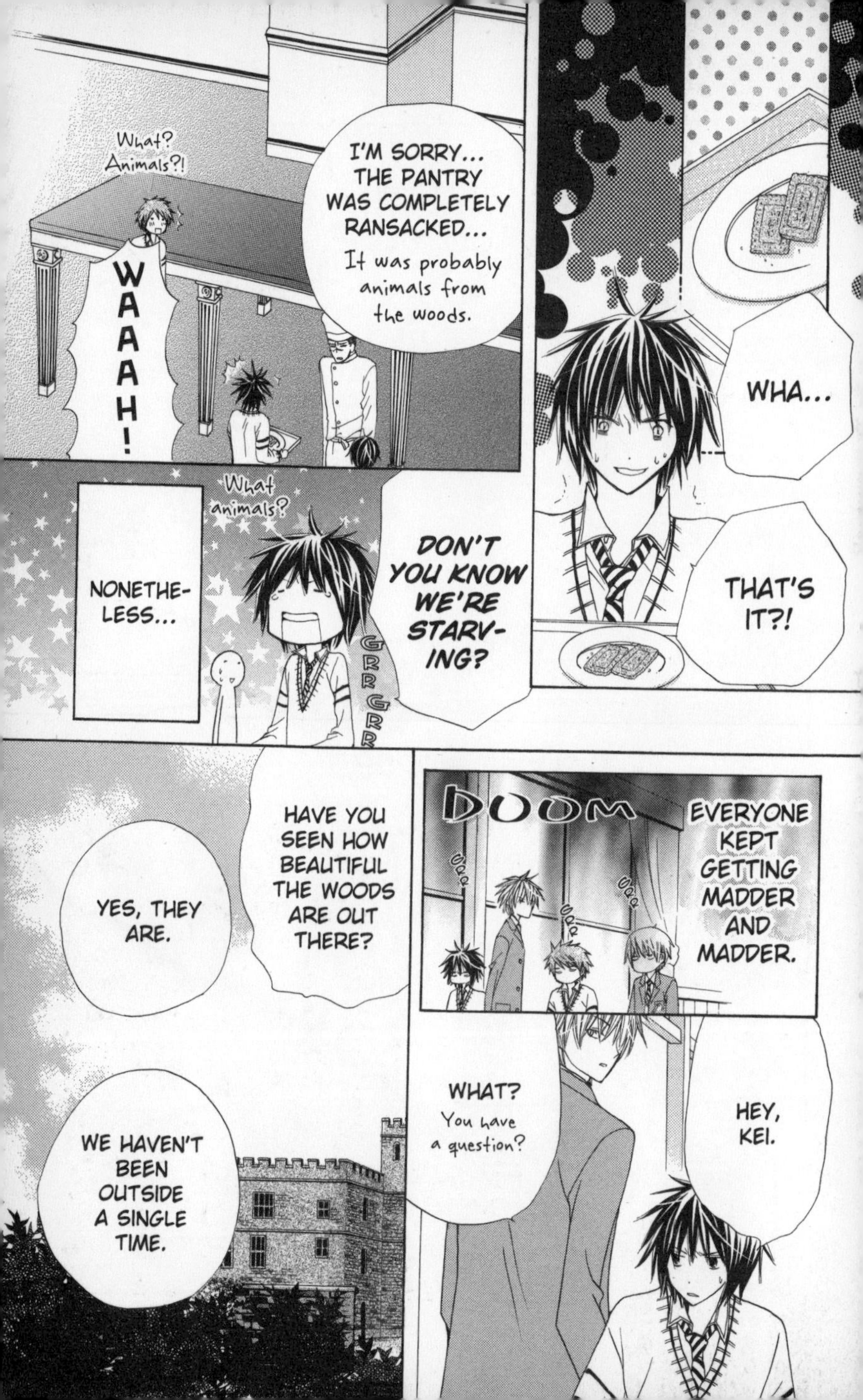
WHA...
THAT'S IT?!
I'M SORRY... THE PANTRY WAS COMPLETELY RANSACKED...
It was probably animals from the woods.
What? Animals?!
WAAAAH!
DON'T YOU KNOW WE'RE STARVING?
GRR GRR
What animals?
NONETHELESS...
EVERYONE KEPT GETTING MADDER AND MADDER.
DOOM
HEY, KEI.
WHAT?
You have a question?
HAVE YOU SEEN HOW BEAUTIFUL THE WOODS ARE OUT THERE?
YES, THEY ARE.
WE HAVEN'T BEEN OUTSIDE A SINGLE TIME.

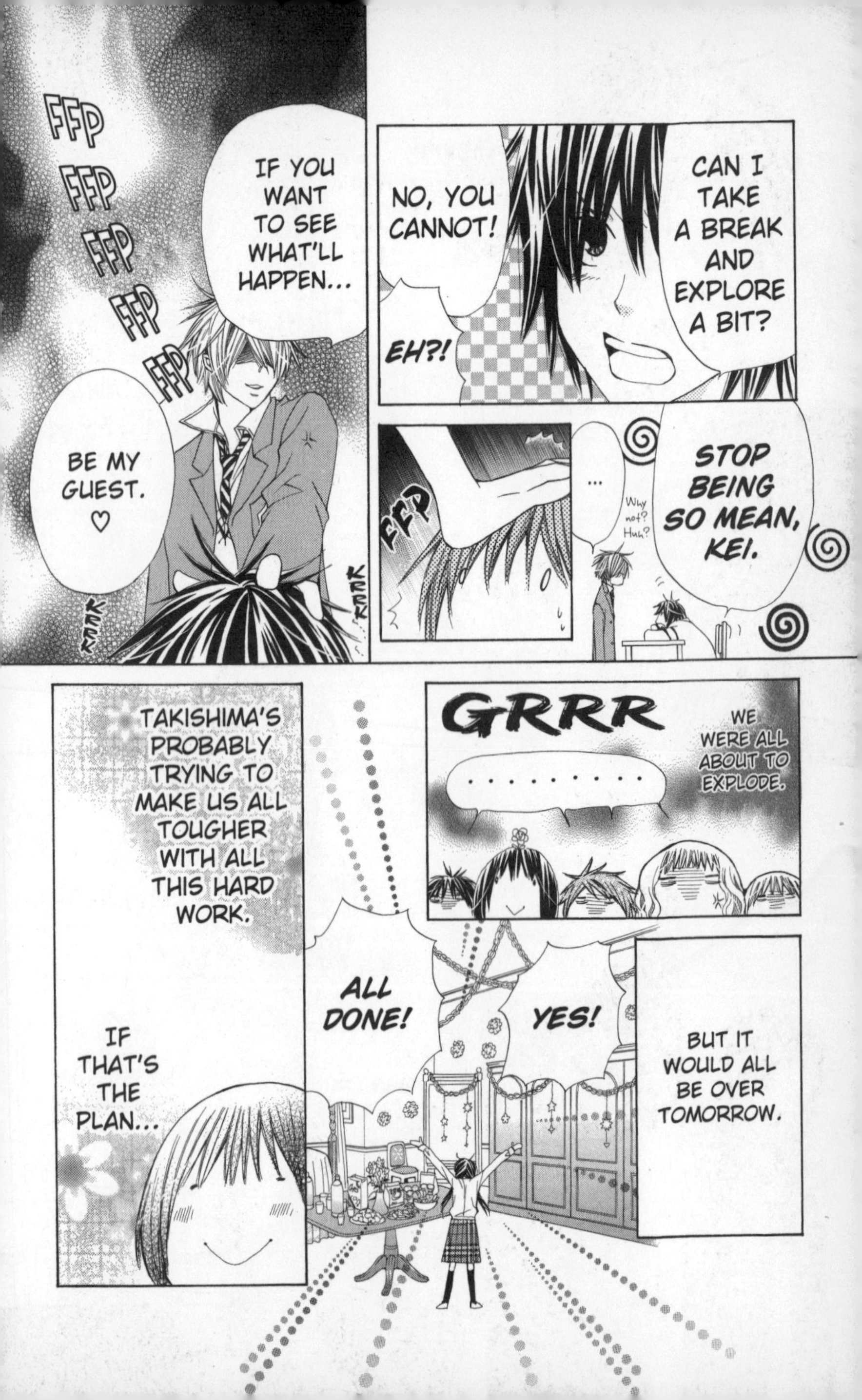
CAN I TAKE A BREAK AND EXPLORE A BIT?
NO, YOU CANNOT!
EH?!
STOP BEING SO MEAN, KEI.
Why not? Huh?
...
FFP
FFP FFP FFP FFP FFP
IF YOU WANT TO SEE WHAT'LL HAPPEN...
BE MY GUEST. ♡
KREK KREK
KREK
GRRR
WE WERE ALL ABOUT TO EXPLODE.
....
BUT IT WOULD ALL BE OVER TOMORROW.
YES!
ALL DONE!
TAKISHIMA'S PROBABLY TRYING TO MAKE US ALL TOUGHER WITH ALL THIS HARD WORK.
IF THAT'S THE PLAN...

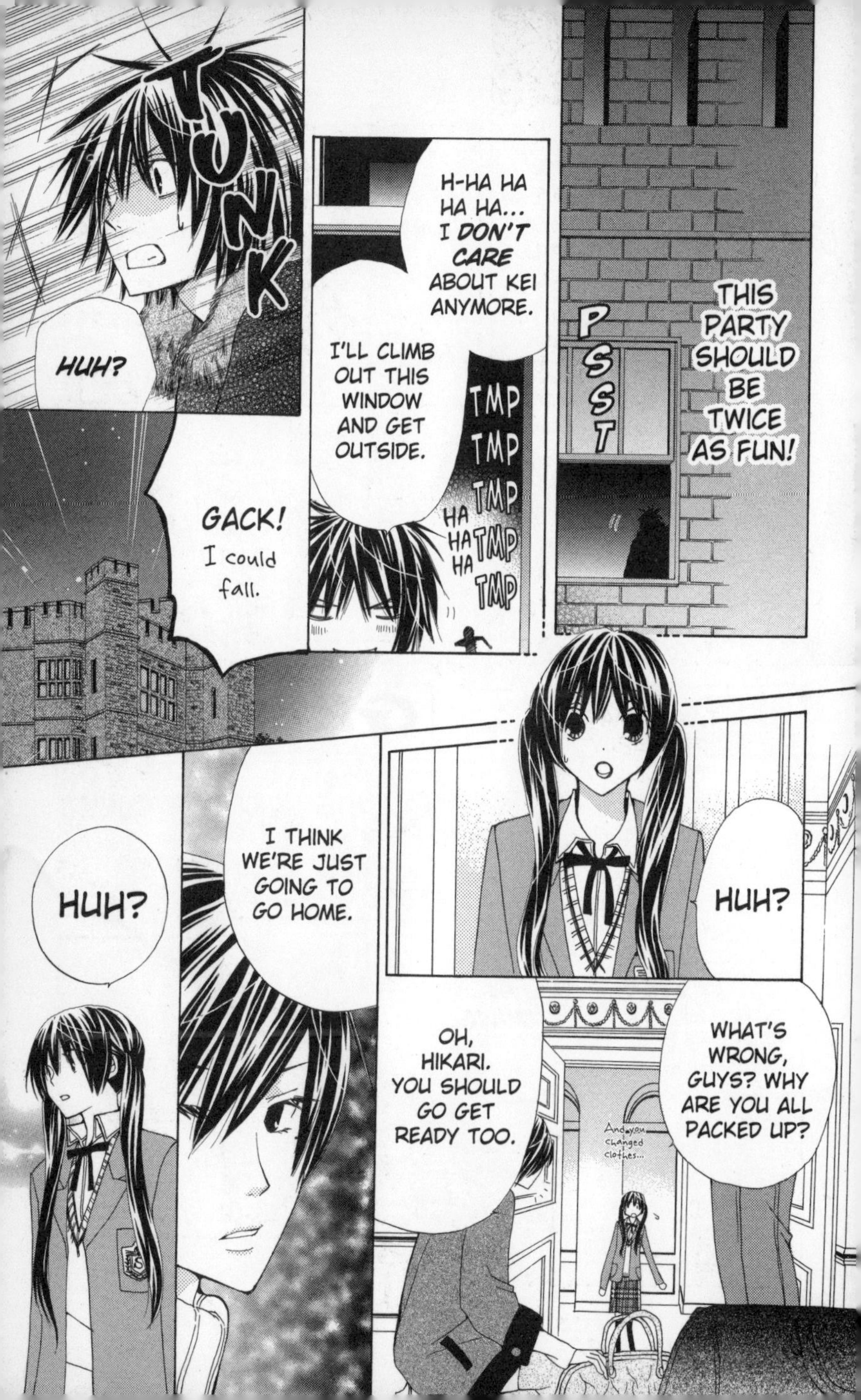
THIS PARTY SHOULD BE TWICE AS FUN!
PSST
H-HA HA HA HA... I DON'T CARE ABOUT KEI ANYMORE.
I'LL CLIMB OUT THIS WINDOW AND GET OUTSIDE.
TMP TMP TMP TMP TMP
HA HA HA
TUNK
HUH?
GACK! I could fall.
HUH?
WHAT'S WRONG, GUYS? WHY ARE YOU ALL PACKED UP?
And you changed clothes...
OH, HIKARI. YOU SHOULD GO GET READY TOO.
I THINK WE'RE JUST GOING TO GO HOME.
HUH?

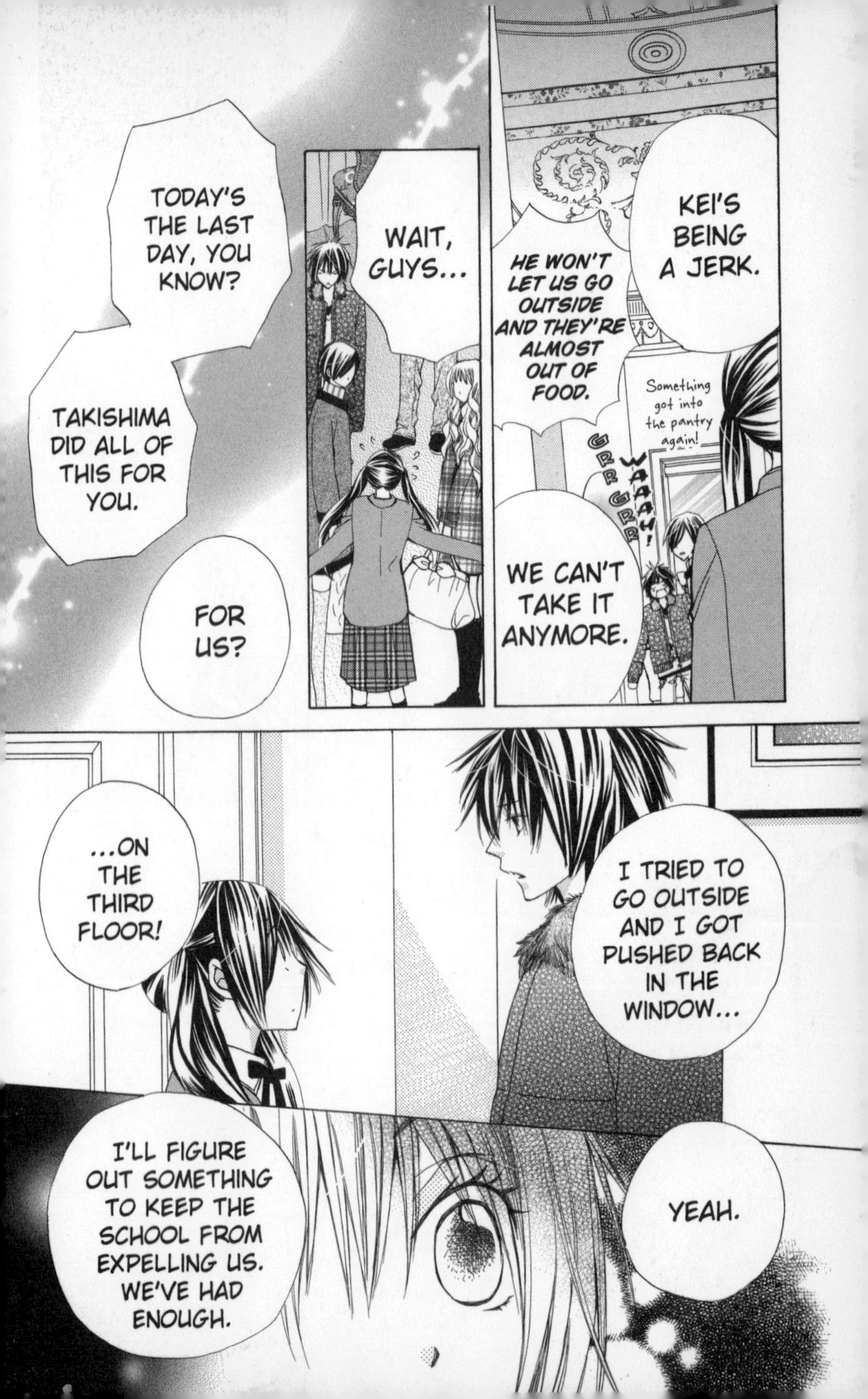
KEI'S BEING A JERK.
HE WON'T LET US GO OUTSIDE AND THEY'RE ALMOST OUT OF FOOD.
Something got into the pantry again!
GRR GRR GRR
WAAAAH!
WE CAN'T TAKE IT ANYMORE.
WAIT, GUYS...
TODAY'S THE LAST DAY, YOU KNOW?
TAKISHIMA DID ALL OF THIS FOR YOU.
FOR US?
I TRIED TO GO OUTSIDE AND I GOT PUSHED BACK IN THE WINDOW...
...ON THE THIRD FLOOR!
YEAH.
I'LL FIGURE OUT SOMETHING TO KEEP THE SCHOOL FROM EXPELLING US. WE'VE HAD ENOUGH.

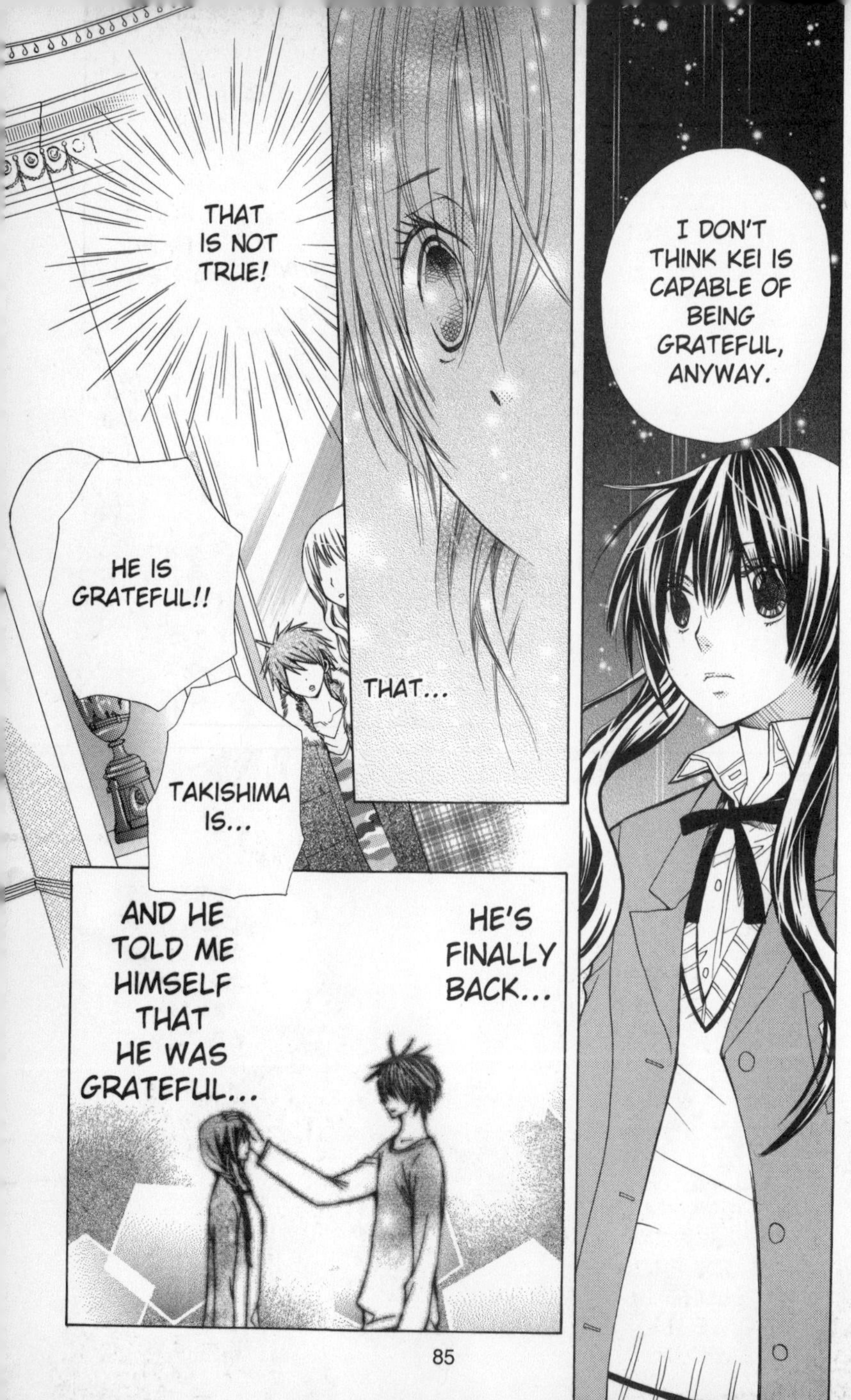
I DON'T THINK KEI IS CAPABLE OF BEING GRATEFUL, ANYWAY.
THAT...
THAT IS NOT TRUE!
HE IS GRATEFUL!!
TAKISHIMA IS...
HE'S FINALLY BACK...
AND HE TOLD ME HIMSELF THAT HE WAS GRATEFUL...

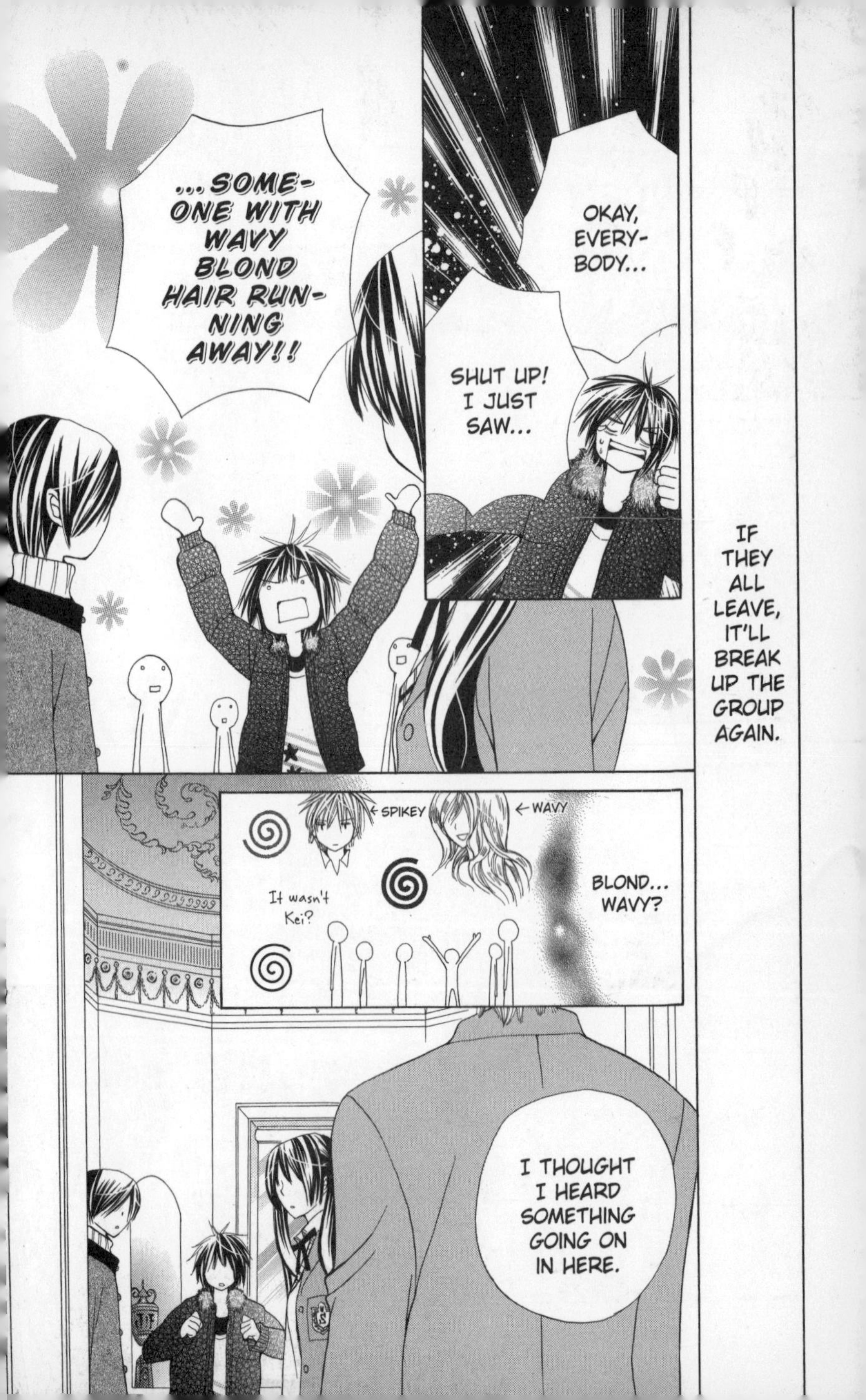
IF THEY ALL LEAVE, IT'LL BREAK UP THE GROUP AGAIN.
OKAY, EVERY-BODY...
SHUT UP! I JUST SAW...
...SOME-ONE WITH WAVY BLOND HAIR RUN-NING AWAY!!
BLOND... WAVY?
WAVY
SPIKEY
It wasn't Kei?
I THOUGHT I HEARD SOMETHING GOING ON IN HERE.

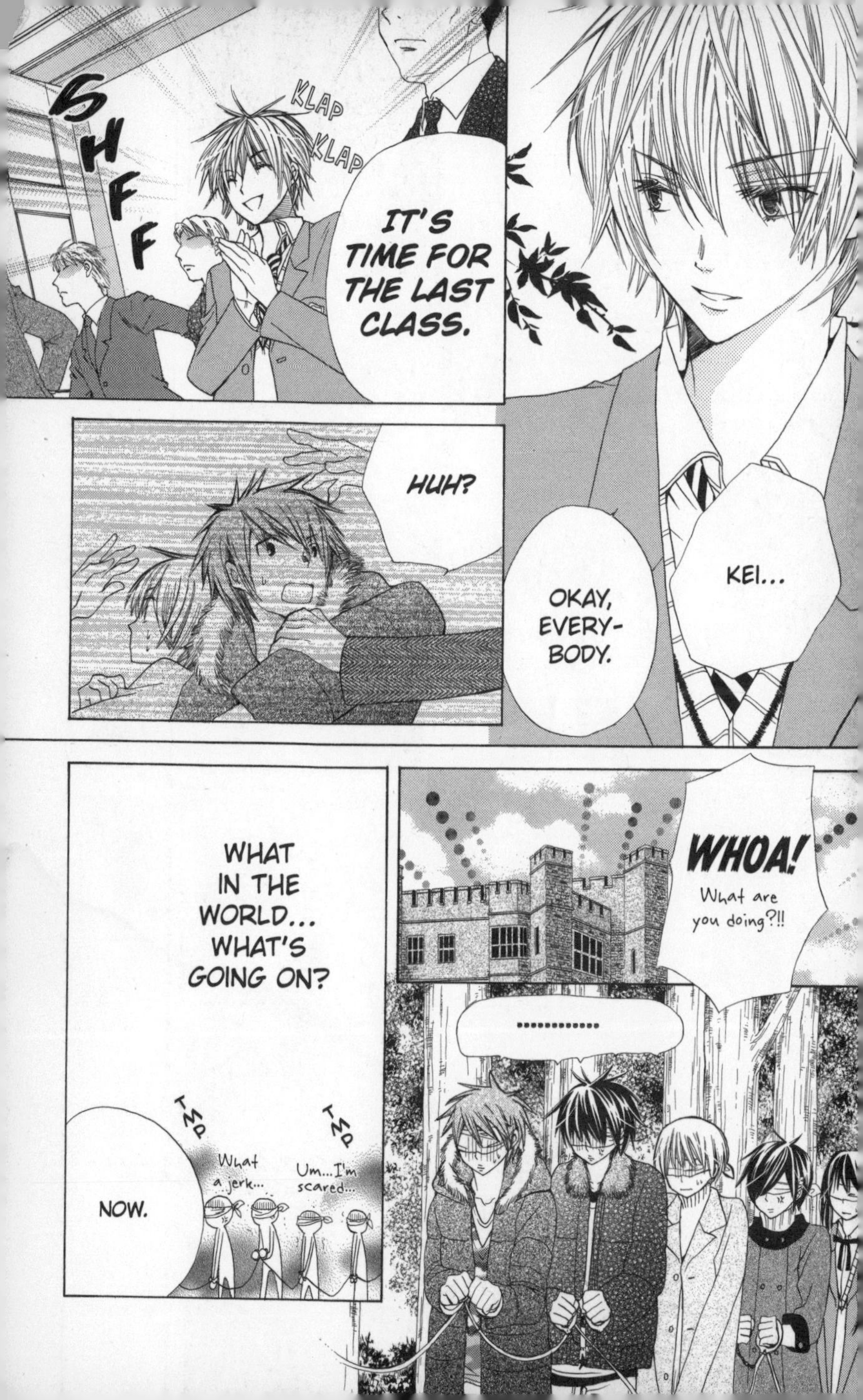

KEI...
OKAY, EVERY-BODY.
SHFF
KLAP
KLAP
IT'S TIME FOR THE LAST CLASS.
HUH?
WHOA!
What are you doing?!!
....
WHAT IN THE WORLD... WHAT'S GOING ON?
TMP
TMP
Um...I'm scared...
What a jerk...
NOW.

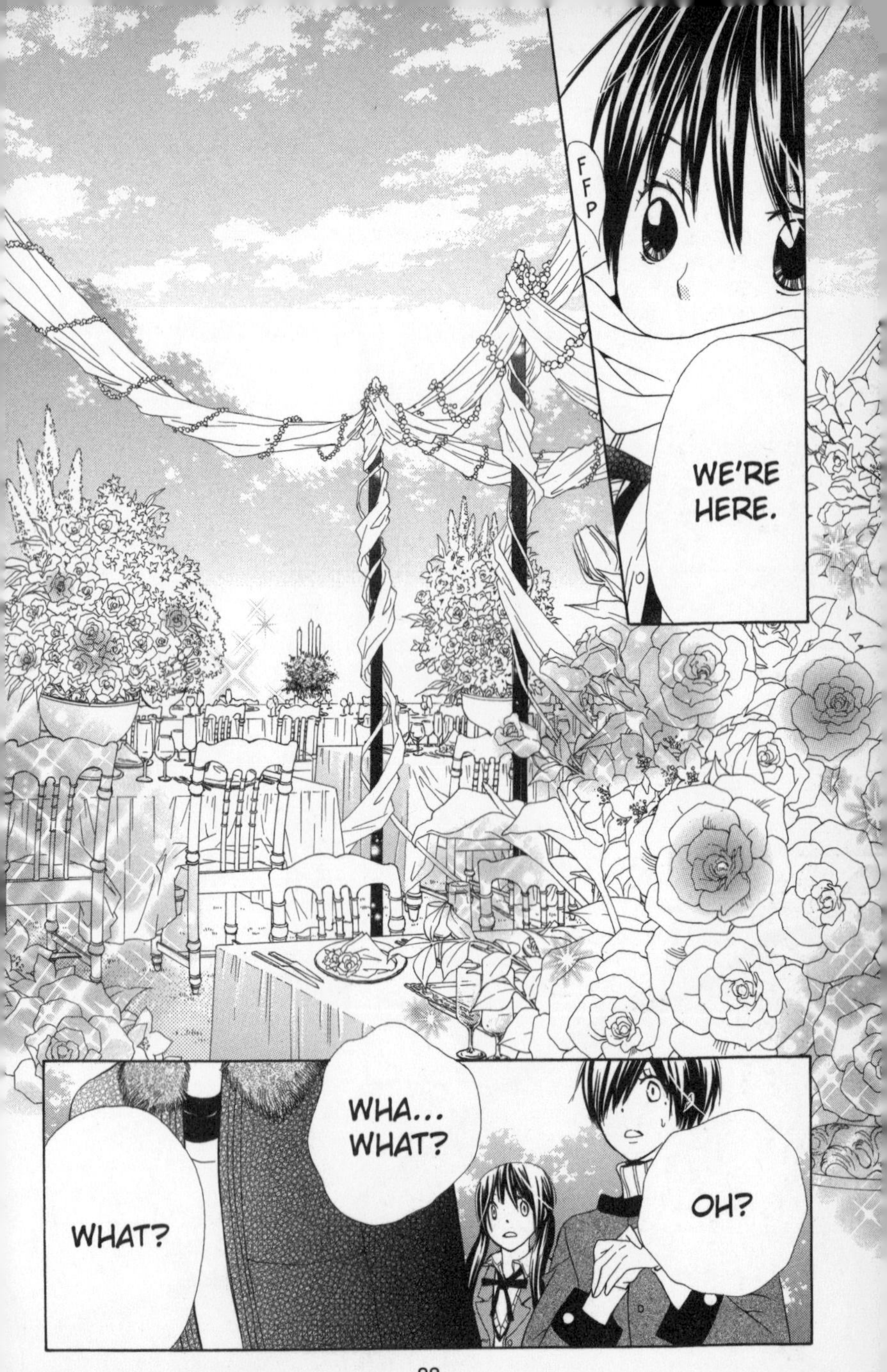
FFP
WE'RE HERE.
OH?
WHA... WHAT?
WHAT?

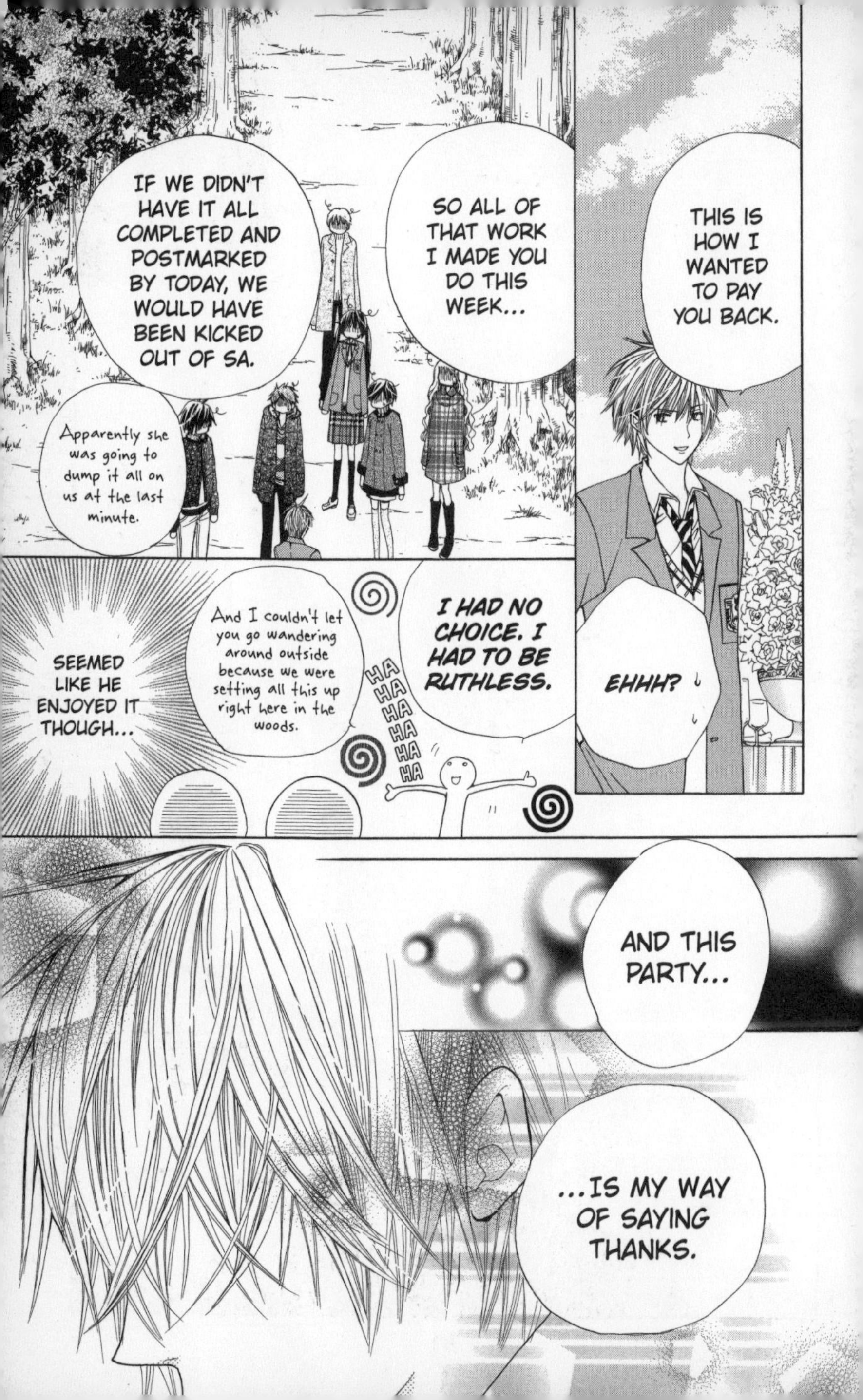
THIS IS HOW I WANTED TO PAY YOU BACK.
EHHH?
SO ALL OF THAT WORK I MADE YOU DO THIS WEEK...
IF WE DIDN'T HAVE IT ALL COMPLETED AND POSTMARKED BY TODAY, WE WOULD HAVE BEEN KICKED OUT OF SA.
Apparently she was going to dump it all on us at the last minute.
I HAD NO CHOICE. I HAD TO BE RUTHLESS.
HA HA HA HA HA HA HA
And I couldn't let you go wandering around outside because we were setting all this up right here in the woods.
SEEMED LIKE HE ENJOYED IT THOUGH...
AND THIS PARTY...
...IS MY WAY OF SAYING THANKS.

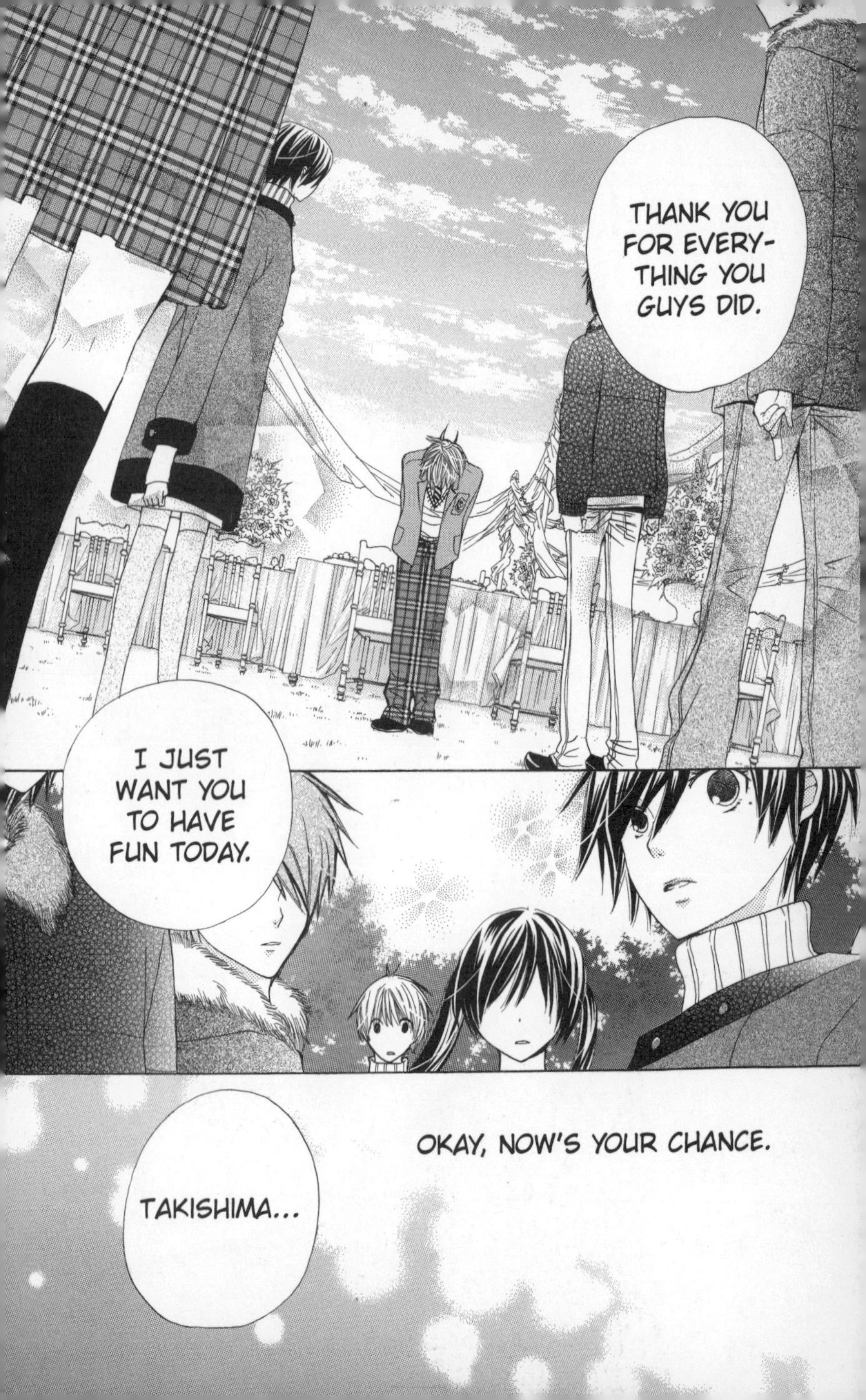
THANK YOU FOR EVERY-THING YOU GUYS DID.
I JUST WANT YOU TO HAVE FUN TODAY.
OKAY, NOW'S YOUR CHANCE.
TAKISHIMA...

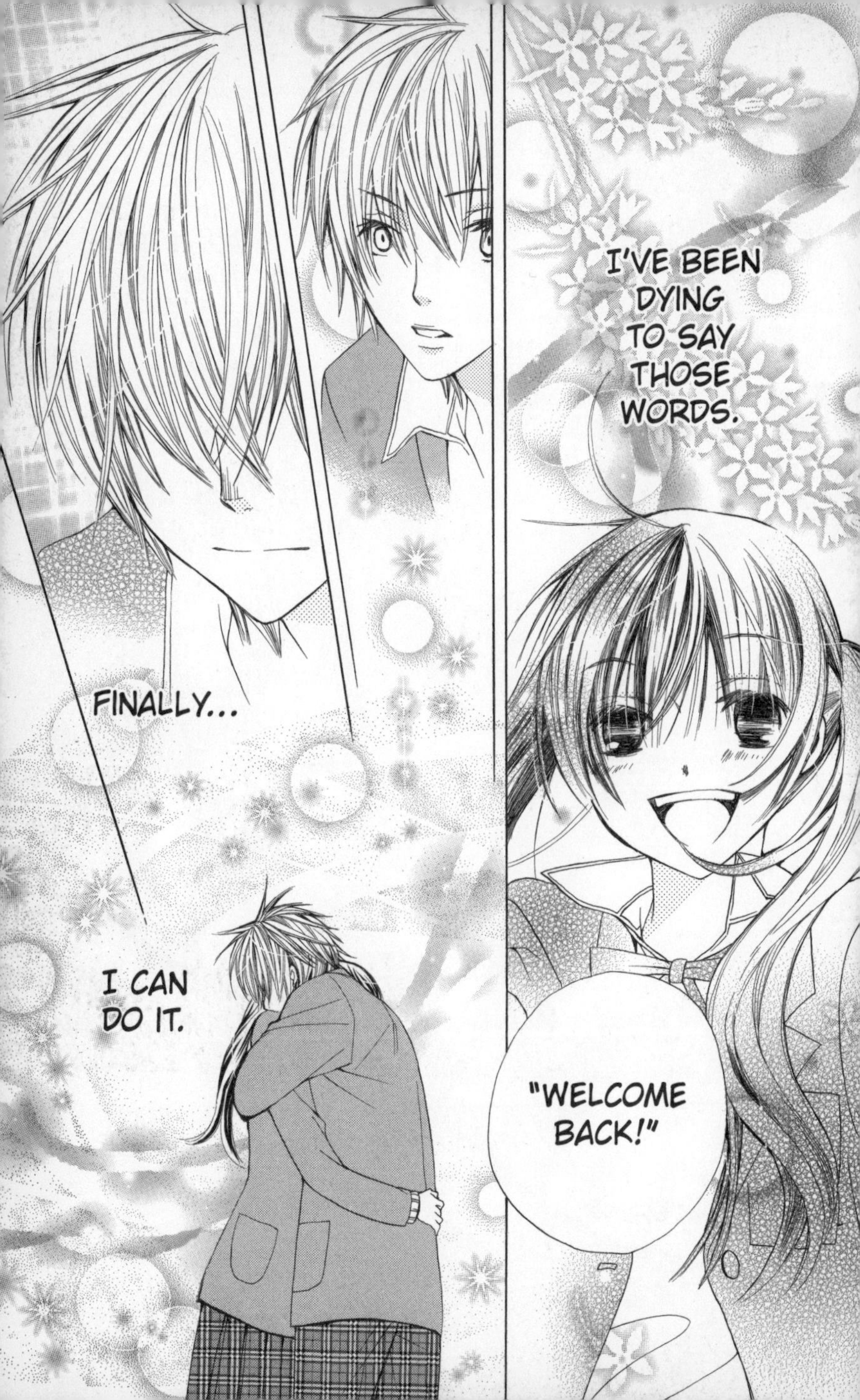
I'VE BEEN DYING TO SAY THOSE WORDS.
"WELCOME BACK!"
FINALLY...
I CAN DO IT.

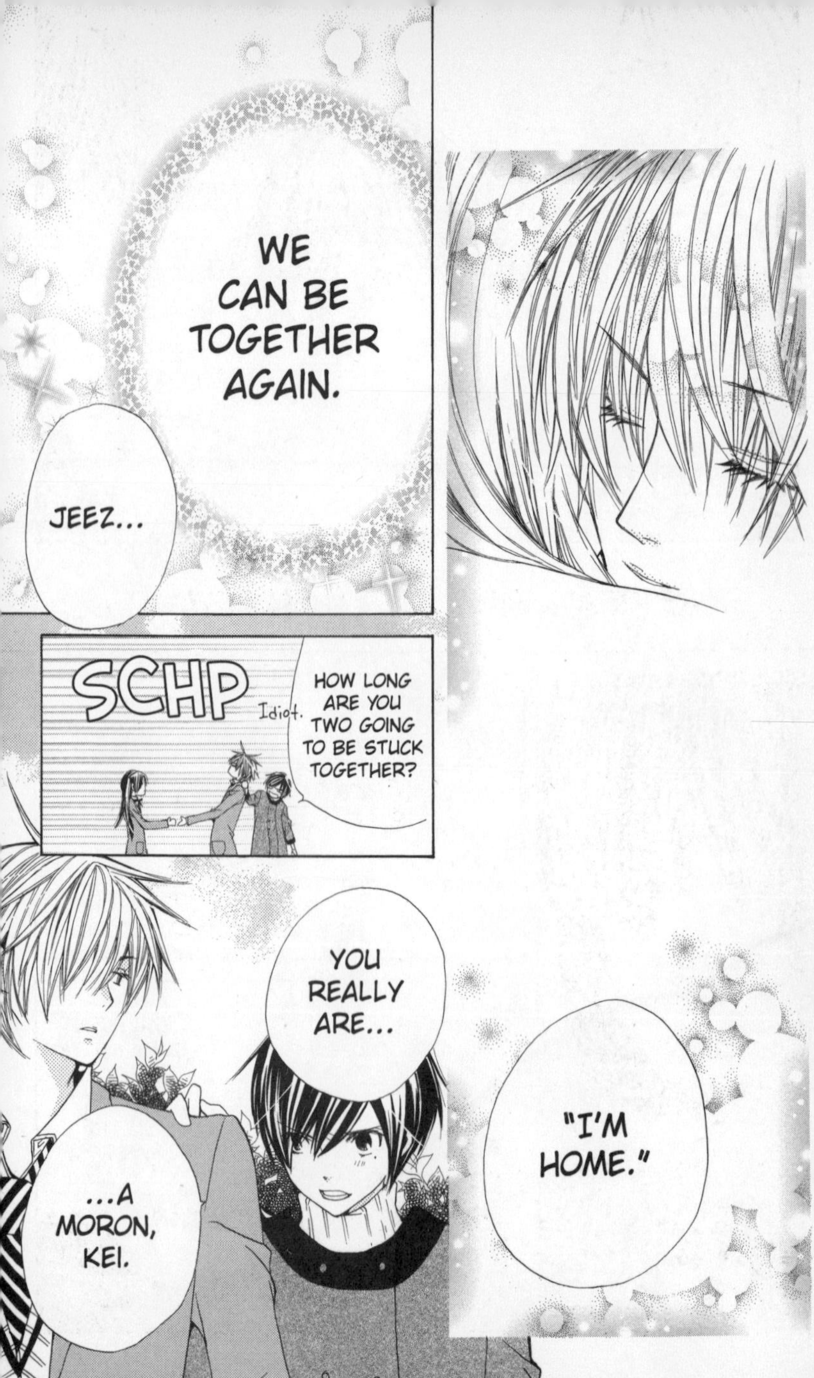
WE CAN BE TOGETHER AGAIN.
JEEZ...
SCHP
HOW LONG ARE YOU TWO GOING TO BE STUCK TOGETHER?
Idiot.
YOU REALLY ARE...
...A MORON, KEI.
"I'M HOME."

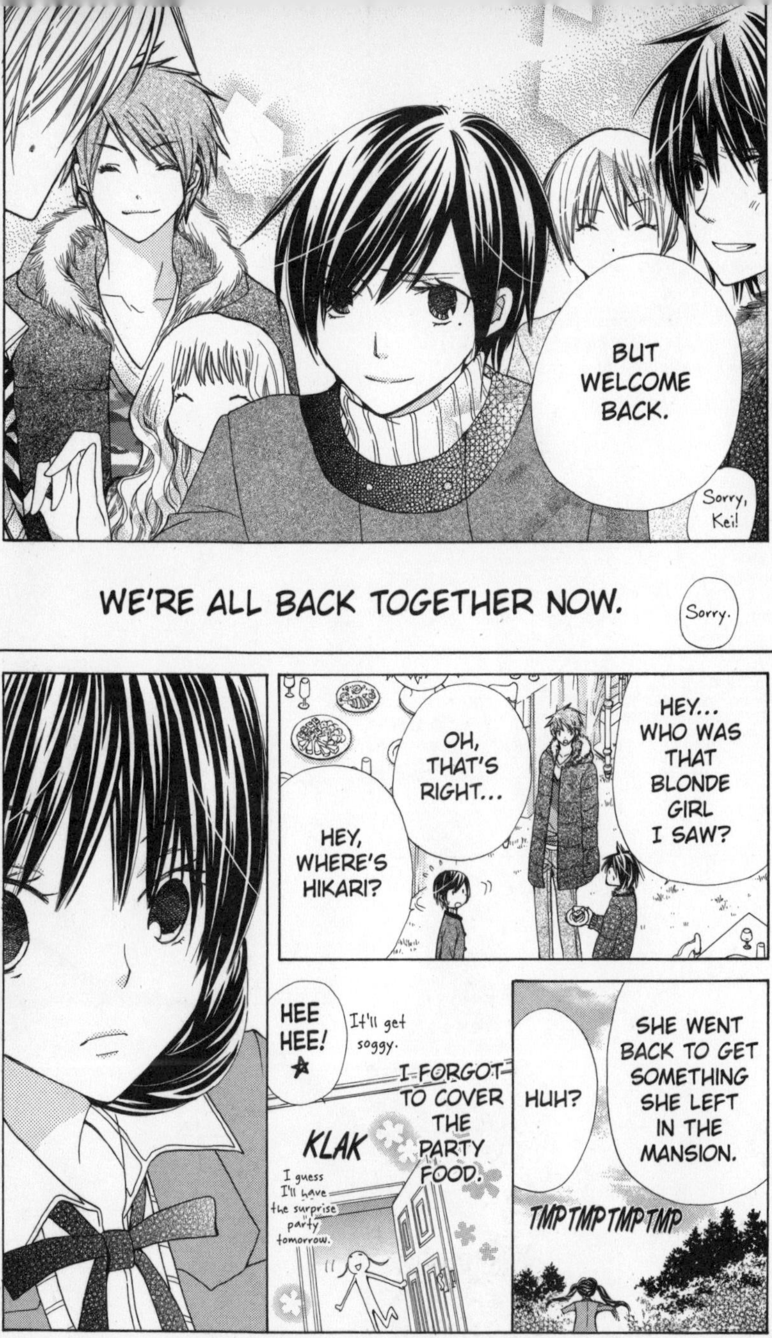
BUT WELCOME BACK.
Sorry, Kei!
Sorry.
WE'RE ALL BACK TOGETHER NOW.
HEY... WHO WAS THAT BLONDE GIRL I SAW?
OH, THAT'S RIGHT...
HEY, WHERE'S HIKARI?
SHE WENT BACK TO GET SOMETHING SHE LEFT IN THE MANSION.
HUH?
TMP TMP TMP TMP
HEE HEE! ☆
It'll get soggy.
I FORGOT TO COVER THE PARTY FOOD.
KLAK
I guess I'll have the surprise party tomorrow.

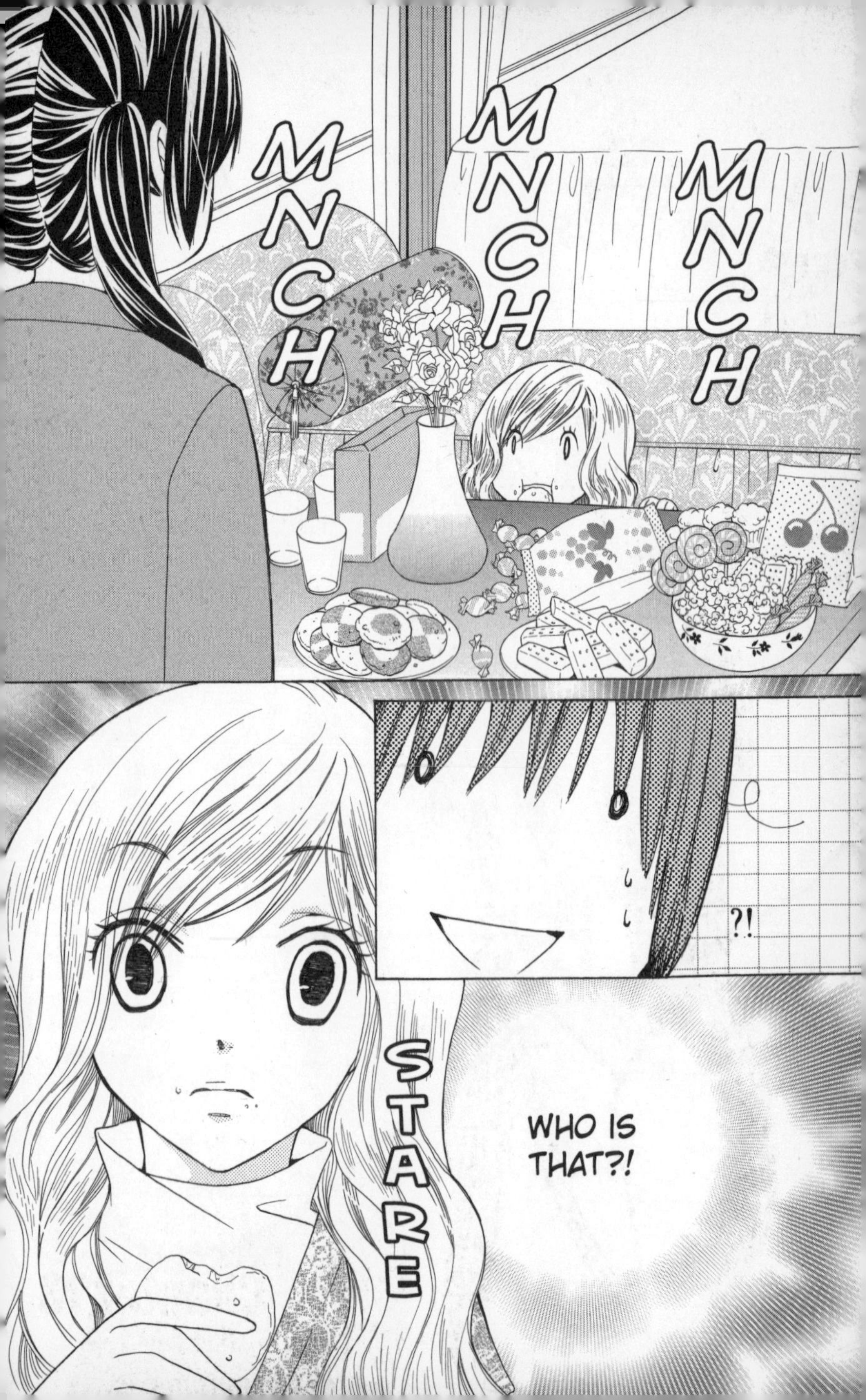
MNCH
MNCH
MNCH
?!
WHO IS THAT?!
STARE

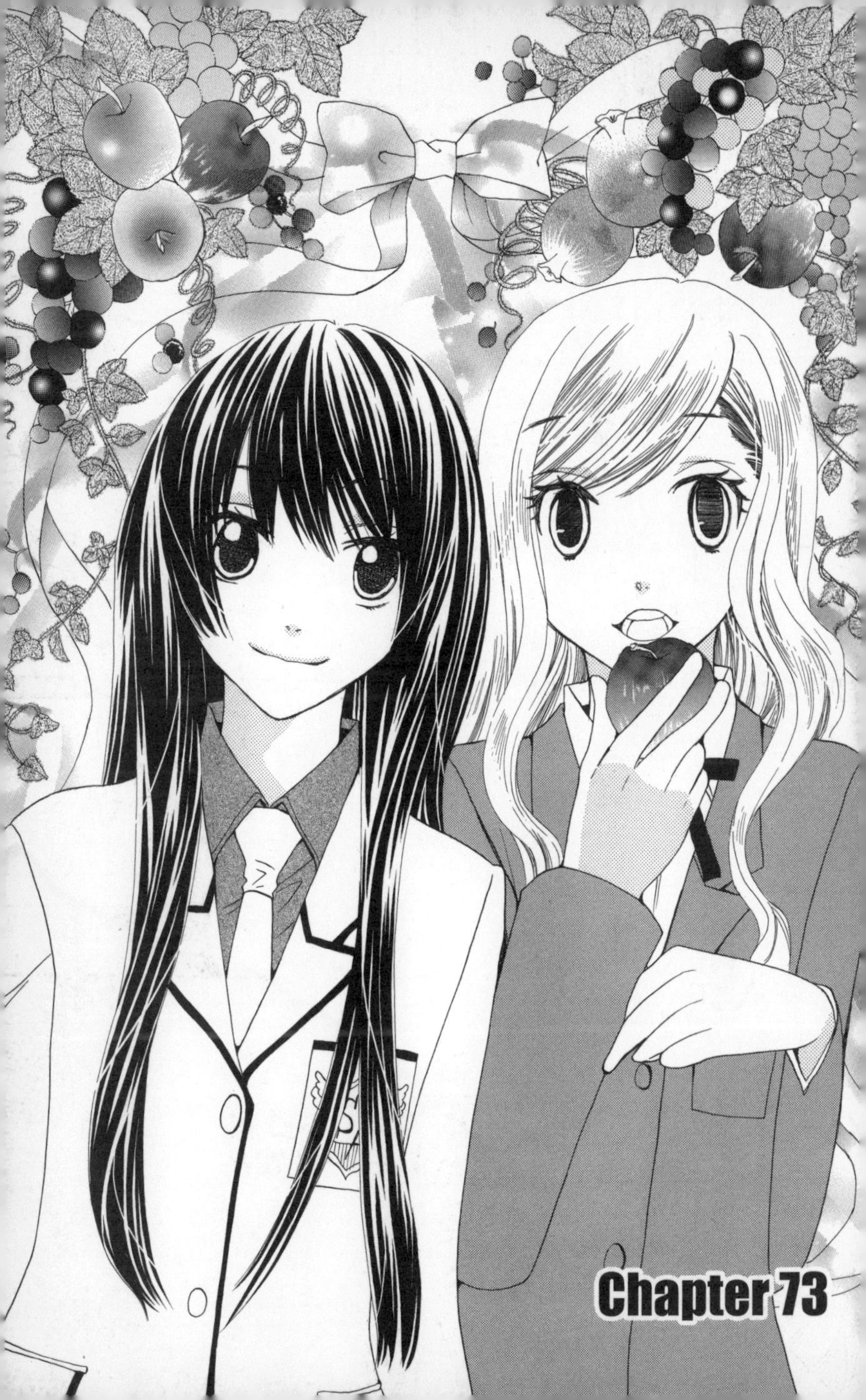
Chapter 73

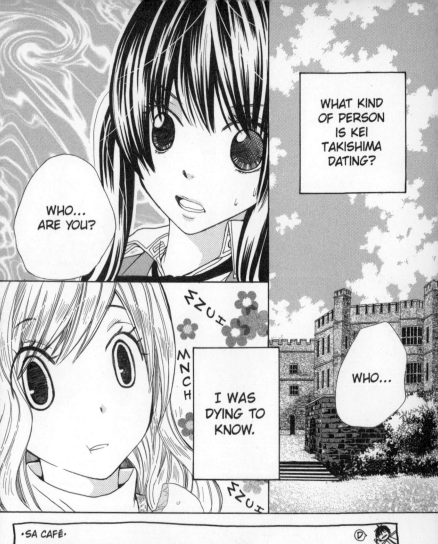

WHAT KIND OF PERSON IS KEI TAKISHIMA DATING?
WHO...
WHO... ARE YOU?
MNCH
I WAS DYING TO KNOW.

•SA CAFÉ•

THERE WERE TONS OF SPECIAL EVENTS WHEN THE ANIME LAUNCHED.
THEY'RE GOING TO HAVE AN *S.A* CAFÉ ON APRIL 19 AND 20 AND SELL SPECIAL DRINKS FOR EACH CHARACTER, AS WELL AS SOME OF THE CONCOCTIONS THE CHARACTERS DRINK IN THE ANIME. AND I HEARD THEY'RE EVEN GOING TO HAVE HIKARI'S CANNONBALL RICE BALLS! THAT'S A-A-A-AWESOME!! AND THE WAITERS WILL ALL BE DRESSED UP LIKE KEI, TADASHI, RYU AND JUN. IT'S GOING TO BE AT A CAFÉ CALLED EDELSTEIN IN AN ALL-BOYS' SCHOOL IN HARAJUKU. A-A-A-AWESOME!!
I STARTED WONDERING WHAT THE SERVICE WOULD BE LIKE...

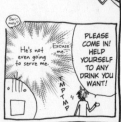

PLEASE COME IN! HELP YOURSELF TO ANY DRINK YOU WANT!
Excuse me.
He's not even going to serve me.
Seriously?
TMP TMP

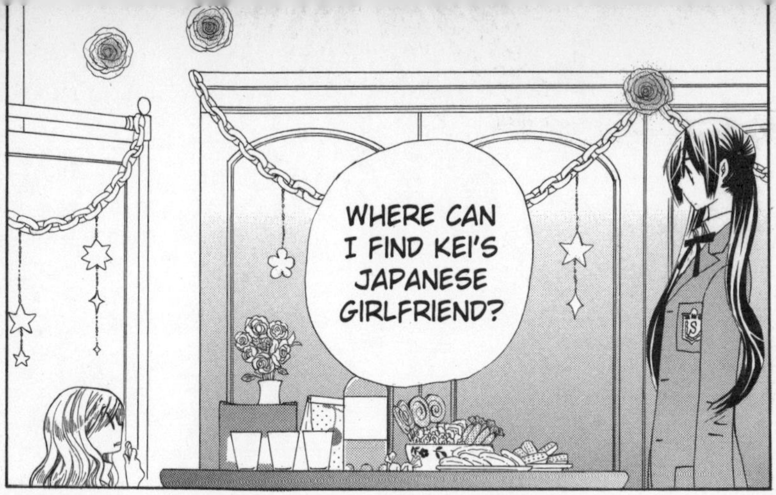
WHERE CAN I FIND KEI'S JAPANESE GIRLFRIEND?

I TRIED JUST ASKING.

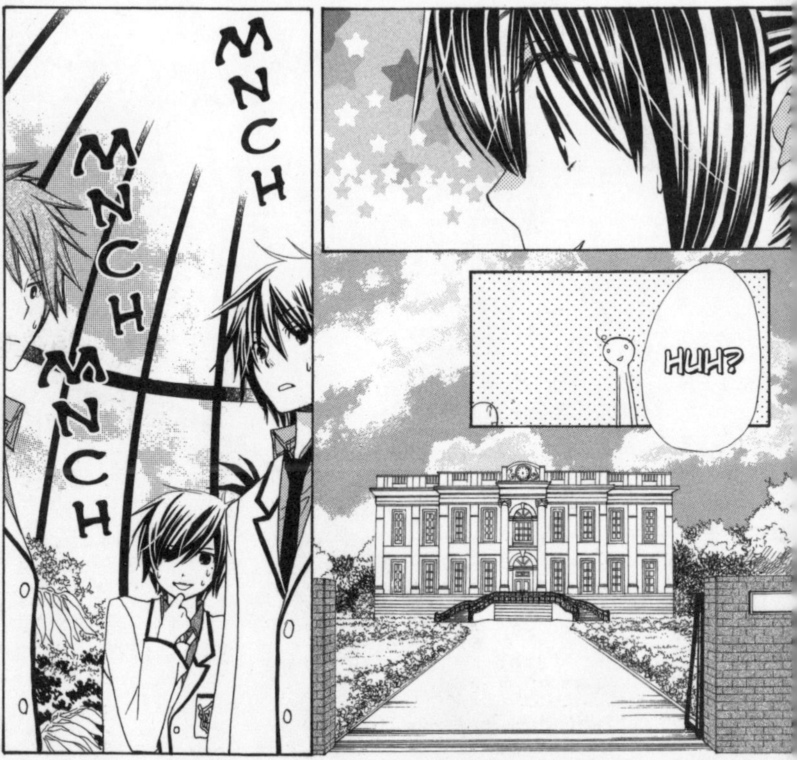
HUH?
MNCH
MNCH
MNCH

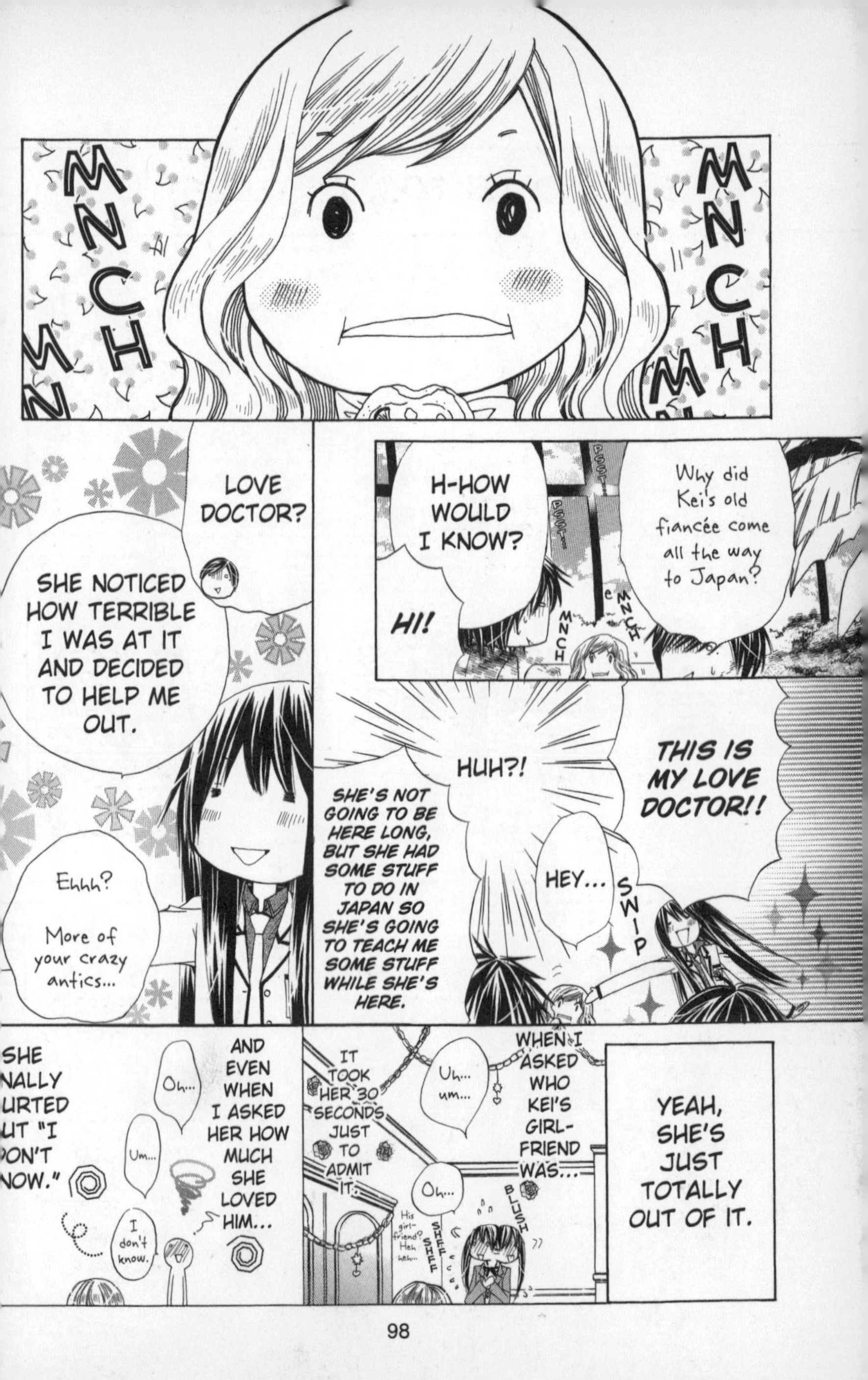
MNCH MNCH
MNCH MNCH
Why did Kei's old fiancée come all the way to Japan?
H-HOW WOULD I KNOW?
PSST PSST...
HI!
MNCH MNCH
THIS IS MY LOVE DOCTOR!!
HUH?!
SHE'S NOT GOING TO BE HERE LONG, BUT SHE HAD SOME STUFF TO DO IN JAPAN SO SHE'S GOING TO TEACH ME SOME STUFF WHILE SHE'S HERE.
HEY...
SWIP
LOVE DOCTOR?
SHE NOTICED HOW TERRIBLE I WAS AT IT AND DECIDED TO HELP ME OUT.
Ehhh? More of your crazy antics...
YEAH, SHE'S JUST TOTALLY OUT OF IT.
WHEN I ASKED WHO KEI'S GIRLFRIEND WAS...
Uh... um...
IT TOOK HER 30 SECONDS JUST TO ADMIT IT.
Oh...
BLUSH
His girlfriend? Heh heh...
SHEFF SHEFF
AND EVEN WHEN I ASKED HER HOW MUCH SHE LOVED HIM...
SHE NALLY URTED UT "I ON'T NOW."
Oh...
Um...
I don't know.

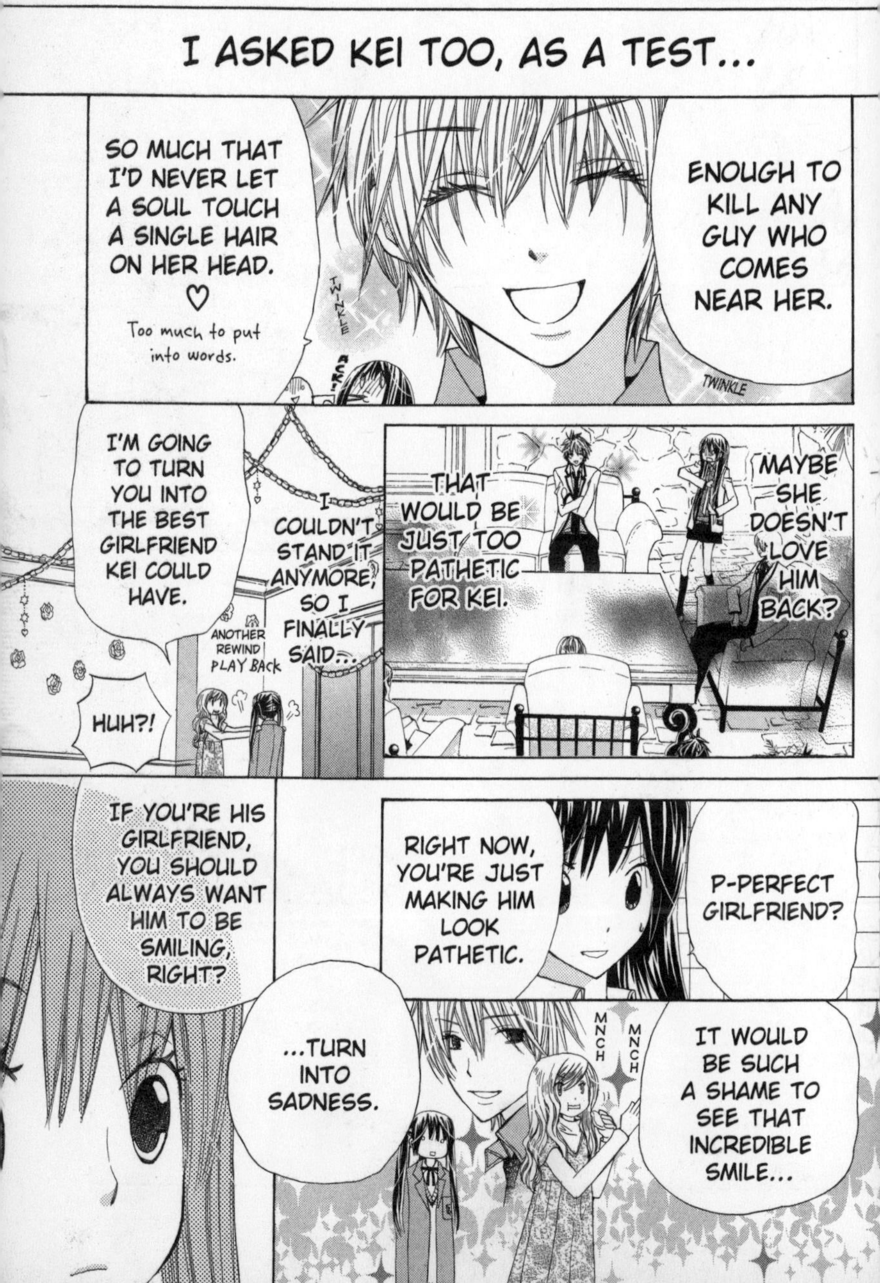
I ASKED KEI TOO, AS A TEST...
ENOUGH TO KILL ANY GUY WHO COMES NEAR HER.
TWINKLE
SO MUCH THAT I'D NEVER LET A SOUL TOUCH A SINGLE HAIR ON HER HEAD. ♡
Too much to put into words.
TWINKLE
ACK!
MAYBE SHE DOESN'T LOVE HIM BACK?
THAT WOULD BE JUST TOO PATHETIC FOR KEI.
I COULDN'T STAND IT ANYMORE, SO I FINALLY SAID...
I'M GOING TO TURN YOU INTO THE BEST GIRLFRIEND KEI COULD HAVE.
ANOTHER REWIND PLAY BACK
HUH?!
P-PERFECT GIRLFRIEND?
RIGHT NOW, YOU'RE JUST MAKING HIM LOOK PATHETIC.
IT WOULD BE SUCH A SHAME TO SEE THAT INCREDIBLE SMILE...
MNCH MNCH
...TURN INTO SADNESS.
IF YOU'RE HIS GIRLFRIEND, YOU SHOULD ALWAYS WANT HIM TO BE SMILING, RIGHT?

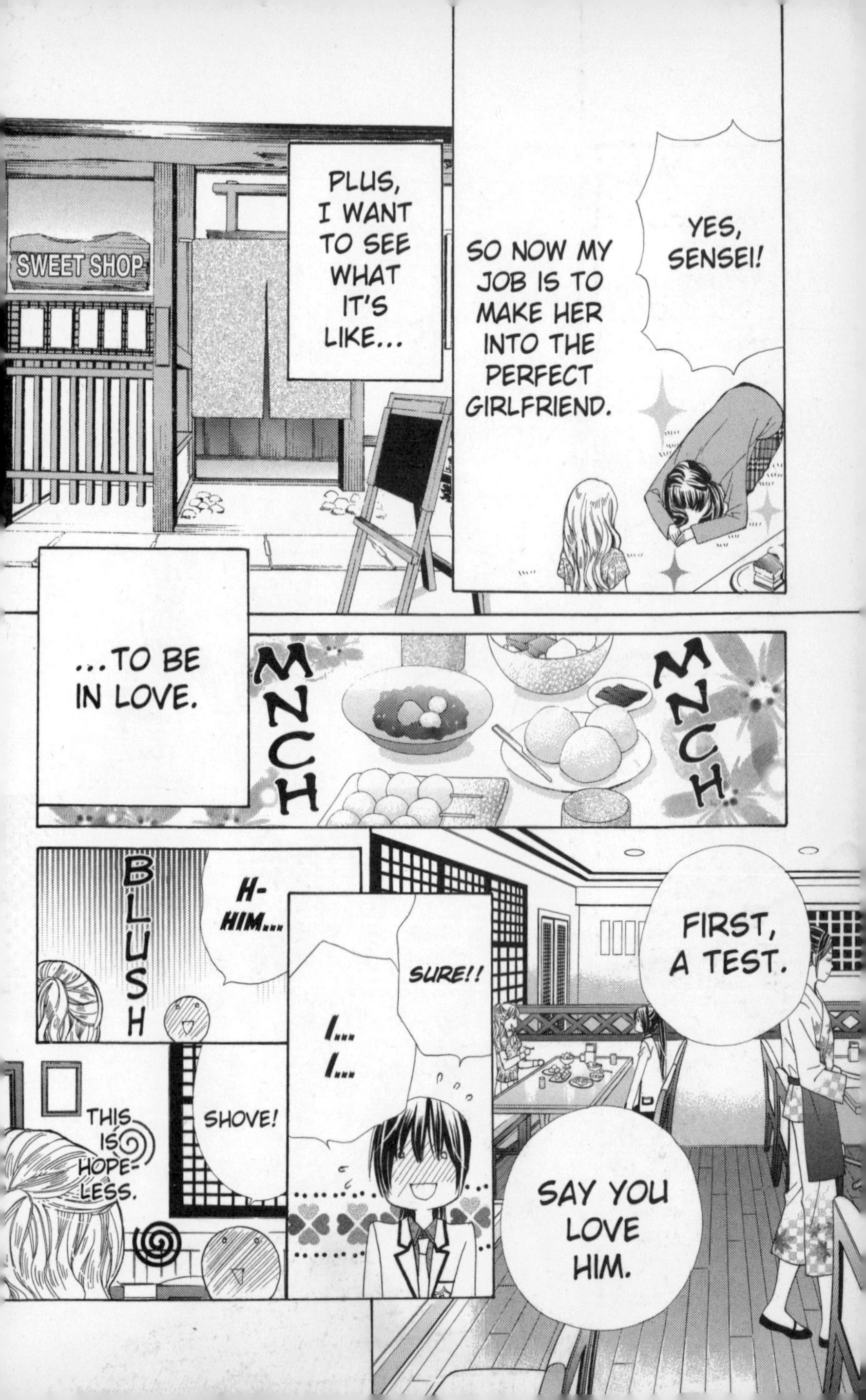
YES, SENSEI!
SO NOW MY JOB IS TO MAKE HER INTO THE PERFECT GIRLFRIEND.
PLUS, I WANT TO SEE WHAT IT'S LIKE...
SWEET SHOP
MNCH
MNCH
...TO BE IN LOVE.
FIRST, A TEST.
SAY YOU LOVE HIM.
SURE!!
I... I...
H- HIM...
BLUSH
SHOVE!
THIS IS HOPE-LESS.

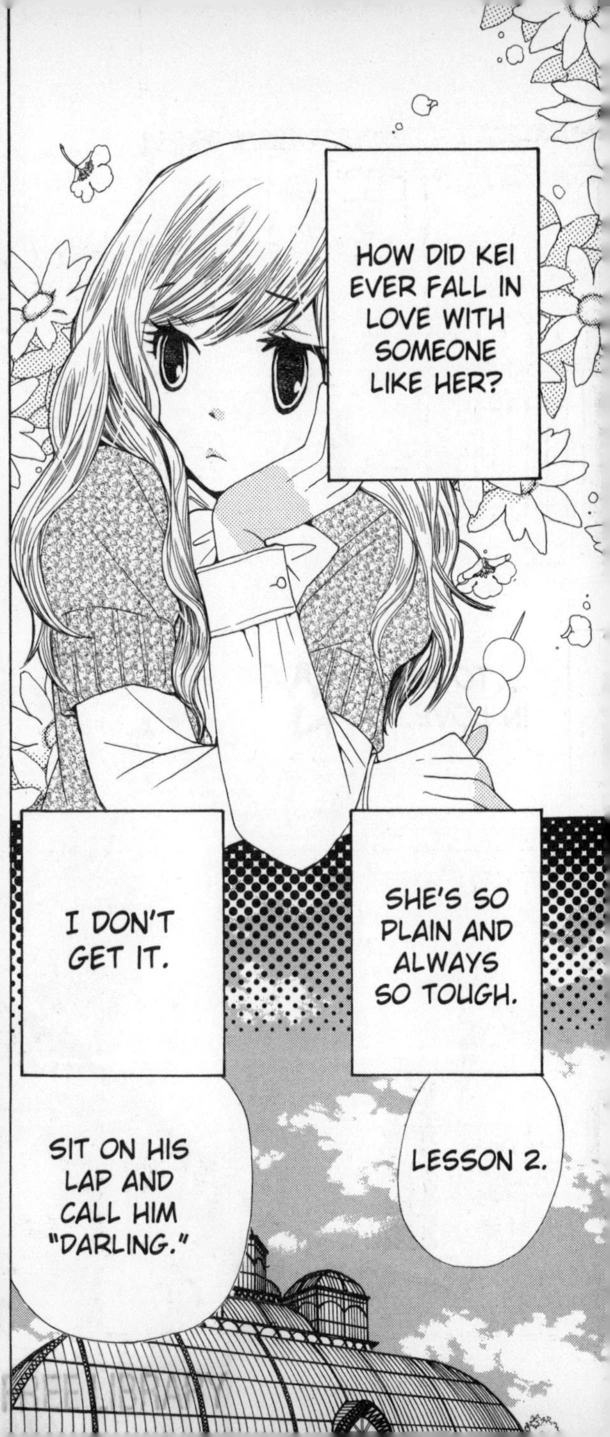
HOW DID KEI EVER FALL IN LOVE WITH SOMEONE LIKE HER?
SHE'S SO PLAIN AND ALWAYS SO TOUGH.
I DON'T GET IT.
LESSON 2.
SIT ON HIS LAP AND CALL HIM "DARLING."

④

• UNCONTROLLABLE CRAVINGS •

ARE THERE CERTAIN FOODS THAT YOU CRAVE UNCONTROLLABLY?

• RAMEN • HAMBURGER •

• OKONOMIYAKI • CRAB •

• CAKE •

• CURRY • CAKE •

• AND... MEAT.

I KEEP HAVING THIS DREAM ABOUT A CAFETERIA WHERE YOU CAN GET EVERYTHING YOU WANT ALL IN ONE PLACE. I DREAM THAT THEY BUILD ONE IN MY NEIGHBORHOOD, REALLY CLOSE TO MY HOUSE.

YEAH... IN MY DREAMS...

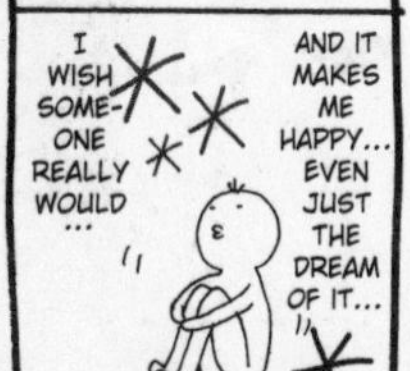
AND IT MAKES ME HAPPY... EVEN JUST THE DREAM OF IT...
I WISH SOME-ONE REALLY WOULD...

...BUILD THE CAFETERIA OF MY DREAMS.
WELL... IT'S A GREAT DREAM...ISN'T IT?
HA HA!

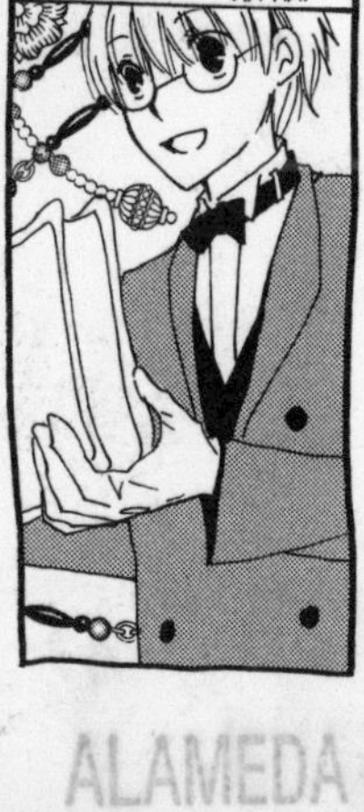

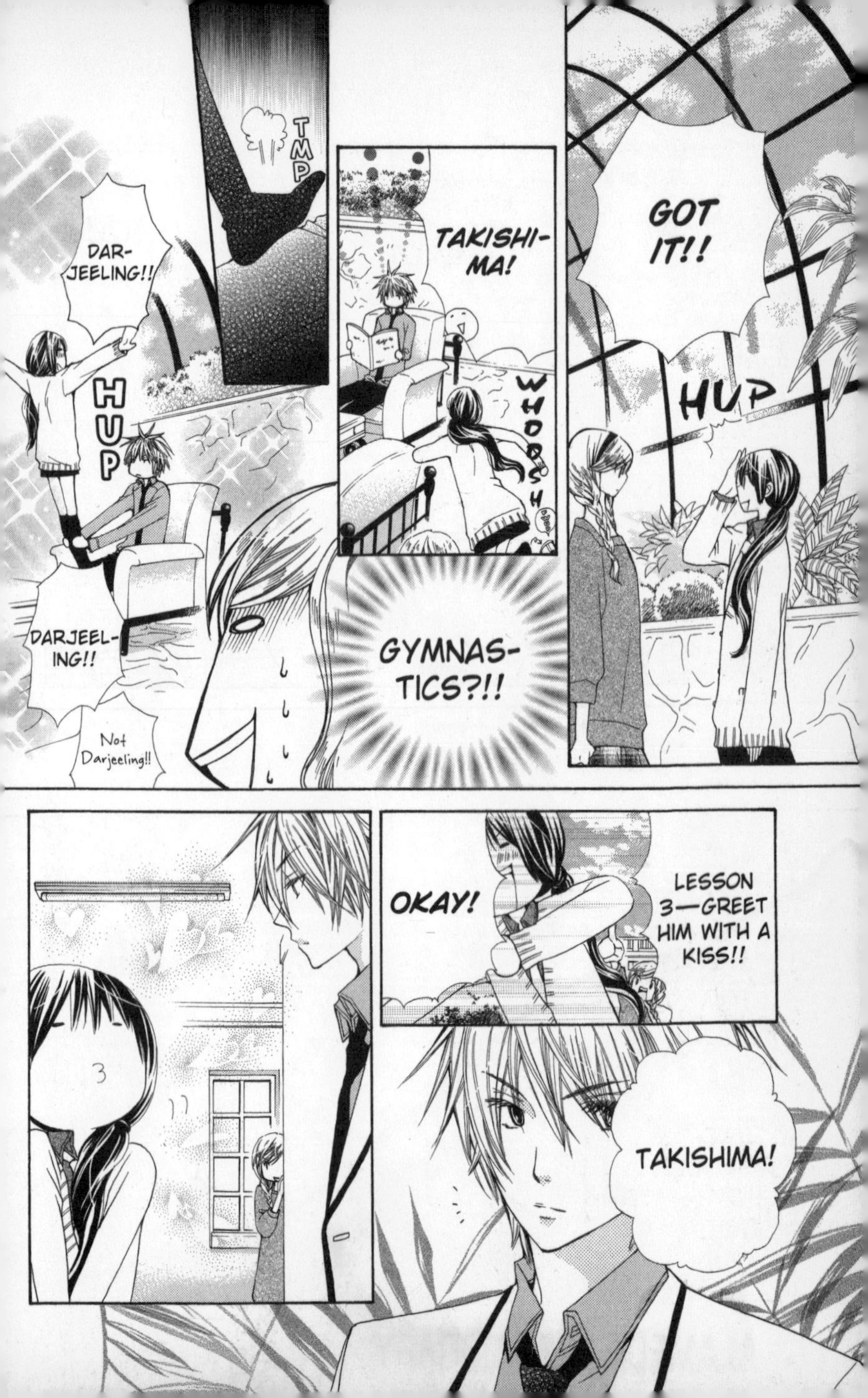
GOT IT!!
HUP
TAKISHIMA!
WHOOSH
TMP
DAR-JEELING!!
HUP
DARJEELING!!
Not Darjeeling!!
GYMNASTICS?!!
LESSON 3—GREET HIM WITH A KISS!!
OKAY!
TAKISHIMA!

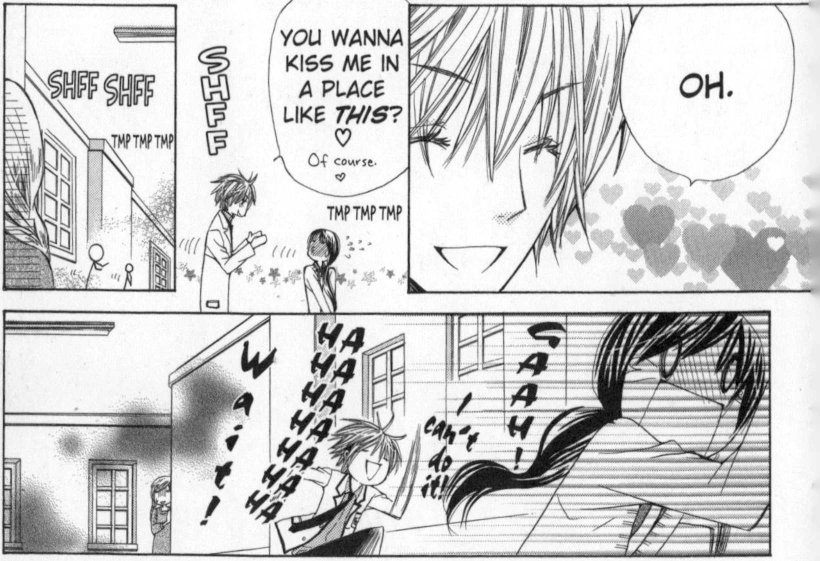
OH.
YOU WANNA KISS ME IN A PLACE LIKE THIS? ♡
Of course. ♡
SHFF
TMP TMP TMP
SHFF SHFF
TMP TMP TMP
GAAH!
I can't do it!
HAHAHAHAHAHAHAHA
Wait!

DOES HIKARI REALLY LOVE KEI?!

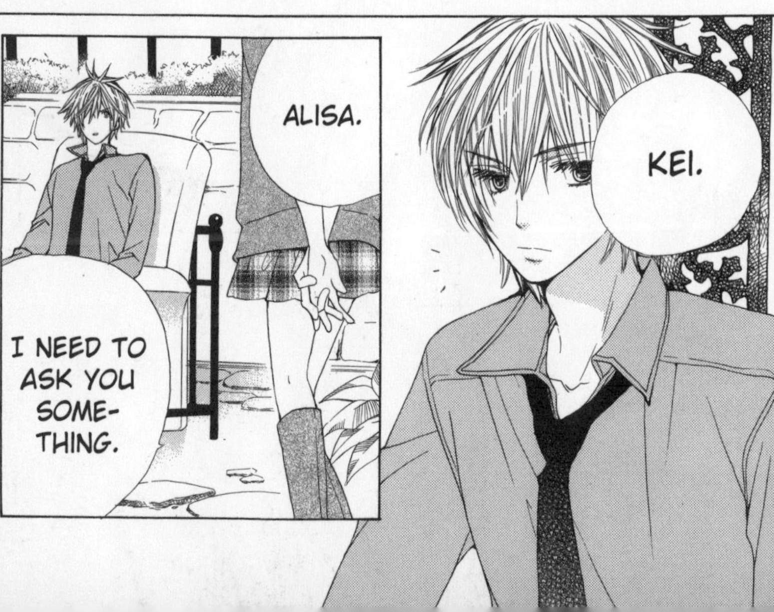
KEI.
ALISA.
I NEED TO ASK YOU SOME-THING.

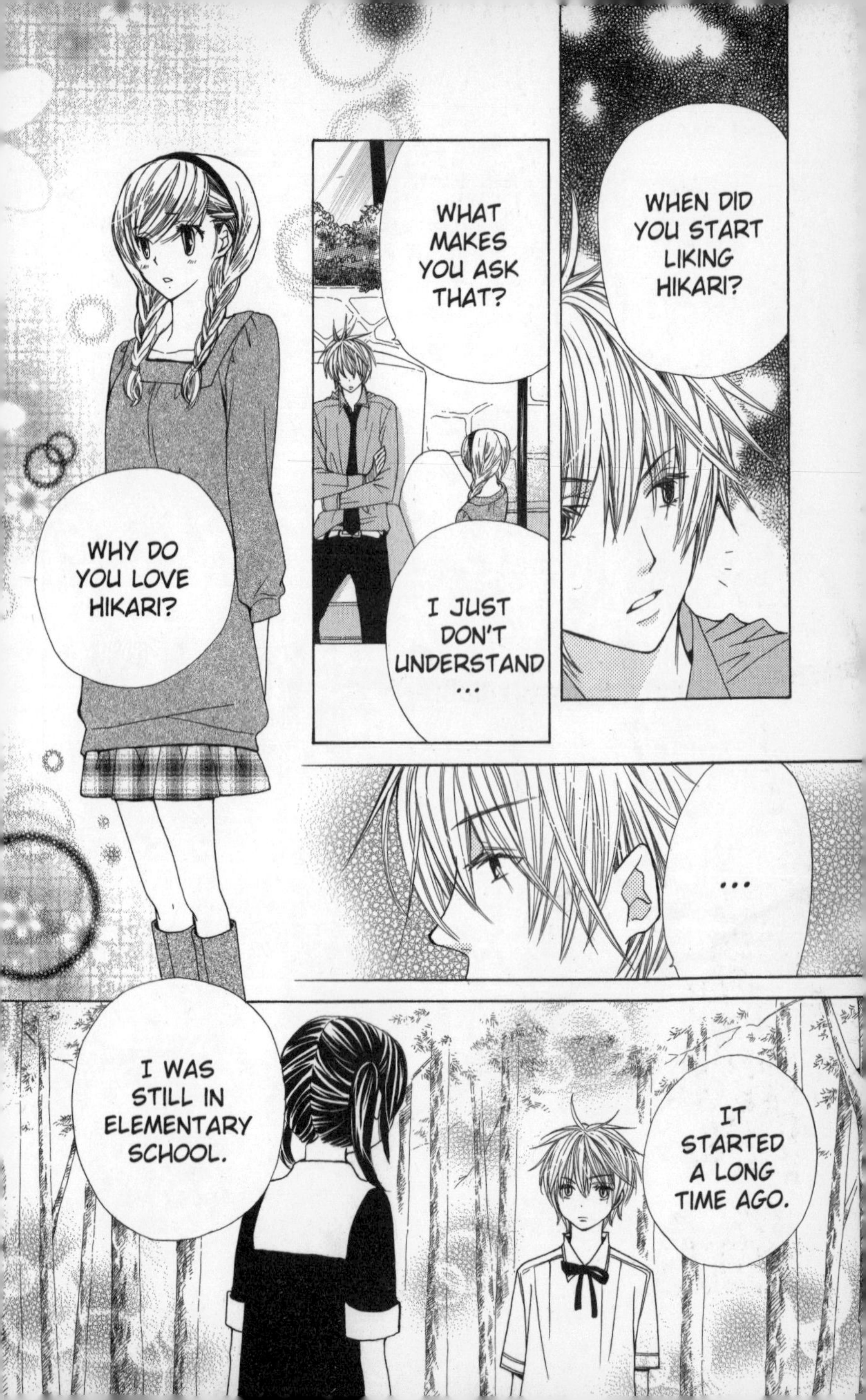
WHEN DID YOU START LIKING HIKARI?
WHAT MAKES YOU ASK THAT?
I JUST DON'T UNDERSTAND...
...
WHY DO YOU LOVE HIKARI?
IT STARTED A LONG TIME AGO.
I WAS STILL IN ELEMENTARY SCHOOL.

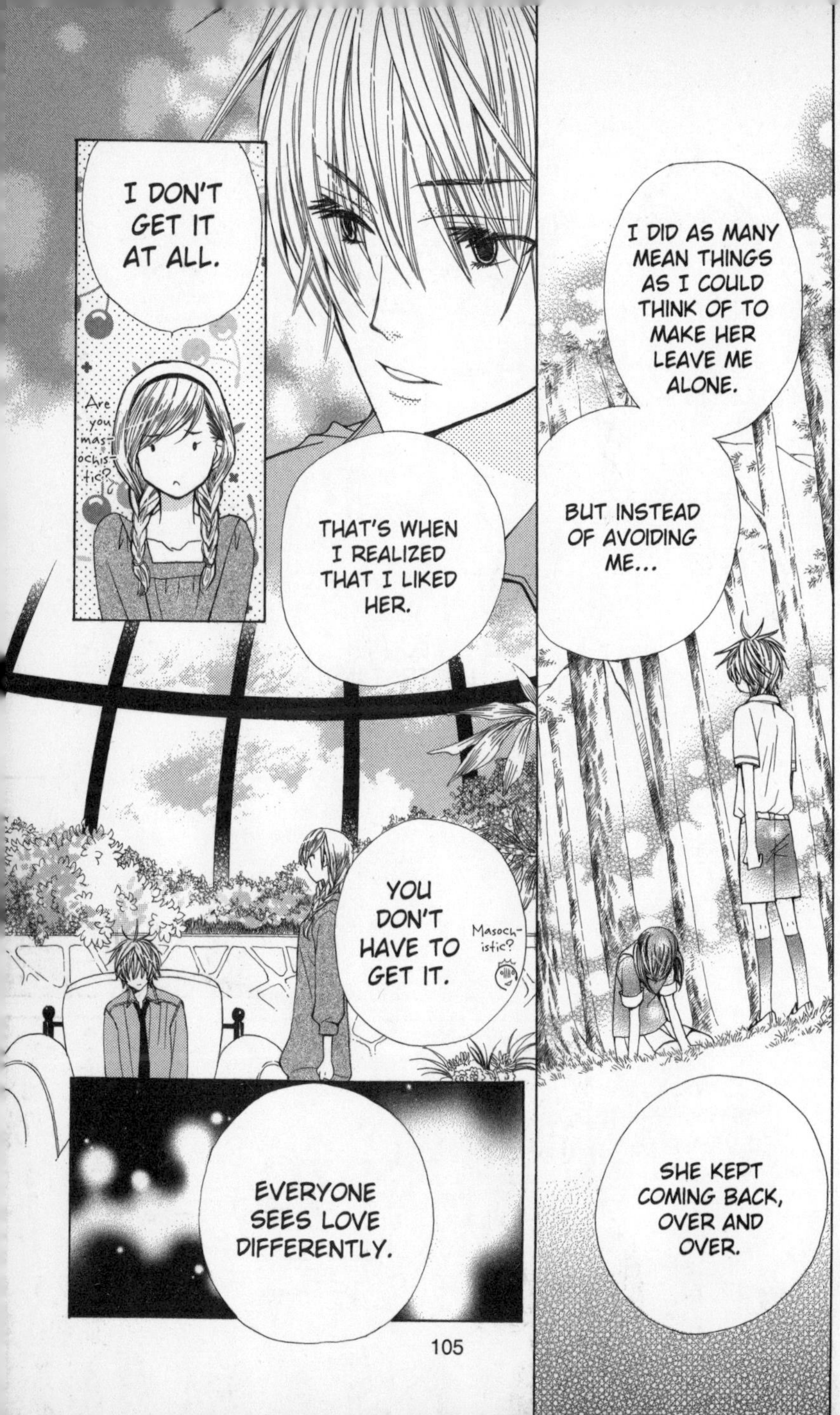
I DID AS MANY MEAN THINGS AS I COULD THINK OF TO MAKE HER LEAVE ME ALONE.
BUT INSTEAD OF AVOIDING ME...
SHE KEPT COMING BACK, OVER AND OVER.
THAT'S WHEN I REALIZED THAT I LIKED HER.
I DON'T GET IT AT ALL.
Are you masochistic?
YOU DON'T HAVE TO GET IT.
Masochistic?
EVERYONE SEES LOVE DIFFERENTLY.

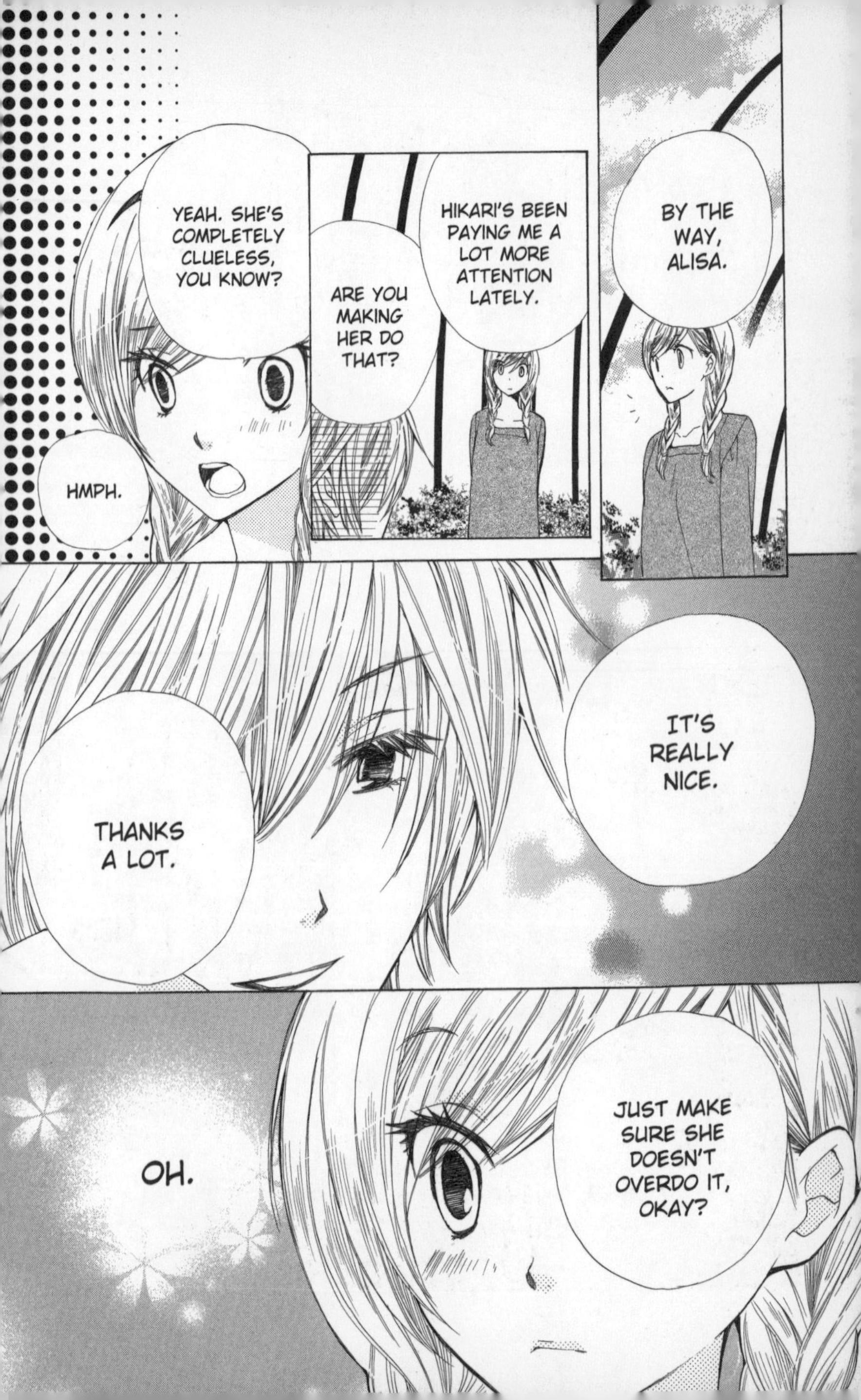
BY THE WAY, ALISA.
HIKARI'S BEEN PAYING ME A LOT MORE ATTENTION LATELY.
ARE YOU MAKING HER DO THAT?
YEAH. SHE'S COMPLETELY CLUELESS, YOU KNOW?
HMPH.
IT'S REALLY NICE.
THANKS A LOT.
JUST MAKE SURE SHE DOESN'T OVERDO IT, OKAY?
OH.

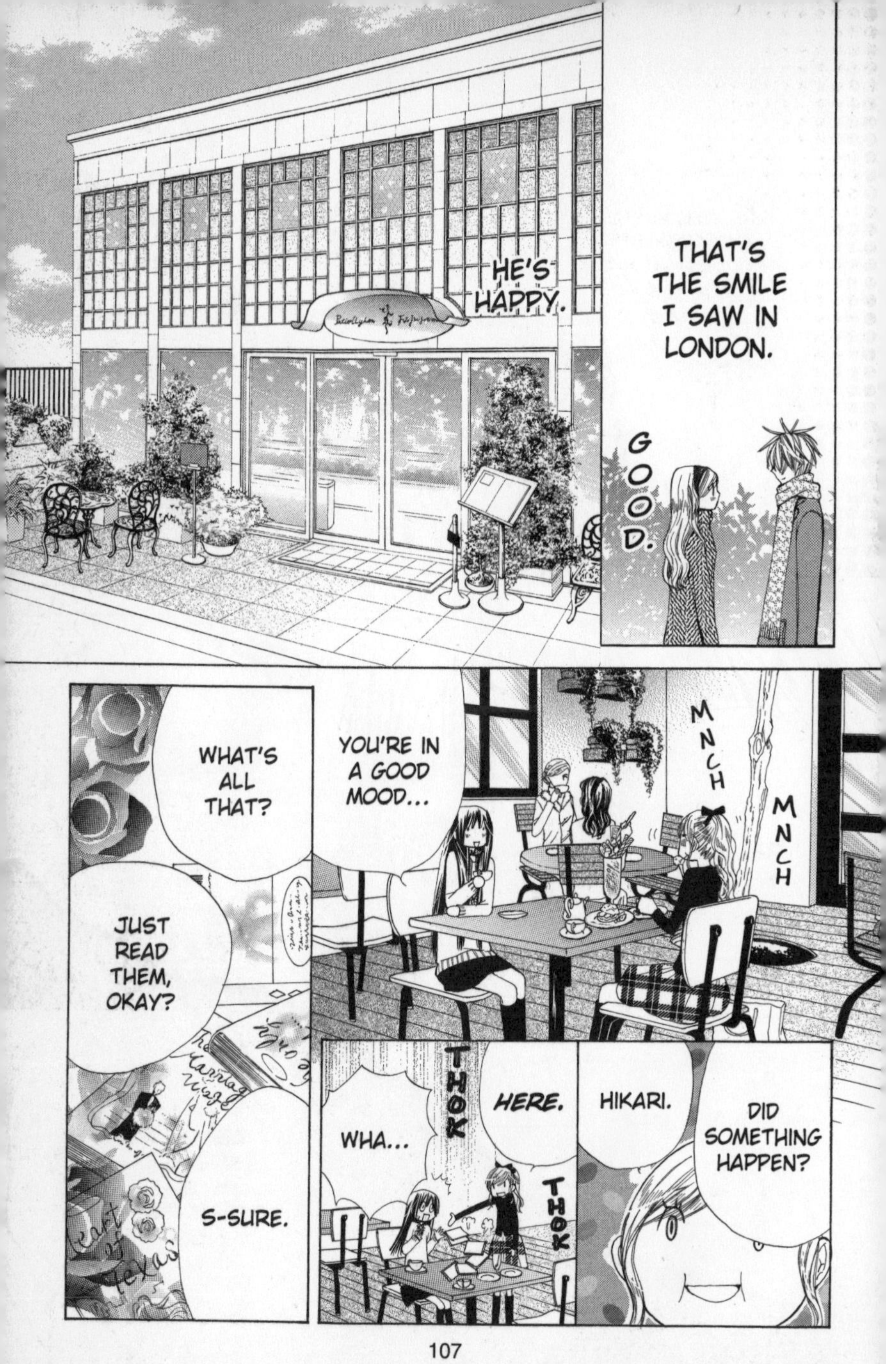
THAT'S THE SMILE I SAW IN LONDON.
GOOD.
HE'S HAPPY.
MNCH
MNCH
YOU'RE IN A GOOD MOOD...
DID SOMETHING HAPPEN?
HIKARI.
HERE.
THOK
THOK
WHA...
WHAT'S ALL THAT?
JUST READ THEM, OKAY?
S-SURE.

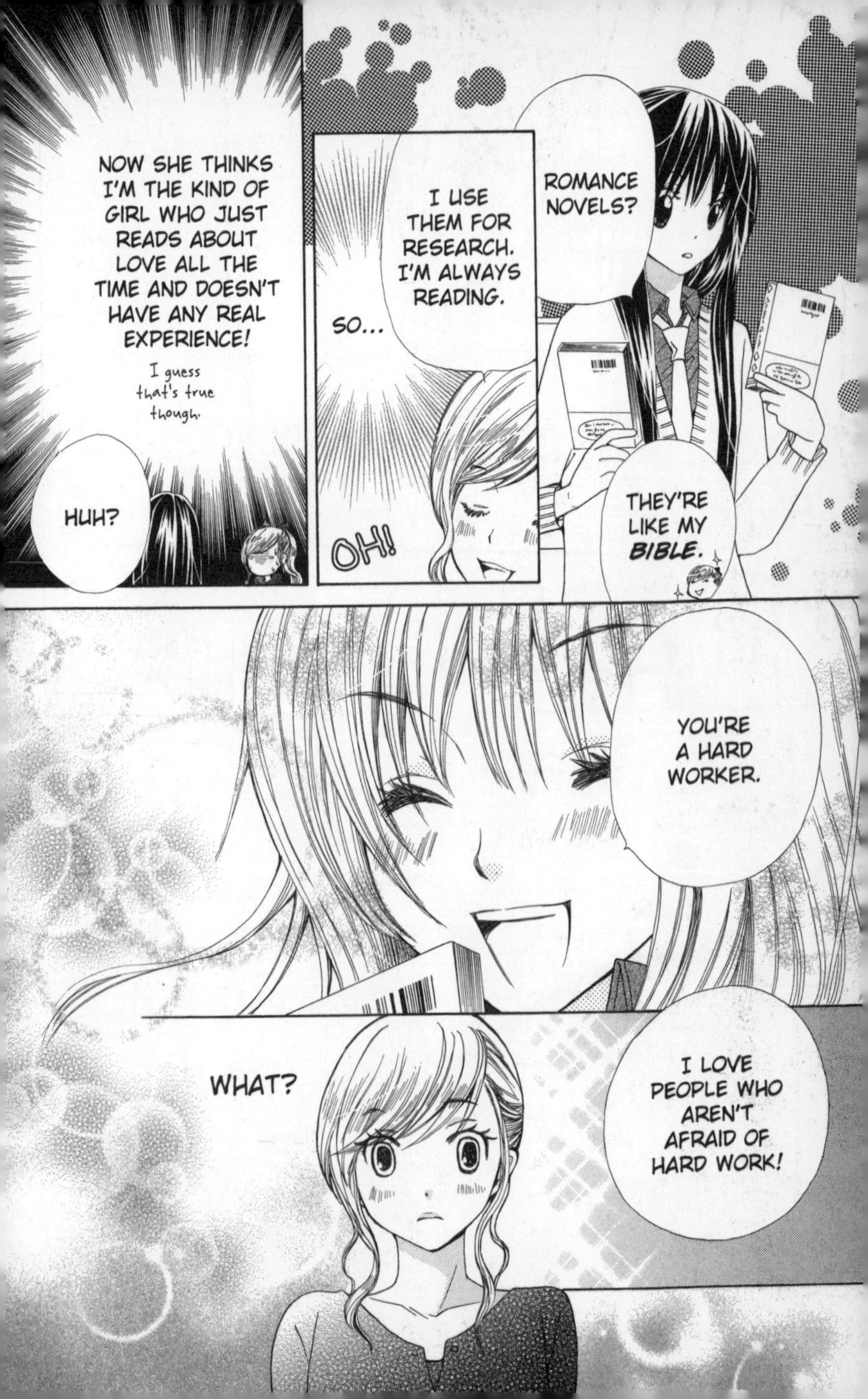
ROMANCE NOVELS?
I USE THEM FOR RESEARCH. I'M ALWAYS READING.
SO...
THEY'RE LIKE MY *BIBLE*.
OH!
NOW SHE THINKS I'M THE KIND OF GIRL WHO JUST READS ABOUT LOVE ALL THE TIME AND DOESN'T HAVE ANY REAL EXPERIENCE!
I guess that's true though.
HUH?
YOU'RE A HARD WORKER.
I LOVE PEOPLE WHO AREN'T AFRAID OF HARD WORK!
WHAT?

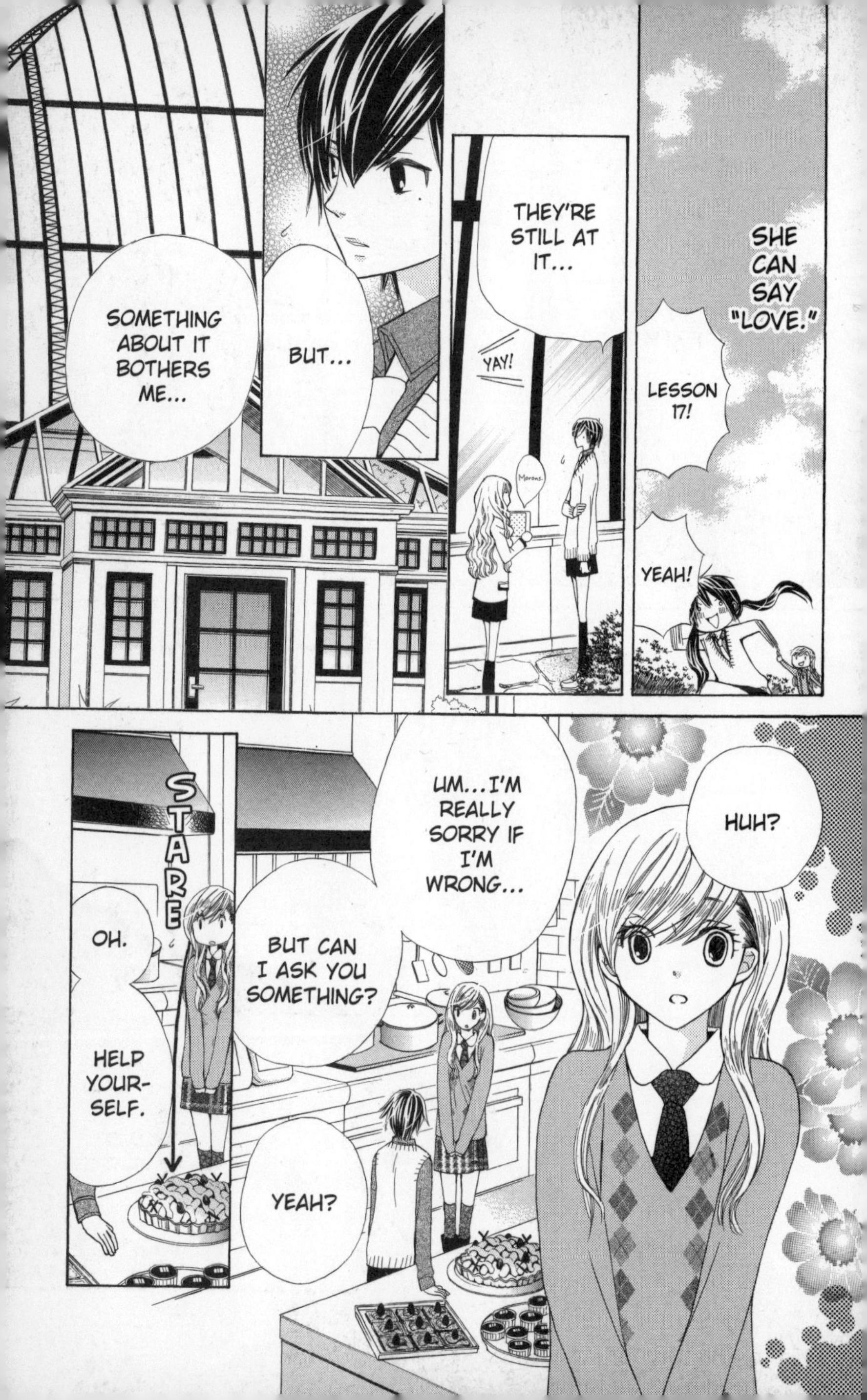
SHE CAN SAY "LOVE."
LESSON 17!
YEAH!
THEY'RE STILL AT IT...
YAY!
Morons.
BUT...
SOMETHING ABOUT IT BOTHERS ME...
HUH?
UM...I'M REALLY SORRY IF I'M WRONG...
BUT CAN I ASK YOU SOMETHING?
YEAH?
STARE
OH.
HELP YOUR-SELF.

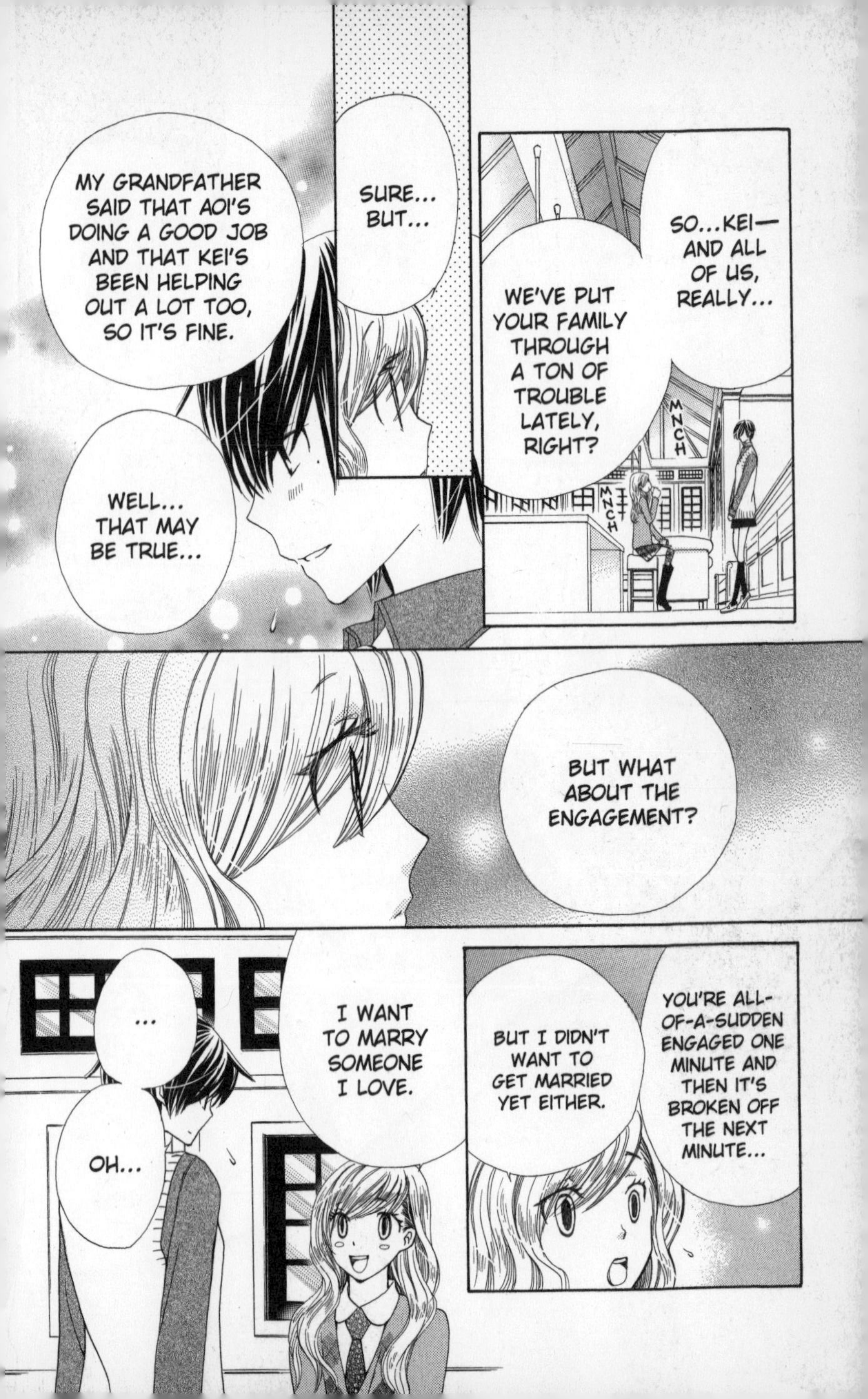
SO...KEI—AND ALL OF US, REALLY...
WE'VE PUT YOUR FAMILY THROUGH A TON OF TROUBLE LATELY, RIGHT?
MNCH
MNCH
SURE... BUT...
MY GRANDFATHER SAID THAT AOI'S DOING A GOOD JOB AND THAT KEI'S BEEN HELPING OUT A LOT TOO, SO IT'S FINE.
WELL... THAT MAY BE TRUE...
BUT WHAT ABOUT THE ENGAGEMENT?
YOU'RE ALL-OF-A-SUDDEN ENGAGED ONE MINUTE AND THEN IT'S BROKEN OFF THE NEXT MINUTE...
BUT I DIDN'T WANT TO GET MARRIED YET EITHER.
I WANT TO MARRY SOMEONE I LOVE.
...
OH...

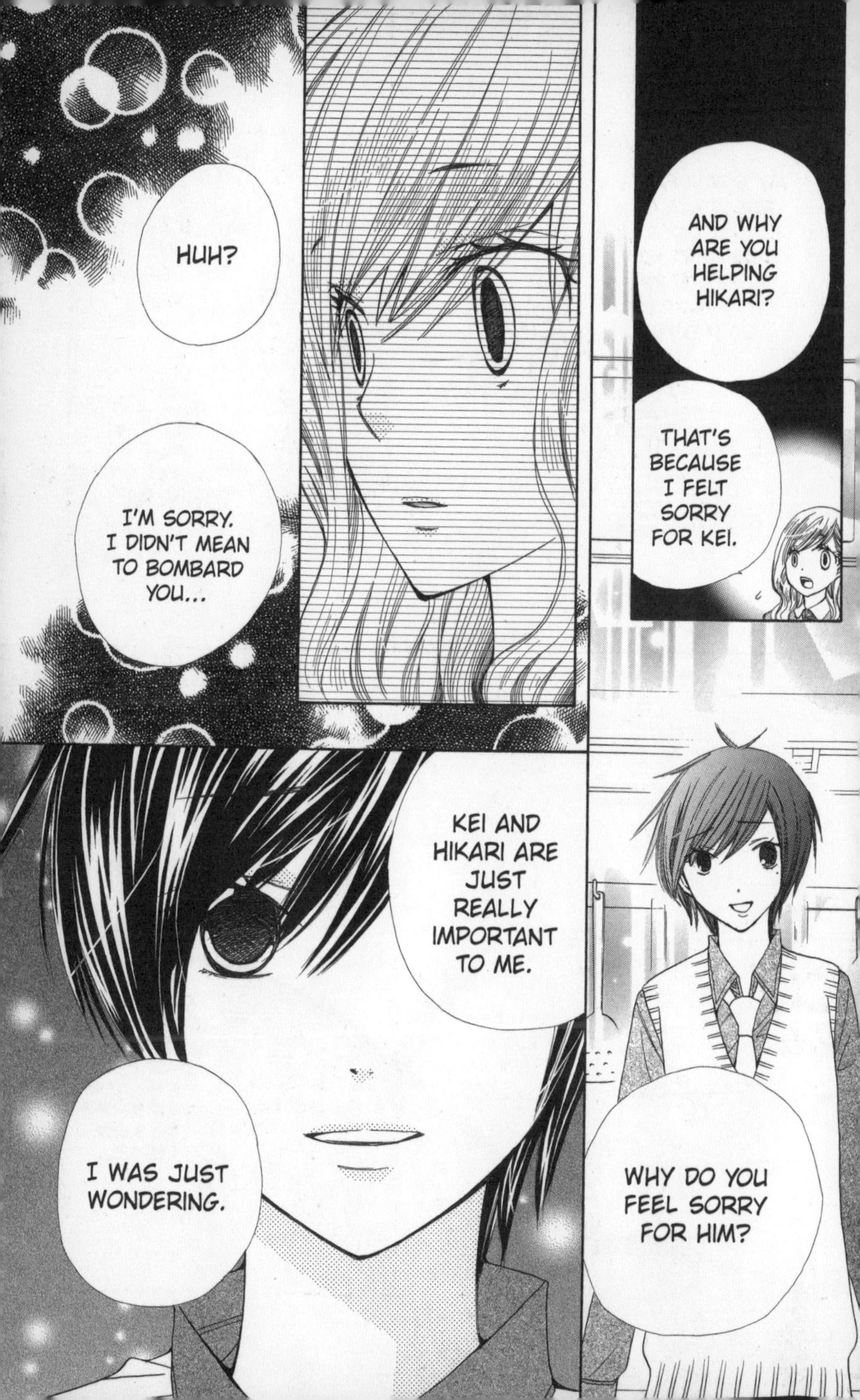
AND WHY ARE YOU HELPING HIKARI?
THAT'S BECAUSE I FELT SORRY FOR KEI.
WHY DO YOU FEEL SORRY FOR HIM?
HUH?
I'M SORRY. I DIDN'T MEAN TO BOMBARD YOU...
KEI AND HIKARI ARE JUST REALLY IMPORTANT TO ME.
I WAS JUST WONDERING.

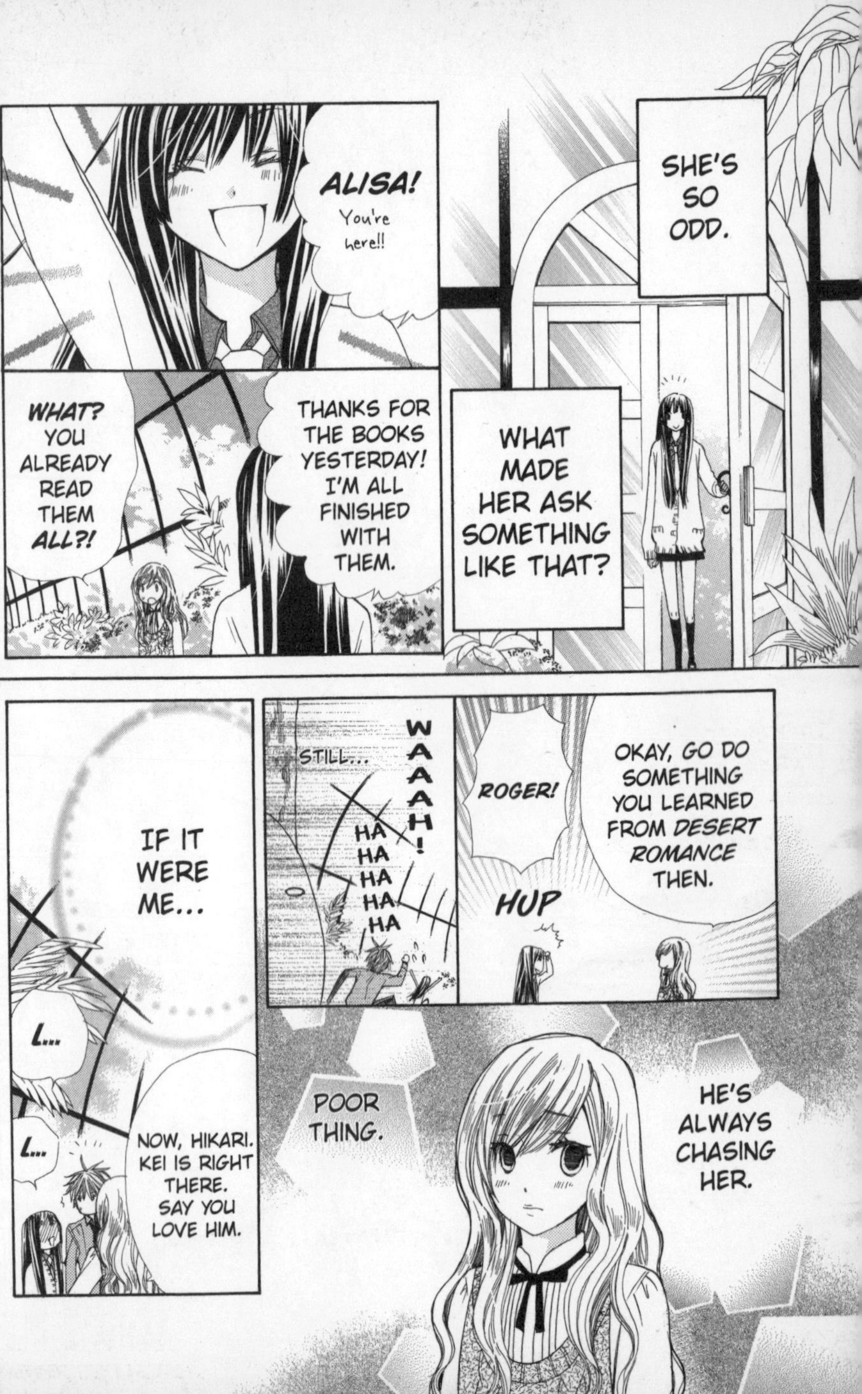
SHE'S SO ODD.
WHAT MADE HER ASK SOMETHING LIKE THAT?
ALISA!
You're here!!
THANKS FOR THE BOOKS YESTERDAY! I'M ALL FINISHED WITH THEM.
WHAT? YOU ALREADY READ THEM ALL?!
OKAY, GO DO SOMETHING YOU LEARNED FROM DESERT ROMANCE THEN.
ROGER!
HUP
WAAAAH!
STILL...
HA HA HA HA HA
HE'S ALWAYS CHASING HER.
POOR THING.
IF IT WERE ME...
L...
NOW, HIKARI. KEI IS RIGHT THERE. SAY YOU LOVE HIM.
L...

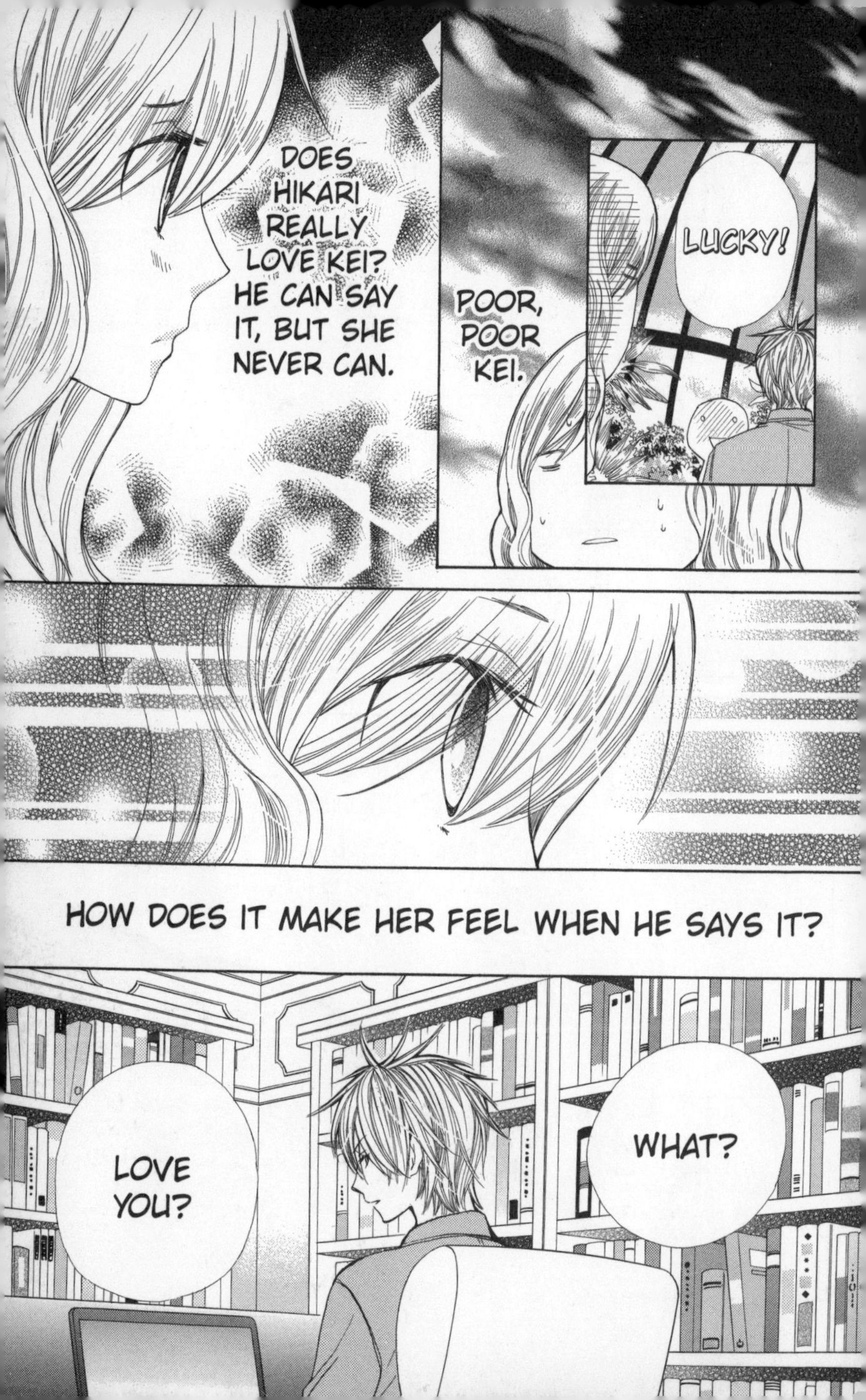
LUCKY!
POOR, POOR KEI.
DOES HIKARI REALLY LOVE KEI? HE CAN SAY IT, BUT SHE NEVER CAN.
HOW DOES IT MAKE HER FEEL WHEN HE SAYS IT?
WHAT?
LOVE YOU?

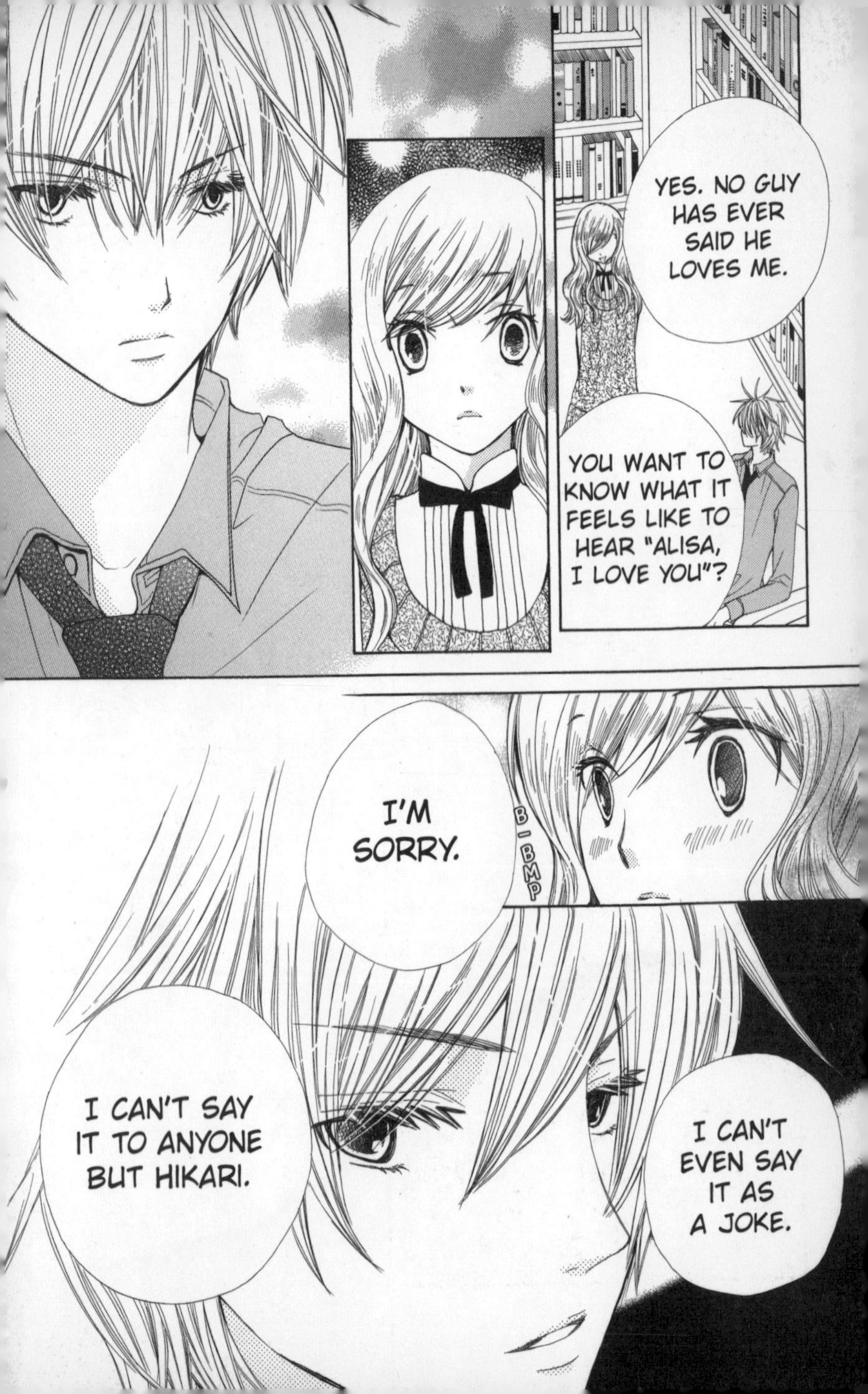
YES. NO GUY HAS EVER SAID HE LOVES ME.
YOU WANT TO KNOW WHAT IT FEELS LIKE TO HEAR "ALISA, I LOVE YOU"?
I'M SORRY.
B-BMP
I CAN'T EVEN SAY IT AS A JOKE.
I CAN'T SAY IT TO ANYONE BUT HIKARI.

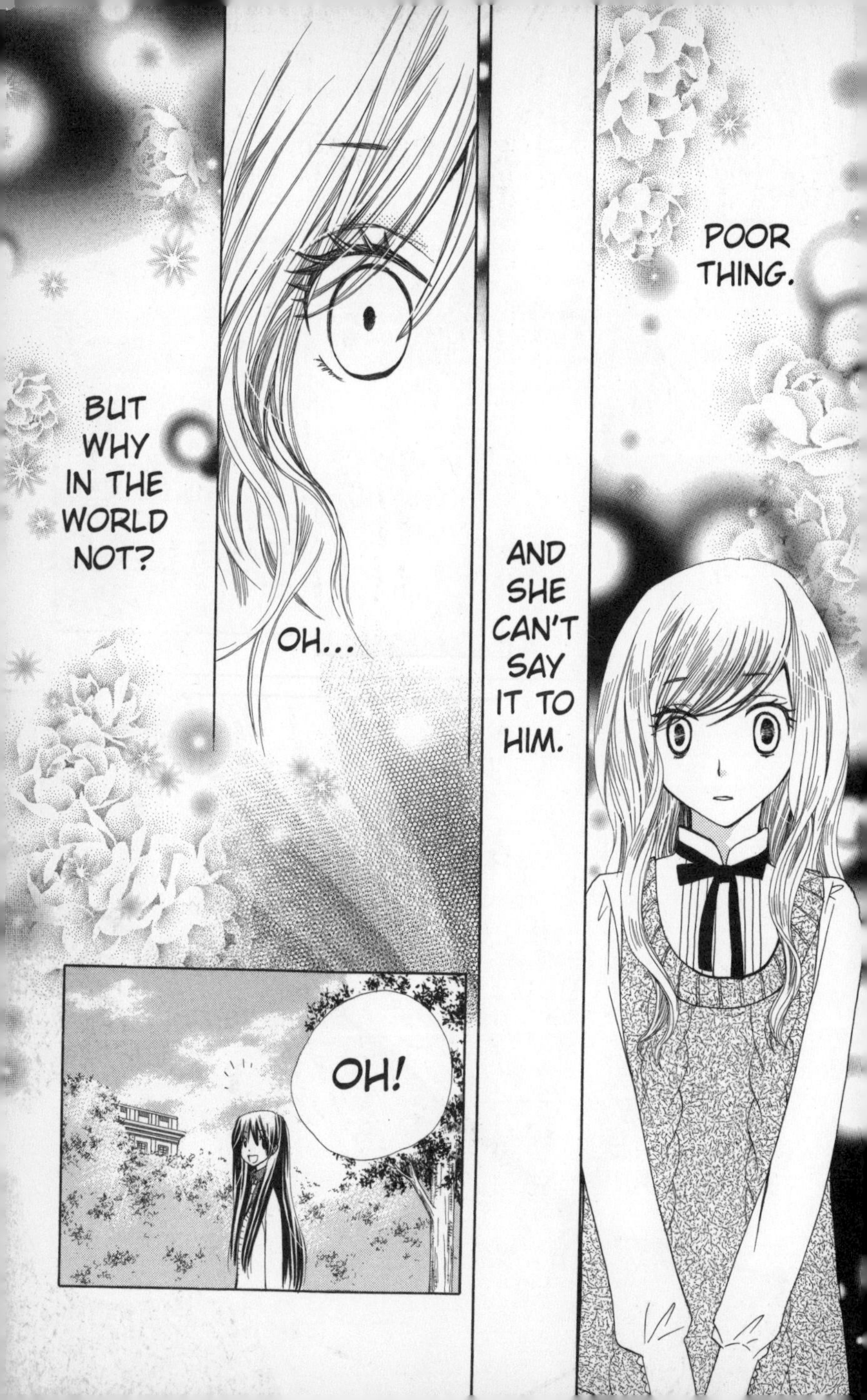
POOR THING.
AND SHE CAN'T SAY IT TO HIM.
OH...
BUT WHY IN THE WORLD NOT?
OH!

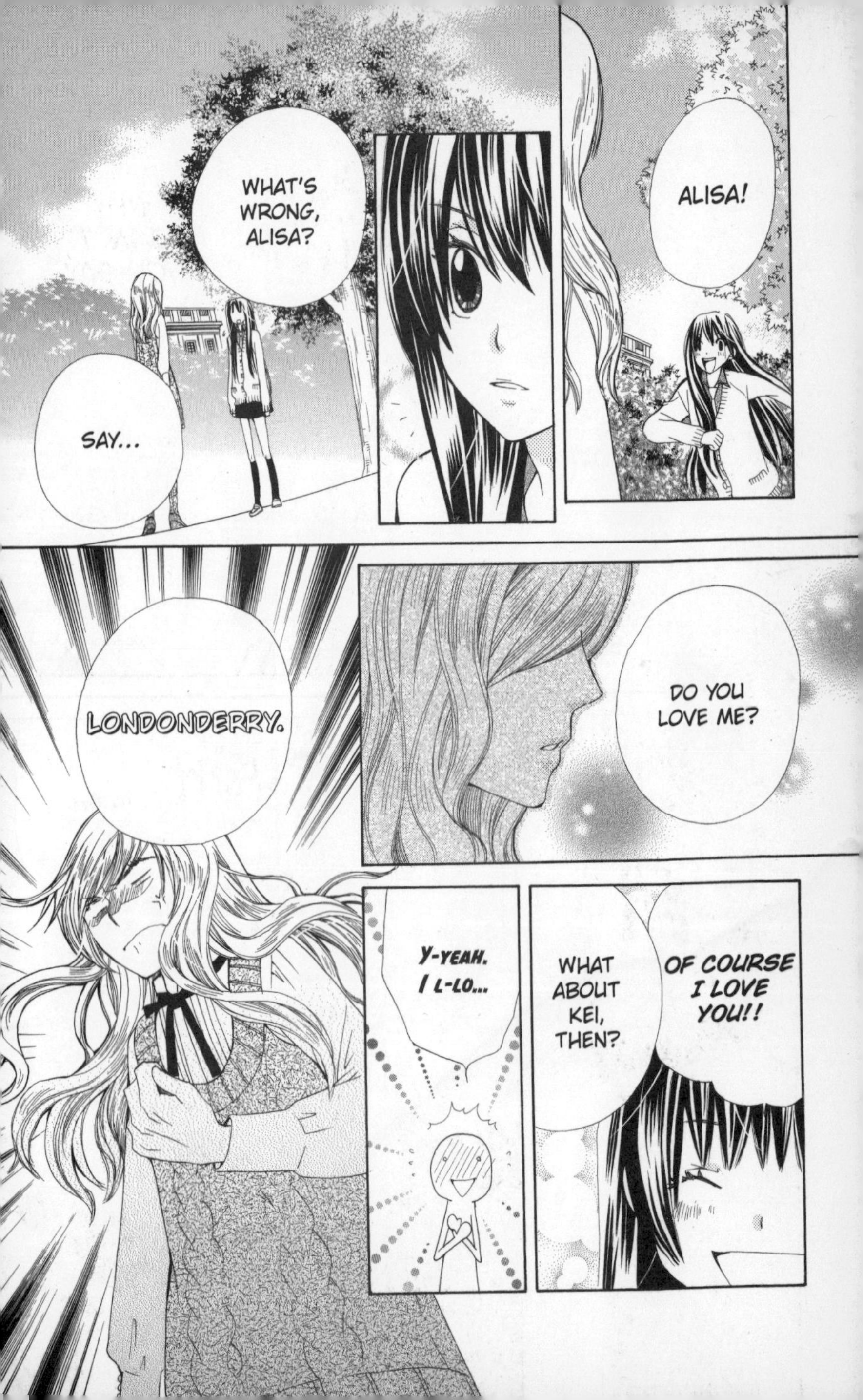
ALISA!
WHAT'S WRONG, ALISA?
SAY...
DO YOU LOVE ME?
LONDONDERRY.
OF COURSE I LOVE YOU!!
WHAT ABOUT KEI, THEN?
Y-YEAH. I L-LO...

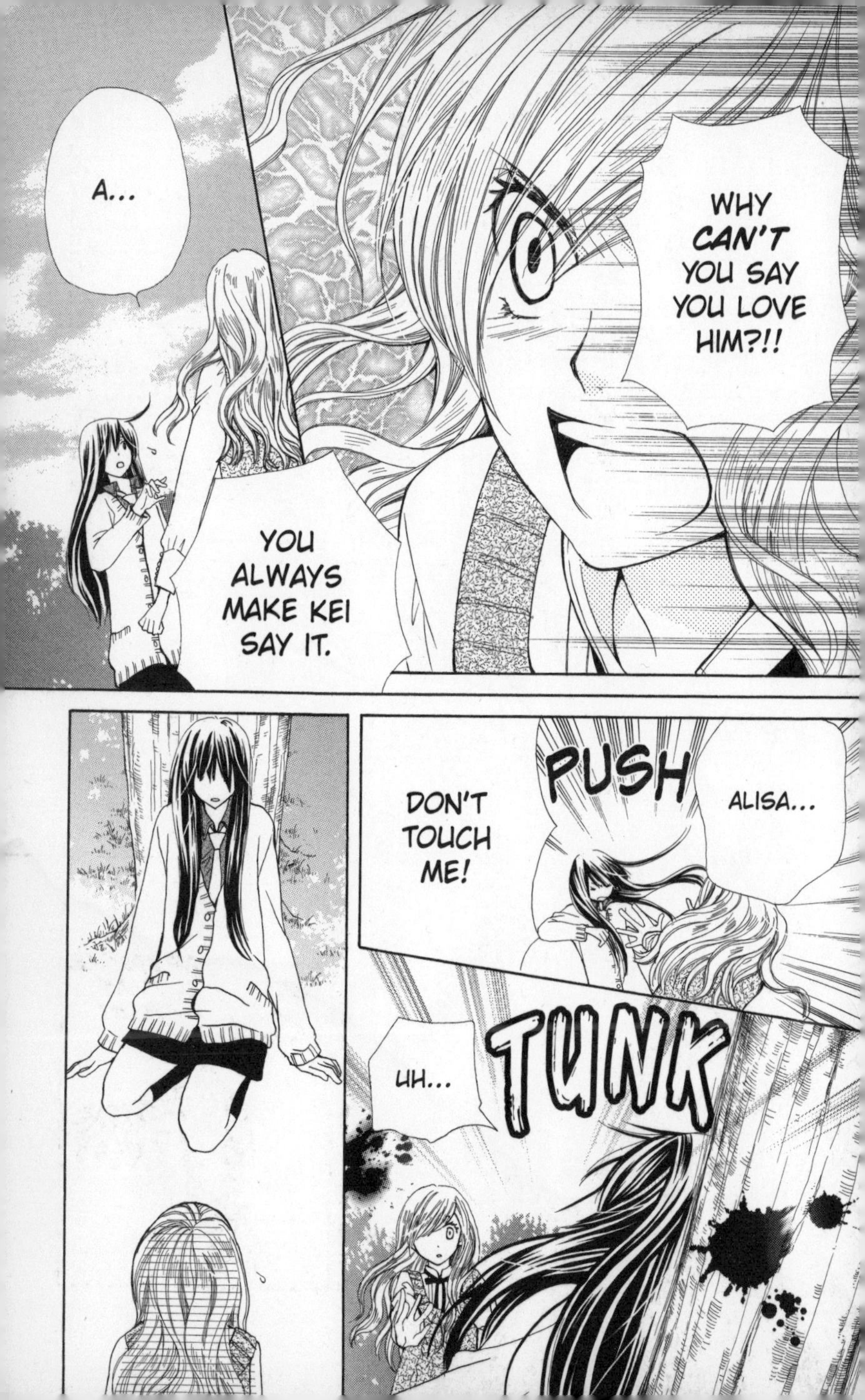
WHY CAN'T YOU SAY YOU LOVE HIM?!!
YOU ALWAYS MAKE KEI SAY IT.
A...
ALISA...
PUSH
DON'T TOUCH ME!
TUNK
UH...

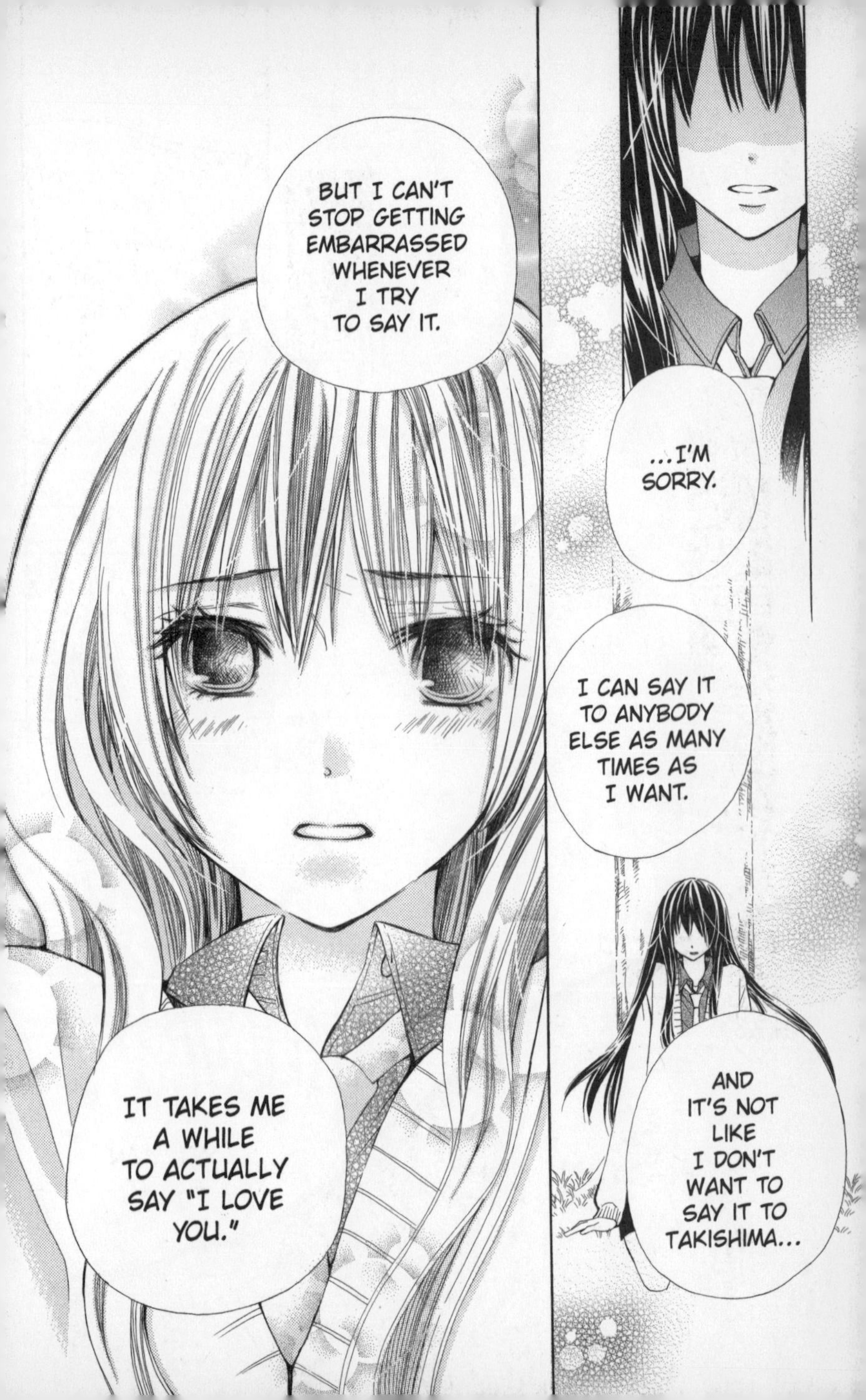
...I'M SORRY.
I CAN SAY IT TO ANYBODY ELSE AS MANY TIMES AS I WANT.
AND IT'S NOT LIKE I DON'T WANT TO SAY IT TO TAKISHIMA...
BUT I CAN'T STOP GETTING EMBARRASSED WHENEVER I TRY TO SAY IT.
IT TAKES ME A WHILE TO ACTUALLY SAY "I LOVE YOU."

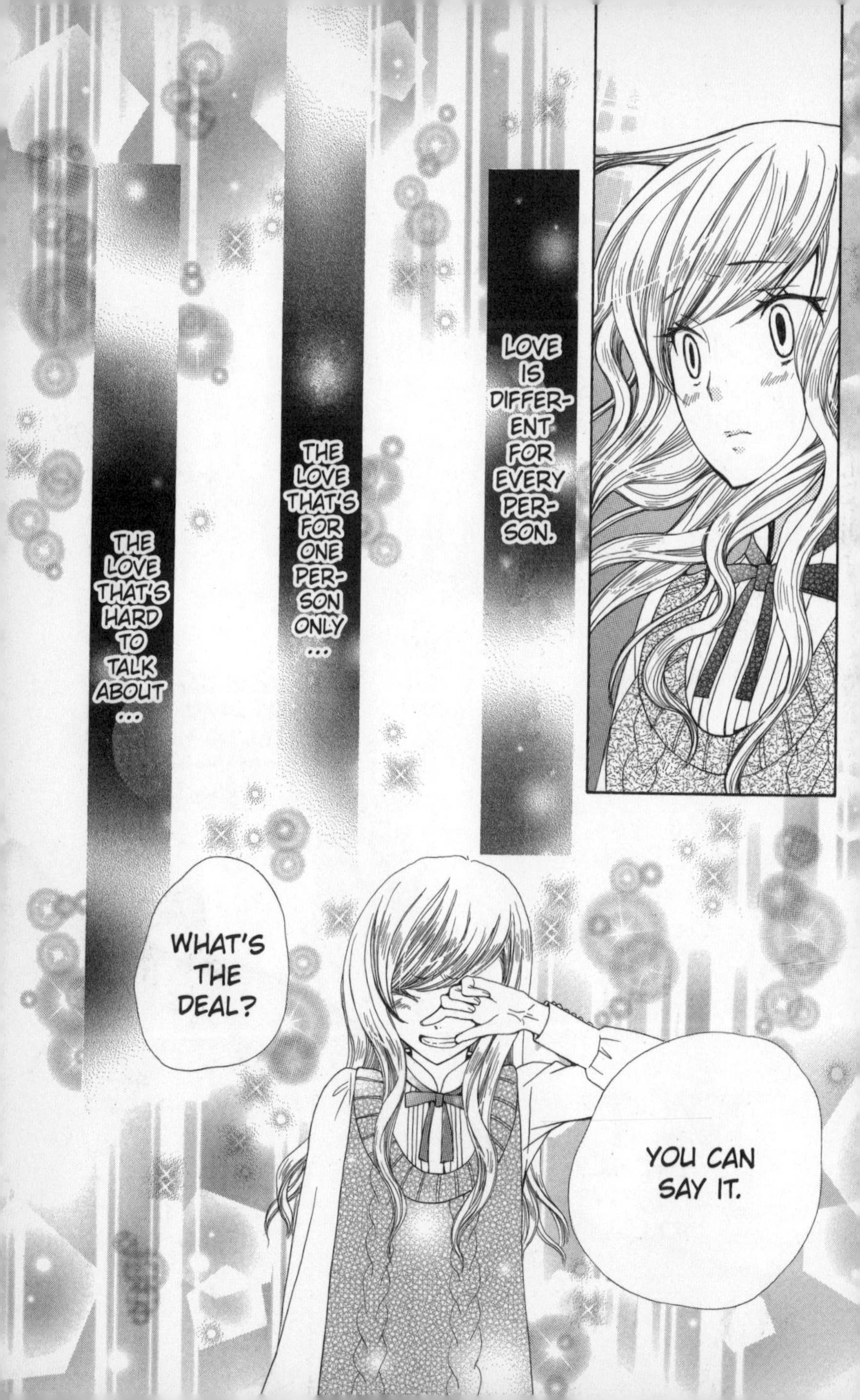

LOVE IS DIFFER-ENT FOR EVERY PER-SON.
THE LOVE THAT'S FOR ONE PER-SON ONLY...
THE LOVE THAT'S HARD TO TALK ABOUT...
WHAT'S THE DEAL?
YOU CAN SAY IT.

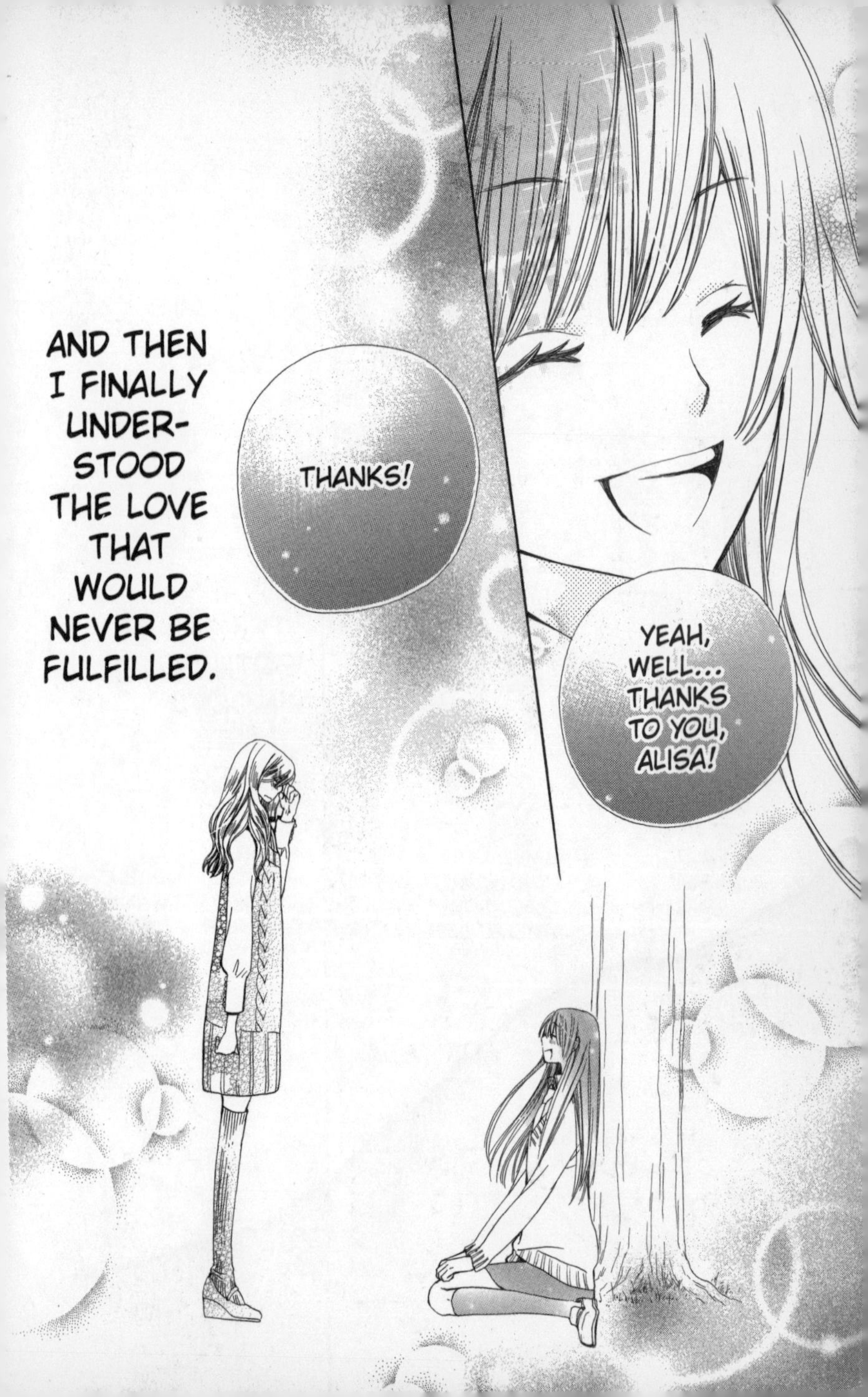
THANKS!
YEAH, WELL... THANKS TO YOU, ALISA!
AND THEN I FINALLY UNDER-STOOD THE LOVE THAT WOULD NEVER BE FULFILLED.

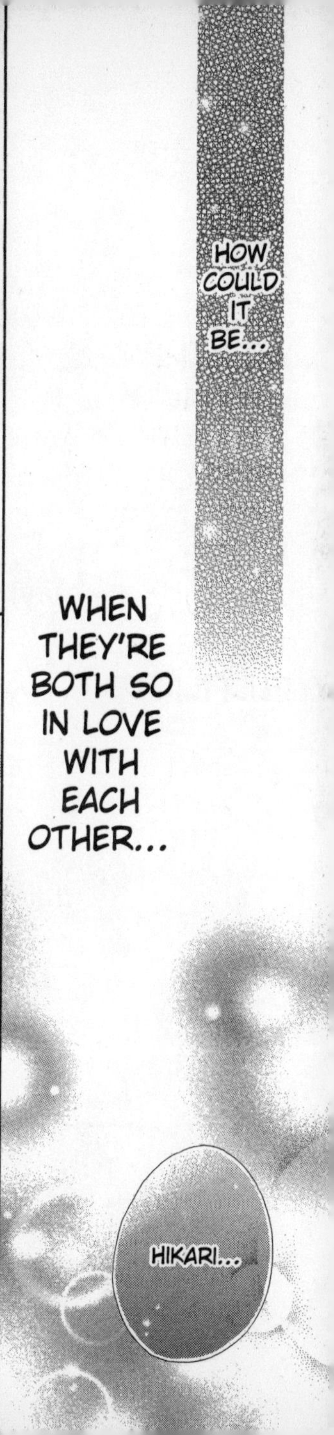
HOW COULD IT BE...
WHEN THEY'RE BOTH SO IN LOVE WITH EACH OTHER...
HIKARI...

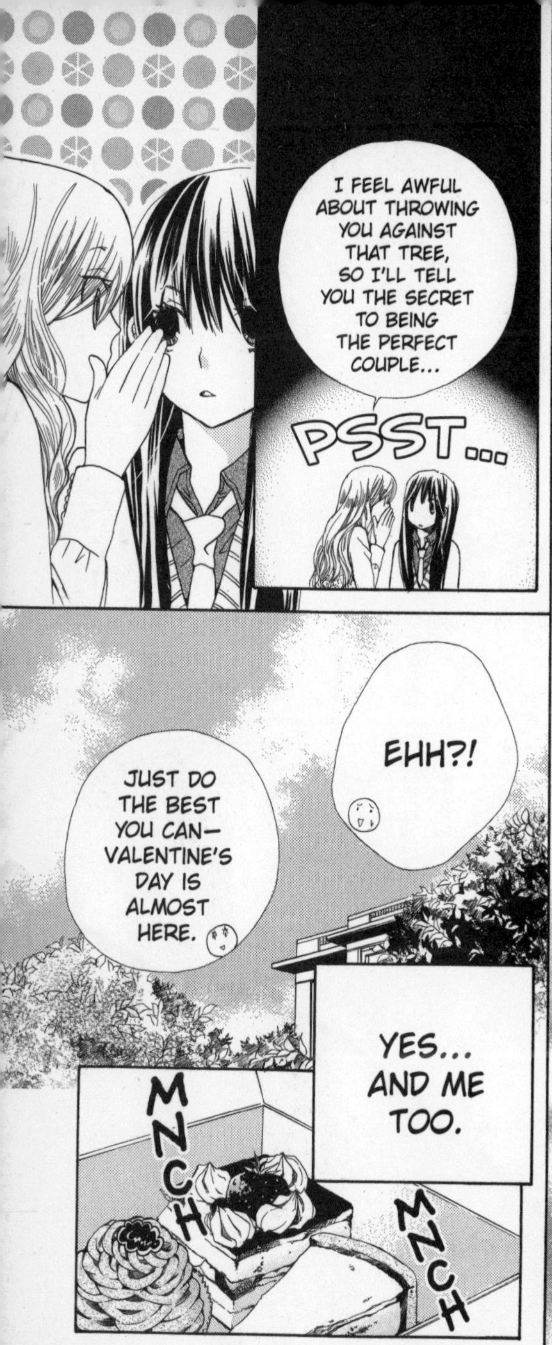
I FEEL AWFUL ABOUT THROWING YOU AGAINST THAT TREE, SO I'LL TELL YOU THE SECRET TO BEING THE PERFECT COUPLE...
PSST...
EHH?!
JUST DO THE BEST YOU CAN— VALENTINE'S DAY IS ALMOST HERE.
YES... AND ME TOO.
MNCH
MNCH

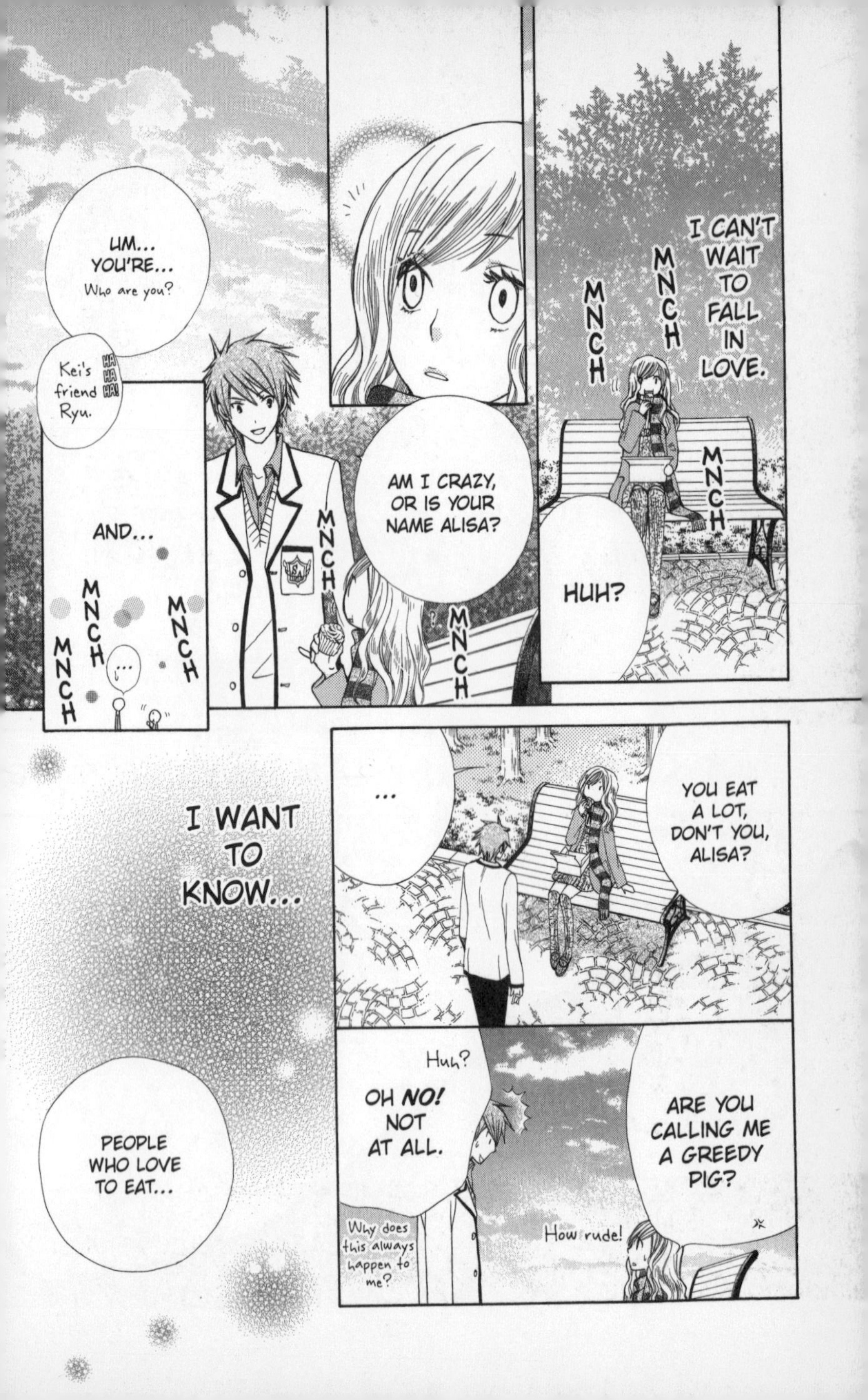
I CAN'T WAIT TO FALL IN LOVE.
MNCH
MNCH
MNCH
HUH?
AM I CRAZY, OR IS YOUR NAME ALISA?
MNCH
MNCH
UM... YOU'RE...
Who are you?
Kei's friend Ryu.
HA HA HA!
AND...
MNCH
MNCH
MNCH
...
YOU EAT A LOT, DON'T YOU, ALISA?
...
ARE YOU CALLING ME A GREEDY PIG?
How rude!
Huh?
OH NO! NOT AT ALL.
Why does this always happen to me?
I WANT TO KNOW...
PEOPLE WHO LOVE TO EAT...

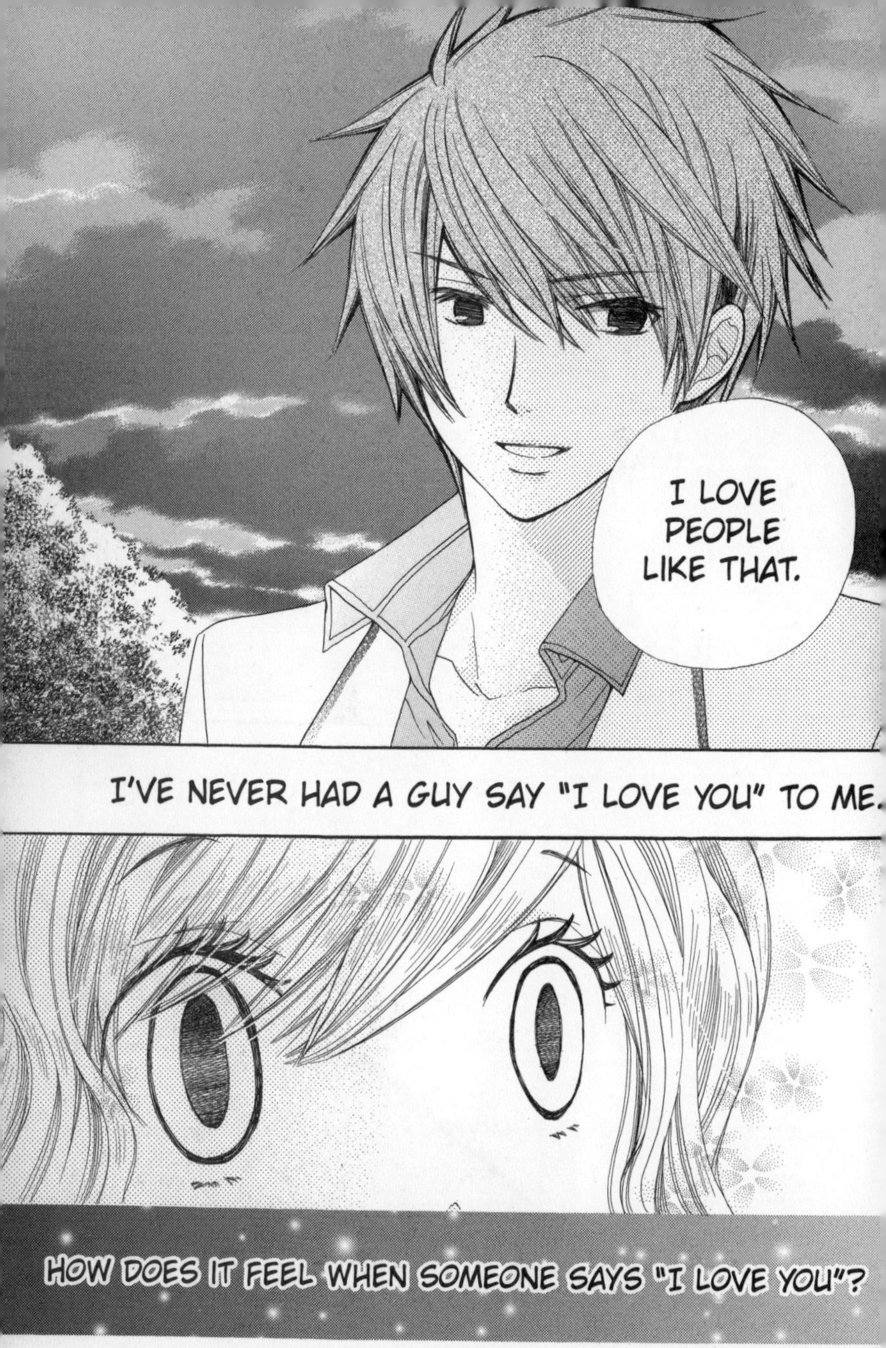
I LOVE PEOPLE LIKE THAT.
I'VE NEVER HAD A GUY SAY "I LOVE YOU" TO ME.
HOW DOES IT FEEL WHEN SOMEONE SAYS "I LOVE YOU"?

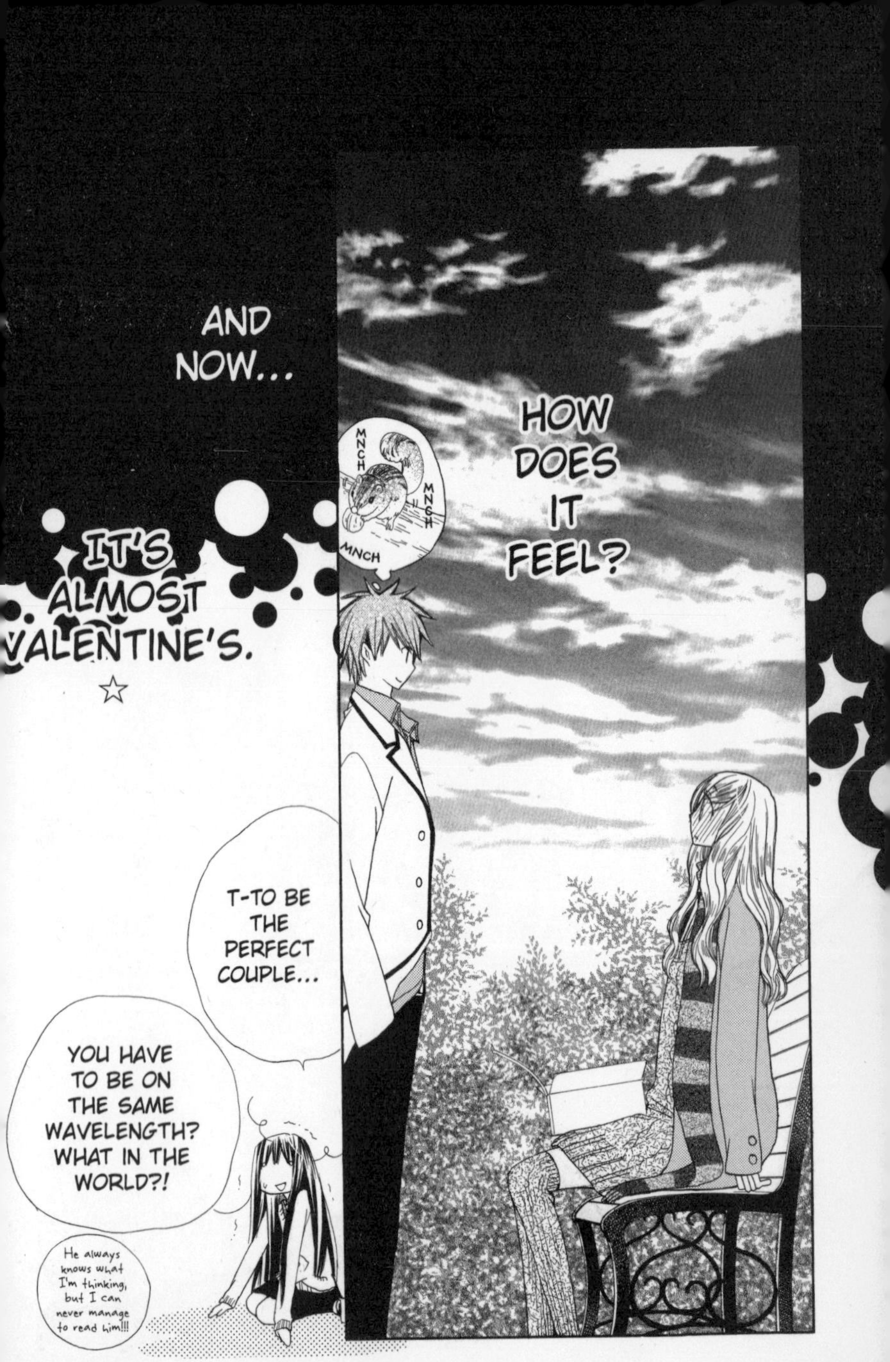
HOW DOES IT FEEL?
MNCH MNCH MNCH
AND NOW...
IT'S ALMOST VALENTINE'S. ☆
T-TO BE THE PERFECT COUPLE...
YOU HAVE TO BE ON THE SAME WAVELENGTH? WHAT IN THE WORLD?!
He always knows what I'm thinking, but I can never manage to read him!!!

Special. A

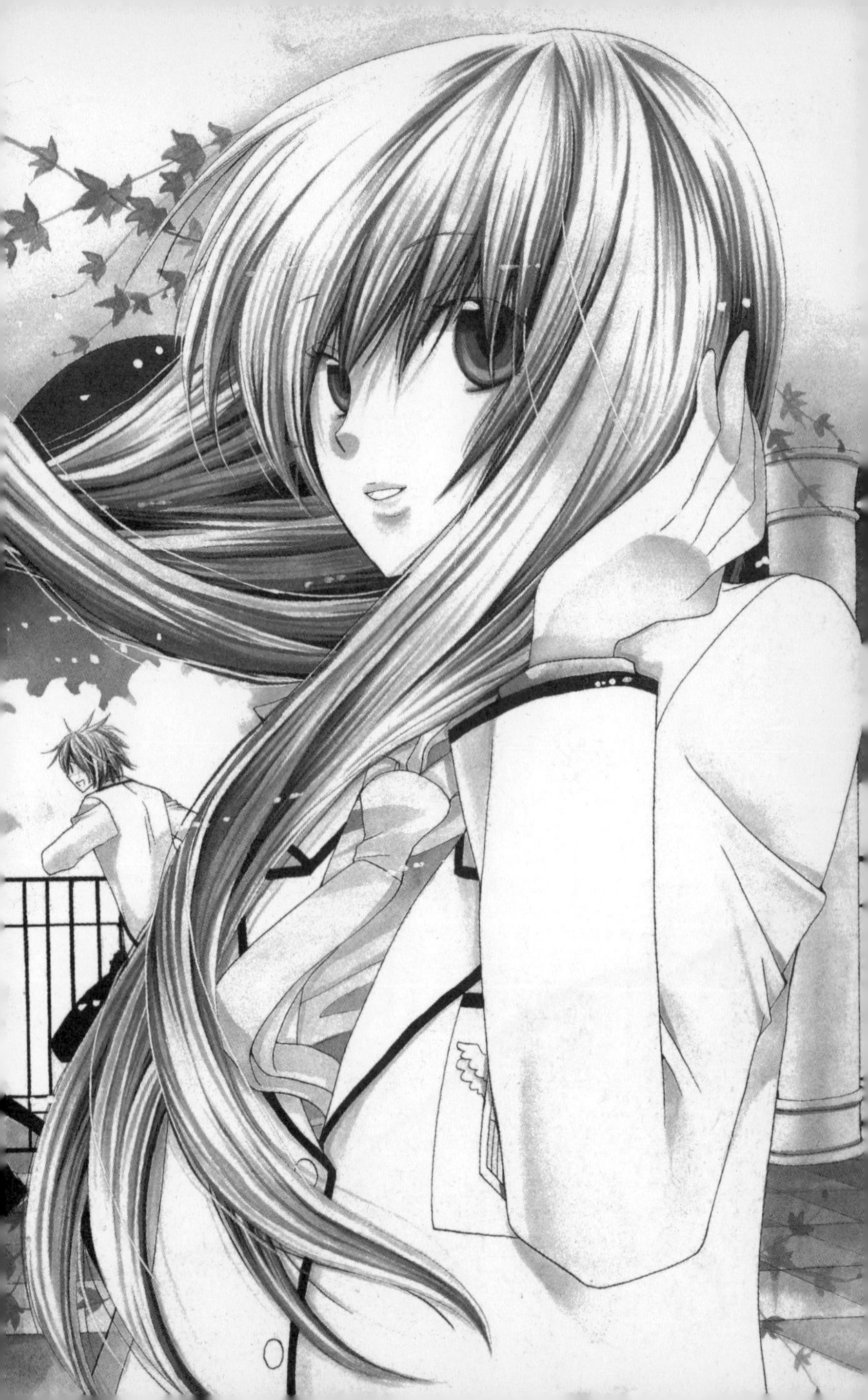

Chapter 74

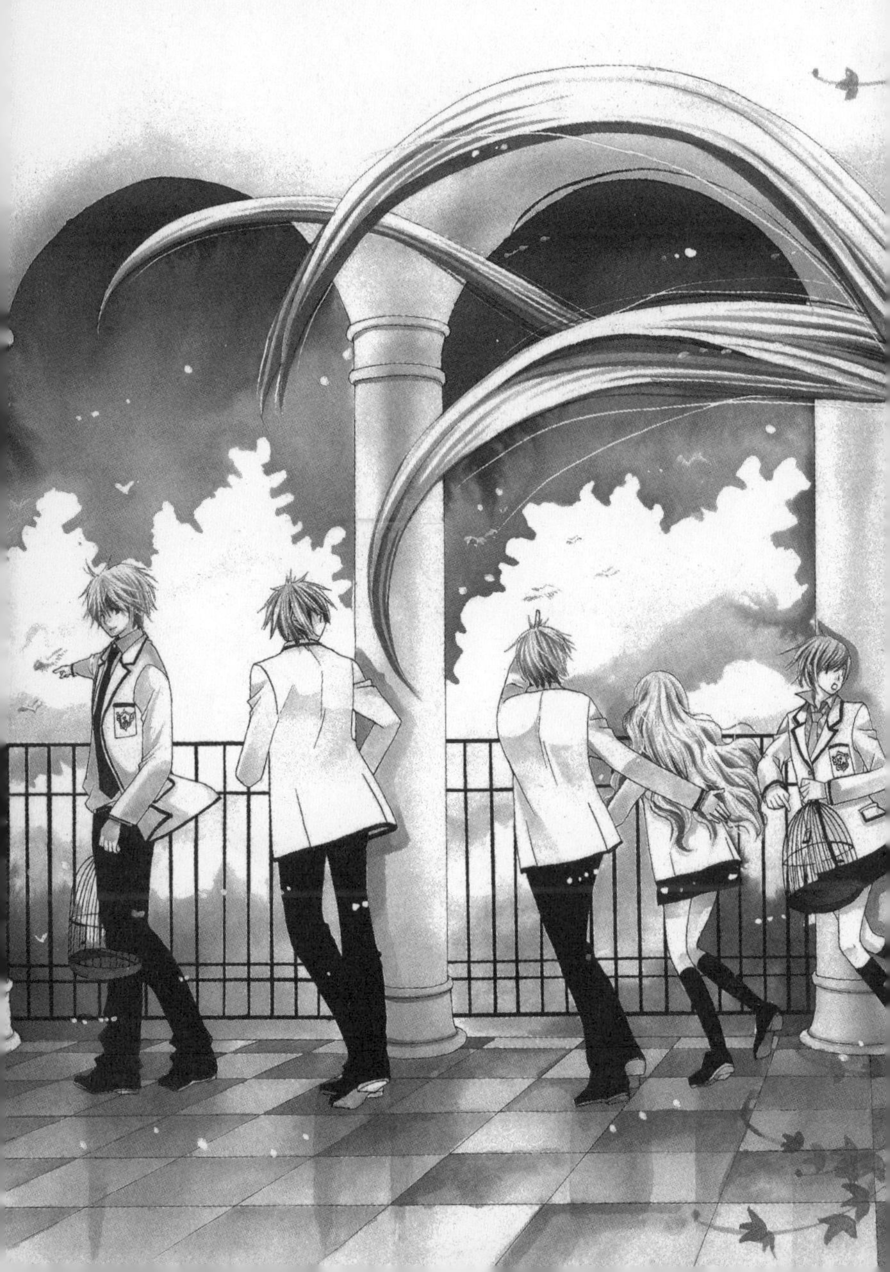

Special.A

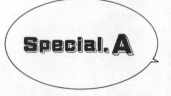

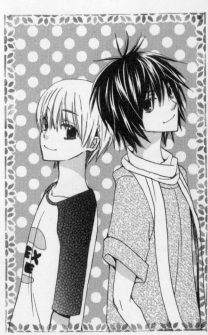

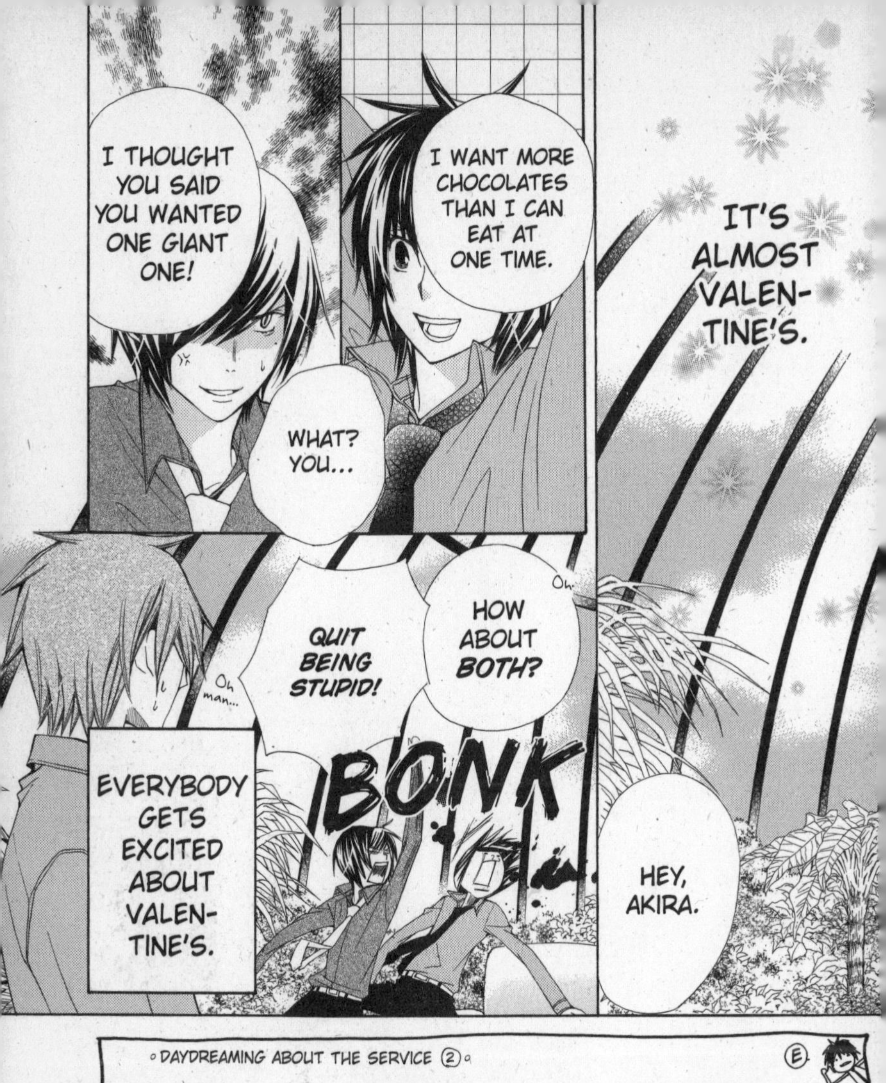
IT'S ALMOST VALEN-TINE'S.
I WANT MORE CHOCOLATES THAN I CAN EAT AT ONE TIME.
I THOUGHT YOU SAID YOU WANTED ONE GIANT ONE!
WHAT? YOU...
HEY, AKIRA.
Oh
HOW ABOUT BOTH?
QUIT BEING STUPID!
BONK
Oh man...
EVERYBODY GETS EXCITED ABOUT VALEN-TINE'S.

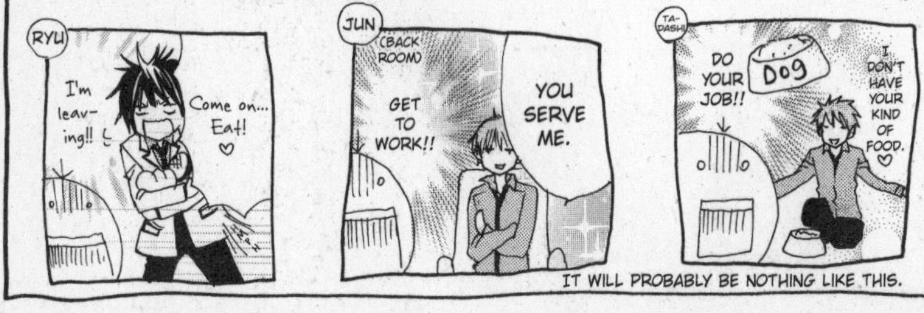
DAYDREAMING ABOUT THE SERVICE ②
E
TADASHI
I DON'T HAVE YOUR KIND OF FOOD.
Dog
DO YOUR JOB!!
JUN
YOU SERVE ME.
(BACK ROOM)
GET TO WORK!!
RYU
Come on... Eat!
I'm leav-ing!!
IT WILL PROBABLY BE NOTHING LIKE THIS.

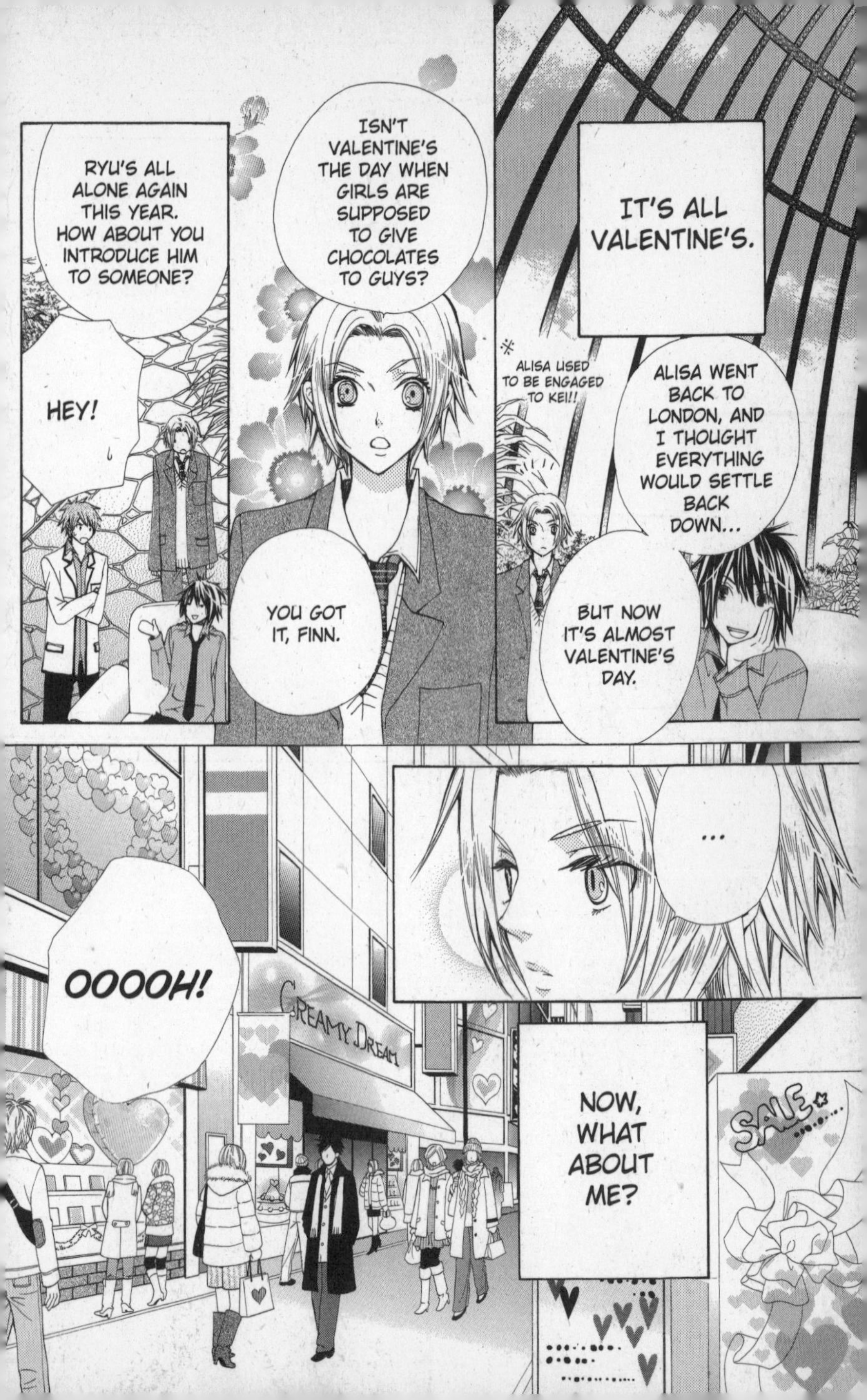
IT'S ALL VALENTINE'S.
ALISA WENT BACK TO LONDON, AND I THOUGHT EVERYTHING WOULD SETTLE BACK DOWN...
※ ALISA USED TO BE ENGAGED TO KEI!!
BUT NOW IT'S ALMOST VALENTINE'S DAY.
ISN'T VALENTINE'S THE DAY WHEN GIRLS ARE SUPPOSED TO GIVE CHOCOLATES TO GUYS?
YOU GOT IT, FINN.
RYU'S ALL ALONE AGAIN THIS YEAR. HOW ABOUT YOU INTRODUCE HIM TO SOMEONE?
HEY!
...
OOOOH!
CREAMY DREAM
NOW, WHAT ABOUT ME?
SALE

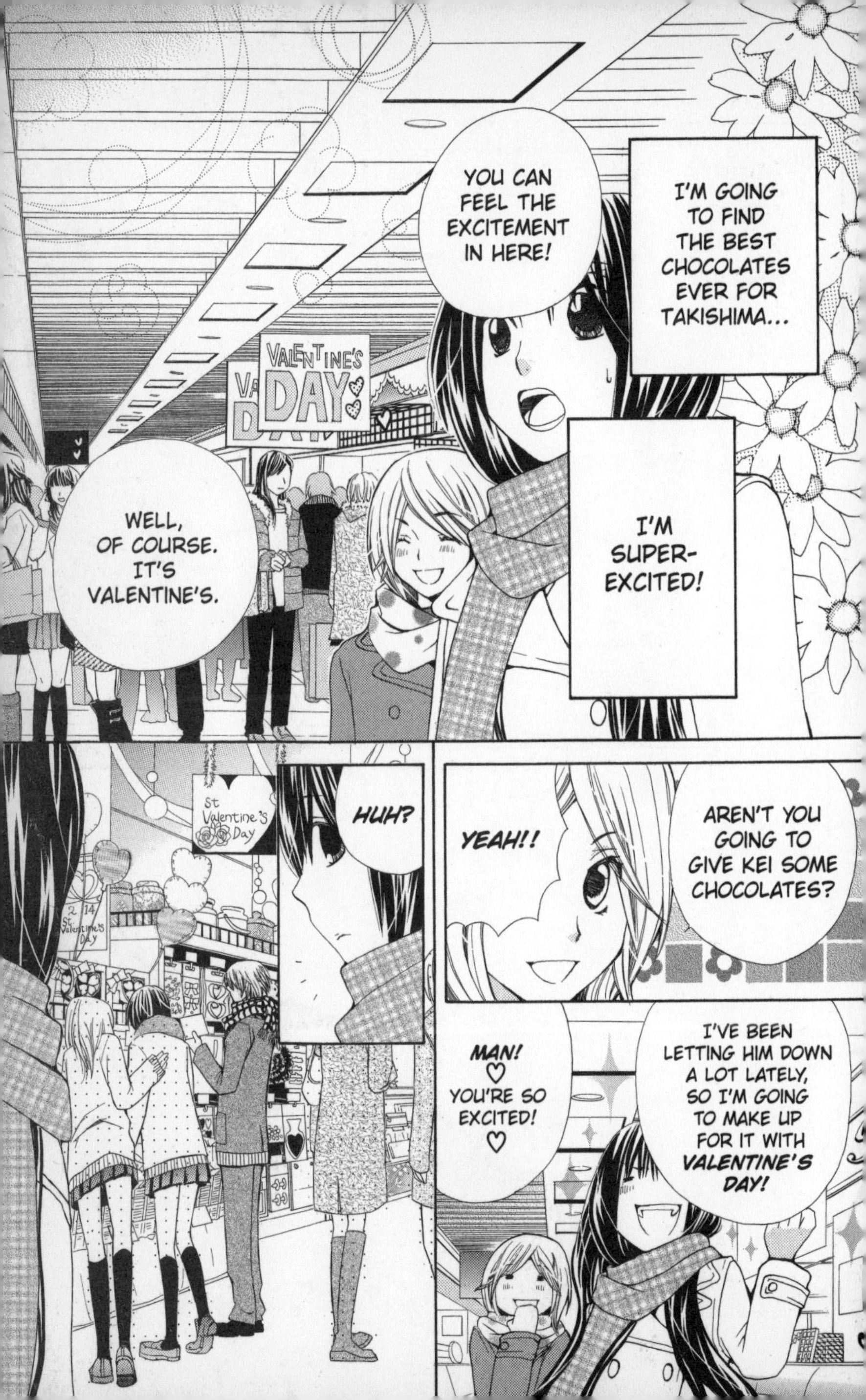
VALENTINE'S DAY
I'M GOING TO FIND THE BEST CHOCOLATES EVER FOR TAKISHIMA...
YOU CAN FEEL THE EXCITEMENT IN HERE!
I'M SUPER-EXCITED!
WELL, OF COURSE. IT'S VALENTINE'S.
AREN'T YOU GOING TO GIVE KEI SOME CHOCOLATES?
YEAH!!
I'VE BEEN LETTING HIM DOWN A LOT LATELY, SO I'M GOING TO MAKE UP FOR IT WITH VALENTINE'S DAY!
MAN! ♡ YOU'RE SO EXCITED! ♡
HUH?
St Valentine's Day
2 14 St. Valentine's Day

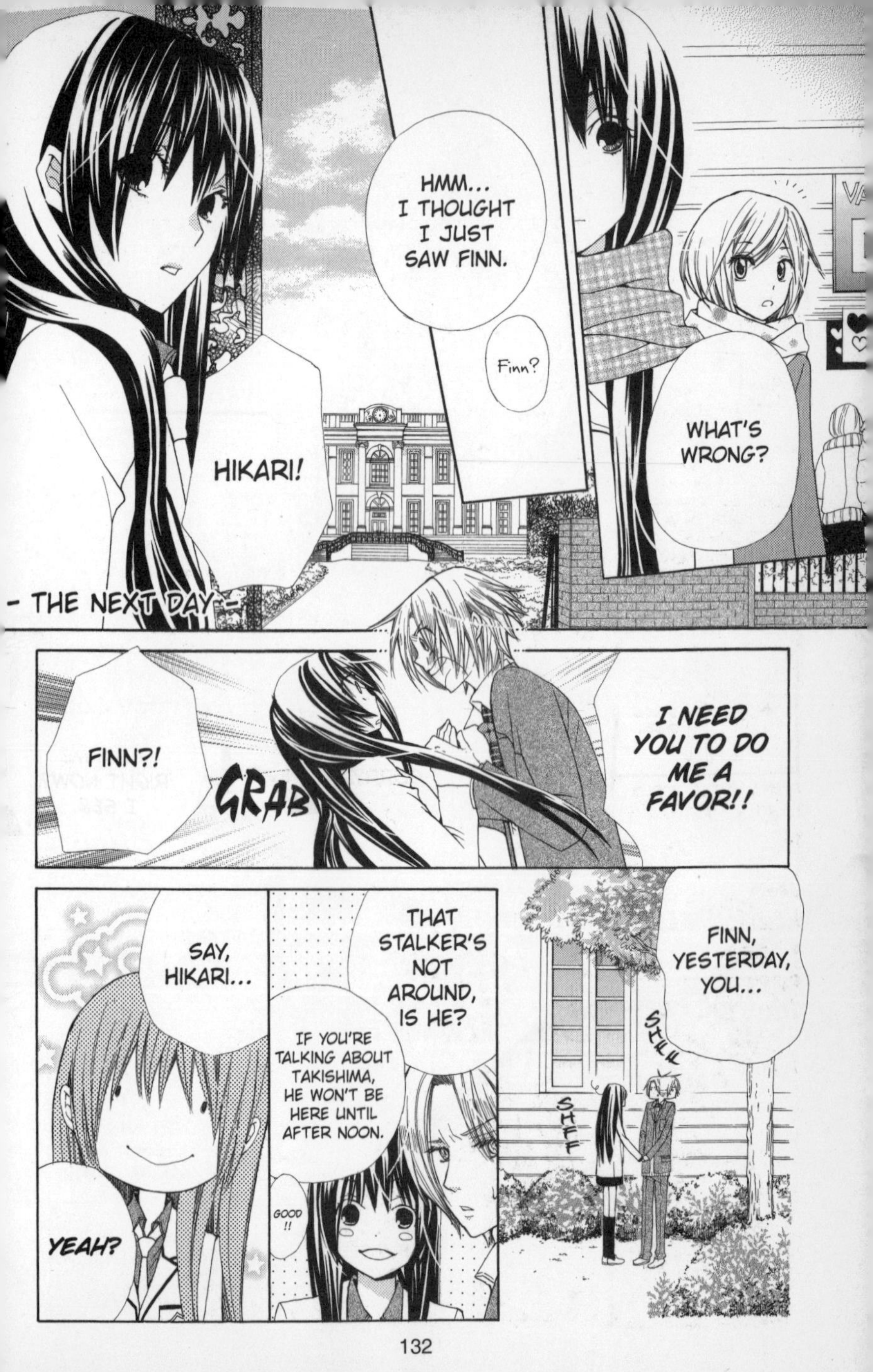
HMM... I THOUGHT I JUST SAW FINN.
Finn?
WHAT'S WRONG?
HIKARI!
- THE NEXT DAY -
I NEED YOU TO DO ME A FAVOR!!
GRAB
FINN?!
FINN, YESTERDAY, YOU...
SHFF
SHFF
THAT STALKER'S NOT AROUND, IS HE?
IF YOU'RE TALKING ABOUT TAKISHIMA, HE WON'T BE HERE UNTIL AFTER NOON.
GOOD!!
SAY, HIKARI...
YEAH?

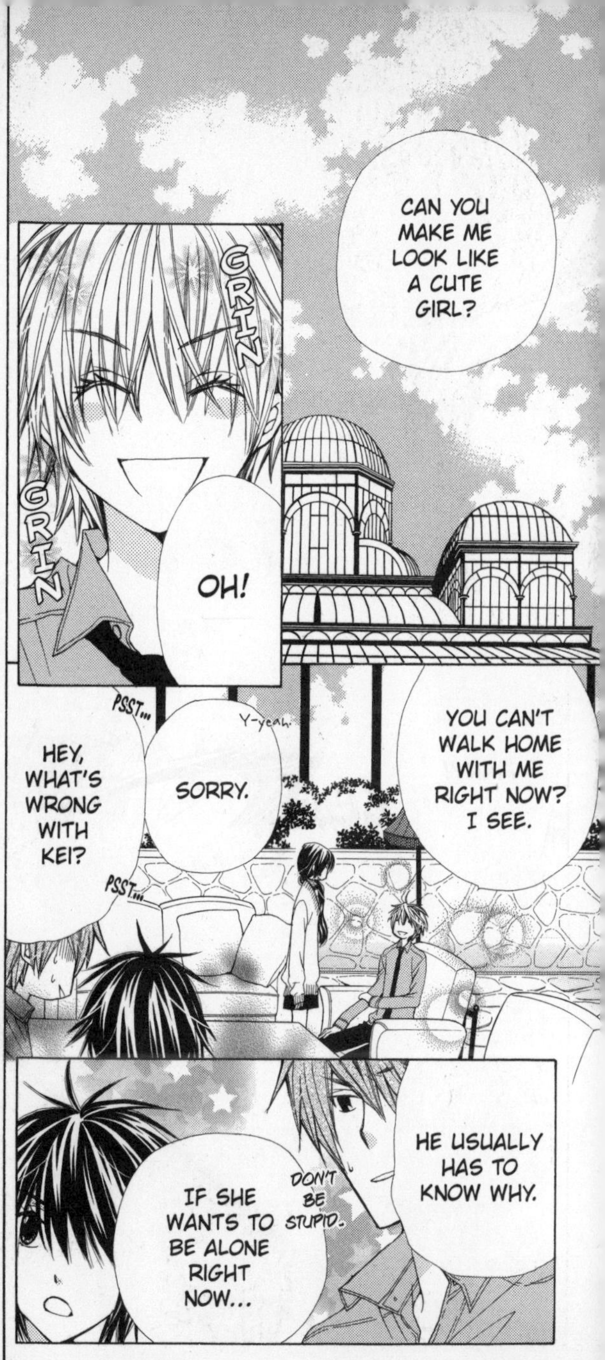
CAN YOU MAKE ME LOOK LIKE A CUTE GIRL?
GRIN
GRIN
OH!
YOU CAN'T WALK HOME WITH ME RIGHT NOW? I SEE.
Y-yeah.
SORRY.
PSST...
HEY, WHAT'S WRONG WITH KEI?
PSST...
HE USUALLY HAS TO KNOW WHY.
DON'T BE STUPID.
IF SHE WANTS TO BE ALONE RIGHT NOW...

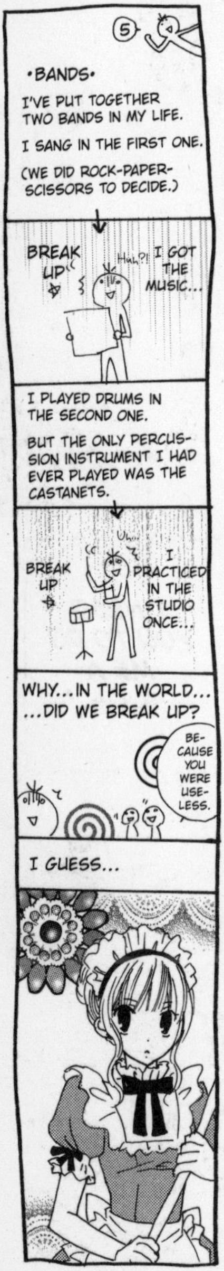
5
•BANDS•
I'VE PUT TOGETHER TWO BANDS IN MY LIFE.
I SANG IN THE FIRST ONE.
(WE DID ROCK-PAPER-SCISSORS TO DECIDE.)
BREAK UP
Huh?!
I GOT THE MUSIC...
I PLAYED DRUMS IN THE SECOND ONE.
BUT THE ONLY PERCUSSION INSTRUMENT I HAD EVER PLAYED WAS THE CASTANETS.
BREAK UP
Uh...
I PRACTICED IN THE STUDIO ONCE...
WHY...IN THE WORLD...
...DID WE BREAK UP?
BECAUSE YOU WERE USELESS.
I GUESS...

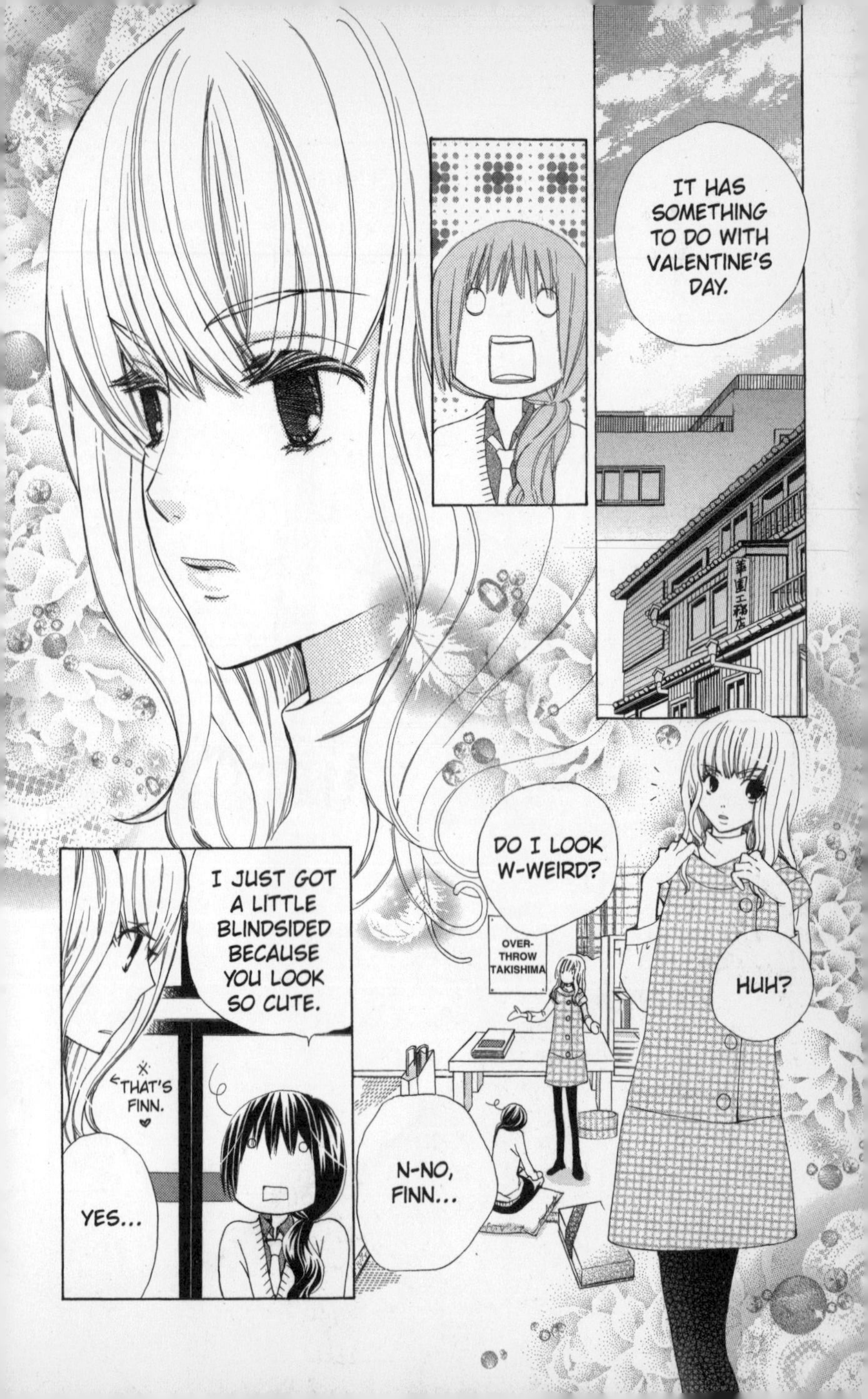
IT HAS SOMETHING TO DO WITH VALENTINE'S DAY.
DO I LOOK W-WEIRD?
HUH?
OVER-THROW TAKISHIMA
N-NO, FINN...
I JUST GOT A LITTLE BLINDSIDED BECAUSE YOU LOOK SO CUTE.
※ ←THAT'S FINN.
YES...

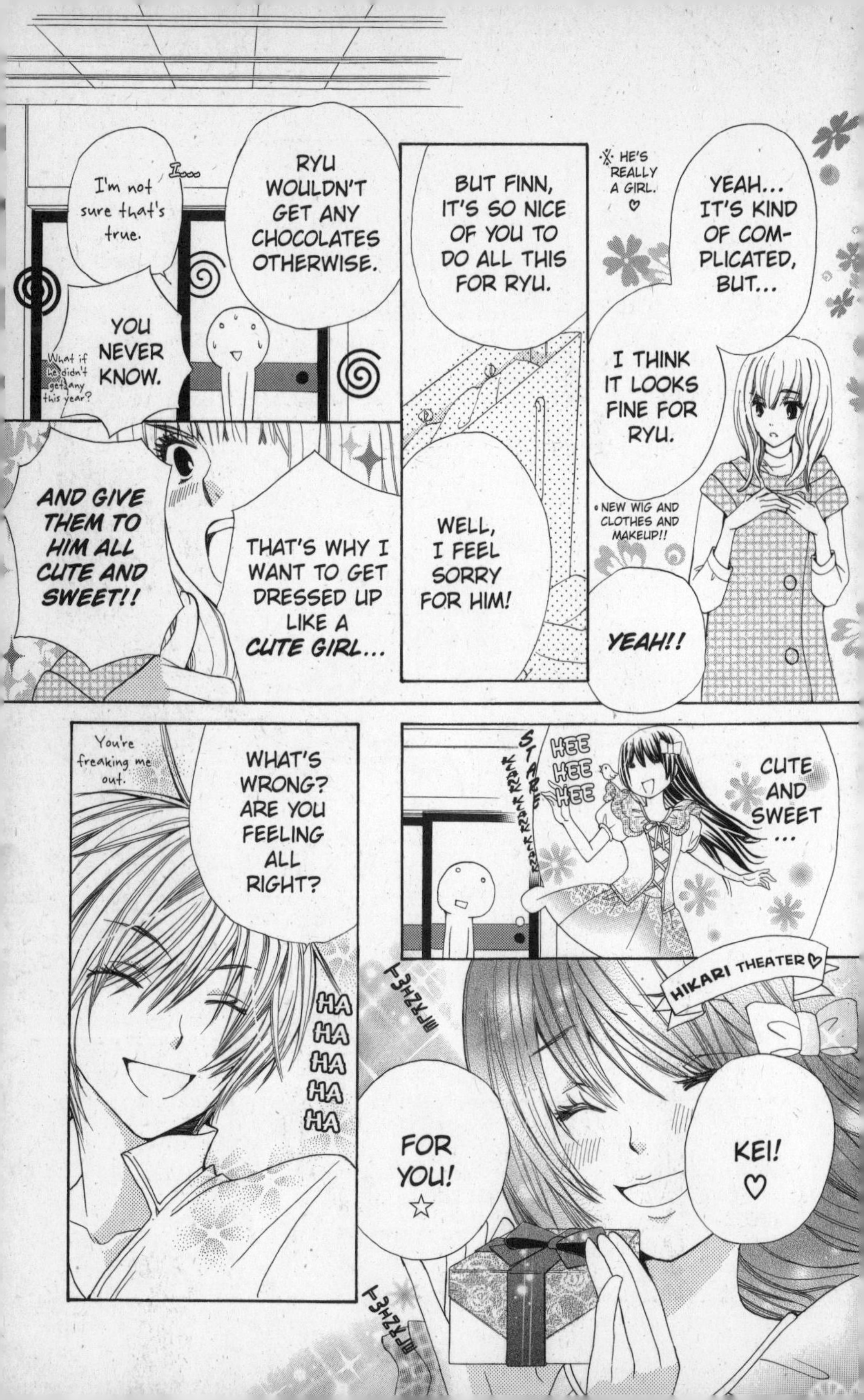
YEAH... IT'S KIND OF COM-PLICATED, BUT...
※ HE'S REALLY A GIRL. ♡
I THINK IT LOOKS FINE FOR RYU.
• NEW WIG AND CLOTHES AND MAKEUP!!
YEAH!!
BUT FINN, IT'S SO NICE OF YOU TO DO ALL THIS FOR RYU.
WELL, I FEEL SORRY FOR HIM!
RYU WOULDN'T GET ANY CHOCOLATES OTHERWISE.
I...
I'm not sure that's true.
YOU NEVER KNOW.
What if he didn't get any this year?
THAT'S WHY I WANT TO GET DRESSED UP LIKE A CUTE GIRL...
AND GIVE THEM TO HIM ALL CUTE AND SWEET!!
CUTE AND SWEET...
HEE HEE HEE
STARE
HIKARI THEATER ♡
KEI! ♡
FOR YOU! ☆
WHAT'S WRONG? ARE YOU FEELING ALL RIGHT?
You're freaking me out.
HA HA HA HA HA

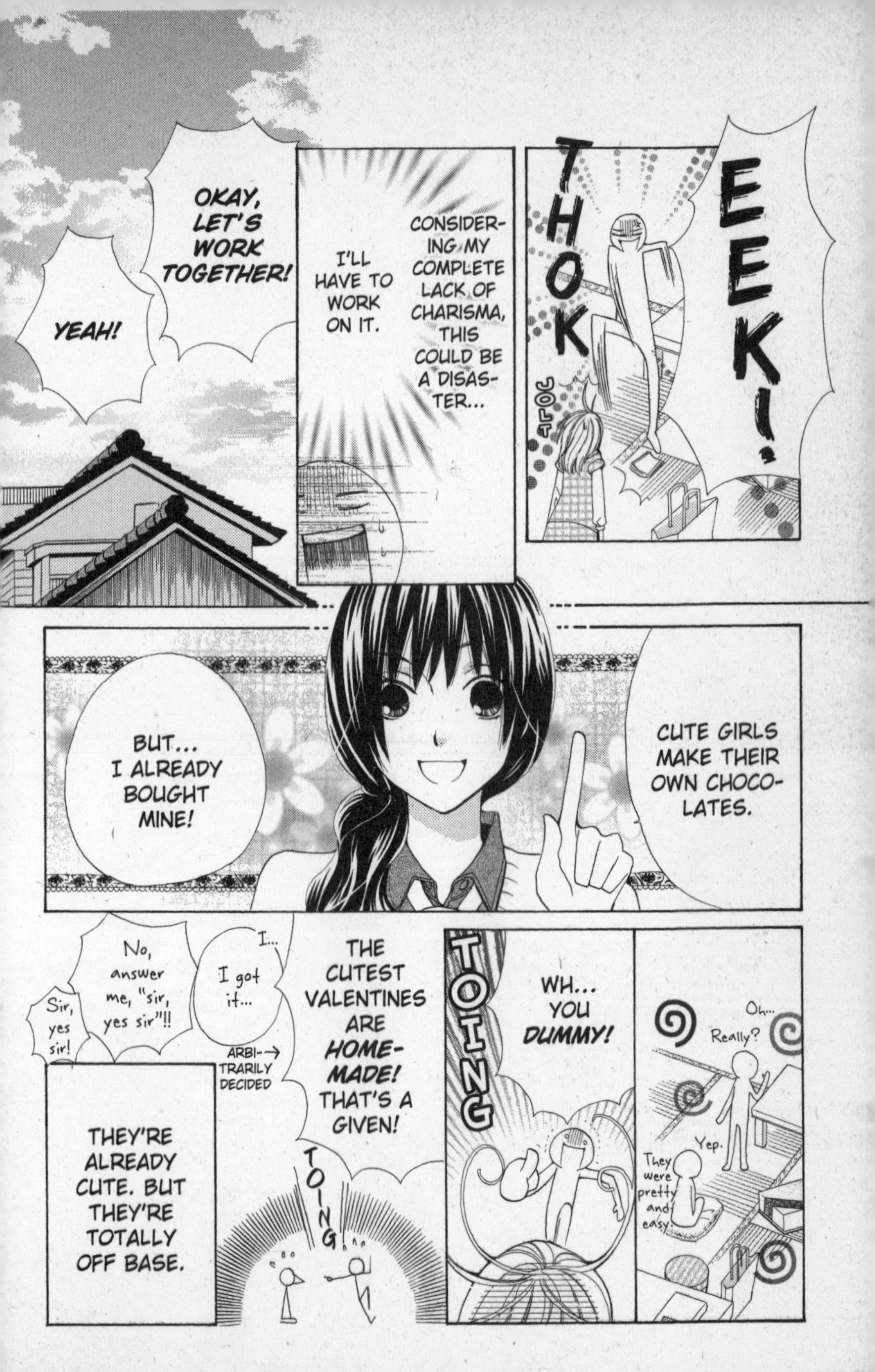
EEK!
THOK
JOLT
CONSIDERING MY COMPLETE LACK OF CHARISMA, THIS COULD BE A DISASTER...
I'LL HAVE TO WORK ON IT.
OKAY, LET'S WORK TOGETHER!
YEAH!
CUTE GIRLS MAKE THEIR OWN CHOCOLATES.
BUT... I ALREADY BOUGHT MINE!
Oh... Really?
Yep.
They were pretty and easy.
WH... YOU DUMMY!
TOING
THE CUTEST VALENTINES ARE HOMEMADE! THAT'S A GIVEN!
ARBITRARILY DECIDED
TOING!
I... I got it...
No, answer me, "sir, yes sir"!!
Sir, yes sir!
THEY'RE ALREADY CUTE. BUT THEY'RE TOTALLY OFF BASE.

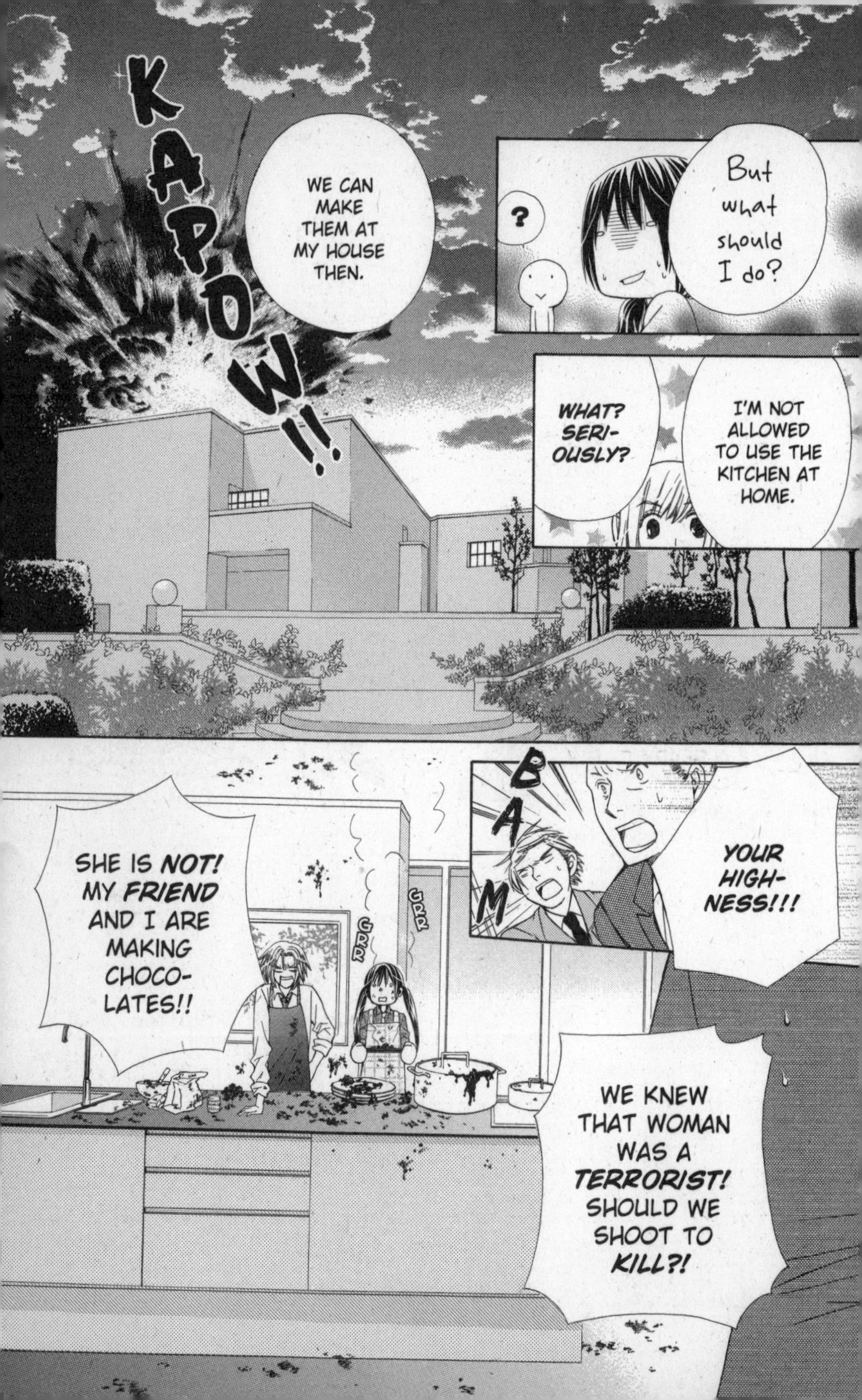
?
But what should I do?
I'M NOT ALLOWED TO USE THE KITCHEN AT HOME.
WHAT? SERI-OUSLY?
WE CAN MAKE THEM AT MY HOUSE THEN.
KAPOW!!
BAM
YOUR HIGHNESS!!!
WE KNEW THAT WOMAN WAS A TERRORIST! SHOULD WE SHOOT TO KILL?!
GRR
GRR
SHE IS NOT! MY FRIEND AND I ARE MAKING CHOCO-LATES!!

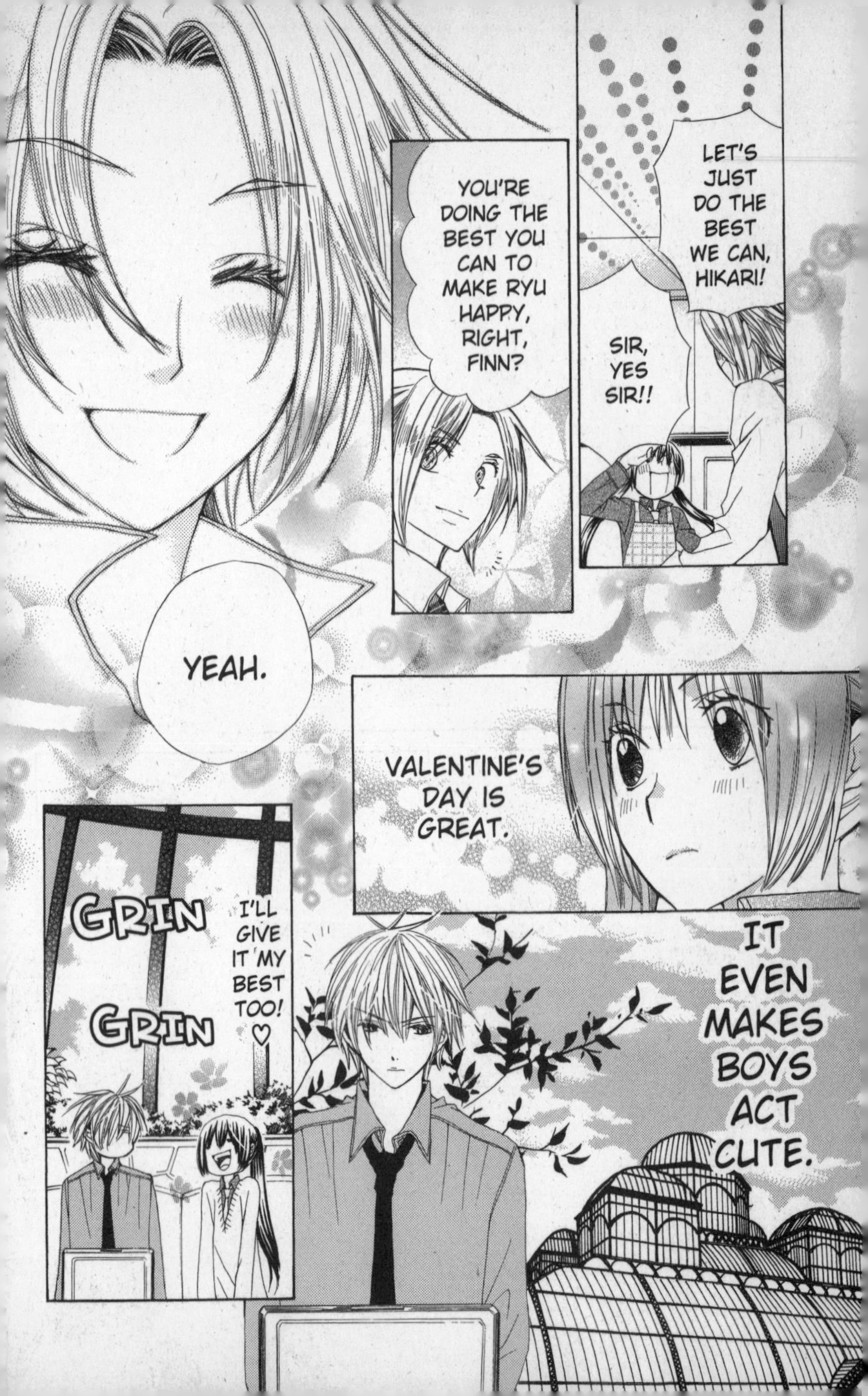
LET'S JUST DO THE BEST WE CAN, HIKARI!
SIR, YES SIR!!
YOU'RE DOING THE BEST YOU CAN TO MAKE RYU HAPPY, RIGHT, FINN?
YEAH.
VALENTINE'S DAY IS GREAT.
IT EVEN MAKES BOYS ACT CUTE.
I'LL GIVE IT MY BEST TOO! ♡
GRIN
GRIN

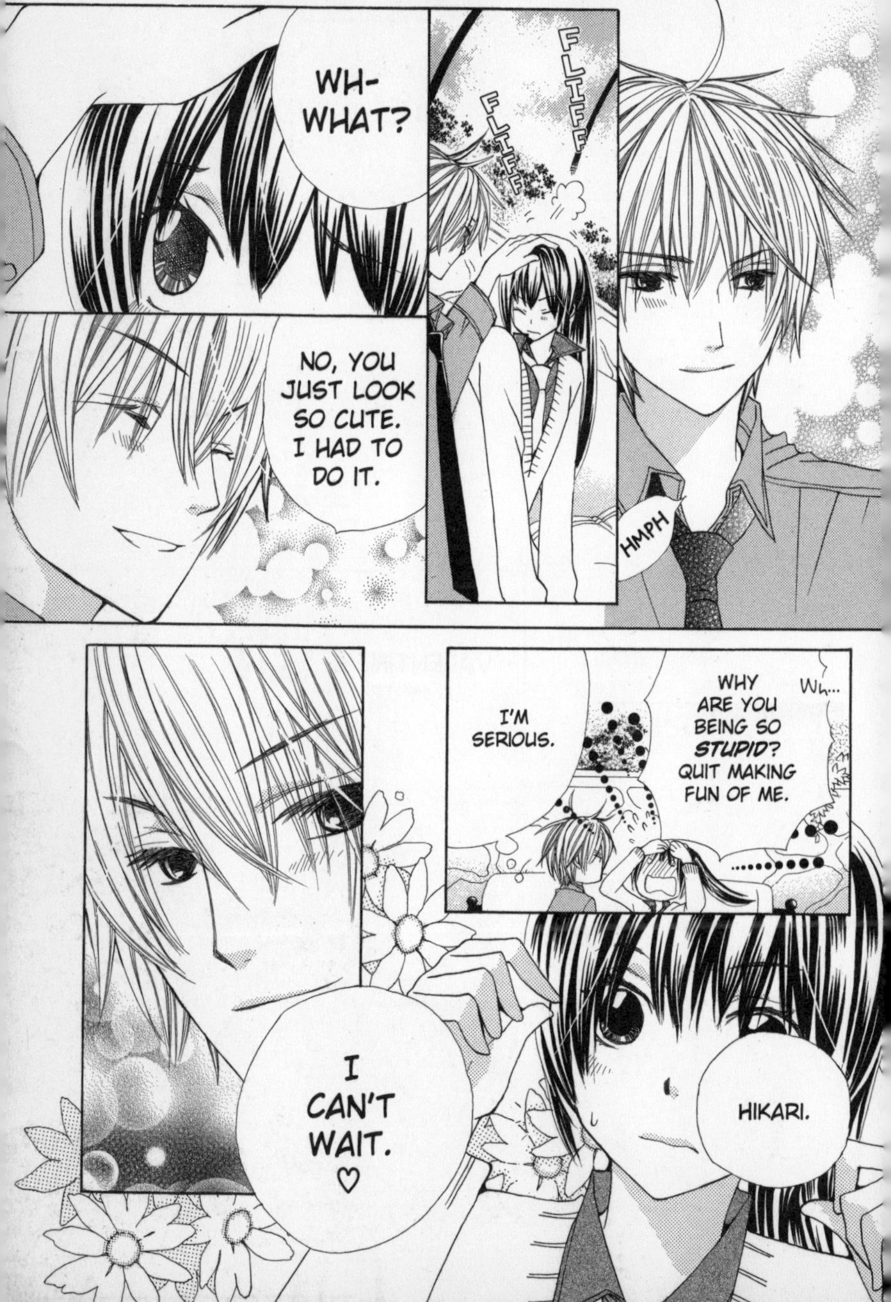
FLIFF
FLIFF
HMPH
WH- WHAT?
NO, YOU JUST LOOK SO CUTE. I HAD TO DO IT.
Wh...
WHY ARE YOU BEING SO STUPID? QUIT MAKING FUN OF ME.
I'M SERIOUS.
......
HIKARI.
I CAN'T WAIT. ♡

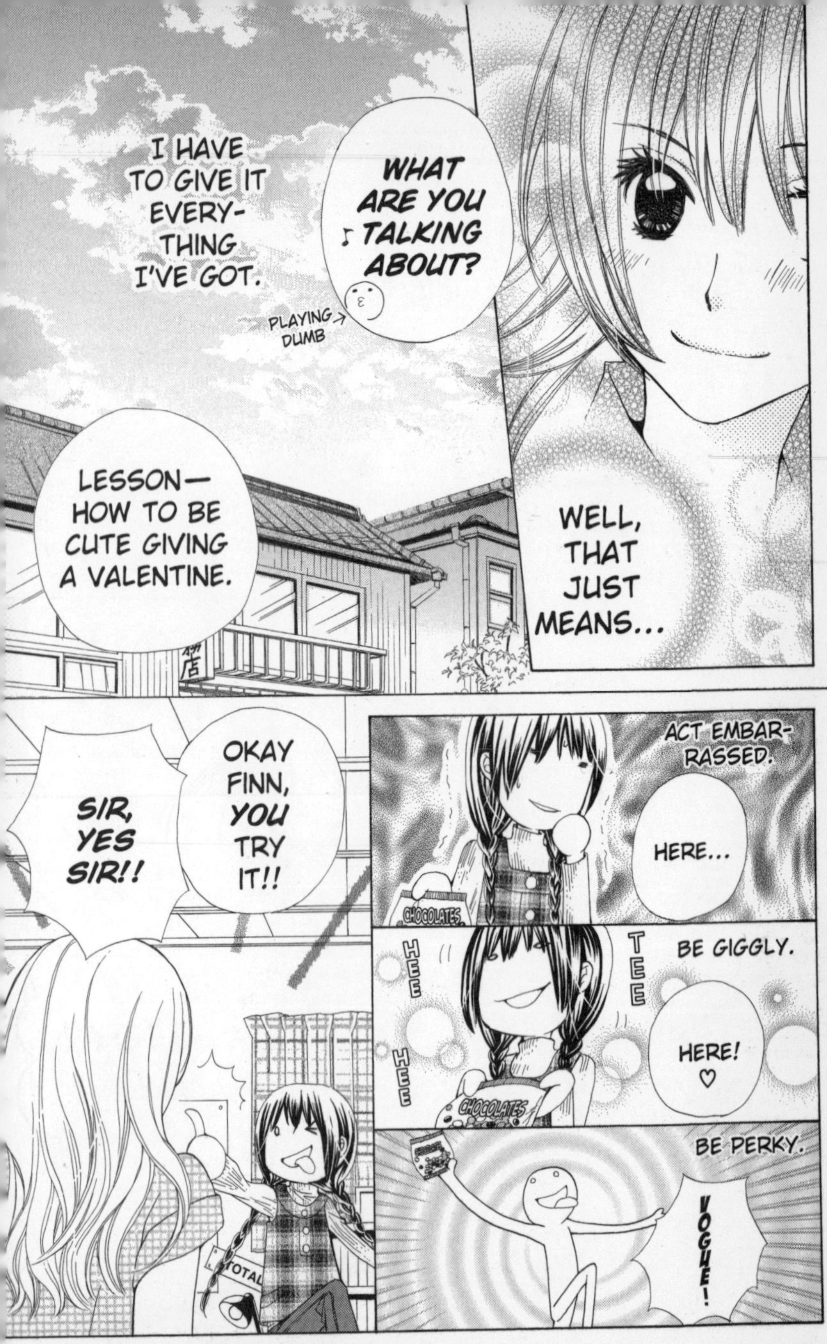
WELL, THAT JUST MEANS...
WHAT ARE YOU TALKING ABOUT? ♪
PLAYING DUMB
I HAVE TO GIVE IT EVERYTHING I'VE GOT.
LESSON—HOW TO BE CUTE GIVING A VALENTINE.
ACT EMBARRASSED.
HERE...
CHOCOLATES
BE GIGGLY.
TEE
HERE! ♡
HEE HEE
CHOCOLATES
BE PERKY.
VOGUE!
OKAY FINN, YOU TRY IT!!
SIR, YES SIR!!
TOTAL

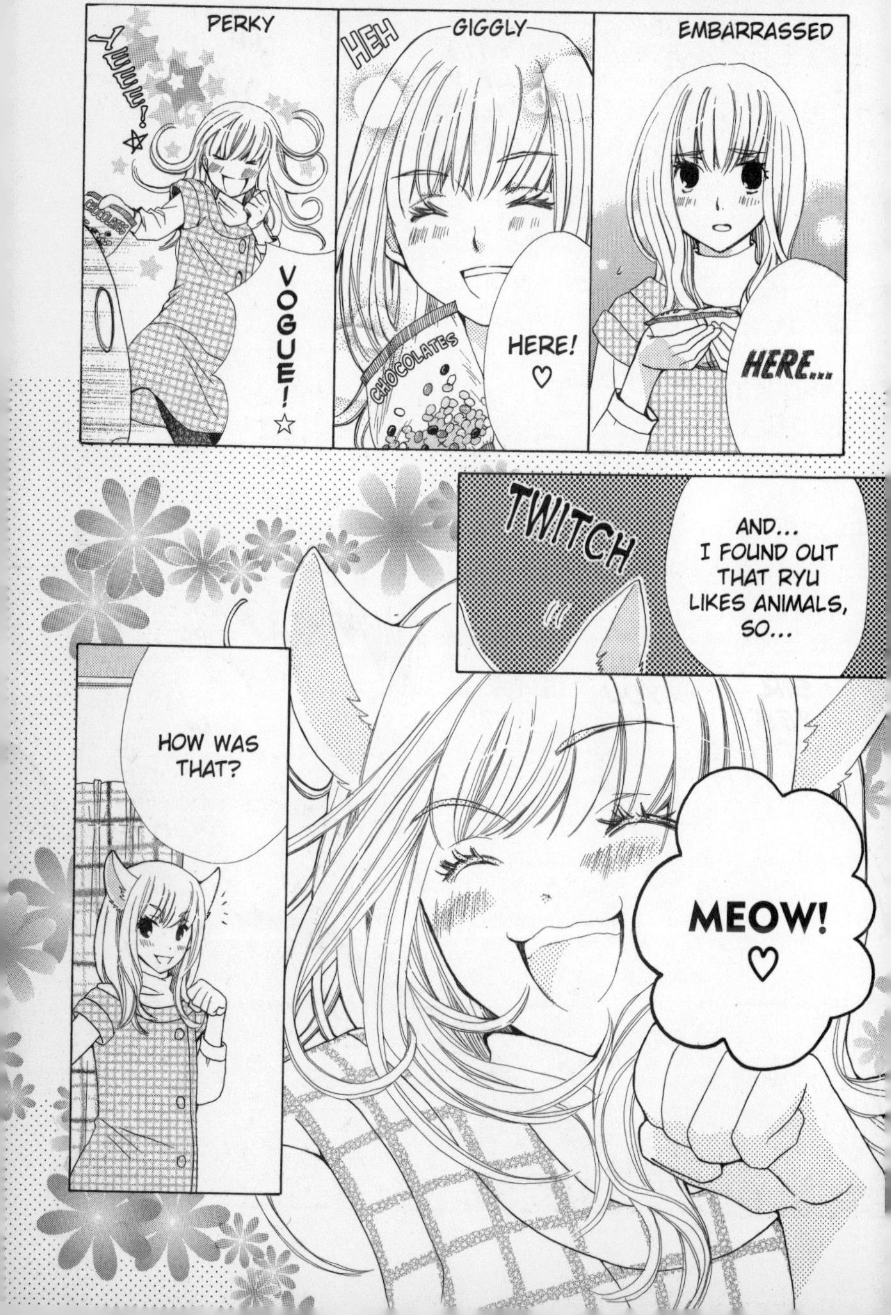
EMBARRASSED
HERE...
HEH
GIGGLY
HERE! ♡
PERKY
YEEEE! ☆
VOGUE! ☆
TWITCH
AND... I FOUND OUT THAT RYU LIKES ANIMALS, SO...
MEOW! ♡
HOW WAS THAT?

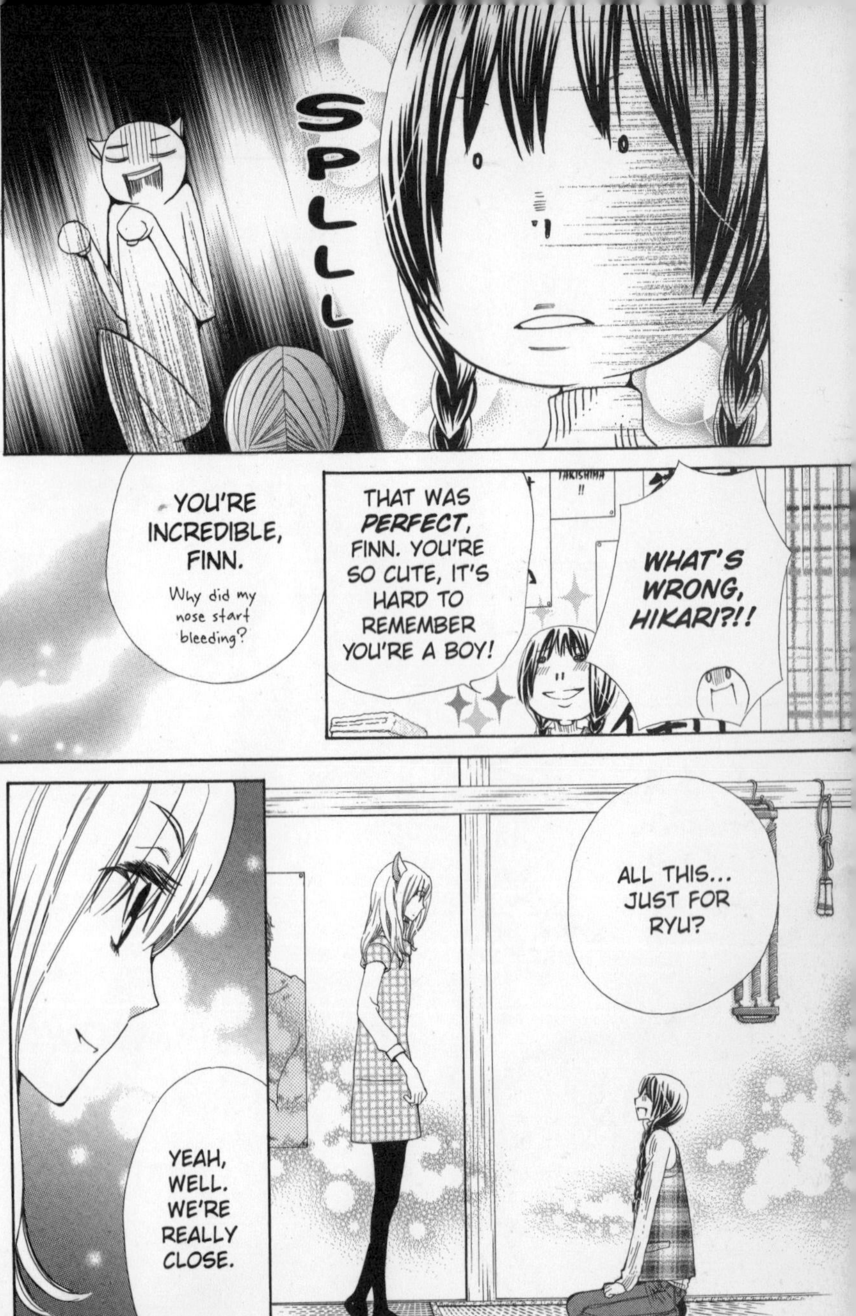
SPLLL
TAKISHIMA !!
WHAT'S WRONG, HIKARI?!!
THAT WAS PERFECT, FINN. YOU'RE SO CUTE, IT'S HARD TO REMEMBER YOU'RE A BOY!
YOU'RE INCREDIBLE, FINN.
Why did my nose start bleeding?
ALL THIS... JUST FOR RYU?
YEAH, WELL. WE'RE REALLY CLOSE.

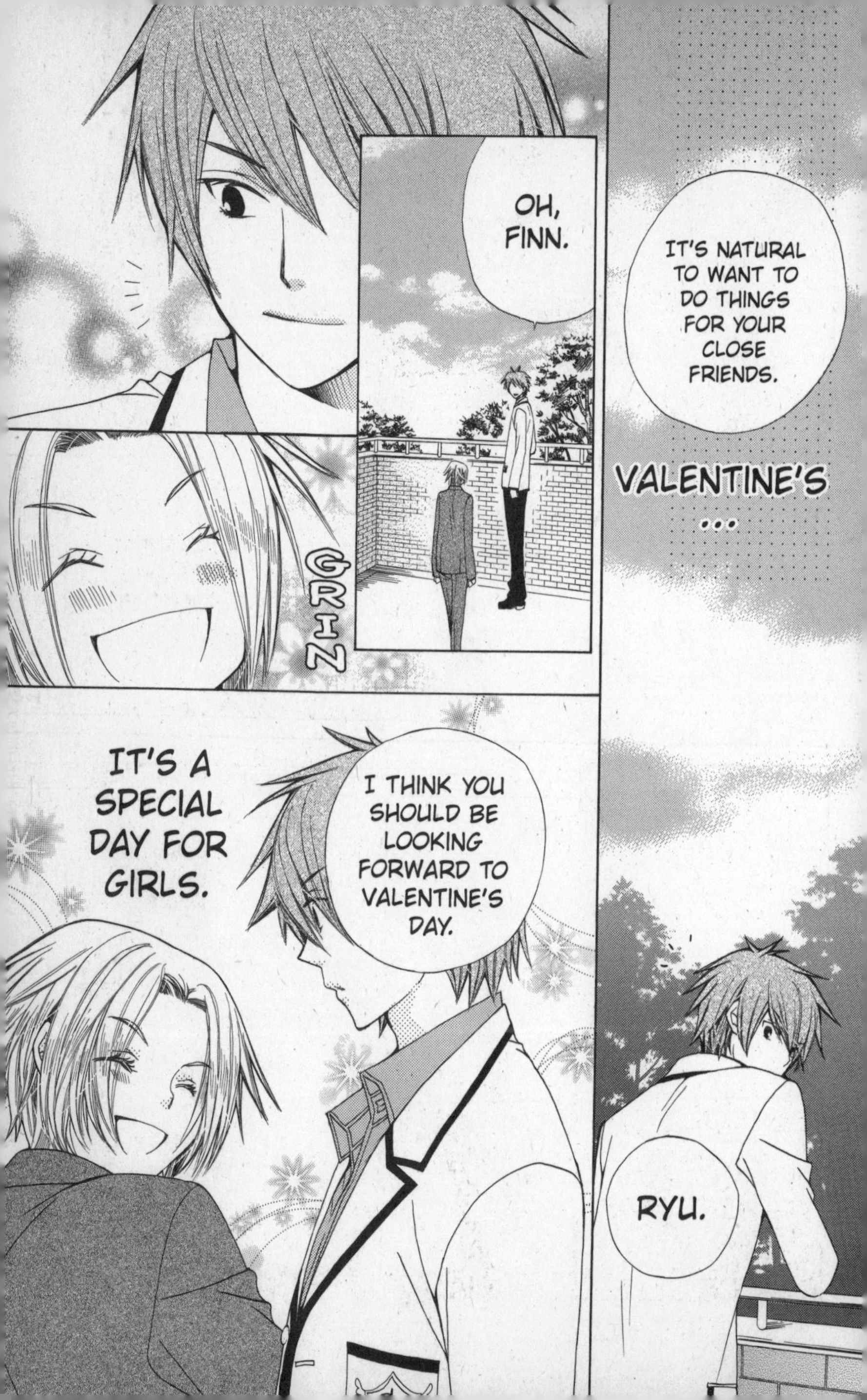
IT'S NATURAL TO WANT TO DO THINGS FOR YOUR CLOSE FRIENDS.
VALENTINE'S...
RYU.
OH, FINN.
GRIN
I THINK YOU SHOULD BE LOOKING FORWARD TO VALENTINE'S DAY.
IT'S A SPECIAL DAY FOR GIRLS.

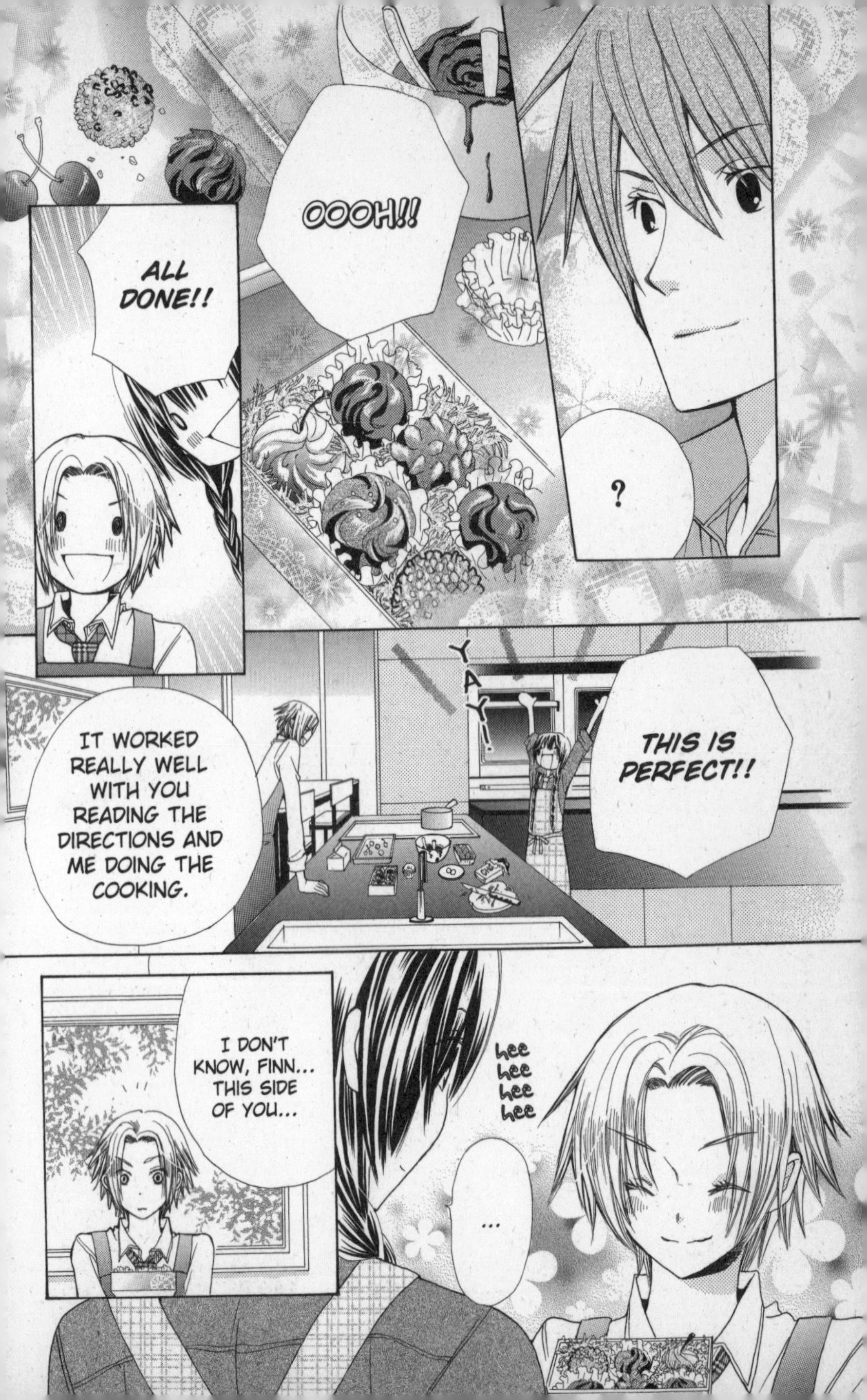
?
OOOH!!
ALL DONE!!
THIS IS PERFECT!!
YAY!
IT WORKED REALLY WELL WITH YOU READING THE DIRECTIONS AND ME DOING THE COOKING.
hee hee hee hee
...
I DON'T KNOW, FINN... THIS SIDE OF YOU...

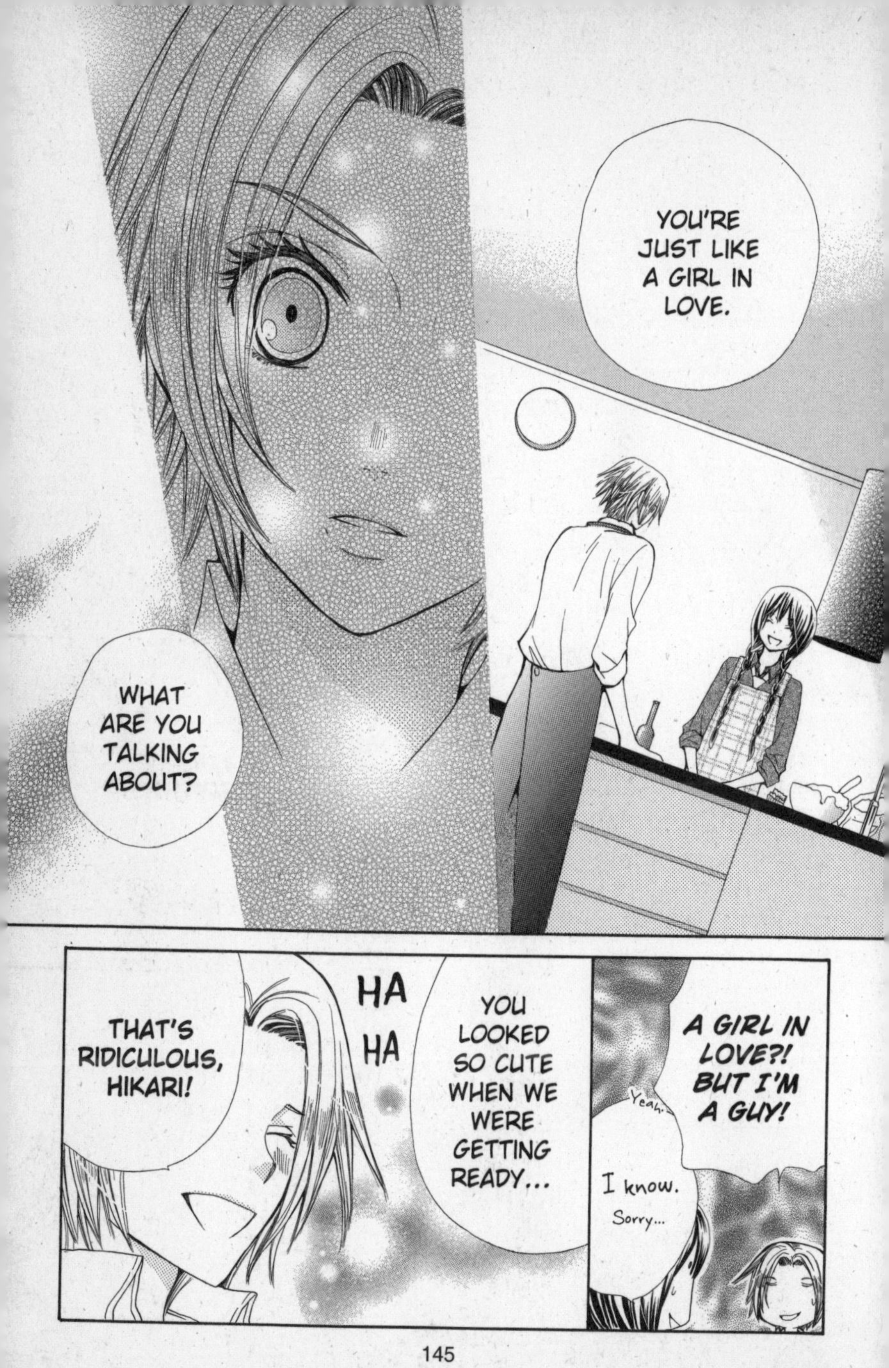
YOU'RE JUST LIKE A GIRL IN LOVE.
WHAT ARE YOU TALKING ABOUT?
A GIRL IN LOVE?! BUT I'M A GUY!
Yeah.
I know.
Sorry...
YOU LOOKED SO CUTE WHEN WE WERE GETTING READY...
HA HA
THAT'S RIDICULOUS, HIKARI!

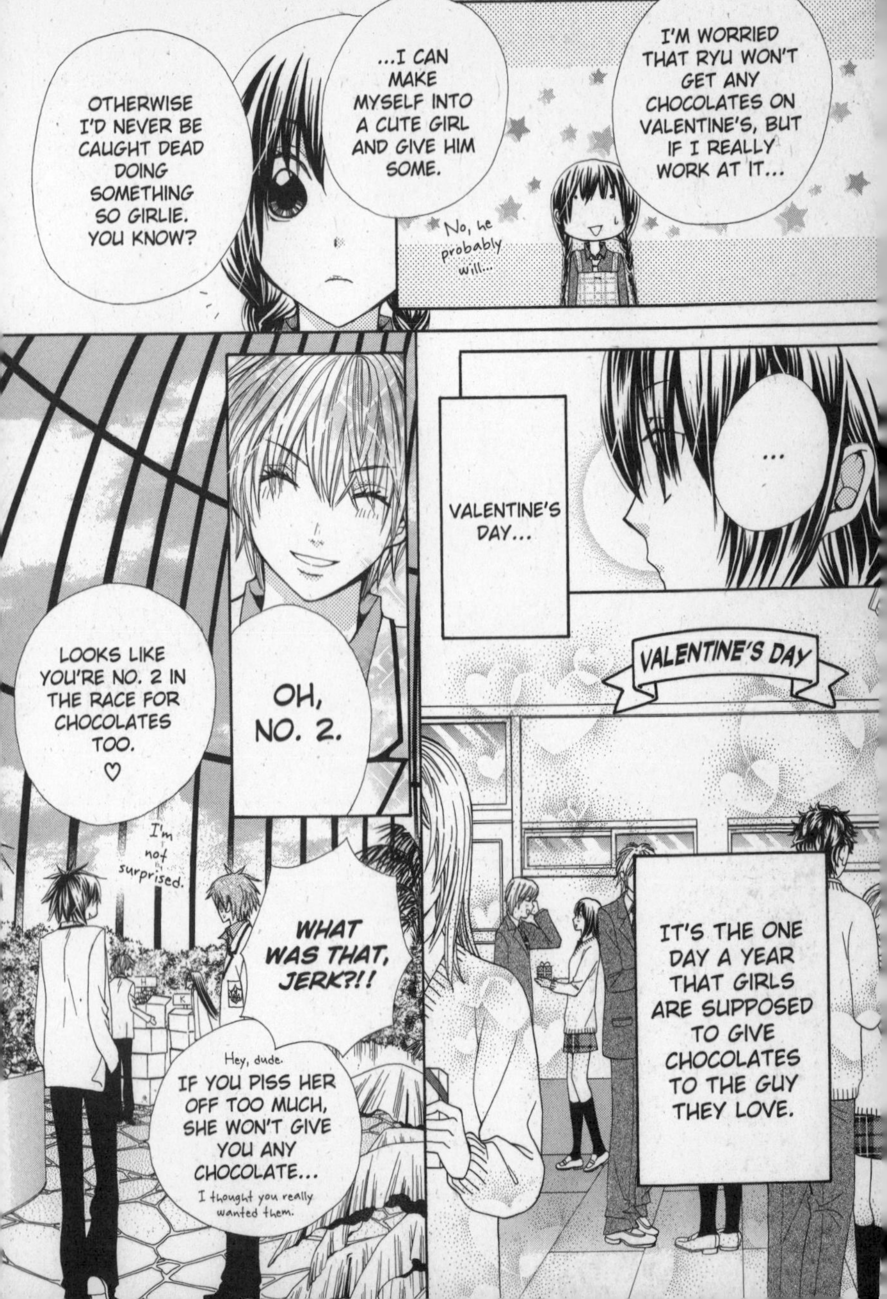
I'M WORRIED THAT RYU WON'T GET ANY CHOCOLATES ON VALENTINE'S, BUT IF I REALLY WORK AT IT...
No, he probably will...
...I CAN MAKE MYSELF INTO A CUTE GIRL AND GIVE HIM SOME.
OTHERWISE I'D NEVER BE CAUGHT DEAD DOING SOMETHING SO GIRLIE. YOU KNOW?
...
VALENTINE'S DAY...
VALENTINE'S DAY
IT'S THE ONE DAY A YEAR THAT GIRLS ARE SUPPOSED TO GIVE CHOCOLATES TO THE GUY THEY LOVE.
LOOKS LIKE YOU'RE NO. 2 IN THE RACE FOR CHOCOLATES TOO. ♡
OH, NO. 2.
I'm not surprised.
WHAT WAS THAT, JERK?!!
Hey, dude.
IF YOU PISS HER OFF TOO MUCH, SHE WON'T GIVE YOU ANY CHOCOLATE...
I thought you really wanted them.

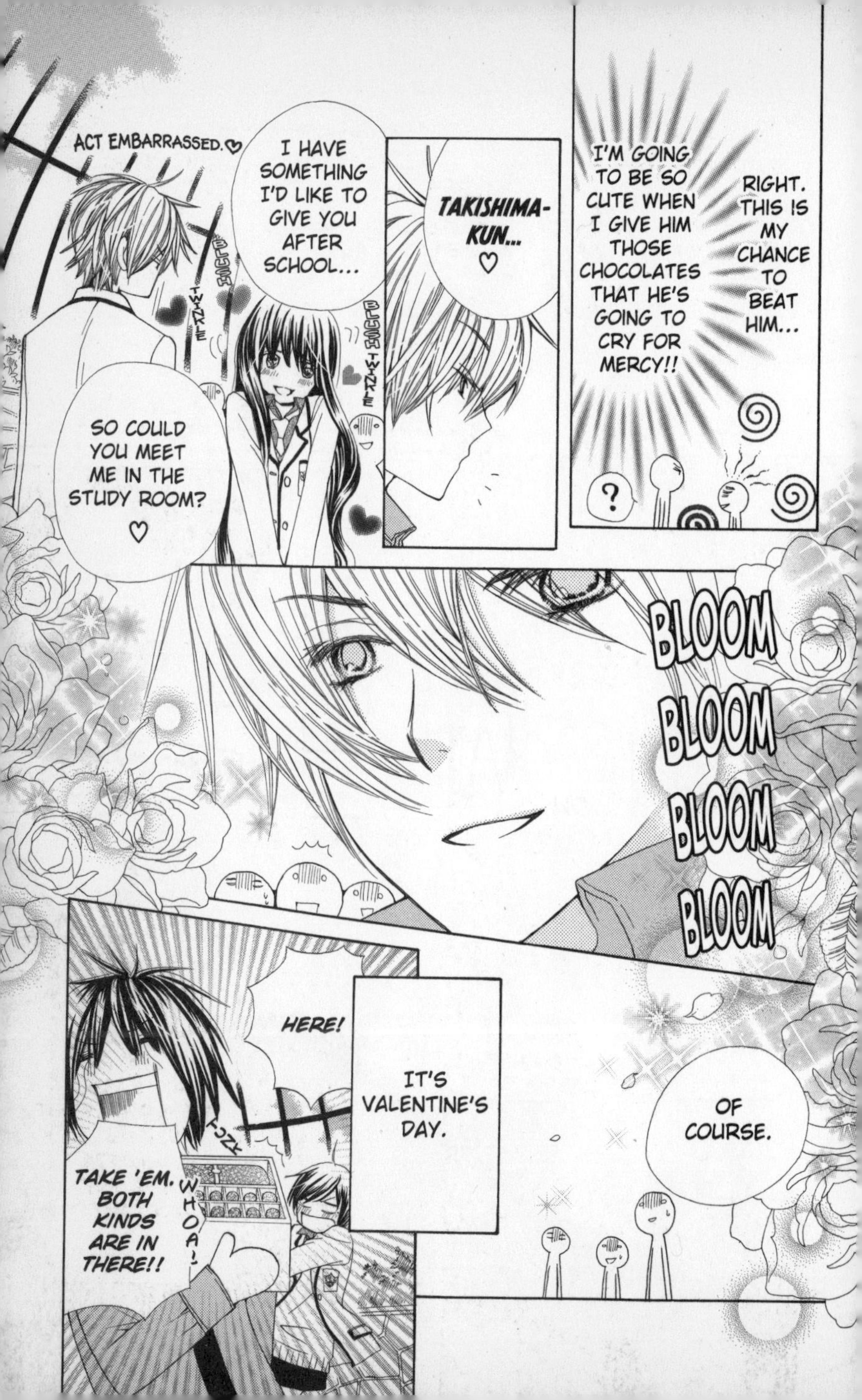
RIGHT. THIS IS MY CHANCE TO BEAT HIM...
I'M GOING TO BE SO CUTE WHEN I GIVE HIM THOSE CHOCOLATES THAT HE'S GOING TO CRY FOR MERCY!!
TAKISHIMA-KUN... ♡
I HAVE SOMETHING I'D LIKE TO GIVE YOU AFTER SCHOOL...
ACT EMBARRASSED. ♡
BLUSH
TWINKLE
BLUSH
TWINKLE
SO COULD YOU MEET ME IN THE STUDY ROOM? ♡
BLOOM
BLOOM
BLOOM
BLOOM
OF COURSE.
IT'S VALENTINE'S DAY.
HERE!
TAKE 'EM. BOTH KINDS ARE IN THERE!!
WHOA!

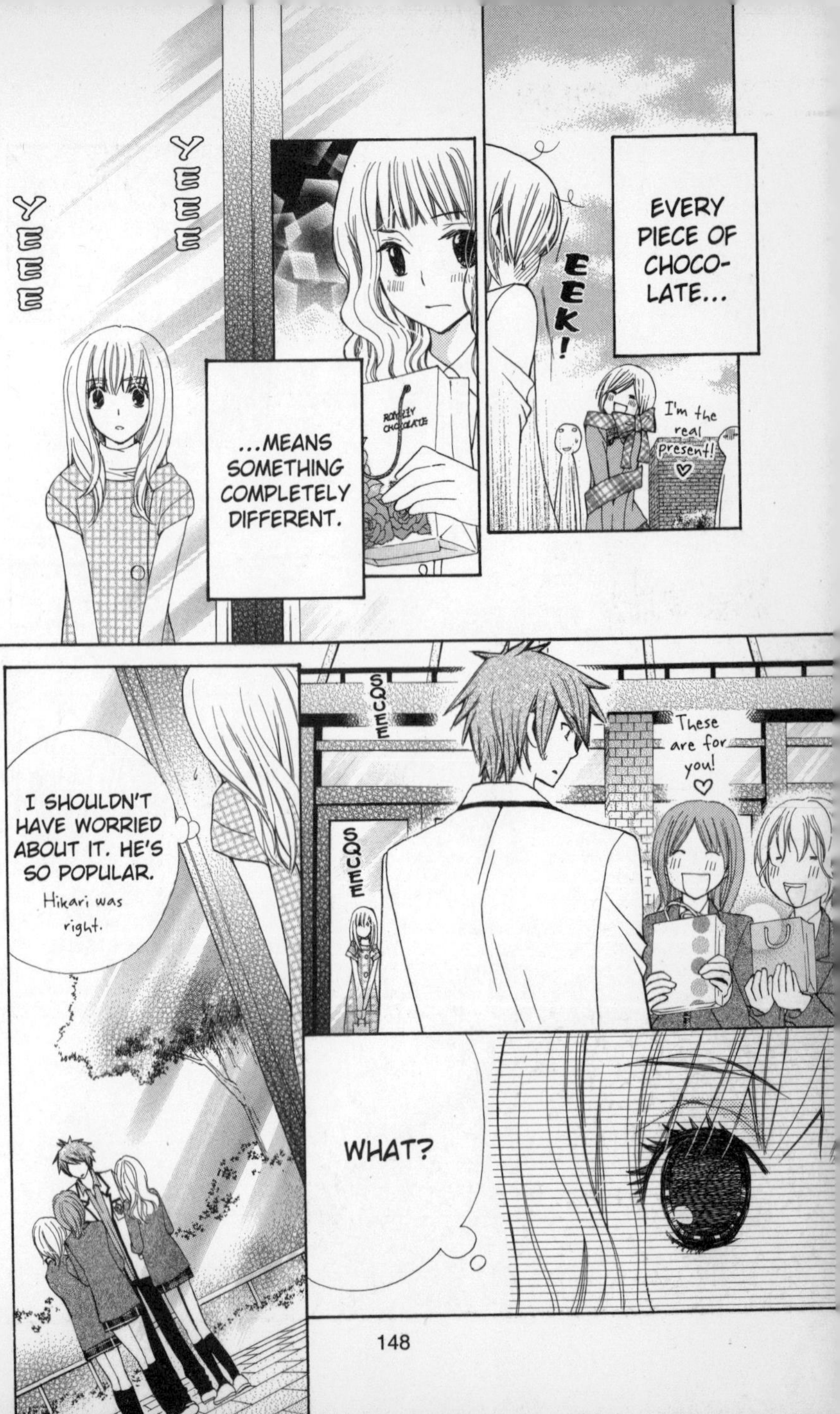
EVERY PIECE OF CHOCOLATE...
EEK!
I'm the real present! ♡
...MEANS SOMETHING COMPLETELY DIFFERENT.
YEEE
YEEE
SQUEE
SQUEE
These are for you! ♡
WHAT?
I SHOULDN'T HAVE WORRIED ABOUT IT. HE'S SO POPULAR.
Hikari was right.

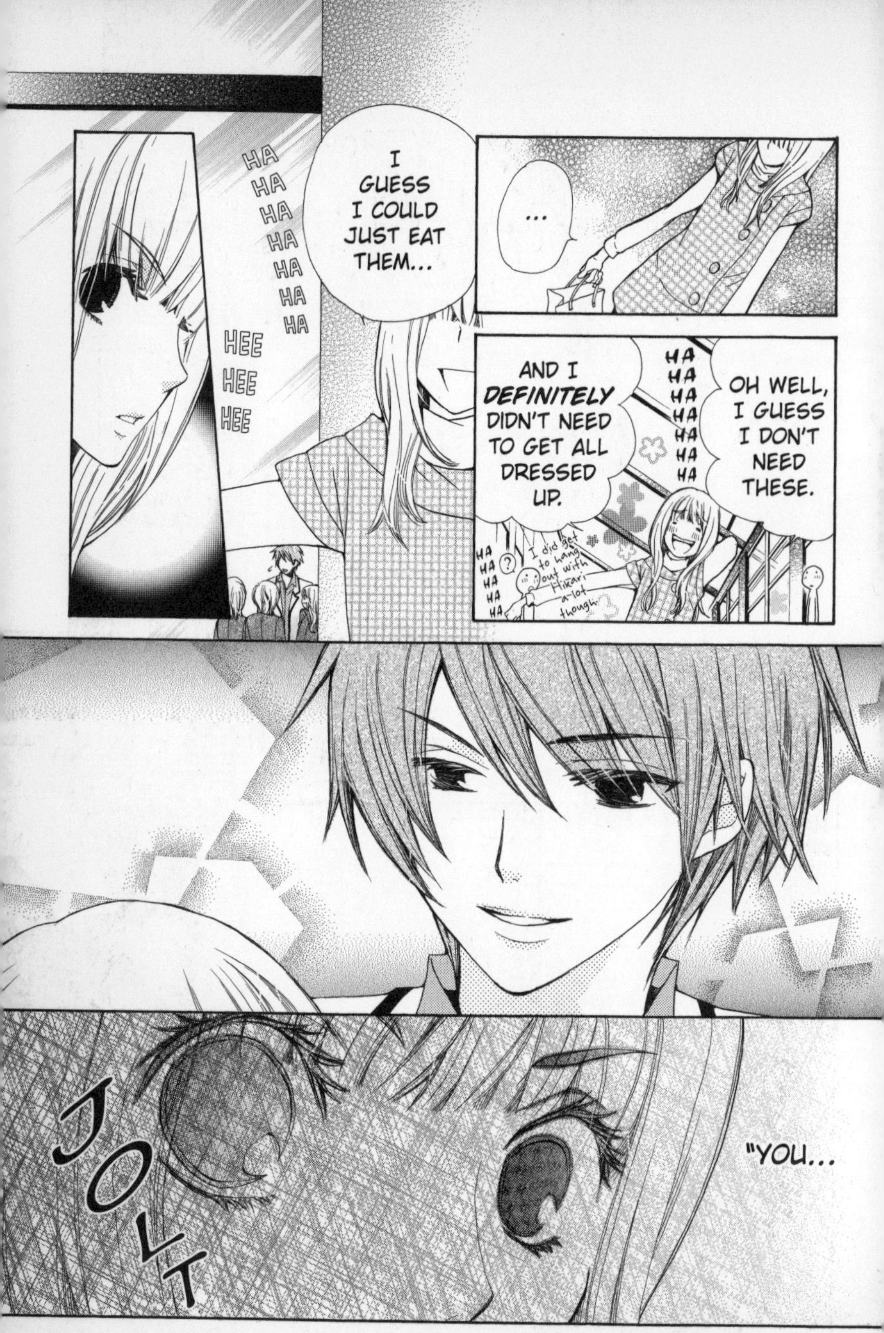
...
OH WELL, I GUESS I DON'T NEED THESE.
HA HA HA HA HA HA HA
AND I *DEFINITELY* DIDN'T NEED TO GET ALL DRESSED UP.
I did get to hang out with Hikari a lot though.
HA HA HA HA HA
I GUESS I COULD JUST EAT THEM...
HA HA HA HA HA HA HA
HEE HEE HEE
JOLT
"YOU...

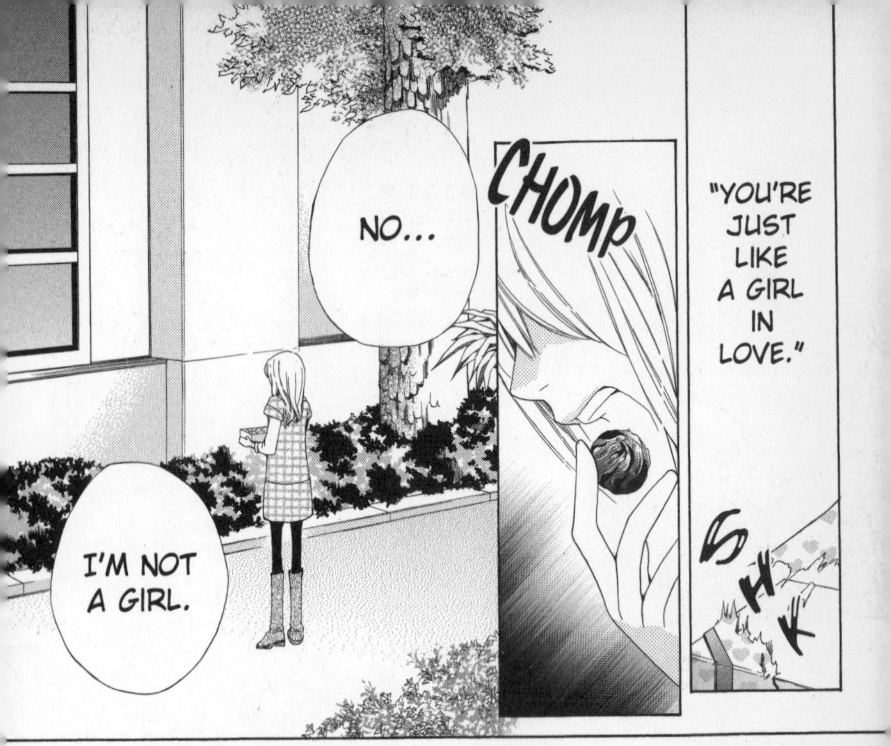
"YOU'RE JUST LIKE A GIRL IN LOVE."
SHK
CHOMP
NO...
I'M NOT A GIRL.

VALENTINE'S DAY IS FOR "GIRLS" TO GIVE CHOCOLATES TO THE "THE GUY THEY LOVE."

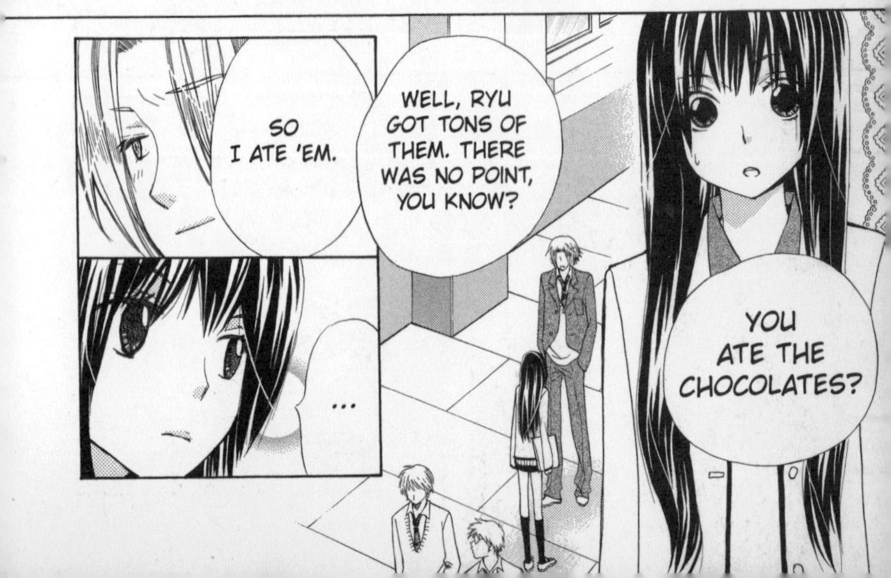
YOU ATE THE CHOCOLATES?
WELL, RYU GOT TONS OF THEM. THERE WAS NO POINT, YOU KNOW?
SO I ATE 'EM.
...

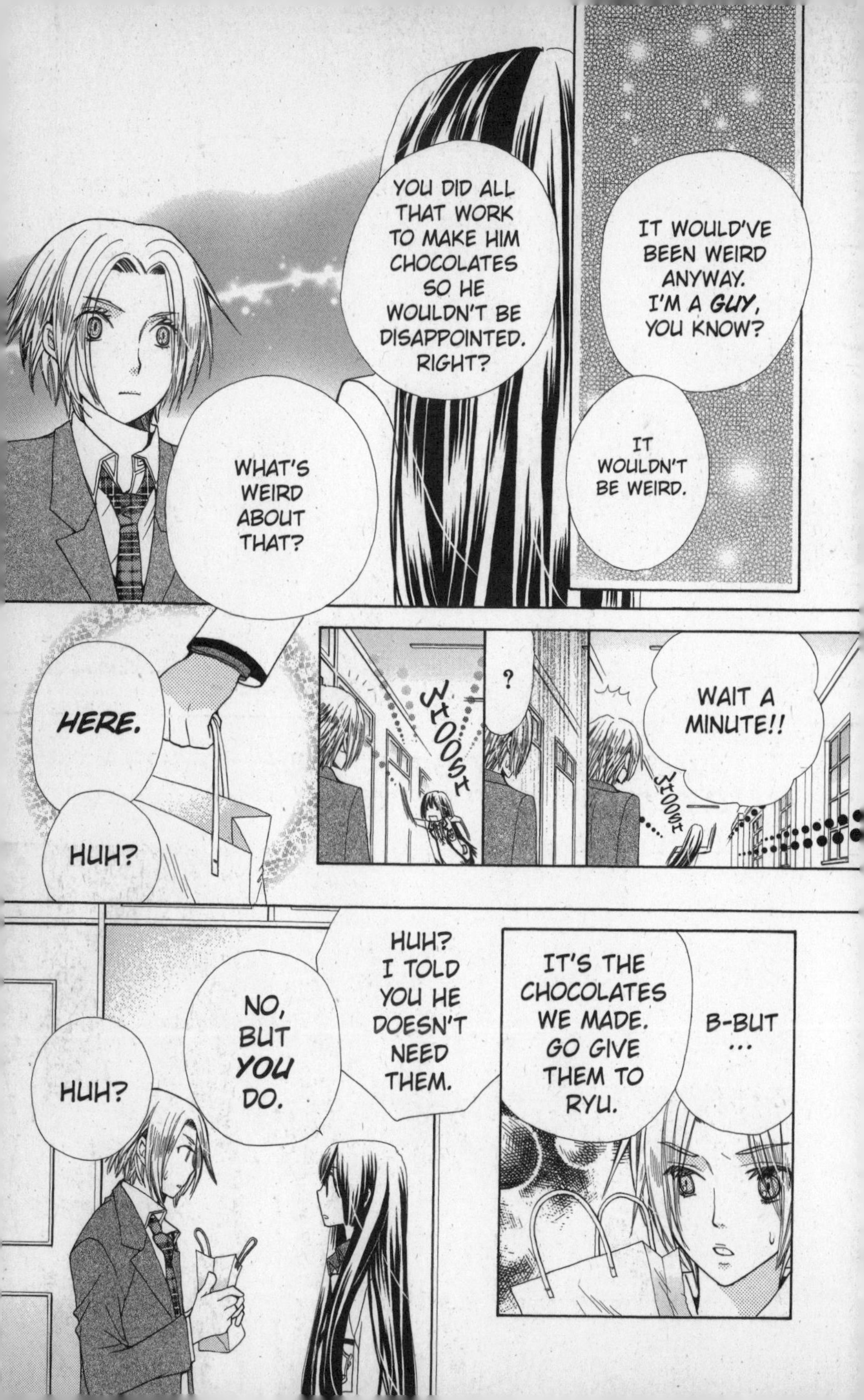
IT WOULD'VE BEEN WEIRD ANYWAY. I'M A *GUY*, YOU KNOW?
YOU DID ALL THAT WORK TO MAKE HIM CHOCOLATES SO HE WOULDN'T BE DISAPPOINTED. RIGHT?
IT WOULDN'T BE WEIRD.
WHAT'S WEIRD ABOUT THAT?
WAIT A MINUTE!!
WHOOSH
?
WHOOSH
HERE.
HUH?
B-BUT ...
IT'S THE CHOCOLATES WE MADE. GO GIVE THEM TO RYU.
HUH? I TOLD YOU HE DOESN'T NEED THEM.
NO, BUT *YOU* DO.
HUH?

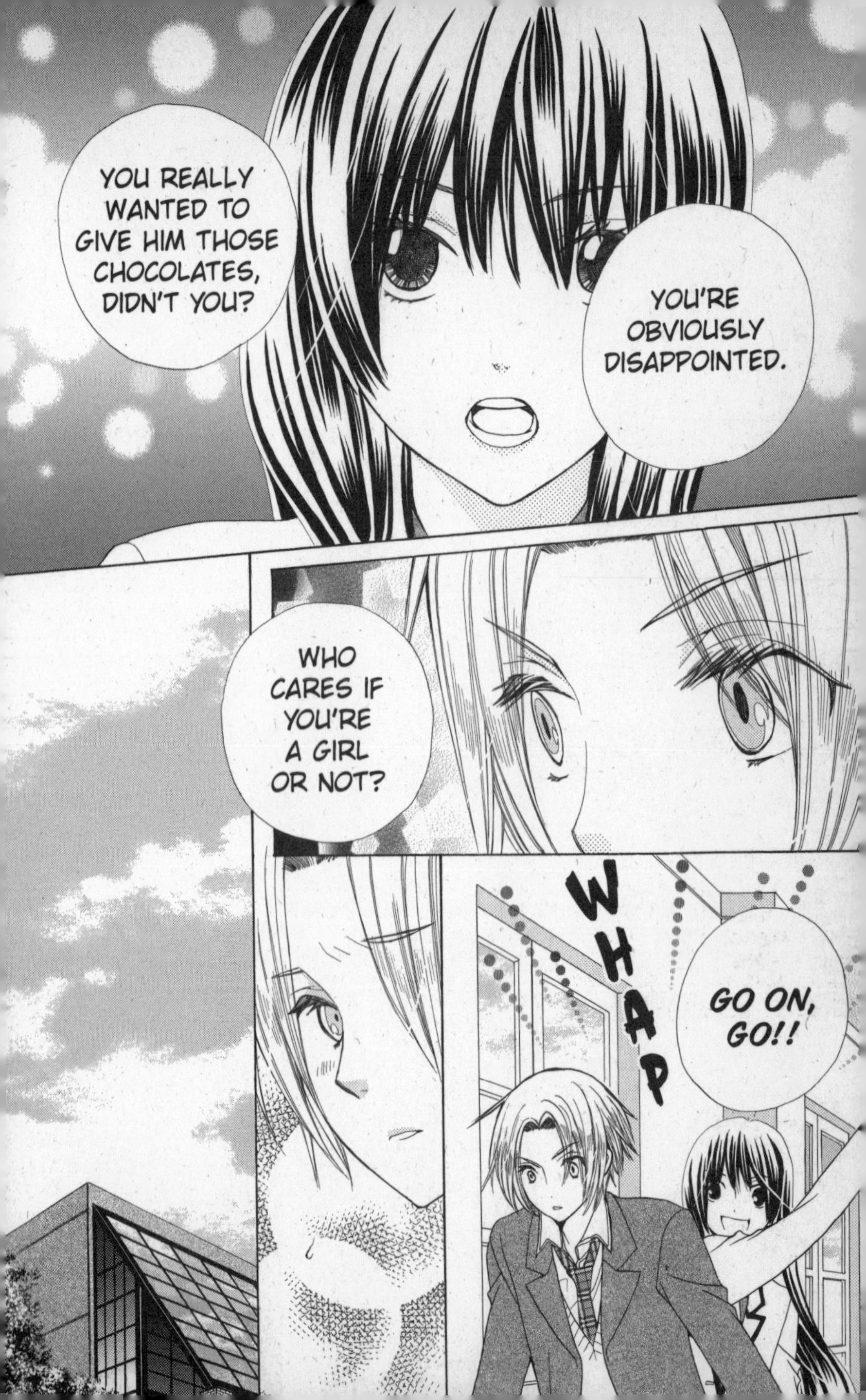
YOU REALLY WANTED TO GIVE HIM THOSE CHOCOLATES, DIDN'T YOU?
YOU'RE OBVIOUSLY DISAPPOINTED.
WHO CARES IF YOU'RE A GIRL OR NOT?
WHAP
GO ON, GO!!

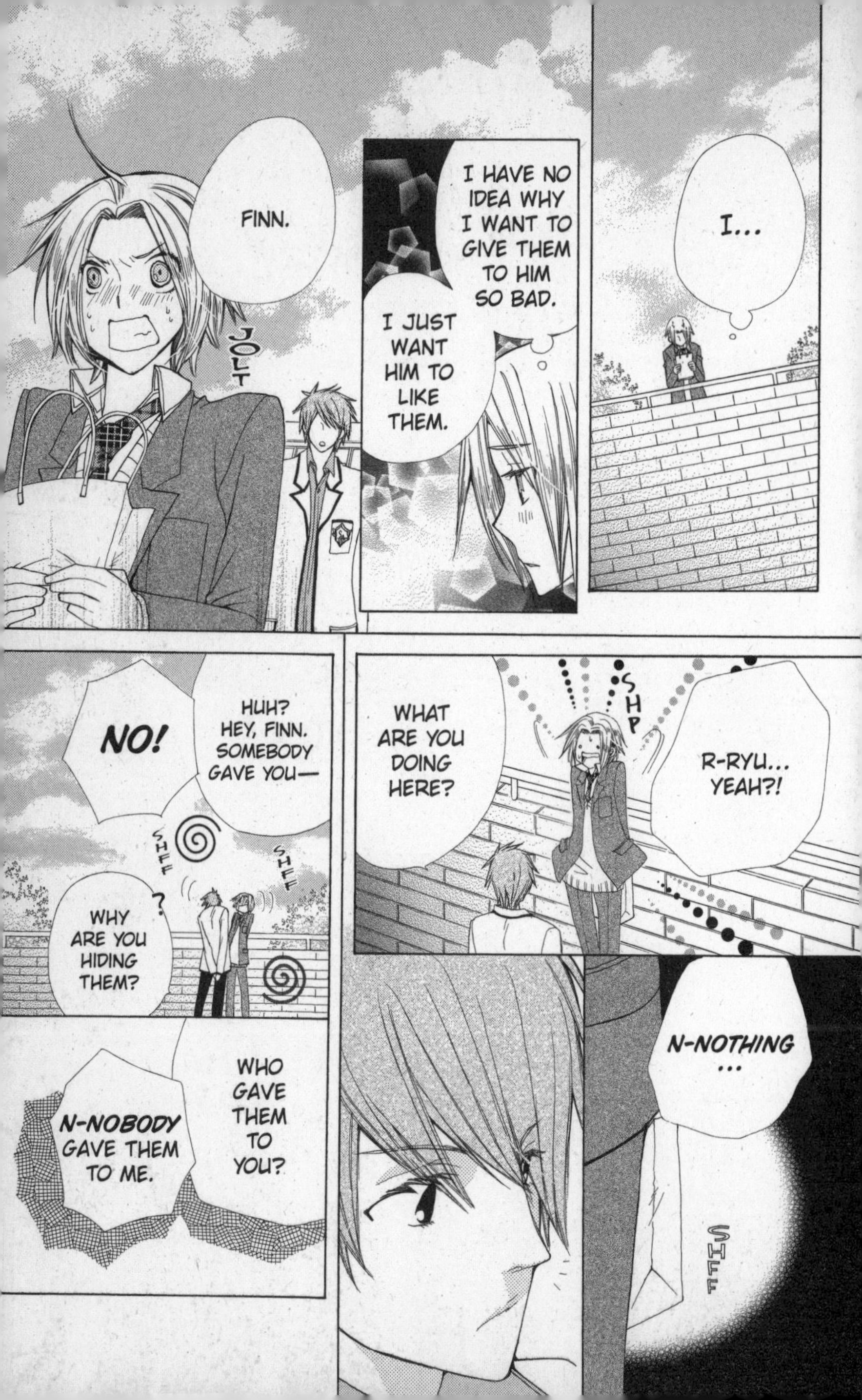
I...
I HAVE NO IDEA WHY I WANT TO GIVE THEM TO HIM SO BAD.
I JUST WANT HIM TO LIKE THEM.
FINN.
JOLT
SHP
R-RYU... YEAH?!
WHAT ARE YOU DOING HERE?
HUH? HEY, FINN. SOMEBODY GAVE YOU—
NO!
SHFF
SHFF
WHY ARE YOU HIDING THEM?
N-NOTHING ...
SHFF
WHO GAVE THEM TO YOU?
N-NOBODY GAVE THEM TO ME.

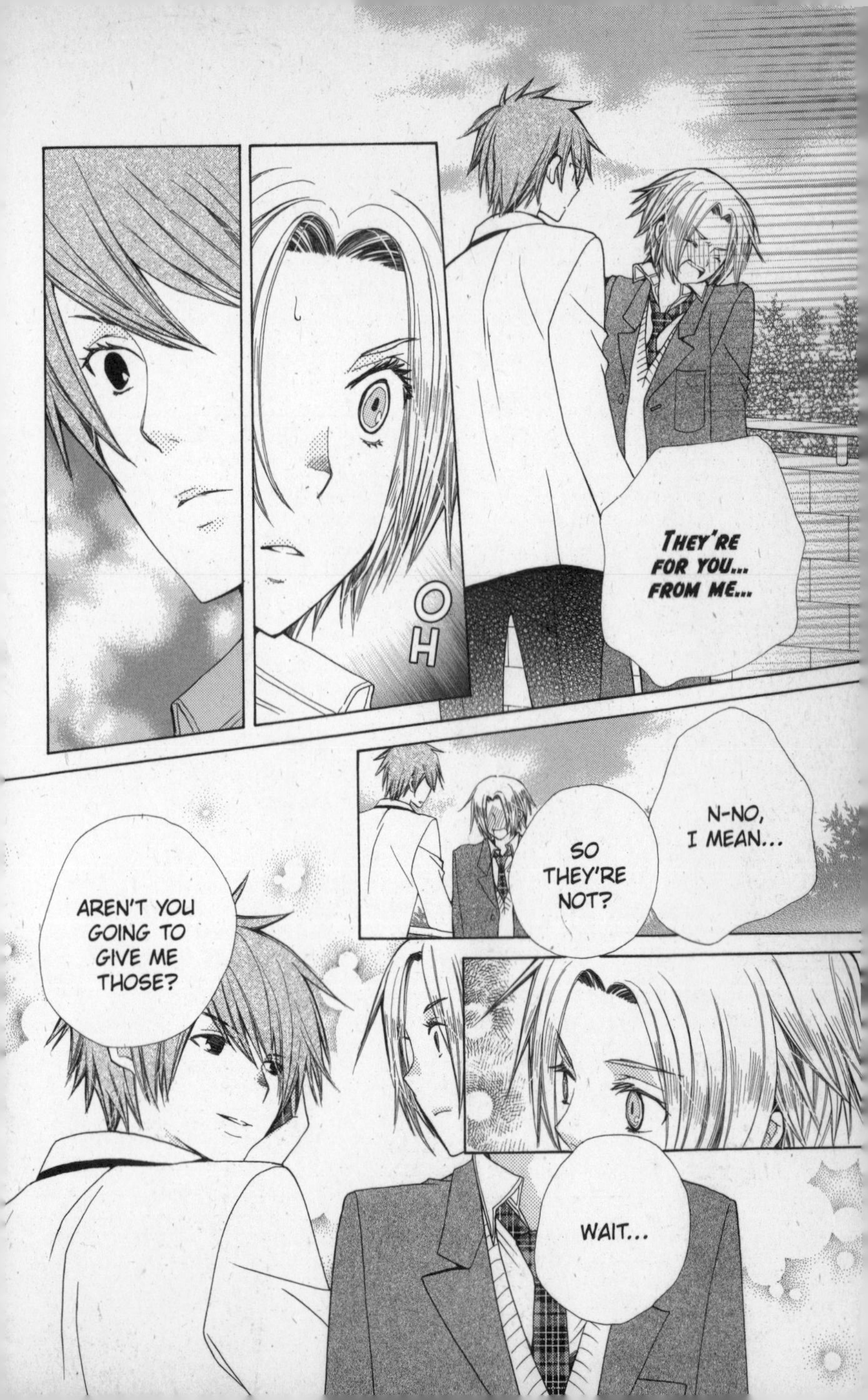

THEY'RE FOR YOU... FROM ME...
OH
N-NO, I MEAN...
SO THEY'RE NOT?
AREN'T YOU GOING TO GIVE ME THOSE?
WAIT...

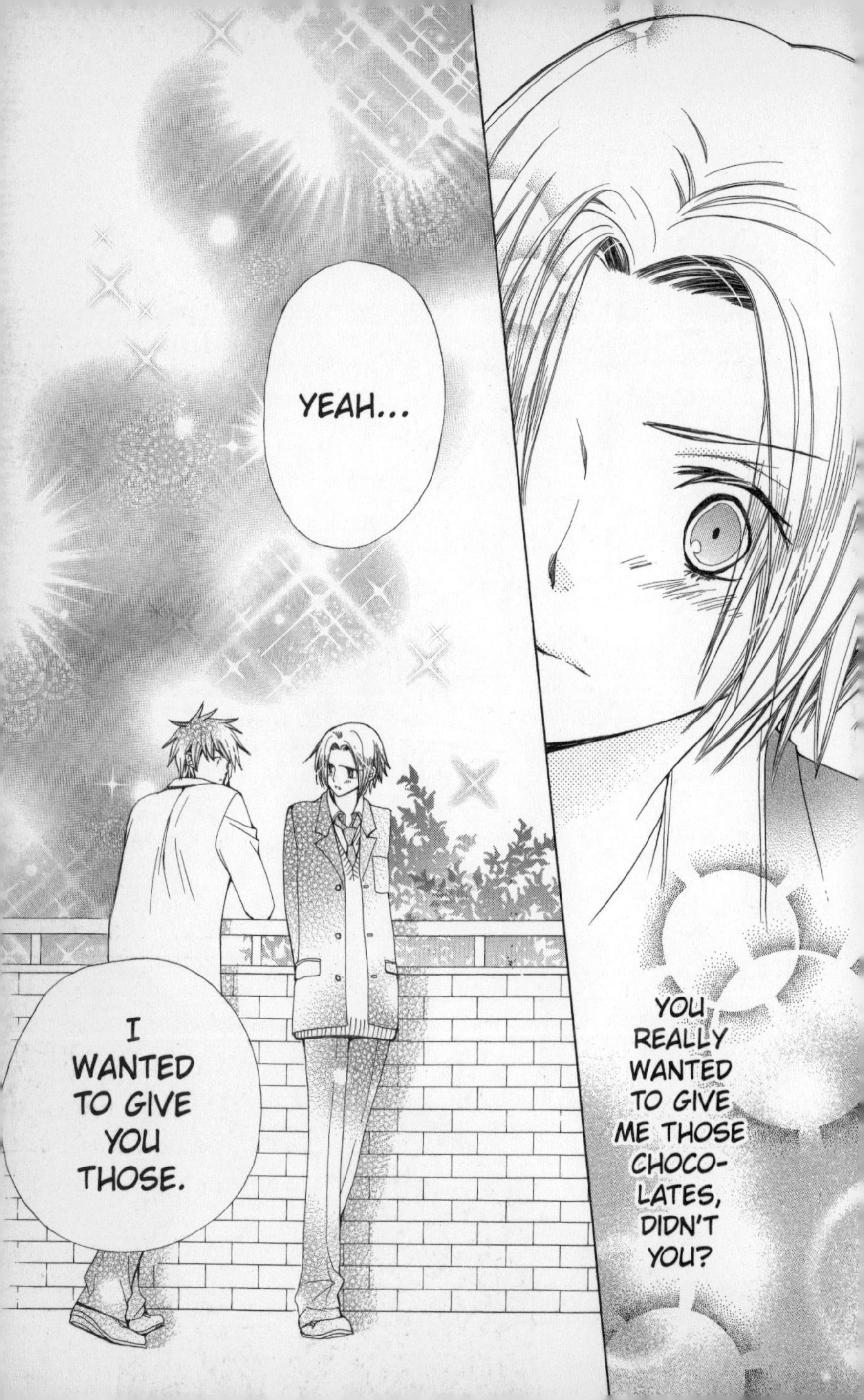
YOU REALLY WANTED TO GIVE ME THOSE CHOCO-LATES, DIDN'T YOU?
YEAH...
I WANTED TO GIVE YOU THOSE.

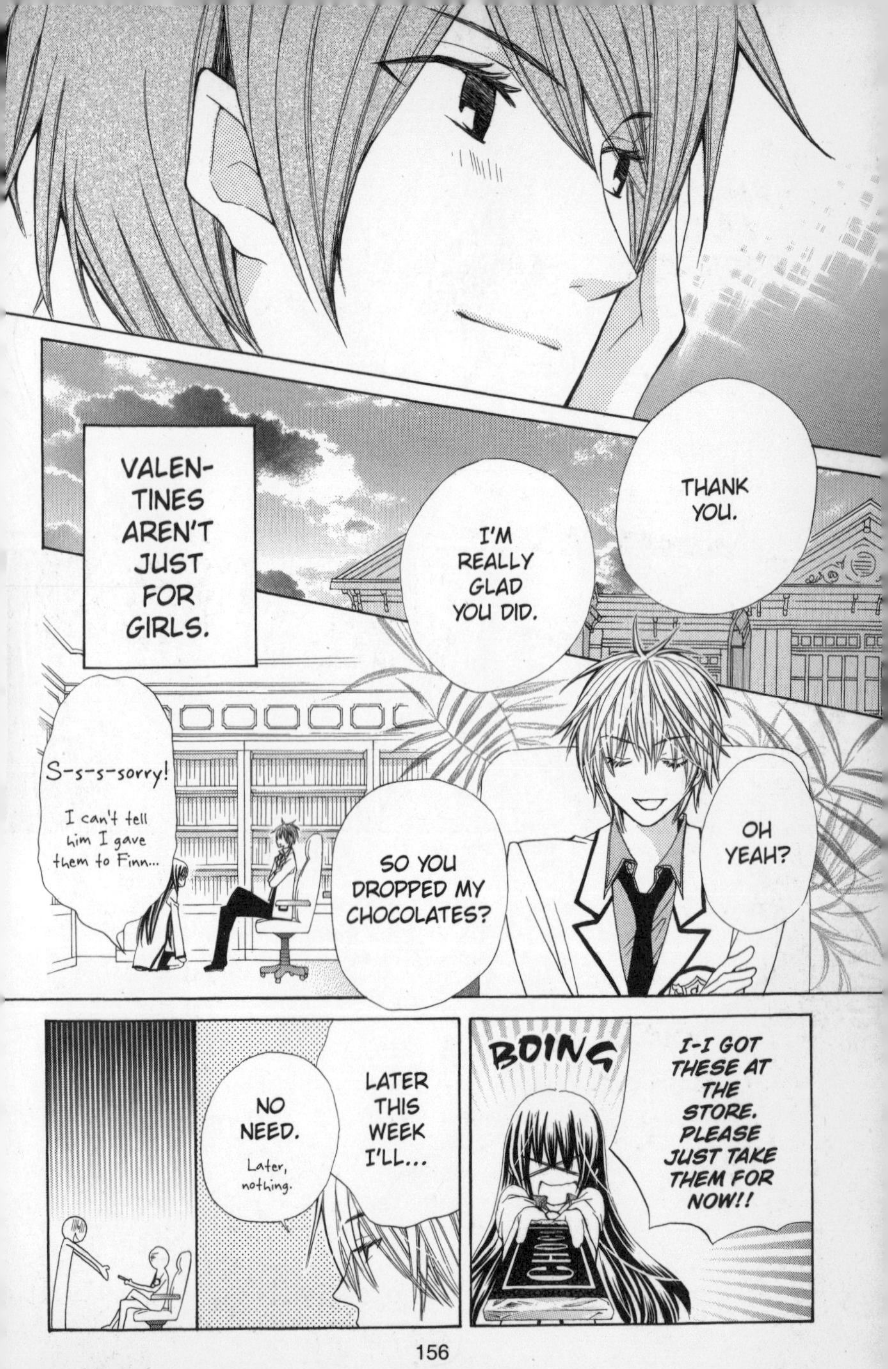
THANK YOU.
I'M REALLY GLAD YOU DID.
VALENTINES AREN'T JUST FOR GIRLS.
OH YEAH?
SO YOU DROPPED MY CHOCOLATES?
S-s-s-sorry!
I can't tell him I gave them to Finn...
BOING
I-I GOT THESE AT THE STORE. PLEASE JUST TAKE THEM FOR NOW!!
LATER THIS WEEK I'LL...
NO NEED.
Later, nothing.

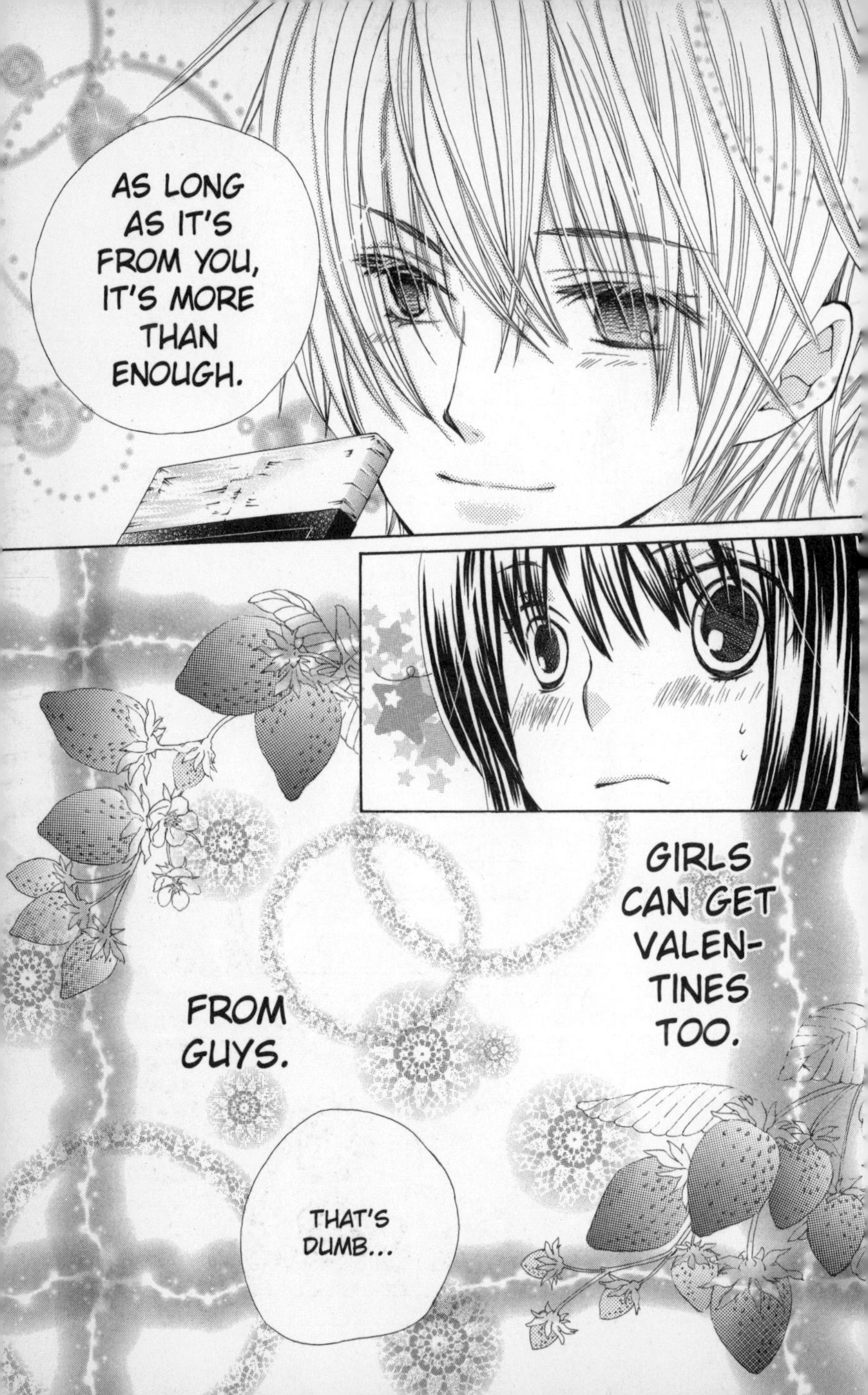
AS LONG AS IT'S FROM YOU, IT'S MORE THAN ENOUGH.
GIRLS CAN GET VALEN- TINES TOO.
FROM GUYS.
THAT'S DUMB...

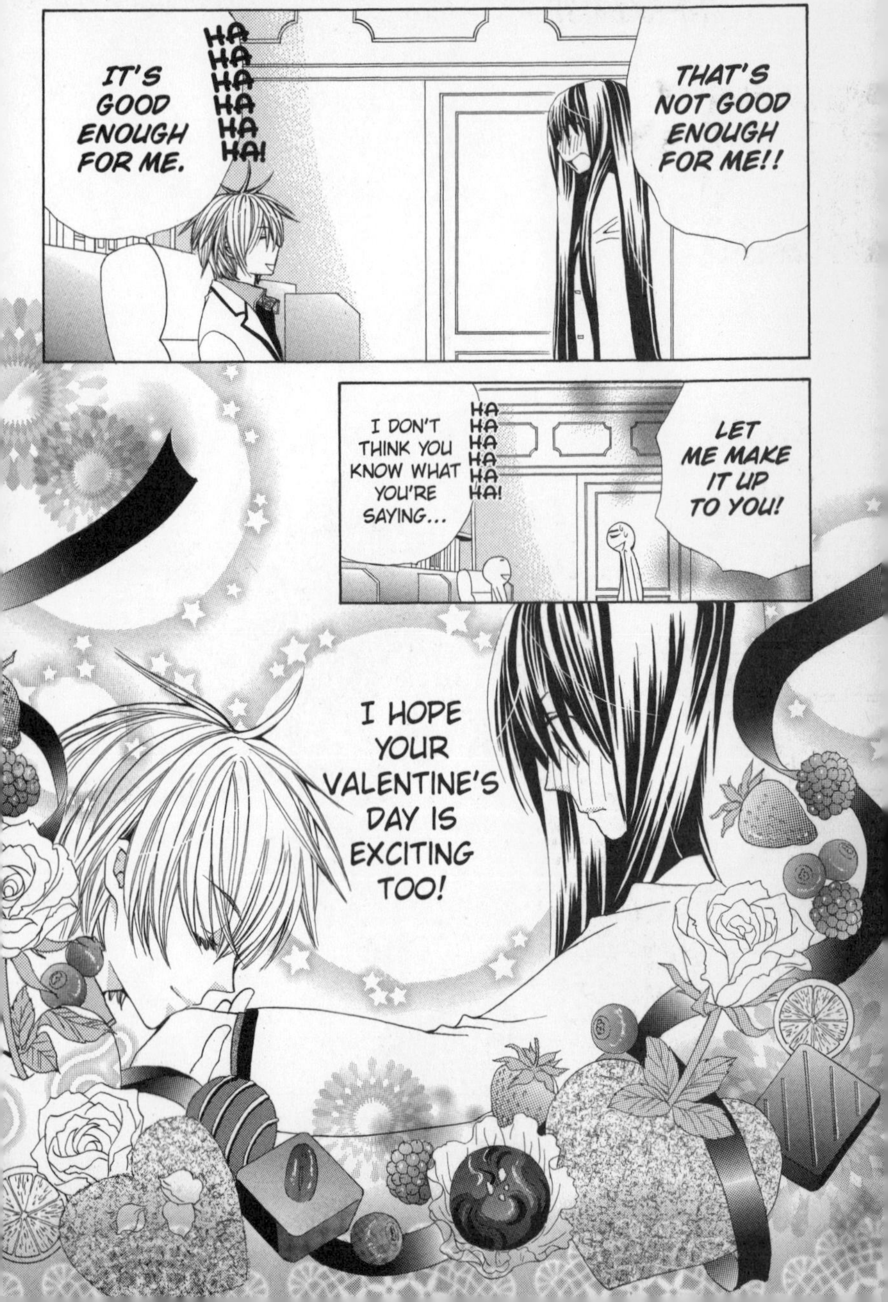
THAT'S NOT GOOD ENOUGH FOR ME!!
HA HA HA HA HA HA!
IT'S GOOD ENOUGH FOR ME.
LET ME MAKE IT UP TO YOU!
HA HA HA HA HA HA!
I DON'T THINK YOU KNOW WHAT YOU'RE SAYING...
I HOPE YOUR VALENTINE'S DAY IS EXCITING TOO!

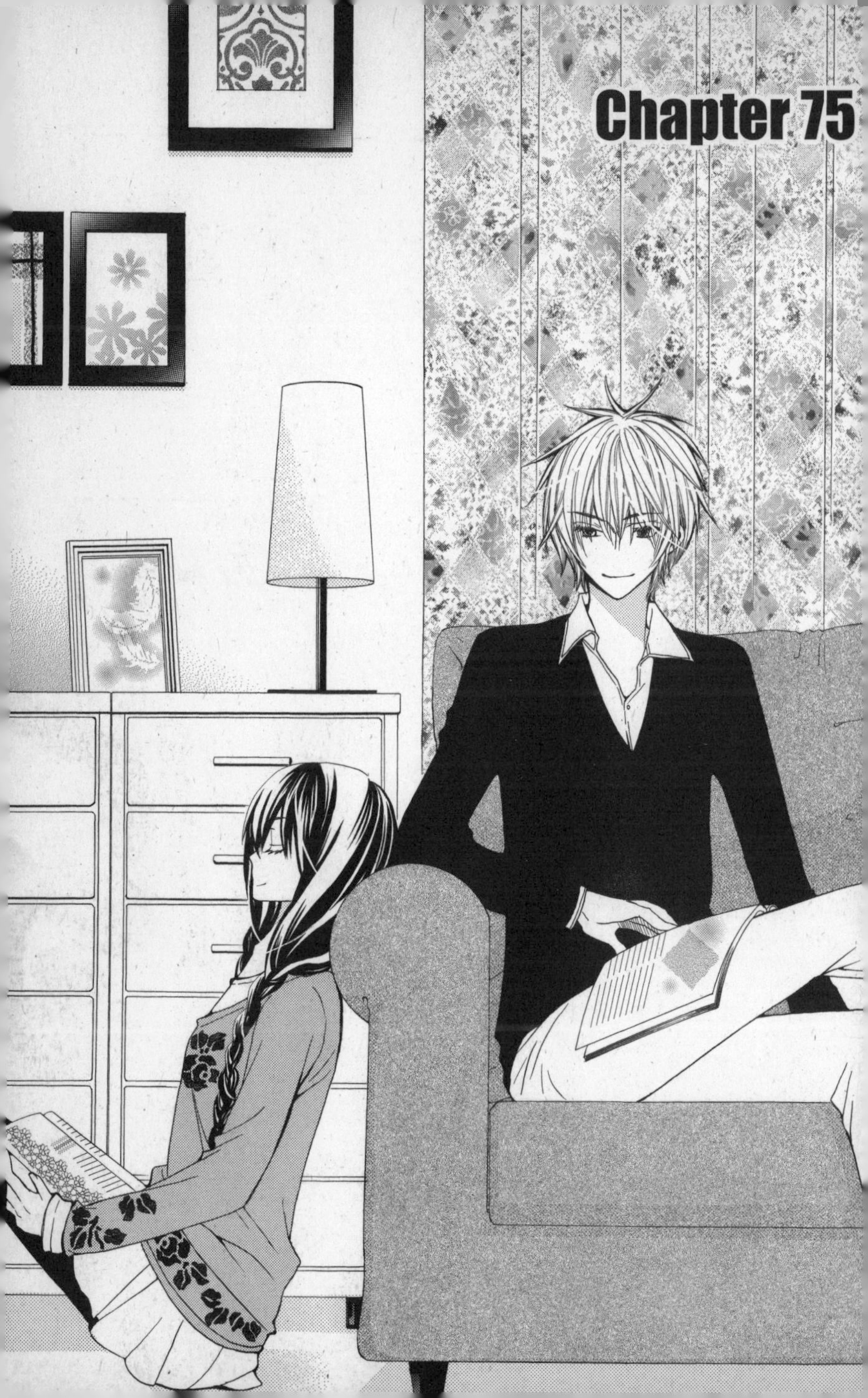
Chapter 75

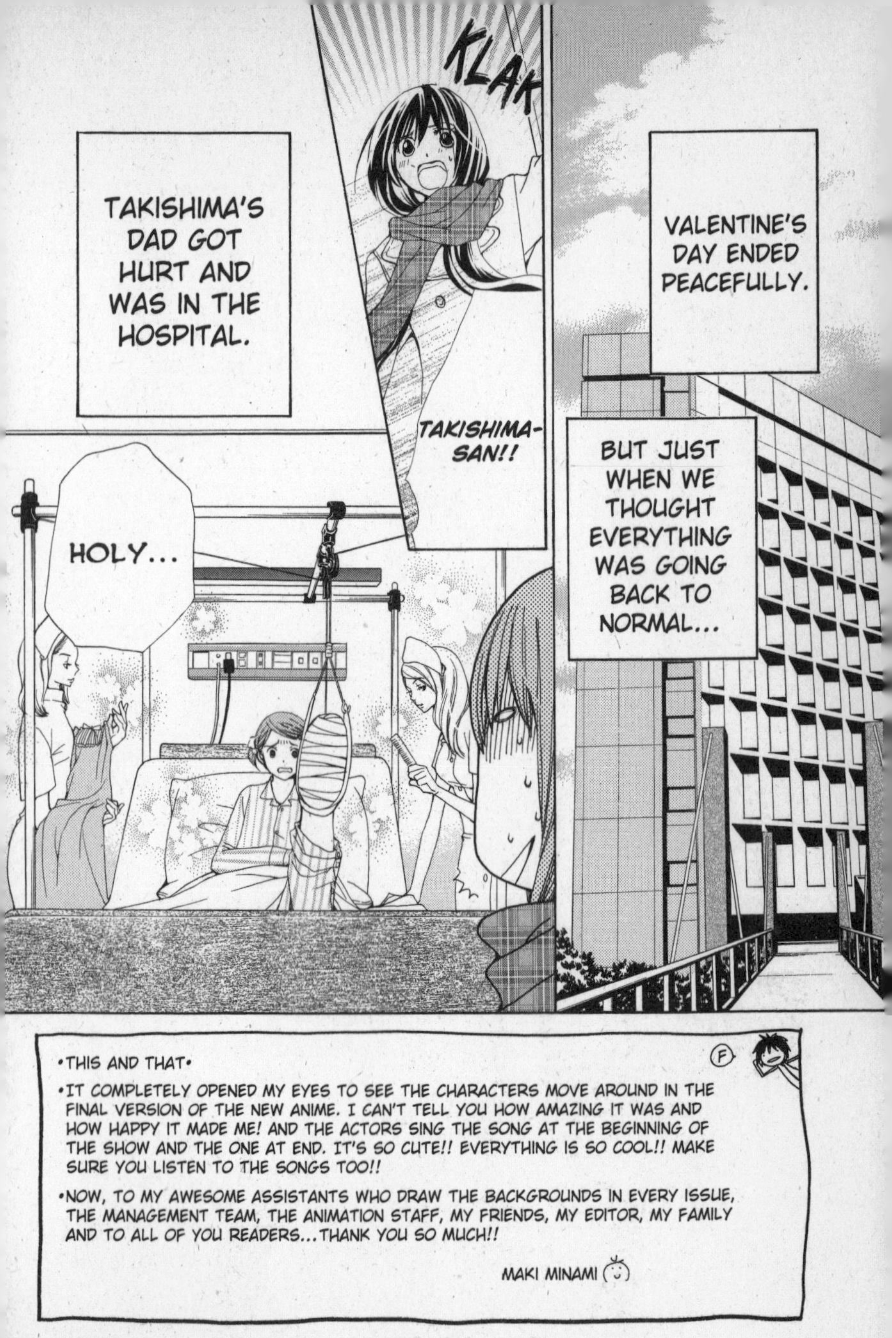
VALENTINE'S DAY ENDED PEACEFULLY.
BUT JUST WHEN WE THOUGHT EVERYTHING WAS GOING BACK TO NORMAL...
KLAK
TAKISHIMA-SAN!!
TAKISHIMA'S DAD GOT HURT AND WAS IN THE HOSPITAL.
HOLY...

•THIS AND THAT•

•IT COMPLETELY OPENED MY EYES TO SEE THE CHARACTERS MOVE AROUND IN THE FINAL VERSION OF THE NEW ANIME. I CAN'T TELL YOU HOW AMAZING IT WAS AND HOW HAPPY IT MADE ME! AND THE ACTORS SING THE SONG AT THE BEGINNING OF THE SHOW AND THE ONE AT END. IT'S SO CUTE!! EVERYTHING IS SO COOL!! MAKE SURE YOU LISTEN TO THE SONGS TOO!!

•NOW, TO MY AWESOME ASSISTANTS WHO DRAW THE BACKGROUNDS IN EVERY ISSUE, THE MANAGEMENT TEAM, THE ANIMATION STAFF, MY FRIENDS, MY EDITOR, MY FAMILY AND TO ALL OF YOU READERS...THANK YOU SO MUCH!!

MAKI MINAMI

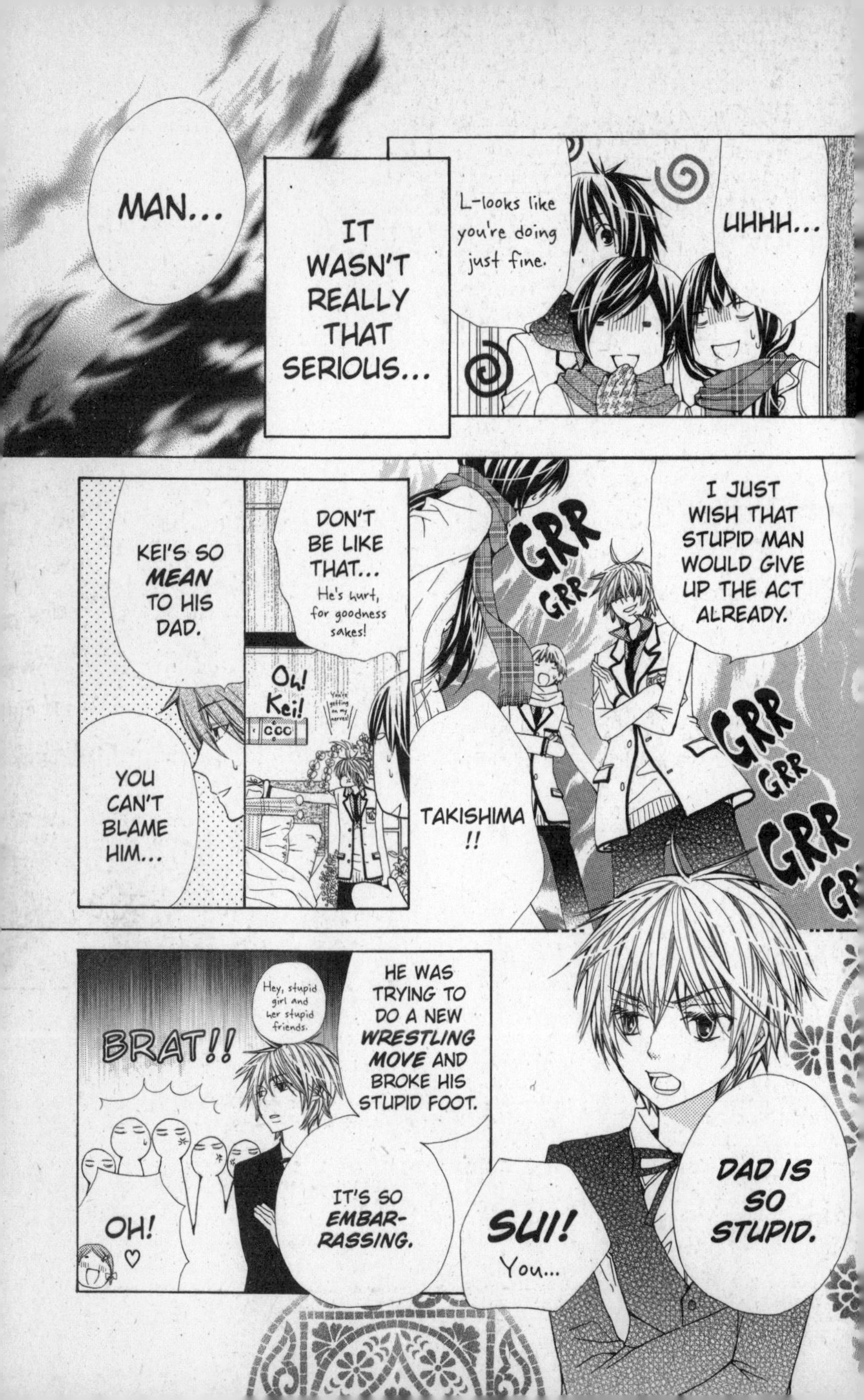
UHHH...
L-looks like you're doing just fine.
IT WASN'T REALLY THAT SERIOUS...
MAN...
I JUST WISH THAT STUPID MAN WOULD GIVE UP THE ACT ALREADY.
GRR GRR
GRR GRR
GRR GR
TAKISHIMA!!
DON'T BE LIKE THAT... He's hurt, for goodness sakes!
Oh! Kei!
You're getting on my nerves!
CCC
KEI'S SO MEAN TO HIS DAD.
YOU CAN'T BLAME HIM...
DAD IS SO STUPID.
SUI! You...
HE WAS TRYING TO DO A NEW WRESTLING MOVE AND BROKE HIS STUPID FOOT.
Hey, stupid girl and her stupid friends.
IT'S SO EMBARRASSING.
BRAT!!
OH! ♥

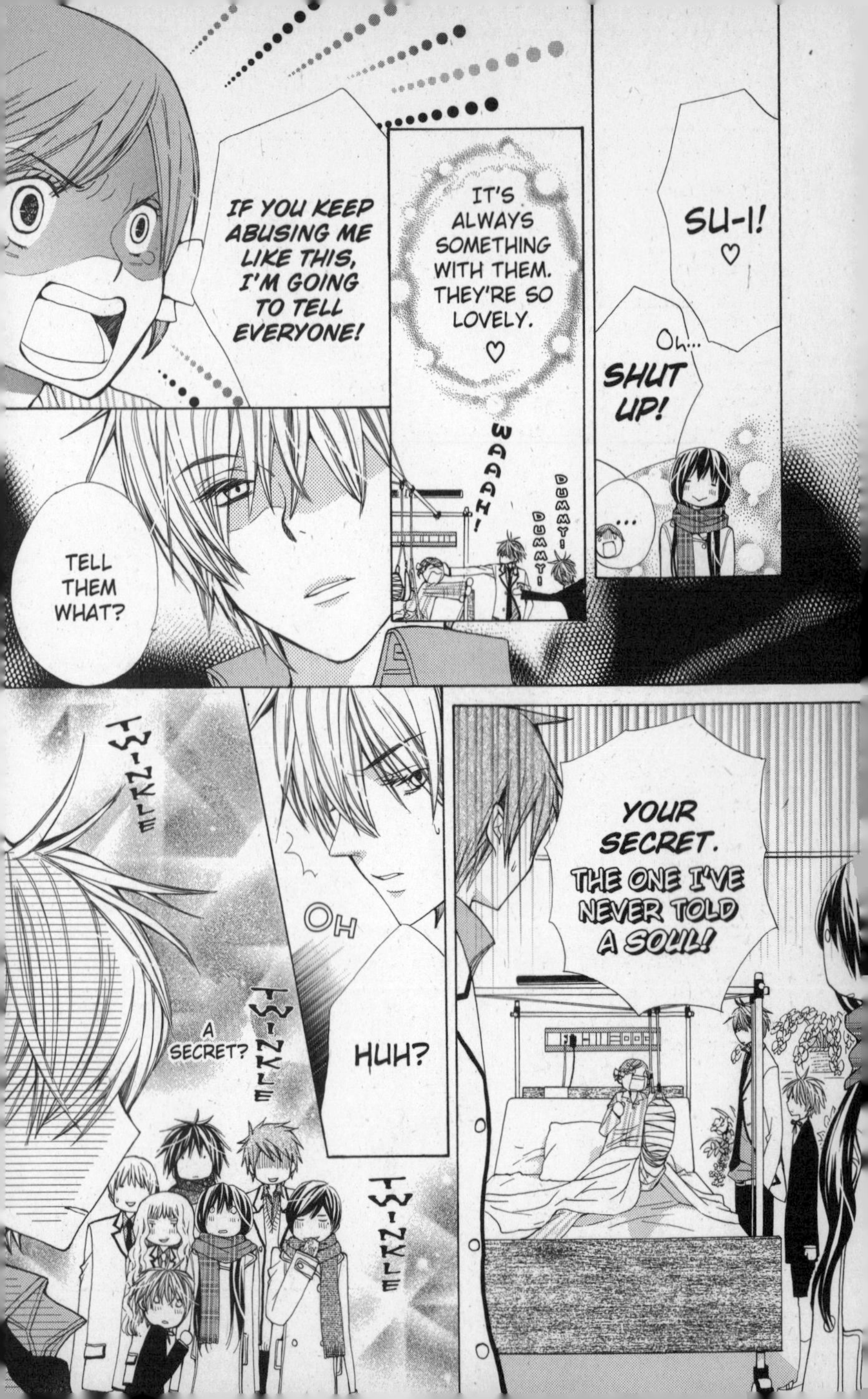
SU-I! ♡
Oh...
SHUT UP!
...
IT'S ALWAYS SOMETHING WITH THEM. THEY'RE SO LOVELY. ♡
WAAAAH!
DUMMY! DUMMY!
IF YOU KEEP ABUSING ME LIKE THIS, I'M GOING TO TELL EVERYONE!
TELL THEM WHAT?
YOUR SECRET. THE ONE I'VE NEVER TOLD A SOUL!
OH
HUH?
TWINKLE
A SECRET?
TWINKLE
TWINKLE

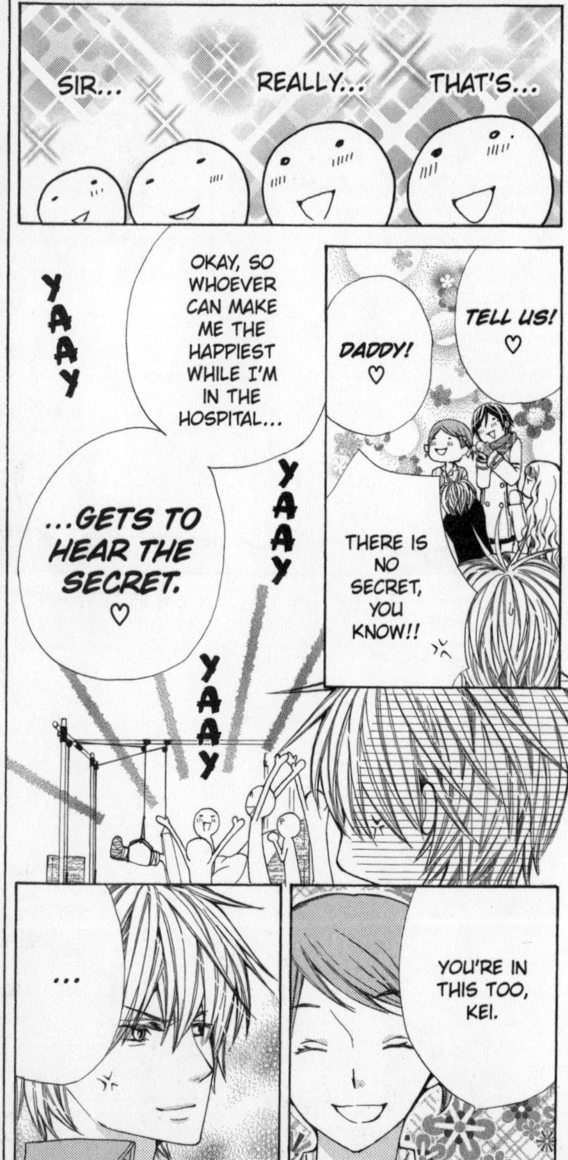

SIR...
REALLY...
THAT'S...
TELL US! ♡
DADDY! ♡
THERE IS NO SECRET, YOU KNOW!!
OKAY, SO WHOEVER CAN MAKE ME THE HAPPIEST WHILE I'M IN THE HOSPITAL...
...GETS TO HEAR THE SECRET. ♡
YAAAY
YAAAY
YAAAY
YOU'RE IN THIS TOO, KEI.
...

⑥

• THIS AND THAT •

• THANK YOU SO MUCH FOR STICKING WITH ME TO THE END OF THE MAIN STORY AND THE LAST QUARTER PAGE!

• THE THEME THIS TIME CAME FROM THE QUESTIONNAIRES THAT THE STAFF GAVE OUT AT THE BOOK SIGNING AT THE BUTLER AND MAID BOOKSTORE IN OSAKA'S KINOKUNIYA. THANK YOU SO, SO MUCH!!

• I LOVE LACE AND RIBBONS.

• THINGS CAN GET REALLY HECTIC IN THE SPRING. BE CAREFUL, EVERYBODY!

• WELL REALLY, THANK YOU SO MUCH FOR READING THIS FAR!!

I HOPE I SEE YOU AGAIN IN VOLUME 14!!

IF YOU'D LIKE TO, LET US KNOW WHAT YOU THINK.

MAKI MINAMI
C/O VIZ MEDIA
SA EDITOR
P.O. BOX 77010
SAN FRANCISCO, CA 94107

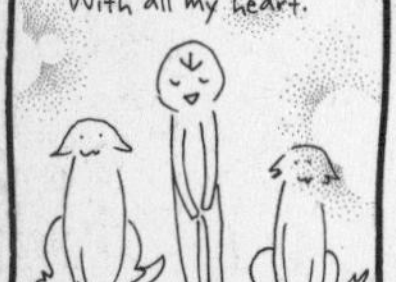

With all my heart.

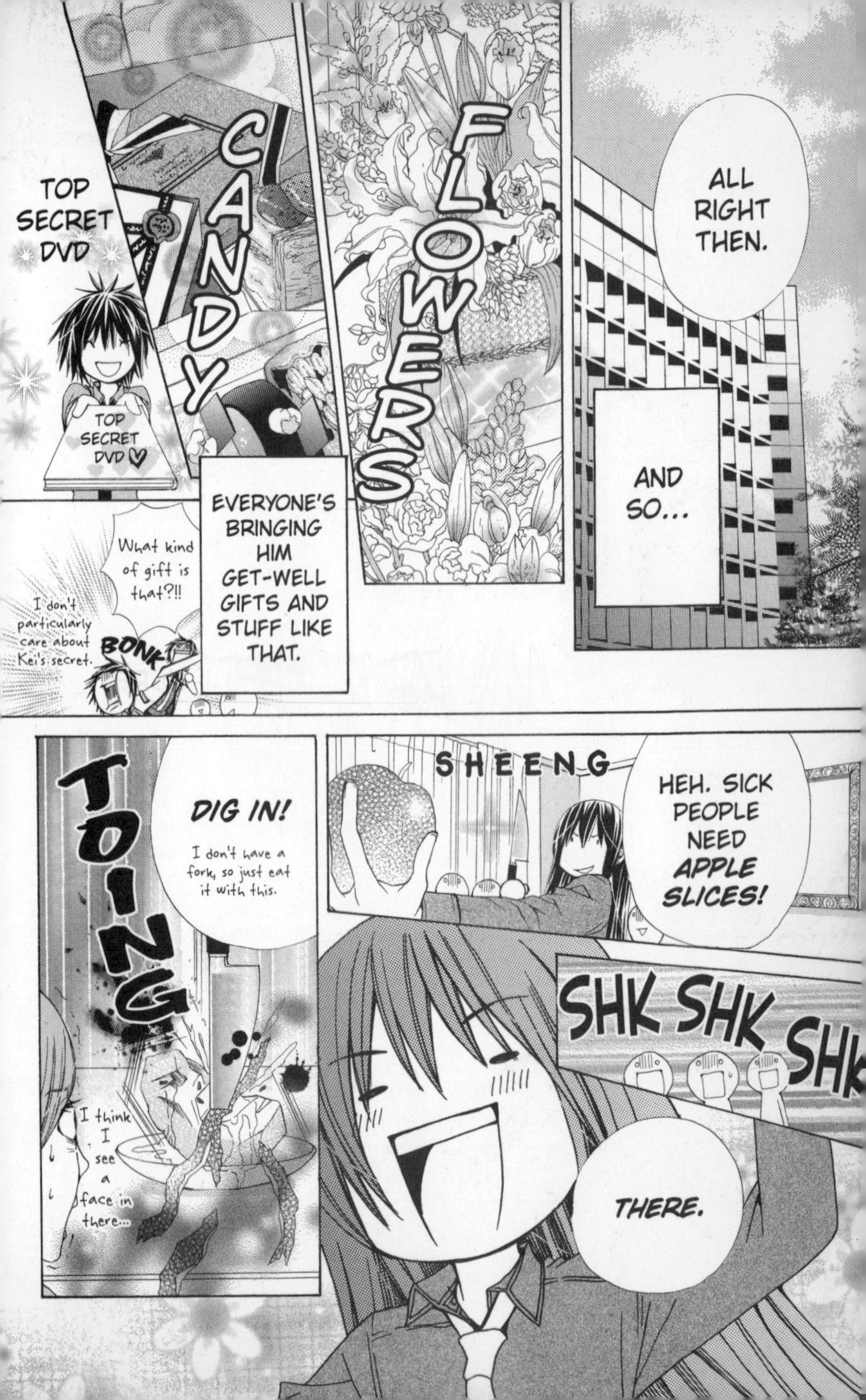
ALL RIGHT THEN.
AND SO...
FLOWERS
EVERYONE'S BRINGING HIM GET-WELL GIFTS AND STUFF LIKE THAT.
CANDY
TOP SECRET DVD
TOP SECRET DVD
What kind of gift is that?!!
BONK
I don't particularly care about Kei's secret.
SHEENG
HEH. SICK PEOPLE NEED APPLE SLICES!
SHK SHK SHK
THERE.
TOING
DIG IN!
I don't have a fork, so just eat it with this.
I think I see a face in there...

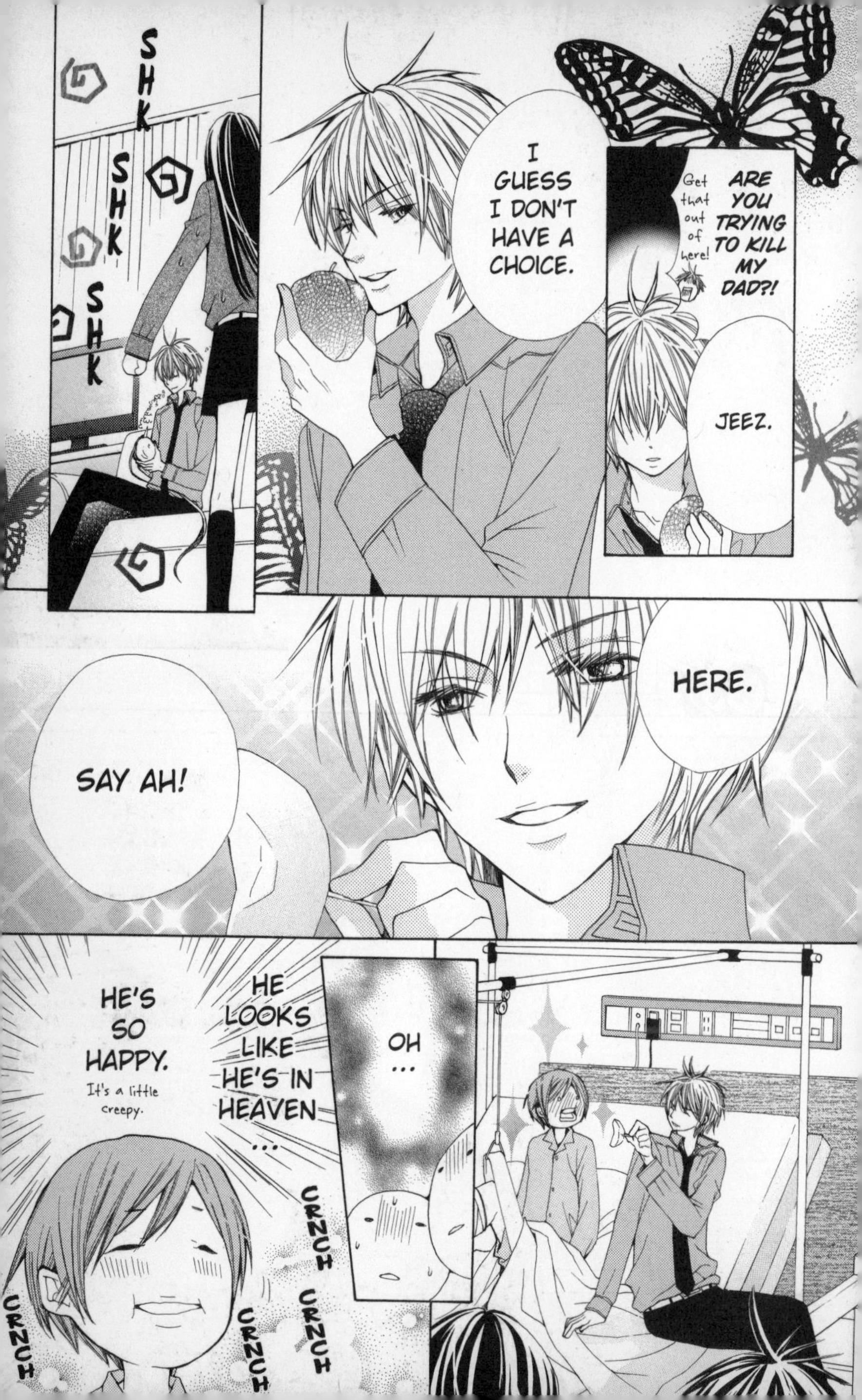
ARE YOU TRYING TO KILL MY DAD?!
Get that out of here!
JEEZ.
I GUESS I DON'T HAVE A CHOICE.
SHK
SHK
SHK
HERE.
SAY AH!
OH...
HE LOOKS LIKE HE'S IN HEAVEN...
HE'S SO HAPPY.
It's a little creepy.
CRNCH
CRNCH
CRNCH
CRNCH

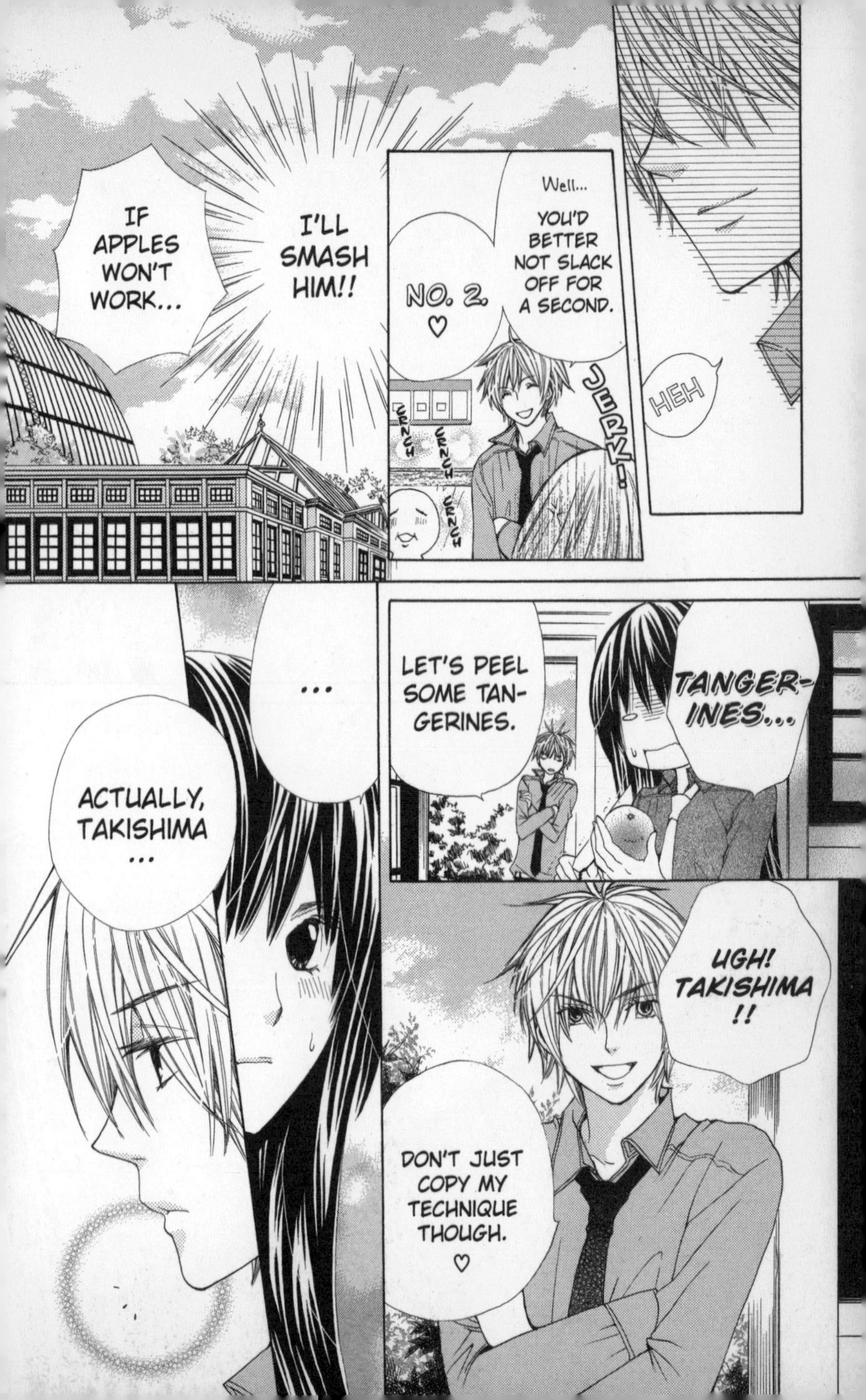
HEH
Well...
YOU'D BETTER NOT SLACK OFF FOR A SECOND.
NO. 2. ♡
JERK!
CRNCH
CRNCH
CRNCH
IF APPLES WON'T WORK...
I'LL SMASH HIM!!
TANGER-INES...
LET'S PEEL SOME TAN-GERINES.
UGH! TAKISHIMA!!
DON'T JUST COPY MY TECHNIQUE THOUGH. ♡
...
ACTUALLY, TAKISHIMA ...

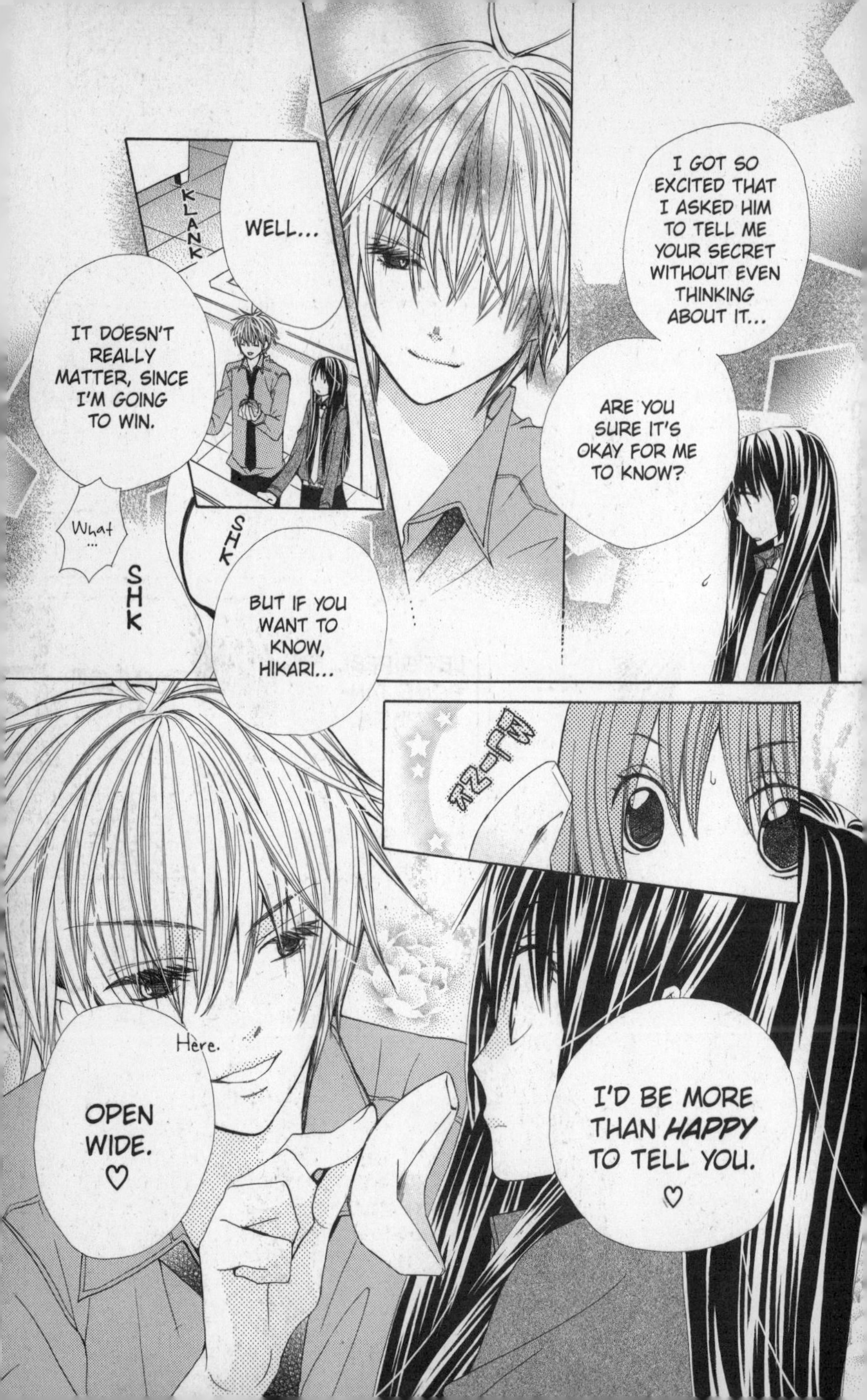

I GOT SO EXCITED THAT I ASKED HIM TO TELL ME YOUR SECRET WITHOUT EVEN THINKING ABOUT IT...
ARE YOU SURE IT'S OKAY FOR ME TO KNOW?
WELL...
KLANK
IT DOESN'T REALLY MATTER, SINCE I'M GOING TO WIN.
What...
SHK
SHK
BUT IF YOU WANT TO KNOW, HIKARI...
I'D BE MORE THAN ***HAPPY*** TO TELL YOU. ♡
Here.
OPEN WIDE. ♡

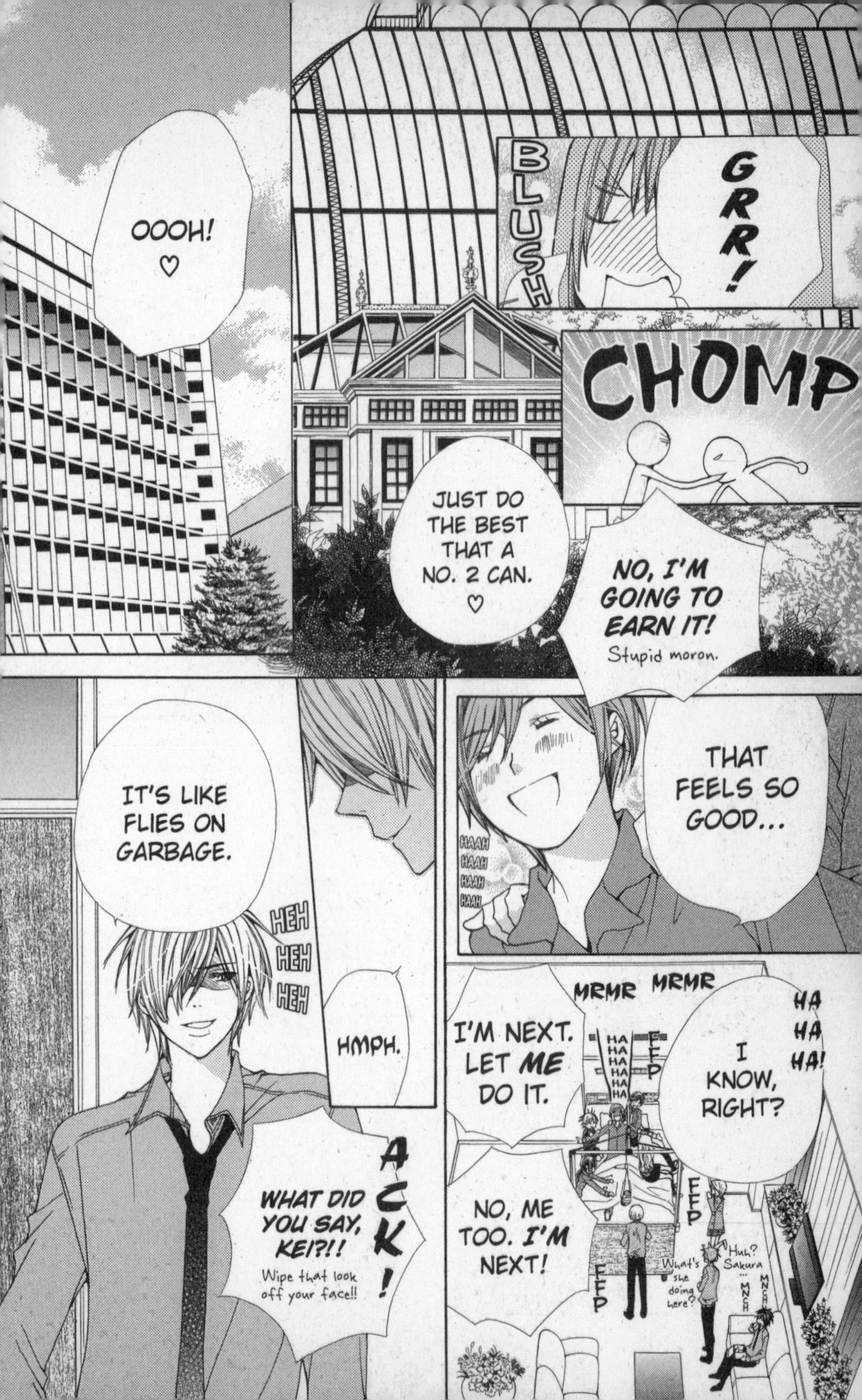
GRR!
BLUSH
CHOMP
JUST DO THE BEST THAT A NO. 2 CAN. ♡
NO, I'M GOING TO EARN IT!
Stupid moron.
OOOH! ♡
THAT FEELS SO GOOD...
HAAH HAAH HAAH HAAH
HA HA HA!
I KNOW, RIGHT?
MRMR MRMR
I'M NEXT. LET ME DO IT.
HA HA HA HA HA HA HA
FFP
FFP
NO, ME TOO. I'M NEXT!
FFP
Huh? Sakura...
What's she doing here?
MNCH MNCH
IT'S LIKE FLIES ON GARBAGE.
HEH HEH HEH
HMPH.
ACK!
WHAT DID YOU SAY, KEI?!!
Wipe that look off your face!!

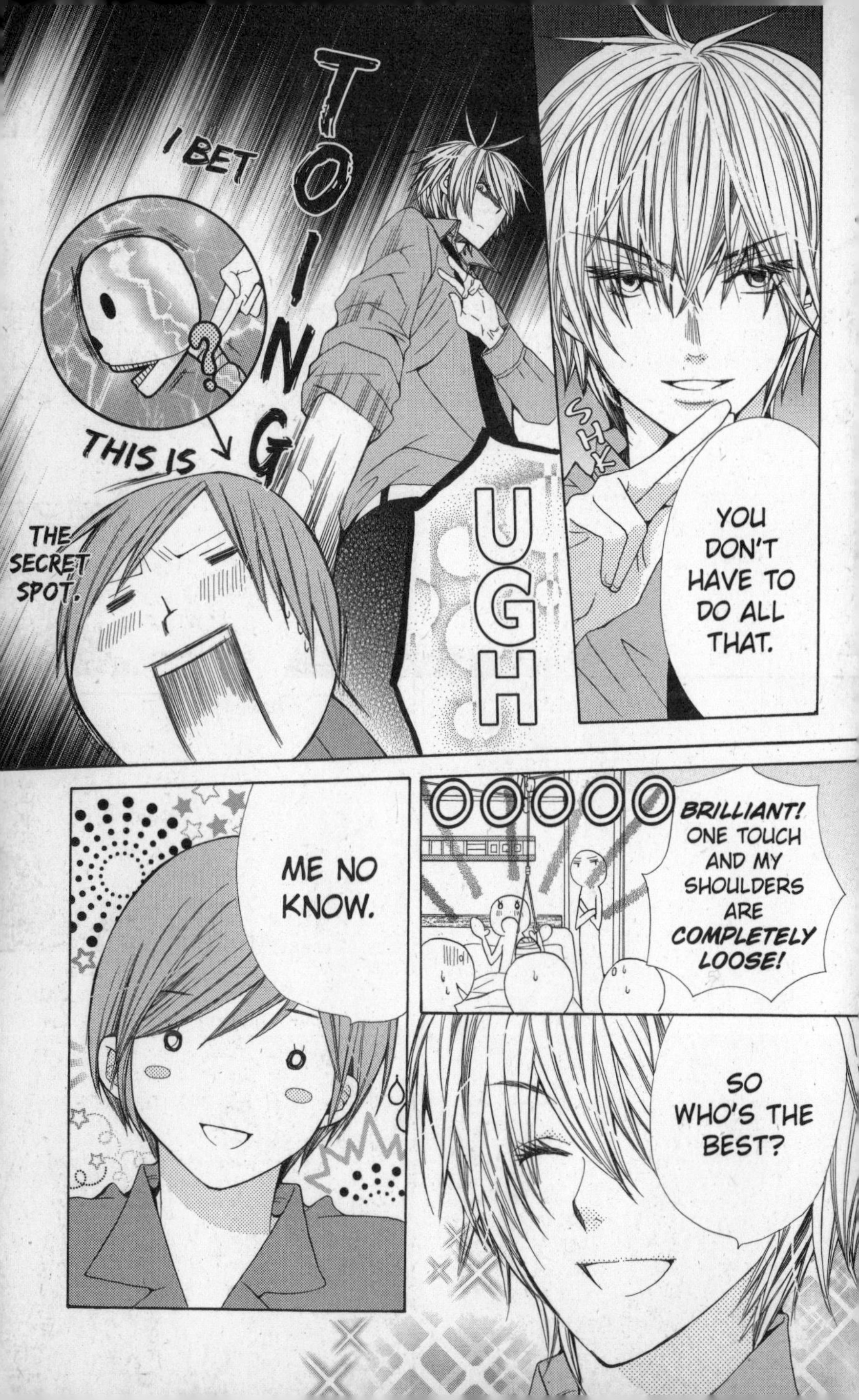
SHK
YOU DON'T HAVE TO DO ALL THAT.
TOING
UGH
I BET
THIS IS
THE SECRET SPOT.
OOOOO
BRILLIANT! ONE TOUCH AND MY SHOULDERS ARE COMPLETELY LOOSE!
SO WHO'S THE BEST?
ME NO KNOW.

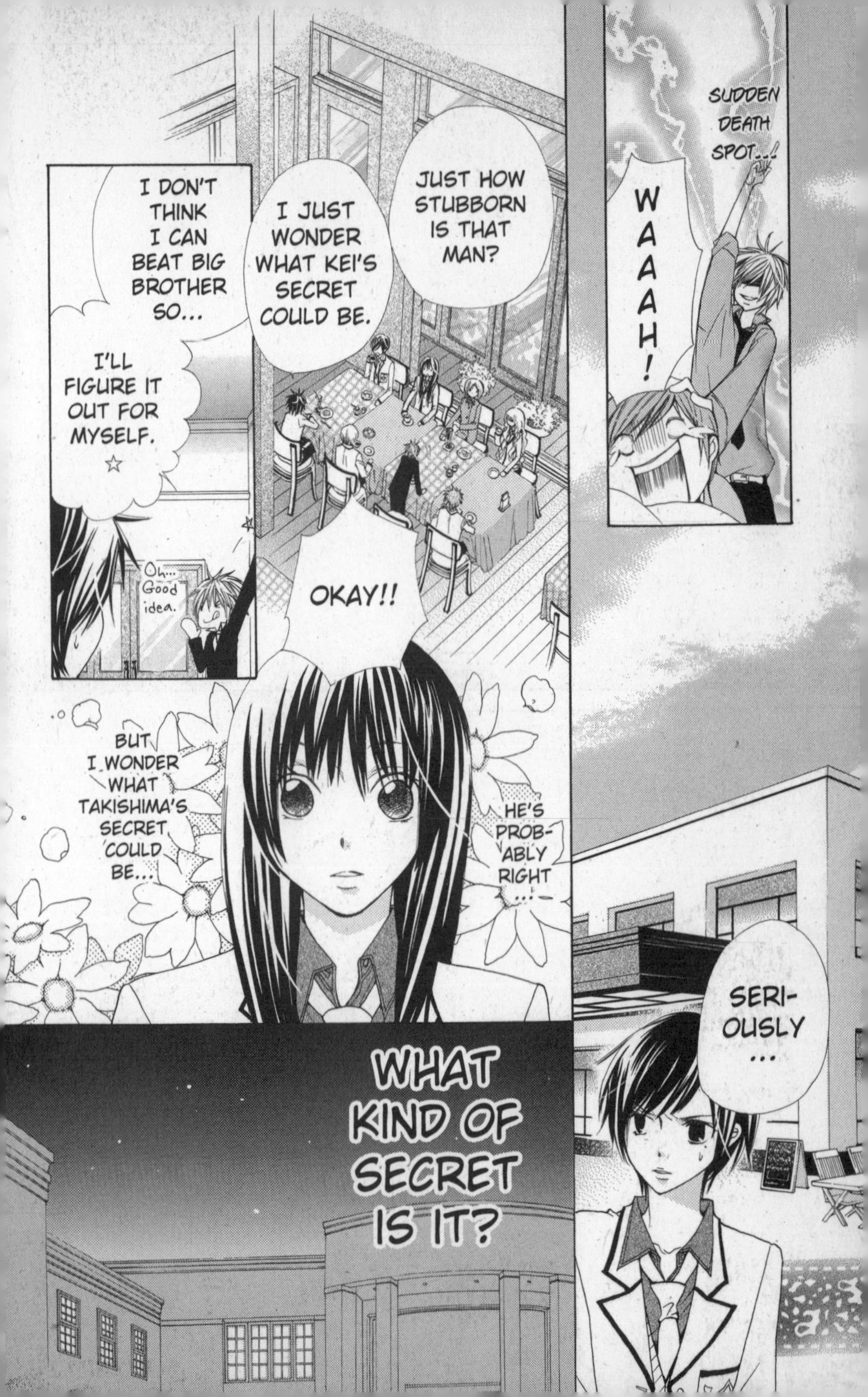
SUDDEN DEATH SPOT...!
WAAAAH!
JUST HOW STUBBORN IS THAT MAN?
I JUST WONDER WHAT KEI'S SECRET COULD BE.
OKAY!!
I DON'T THINK I CAN BEAT BIG BROTHER SO...
I'LL FIGURE IT OUT FOR MYSELF. ☆
Oh... Good idea.
SERI-OUSLY...
HE'S PROB-ABLY RIGHT...
BUT I WONDER WHAT TAKISHIMA'S SECRET COULD BE...
WHAT KIND OF SECRET IS IT?

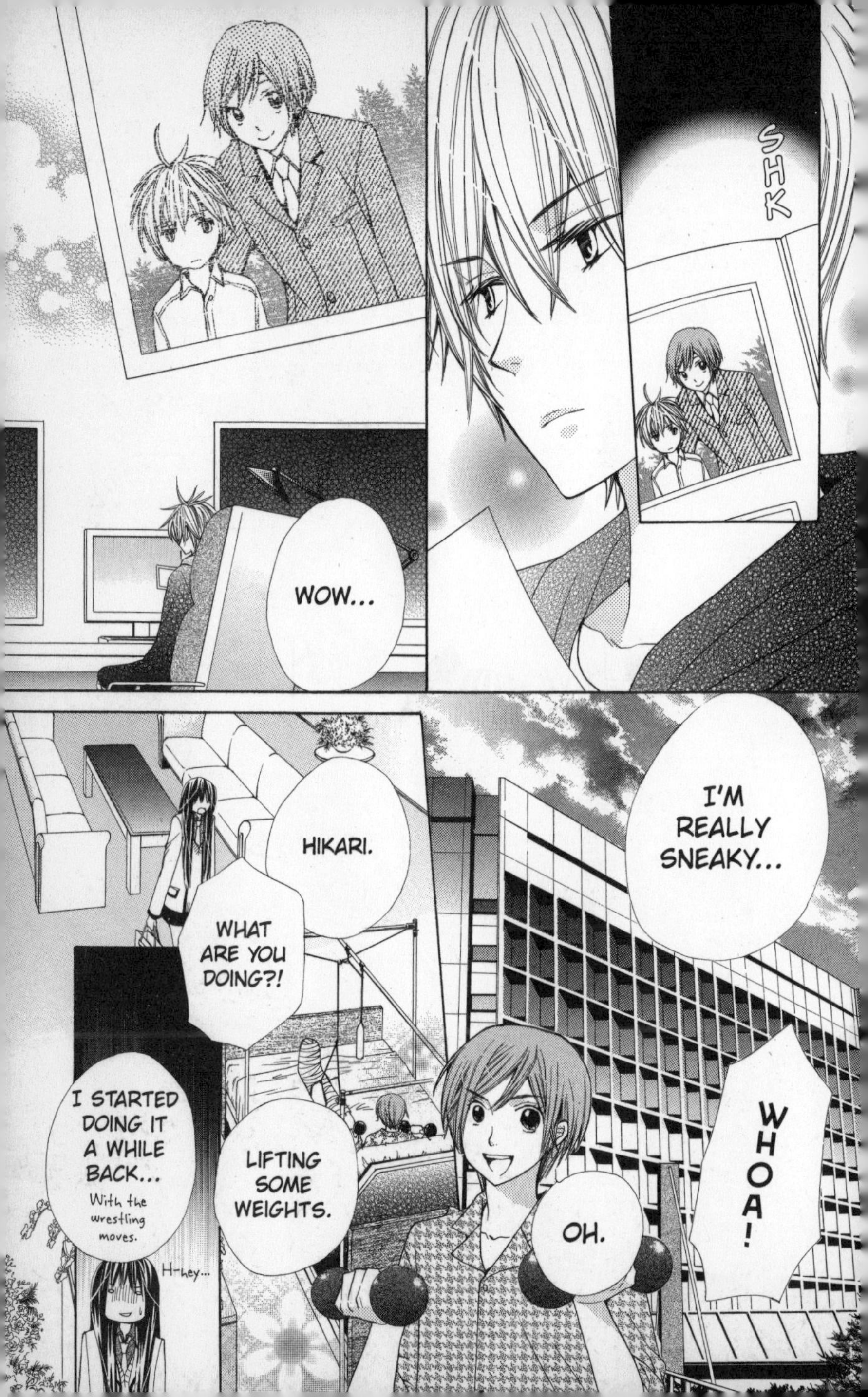
SHK
WOW...
I'M REALLY SNEAKY...
HIKARI.
WHAT ARE YOU DOING?!
WHOA!
OH.
LIFTING SOME WEIGHTS.
I STARTED DOING IT A WHILE BACK...
With the wrestling moves.
H-hey...

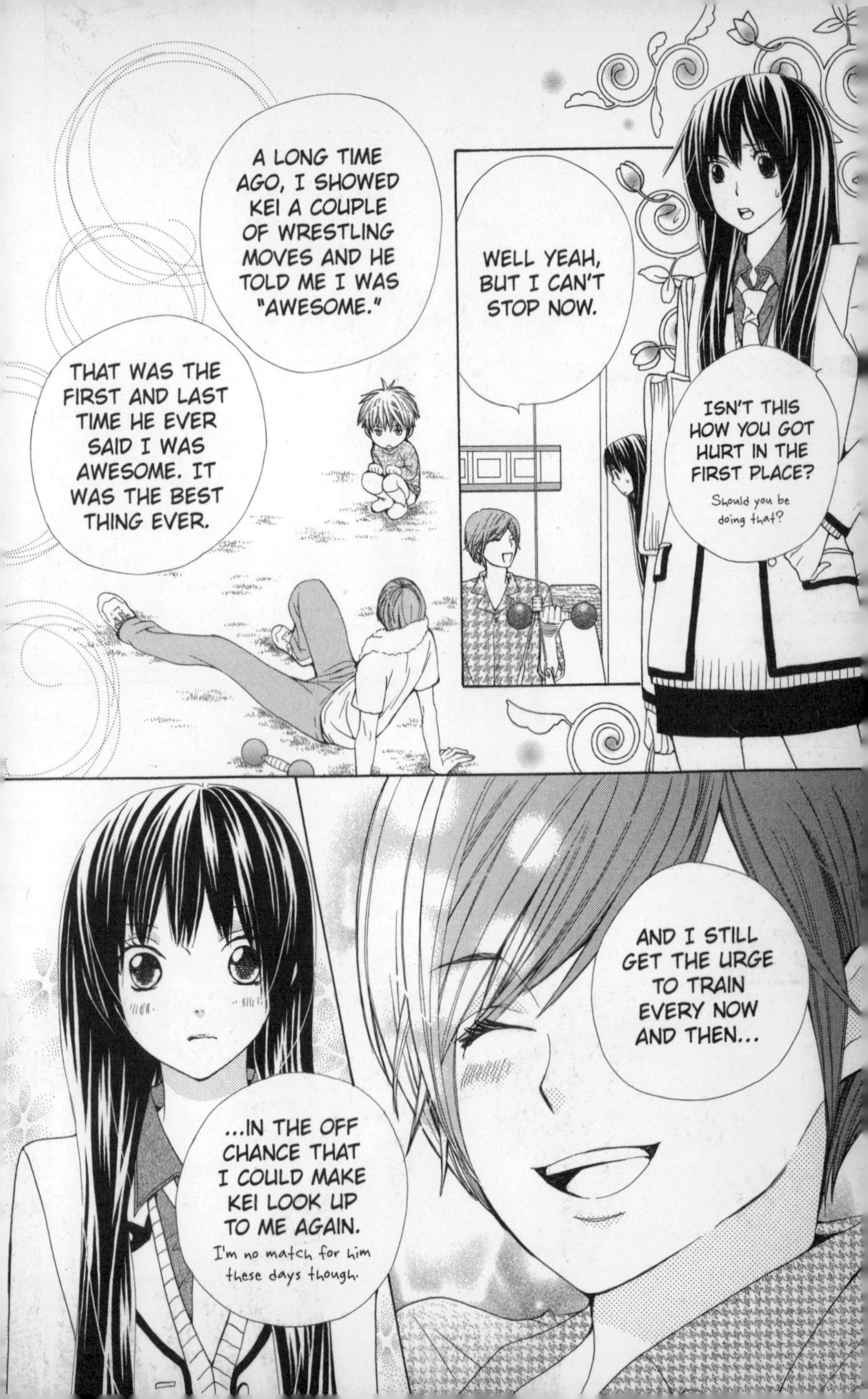
ISN'T THIS HOW YOU GOT HURT IN THE FIRST PLACE?
Should you be doing that?
WELL YEAH, BUT I CAN'T STOP NOW.
A LONG TIME AGO, I SHOWED KEI A COUPLE OF WRESTLING MOVES AND HE TOLD ME I WAS "AWESOME."
THAT WAS THE FIRST AND LAST TIME HE EVER SAID I WAS AWESOME. IT WAS THE BEST THING EVER.
AND I STILL GET THE URGE TO TRAIN EVERY NOW AND THEN...
...IN THE OFF CHANCE THAT I COULD MAKE KEI LOOK UP TO ME AGAIN.
I'm no match for him these days though.

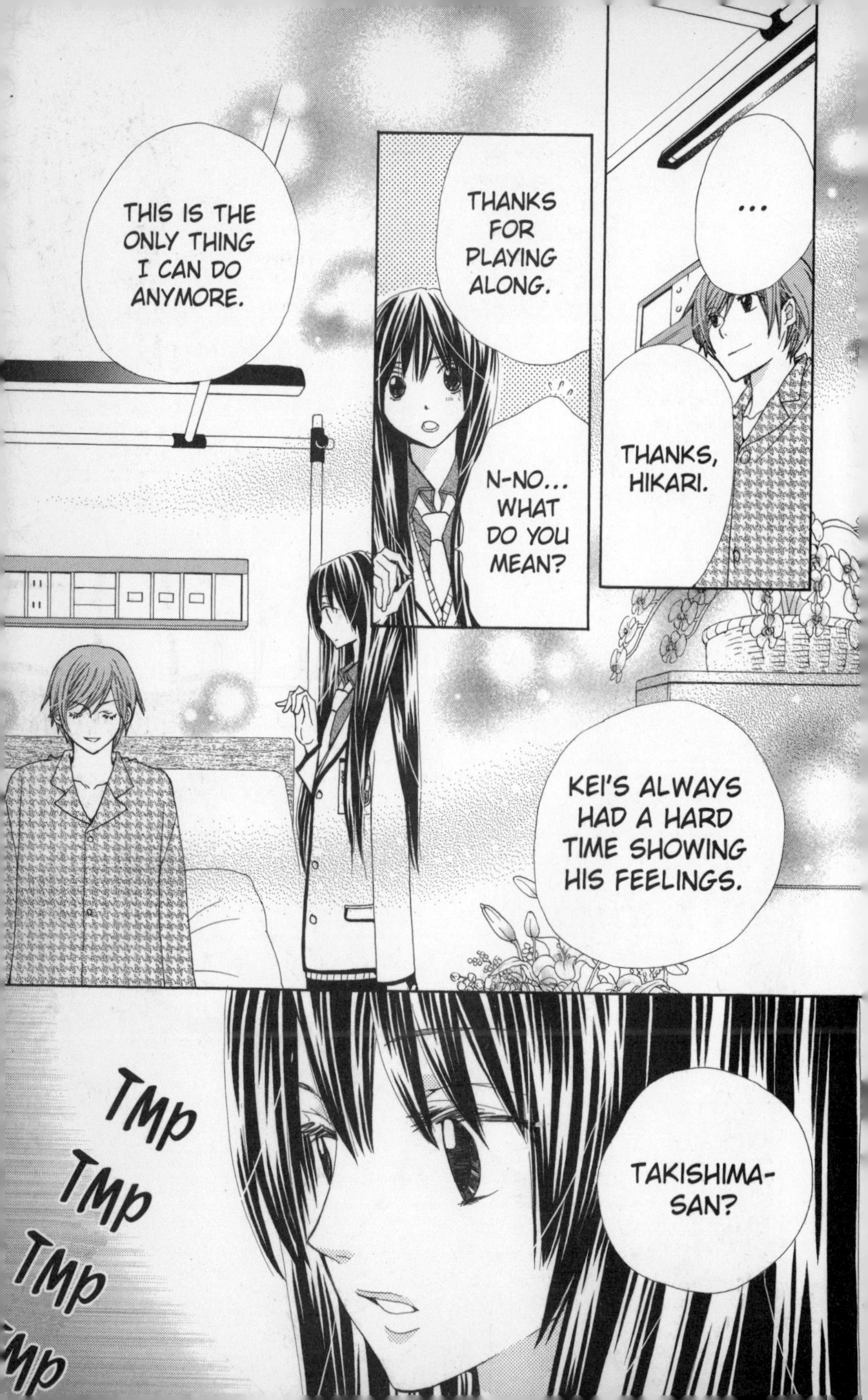
...
THANKS, HIKARI.
THANKS FOR PLAYING ALONG.
N-NO... WHAT DO YOU MEAN?
THIS IS THE ONLY THING I CAN DO ANYMORE.
KEI'S ALWAYS HAD A HARD TIME SHOWING HIS FEELINGS.
TAKISHIMA-SAN?
TMP
TMP
TMP
TMP

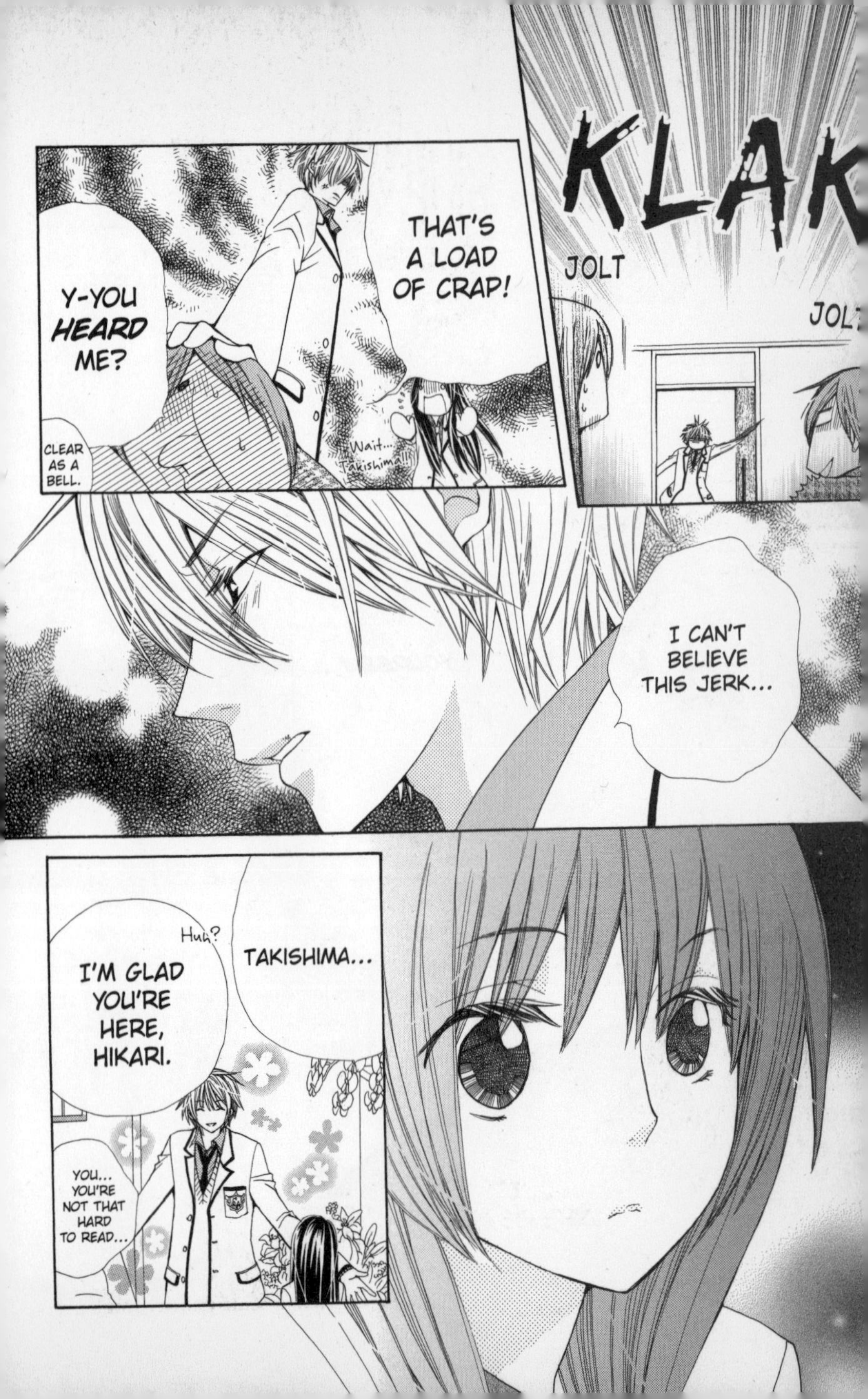
KLAK
JOLT
JOLT
THAT'S A LOAD OF CRAP!
Y-YOU **HEARD** ME?
Wait... Takishima!!
CLEAR AS A BELL.
I CAN'T BELIEVE THIS JERK...
TAKISHIMA...
Huh?
I'M GLAD YOU'RE HERE, HIKARI.
YOU... YOU'RE NOT THAT HARD TO READ...

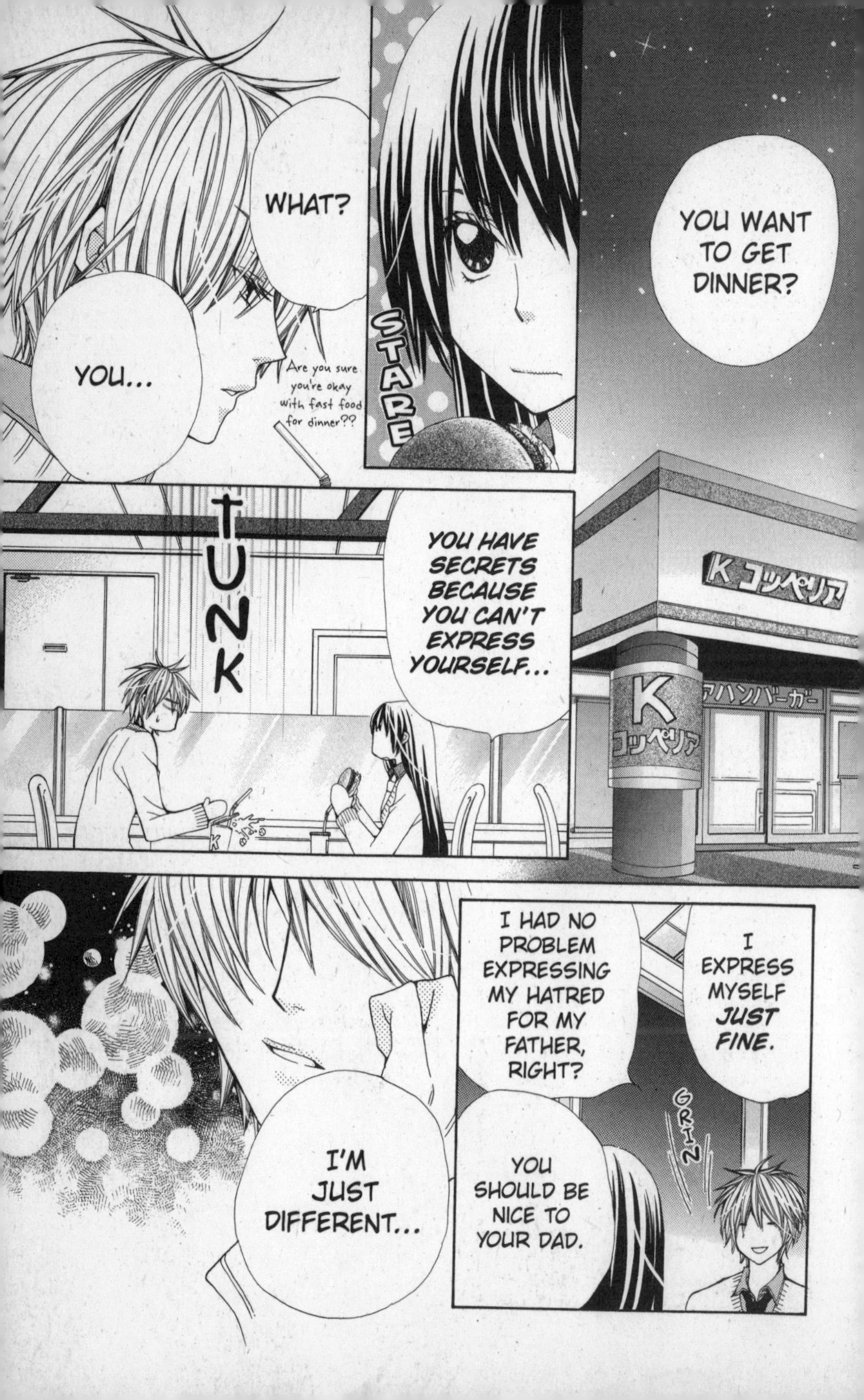
YOU WANT TO GET DINNER?
K コッペリア
K コッペリア
アハンバーガー
STARE
WHAT?
YOU...
Are you sure you're okay with fast food for dinner??
YOU HAVE SECRETS BECAUSE YOU CAN'T EXPRESS YOURSELF...
TUNK
I EXPRESS MYSELF JUST FINE.
I HAD NO PROBLEM EXPRESSING MY HATRED FOR MY FATHER, RIGHT?
GRIN
YOU SHOULD BE NICE TO YOUR DAD.
I'M JUST DIFFERENT...

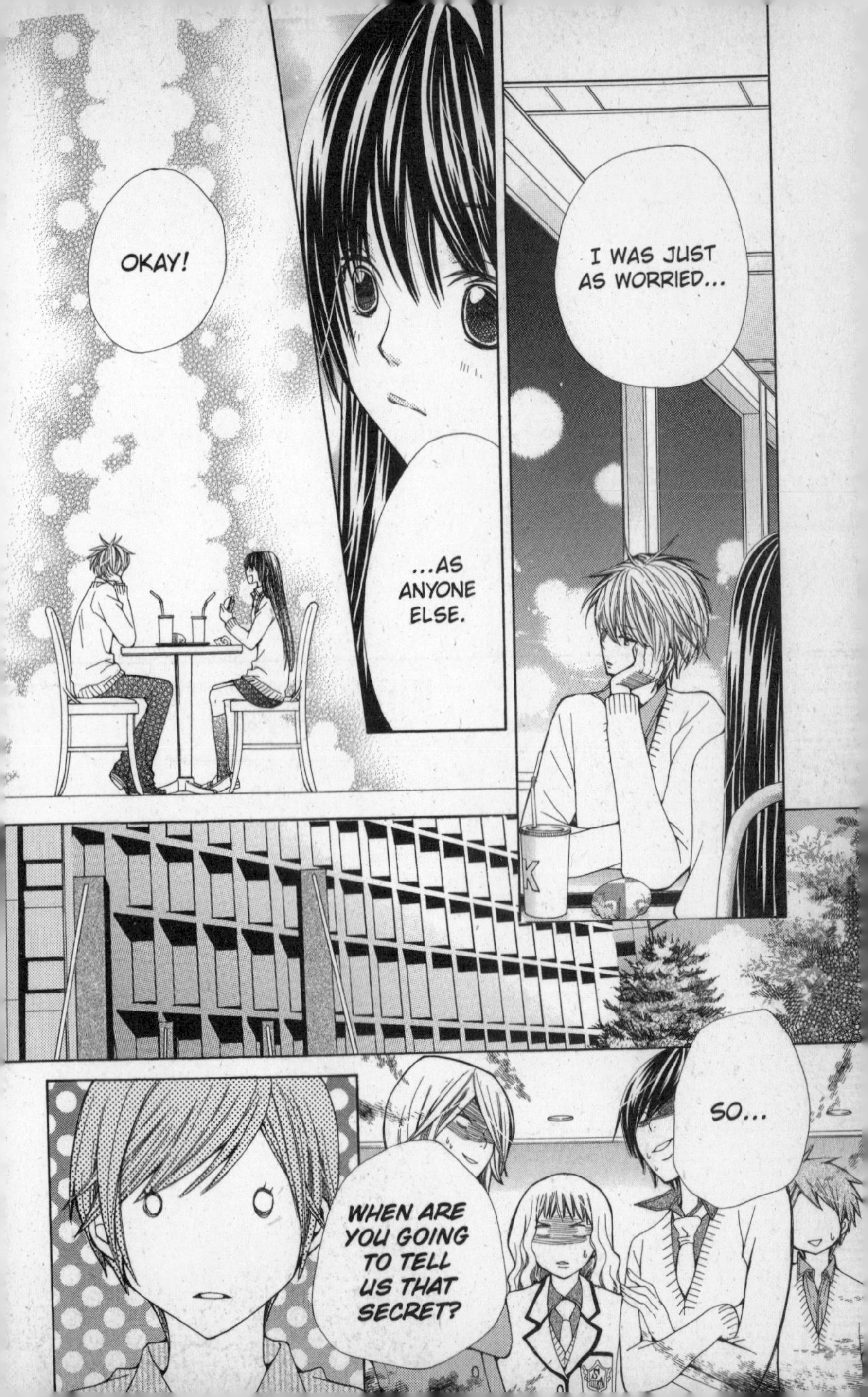
I WAS JUST AS WORRIED...
...AS ANYONE ELSE.
OKAY!
SO...
WHEN ARE YOU GOING TO TELL US THAT SECRET?

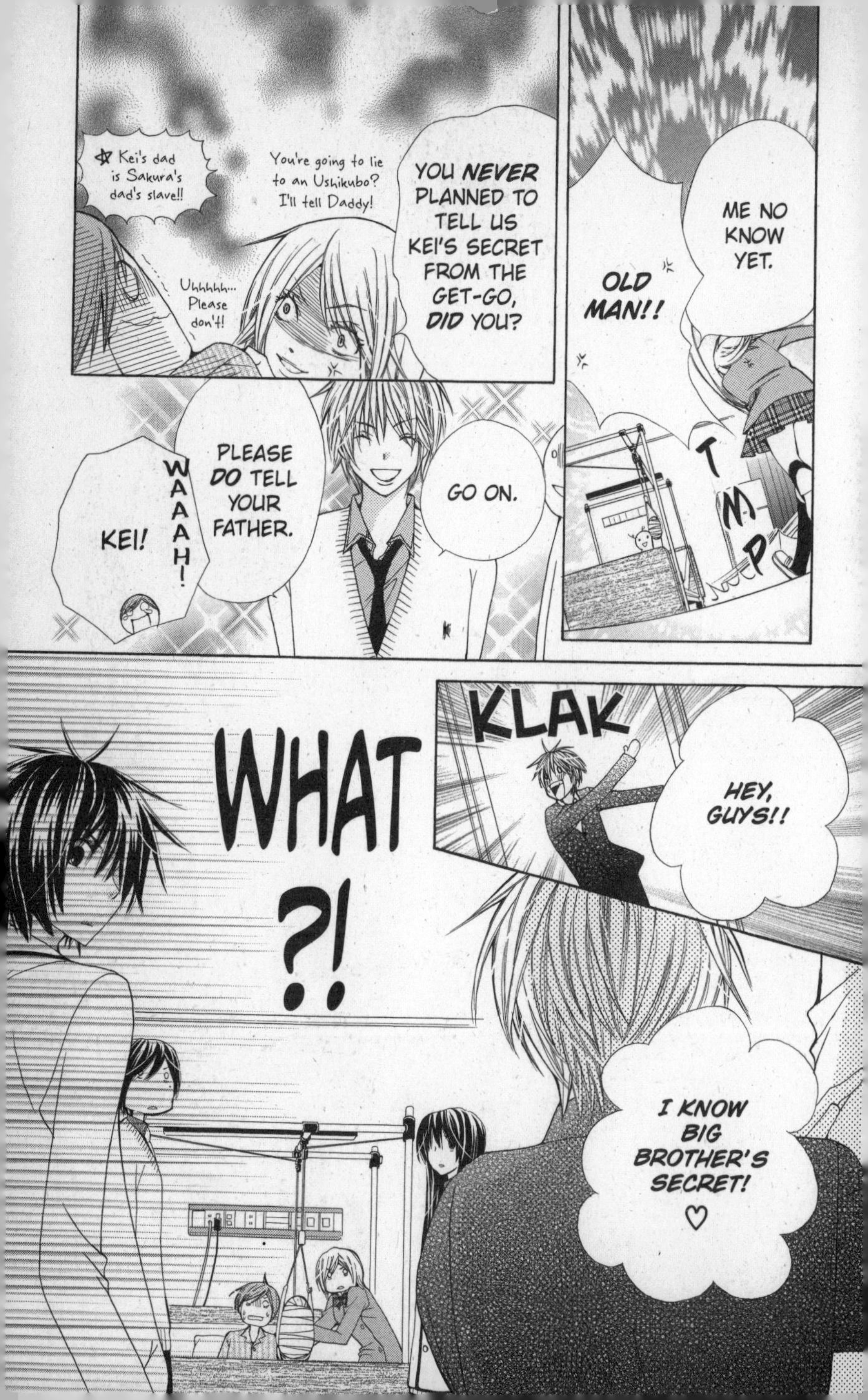
ME NO KNOW YET.
OLD MAN!!
TMP
YOU NEVER PLANNED TO TELL US KEI'S SECRET FROM THE GET-GO, DID YOU?
You're going to lie to an Ushikubo? I'll tell Daddy!
Kei's dad is Sakura's dad's slave!!
Uhhhhh... Please don't!
GO ON.
PLEASE DO TELL YOUR FATHER.
WAAAAH!
KEI!
KLAK
HEY, GUYS!!
I KNOW BIG BROTHER'S SECRET! ♡
WHAT?!

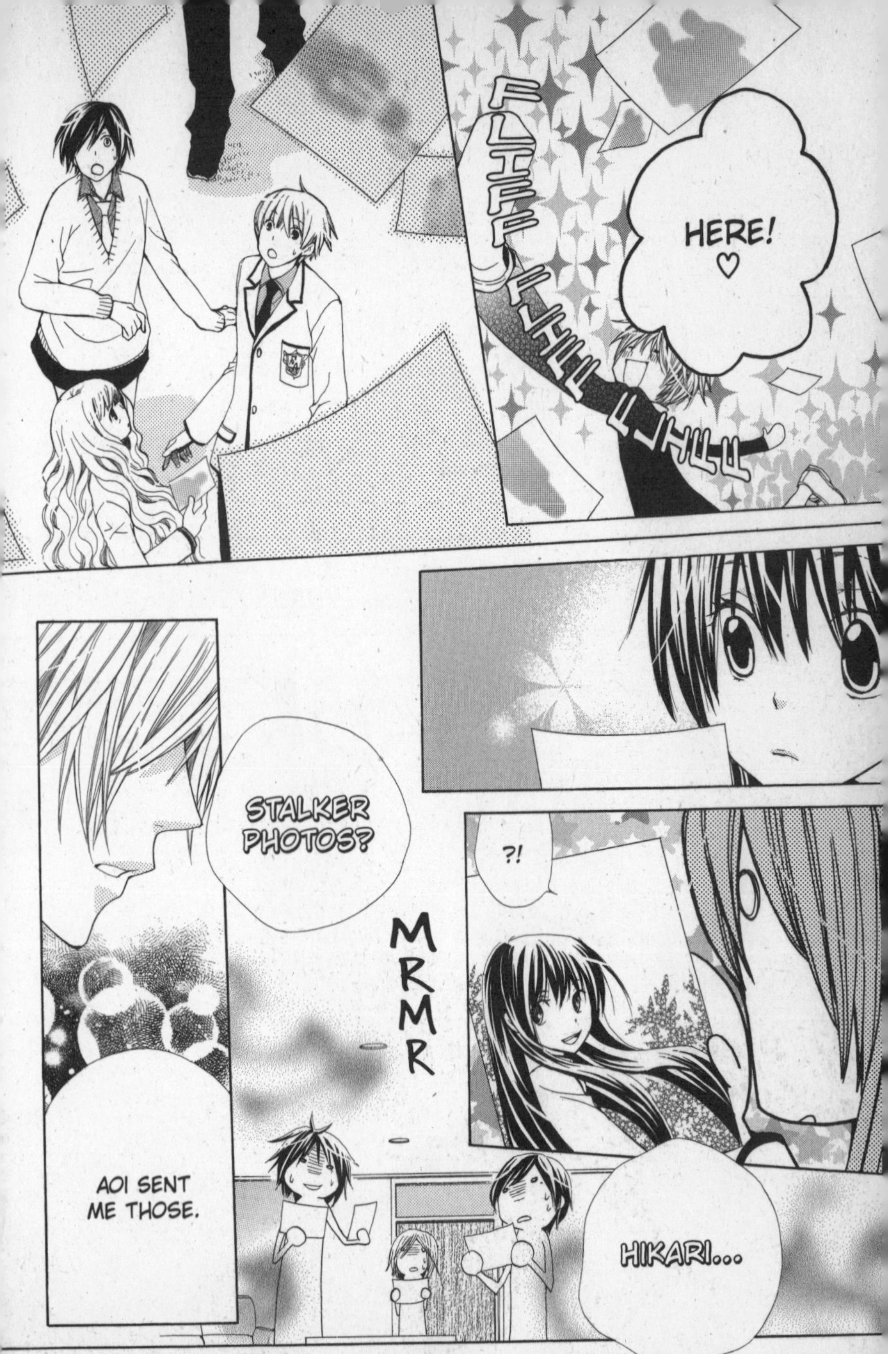
HERE! ♡
FLIFF
FLIFF
FLIFF
?!
HIKARI...
MRMR
STALKER PHOTOS?
AOI SENT ME THOSE.

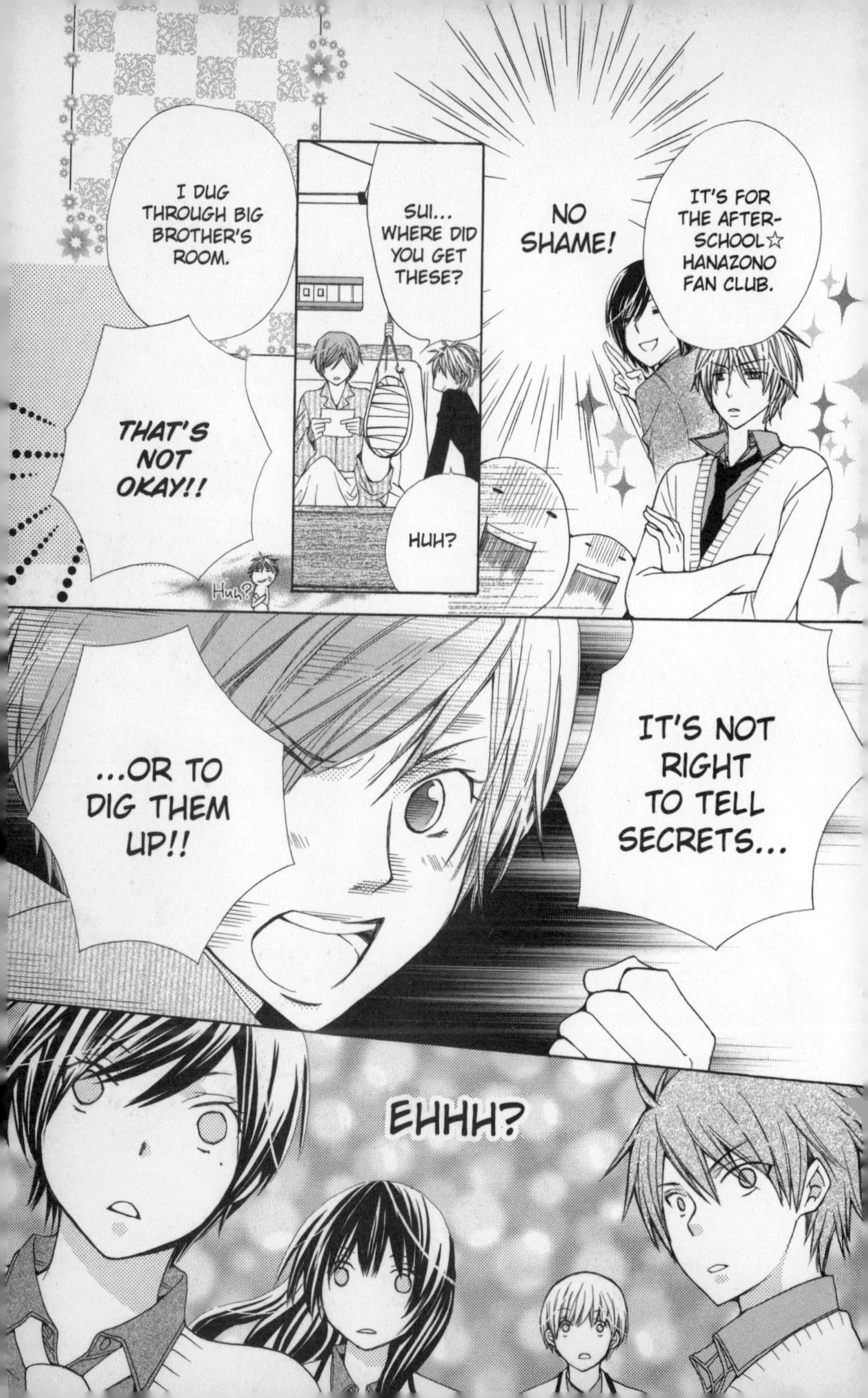
IT'S FOR THE AFTER-SCHOOL☆ HANAZONO FAN CLUB.
NO SHAME!
SUI... WHERE DID YOU GET THESE?
HUH?
I DUG THROUGH BIG BROTHER'S ROOM.
THAT'S NOT OKAY!!
Huh?
IT'S NOT RIGHT TO TELL SECRETS...
...OR TO DIG THEM UP!!
EHHH?

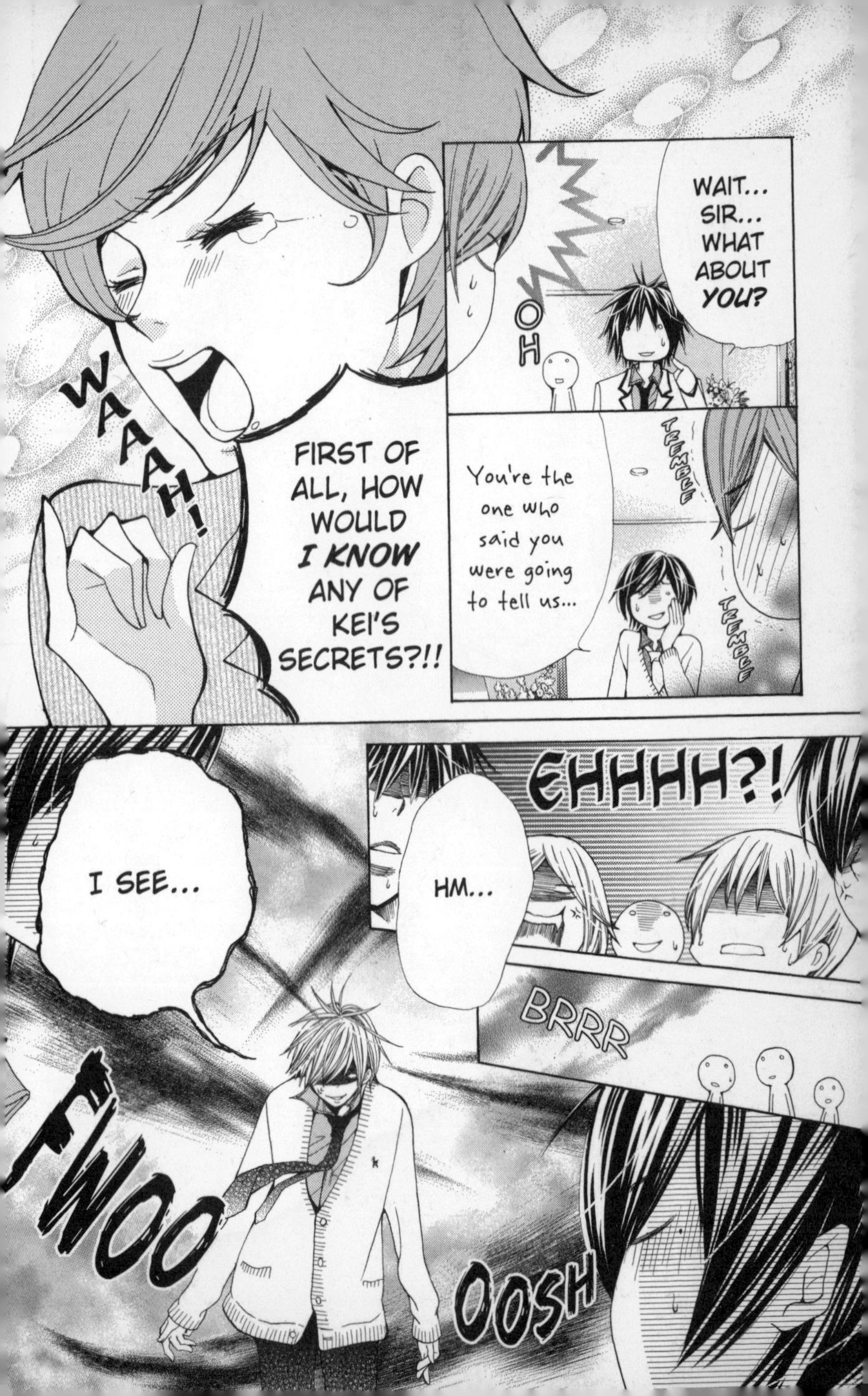
WAIT... SIR... WHAT ABOUT *YOU?*
OH
You're the one who said you were going to tell us...
TREMBLE
TREMBLE
WAAAH!
FIRST OF ALL, HOW WOULD ***I KNOW*** ANY OF KEI'S SECRETS?!!
EHHHH?!
HM...
BRRR
I SEE...
FWOO
OOSH

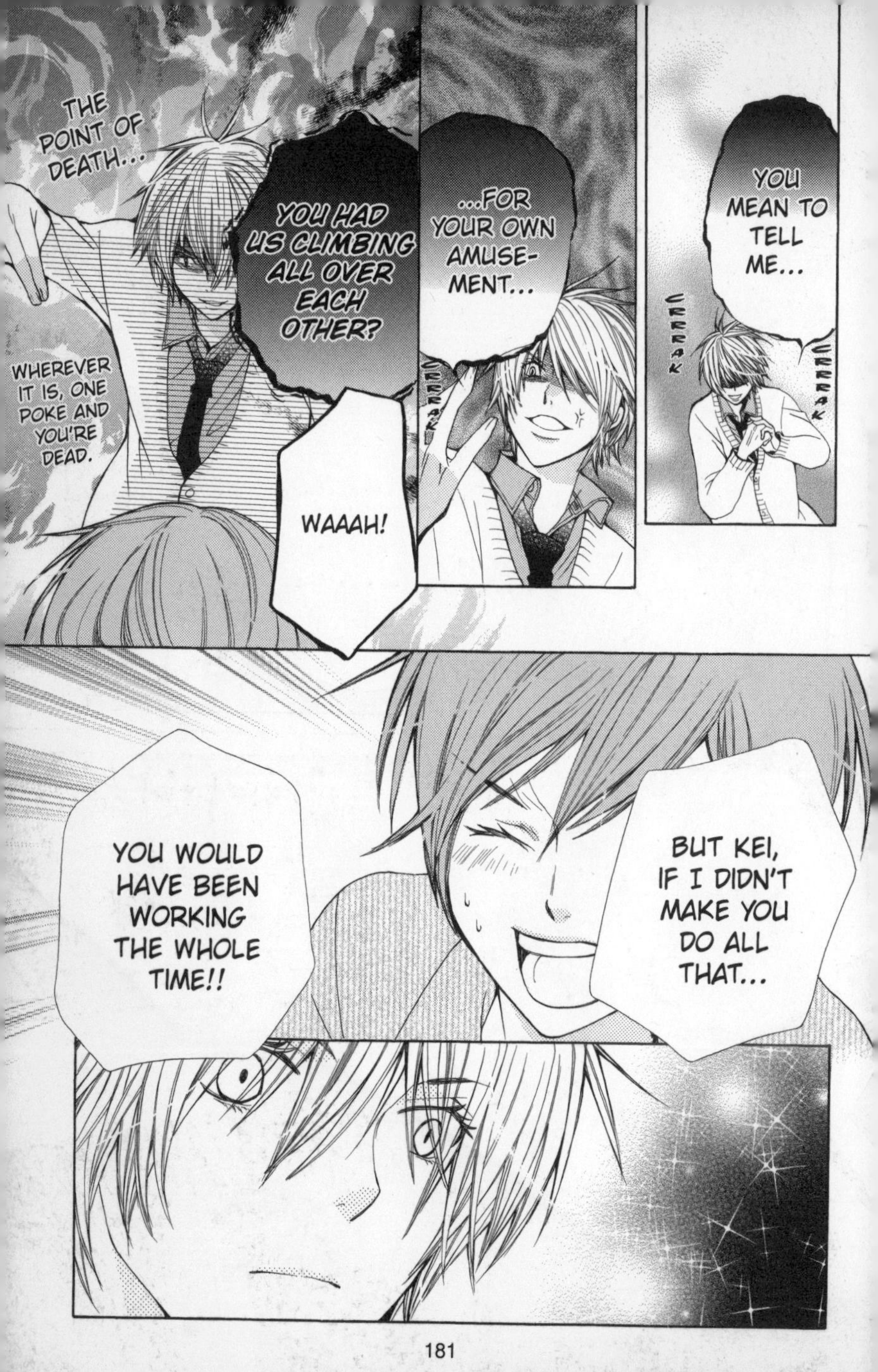

YOU MEAN TO TELL ME...
CRRRAK
CRRRAK
...FOR YOUR OWN AMUSE-MENT...
CRRRAK
YOU HAD US CLIMBING ALL OVER EACH OTHER?
THE POINT OF DEATH...
WAAAH!
WHEREVER IT IS, ONE POKE AND YOU'RE DEAD.
BUT KEI, IF I DIDN'T MAKE YOU DO ALL THAT...
YOU WOULD HAVE BEEN WORKING THE WHOLE TIME!!

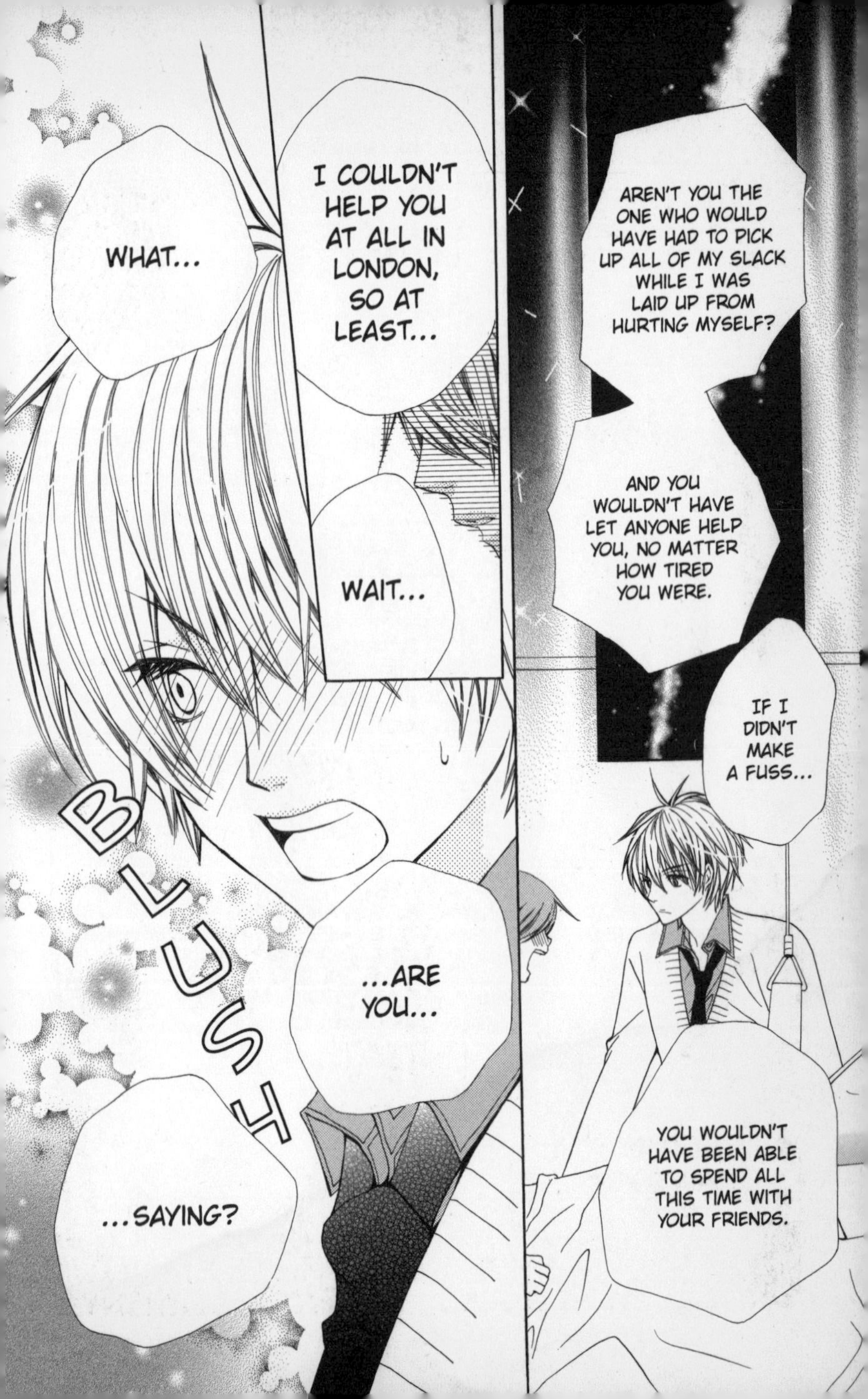
AREN'T YOU THE ONE WHO WOULD HAVE HAD TO PICK UP ALL OF MY SLACK WHILE I WAS LAID UP FROM HURTING MYSELF?
AND YOU WOULDN'T HAVE LET ANYONE HELP YOU, NO MATTER HOW TIRED YOU WERE.
IF I DIDN'T MAKE A FUSS...
YOU WOULDN'T HAVE BEEN ABLE TO SPEND ALL THIS TIME WITH YOUR FRIENDS.
I COULDN'T HELP YOU AT ALL IN LONDON, SO AT LEAST...
WAIT...
WHAT...
BLUSH
...ARE YOU...
...SAYING?

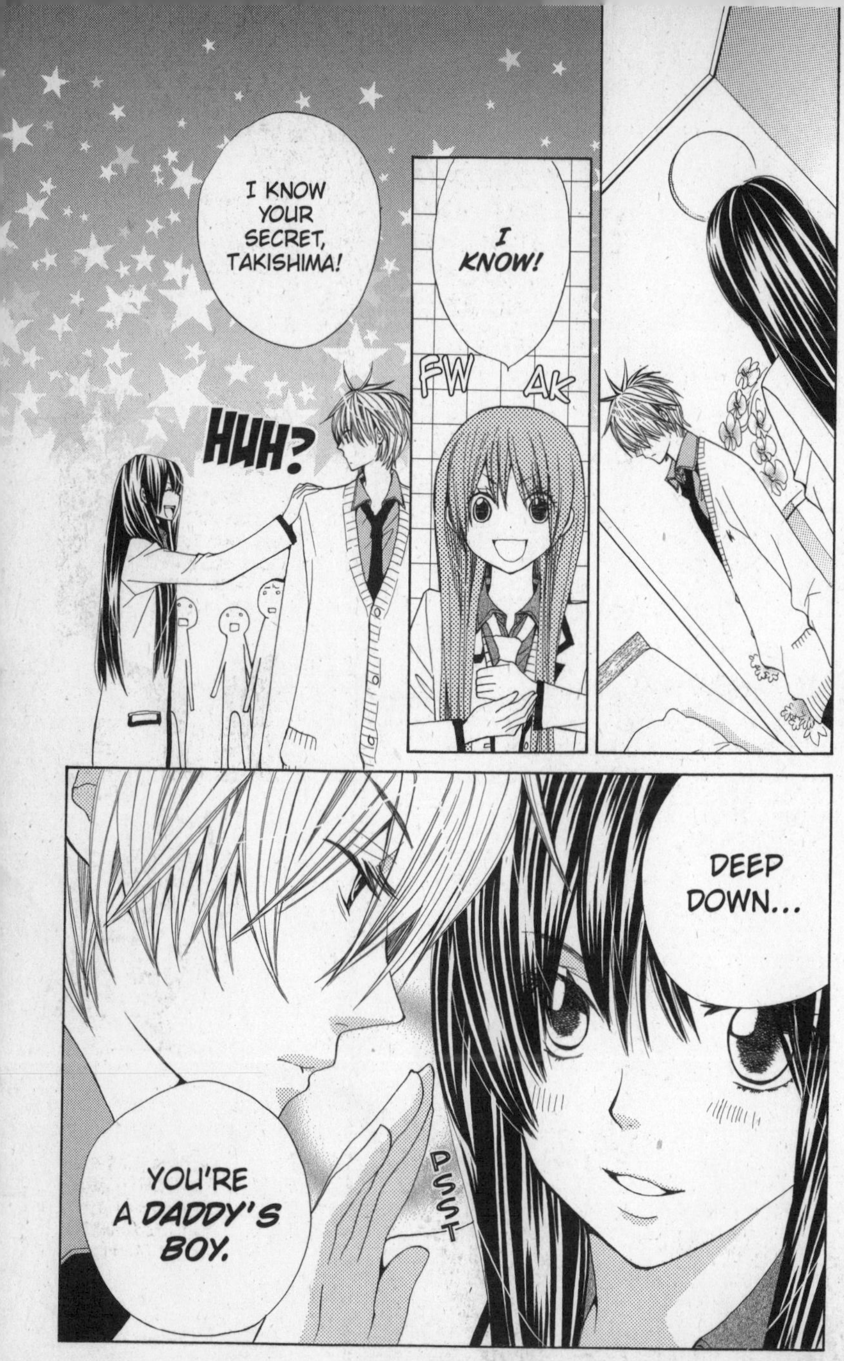
I KNOW!
FW AK
I KNOW YOUR SECRET, TAKISHIMA!
HUH?
DEEP DOWN...
PSST
YOU'RE A DADDY'S BOY.

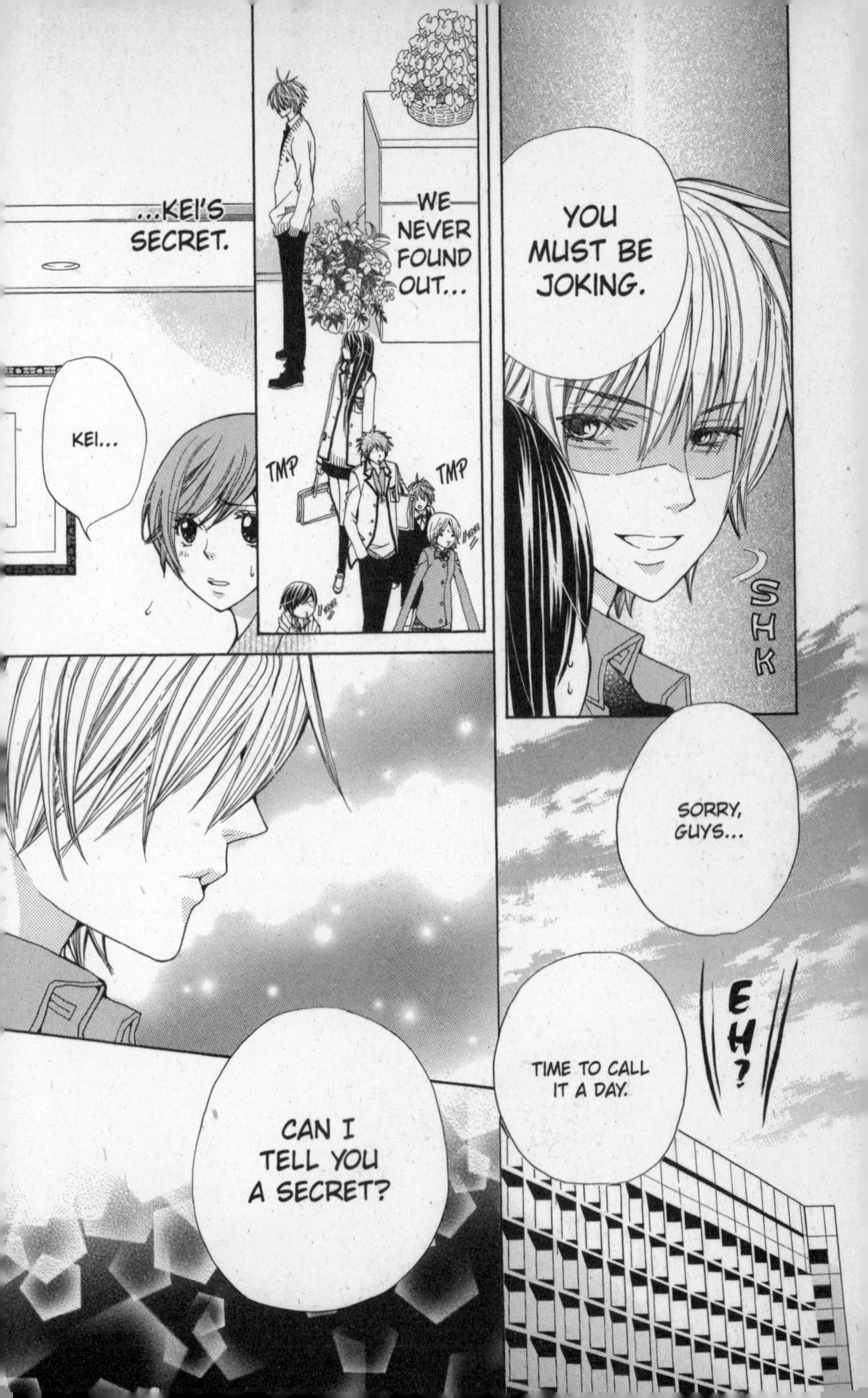
YOU MUST BE JOKING.
SHK
WE NEVER FOUND OUT...
TMP
TMP
...KEI'S SECRET.
KEI...
SORRY, GUYS...
EH?
TIME TO CALL IT A DAY.
CAN I TELL YOU A SECRET?

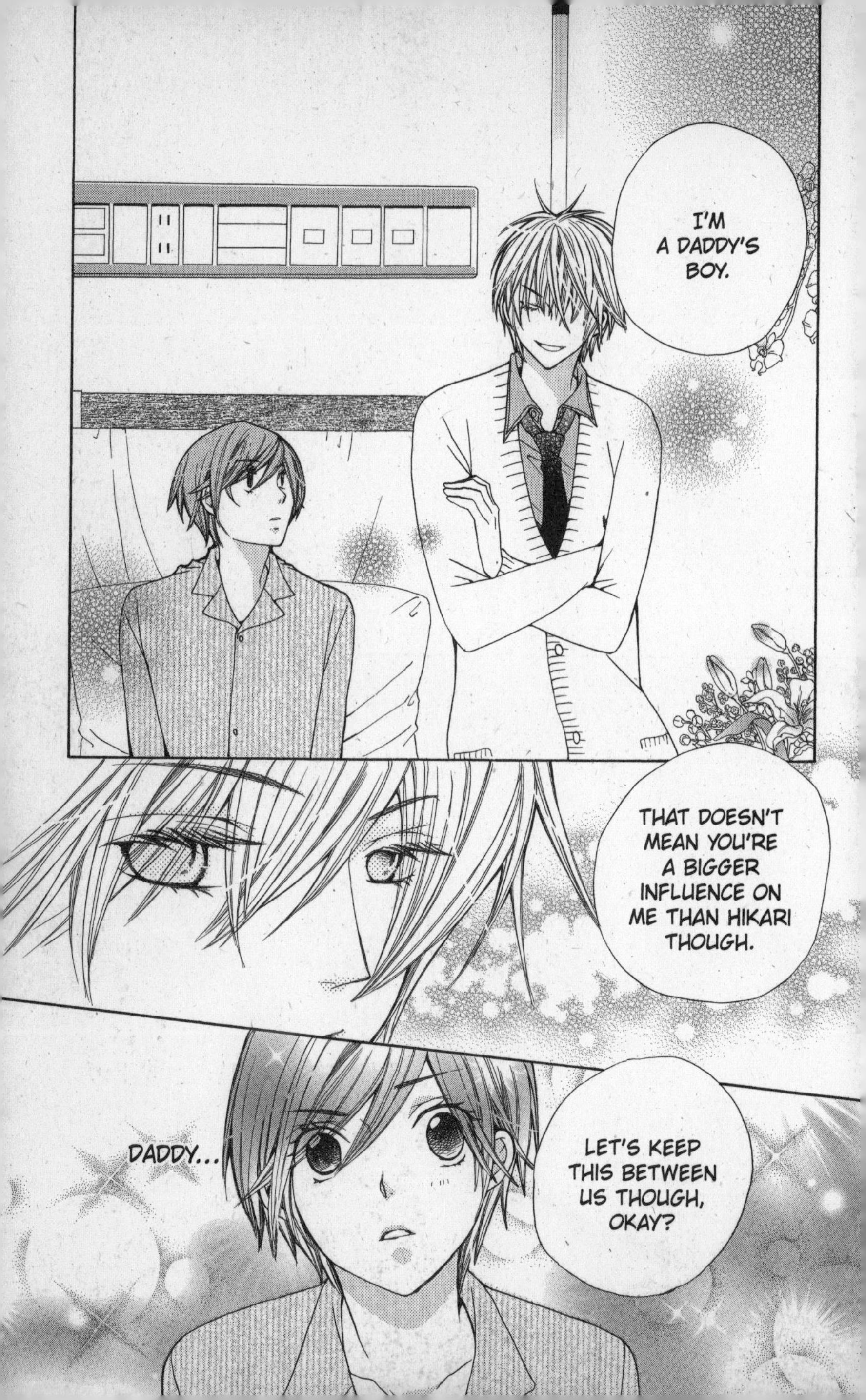
I'M A DADDY'S BOY.
THAT DOESN'T MEAN YOU'RE A BIGGER INFLUENCE ON ME THAN HIKARI THOUGH.
LET'S KEEP THIS BETWEEN US THOUGH, OKAY?
DADDY...

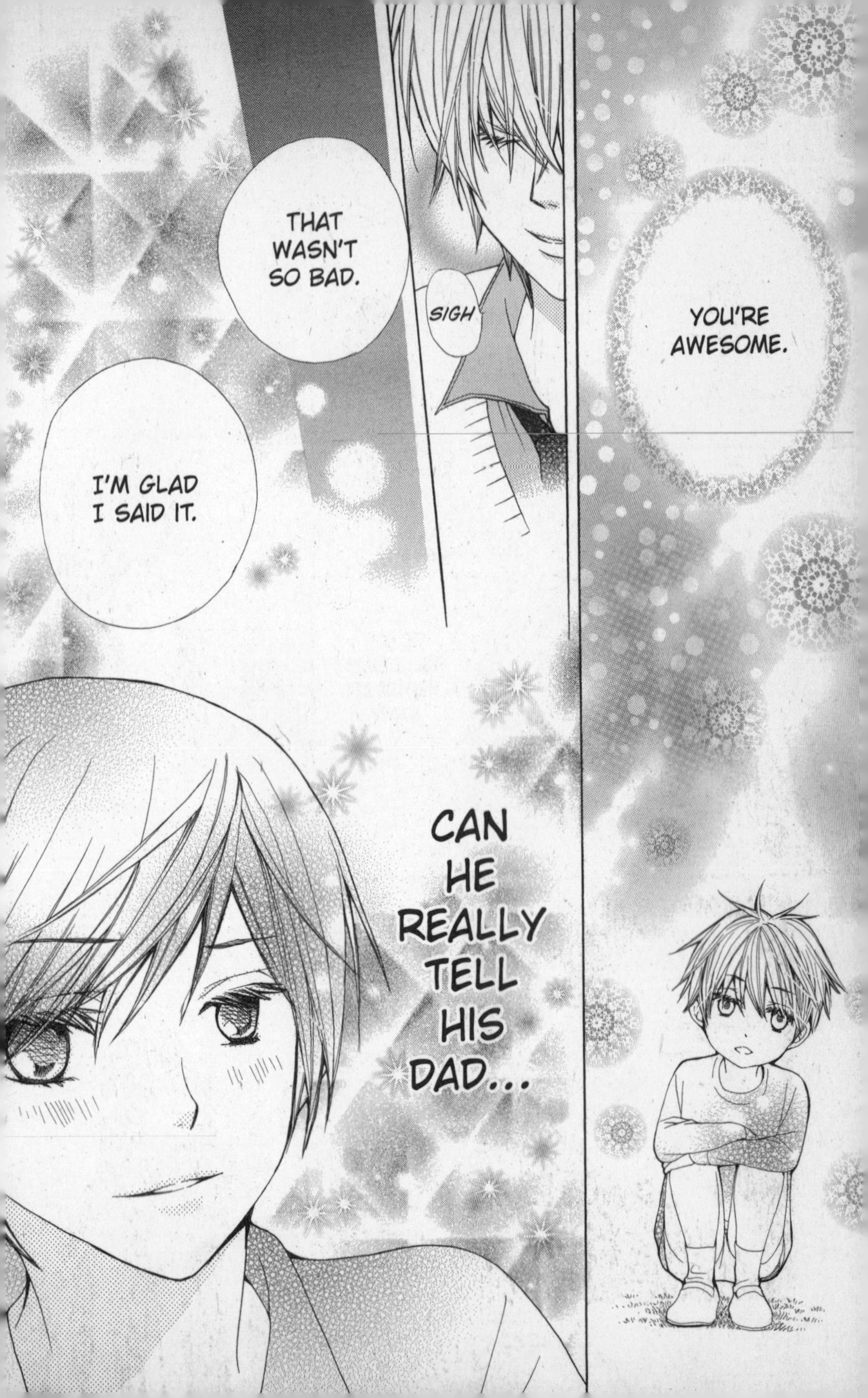
YOU'RE AWESOME.
SIGH
THAT WASN'T SO BAD.
I'M GLAD I SAID IT.
CAN HE REALLY TELL HIS DAD...

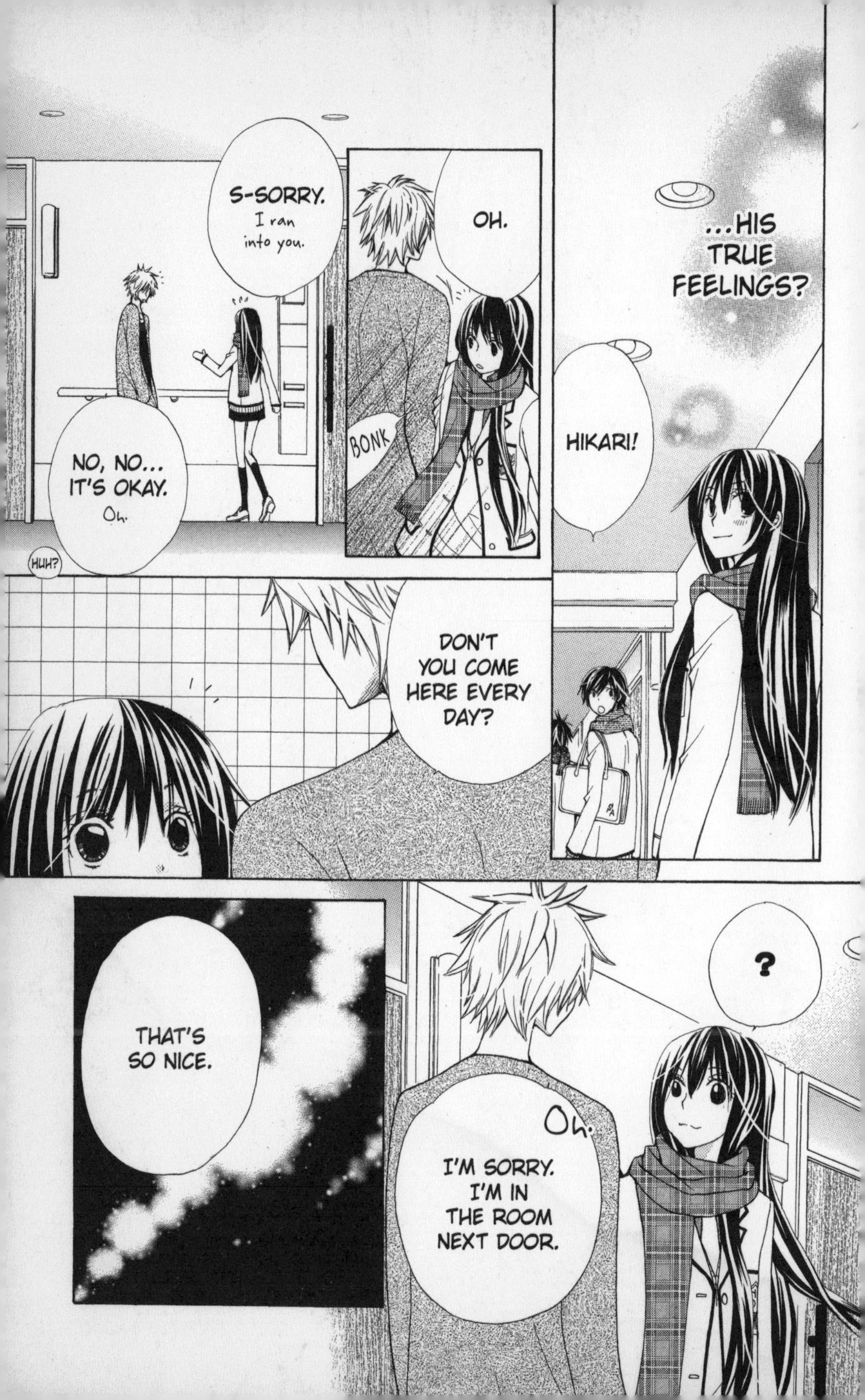
...HIS TRUE FEELINGS?
HIKARI!
OH.
BONK
S-SORRY. I ran into you.
NO, NO... IT'S OKAY. Oh.
HUH?
DON'T YOU COME HERE EVERY DAY?
?
Oh.
I'M SORRY. I'M IN THE ROOM NEXT DOOR.
THAT'S SO NICE.

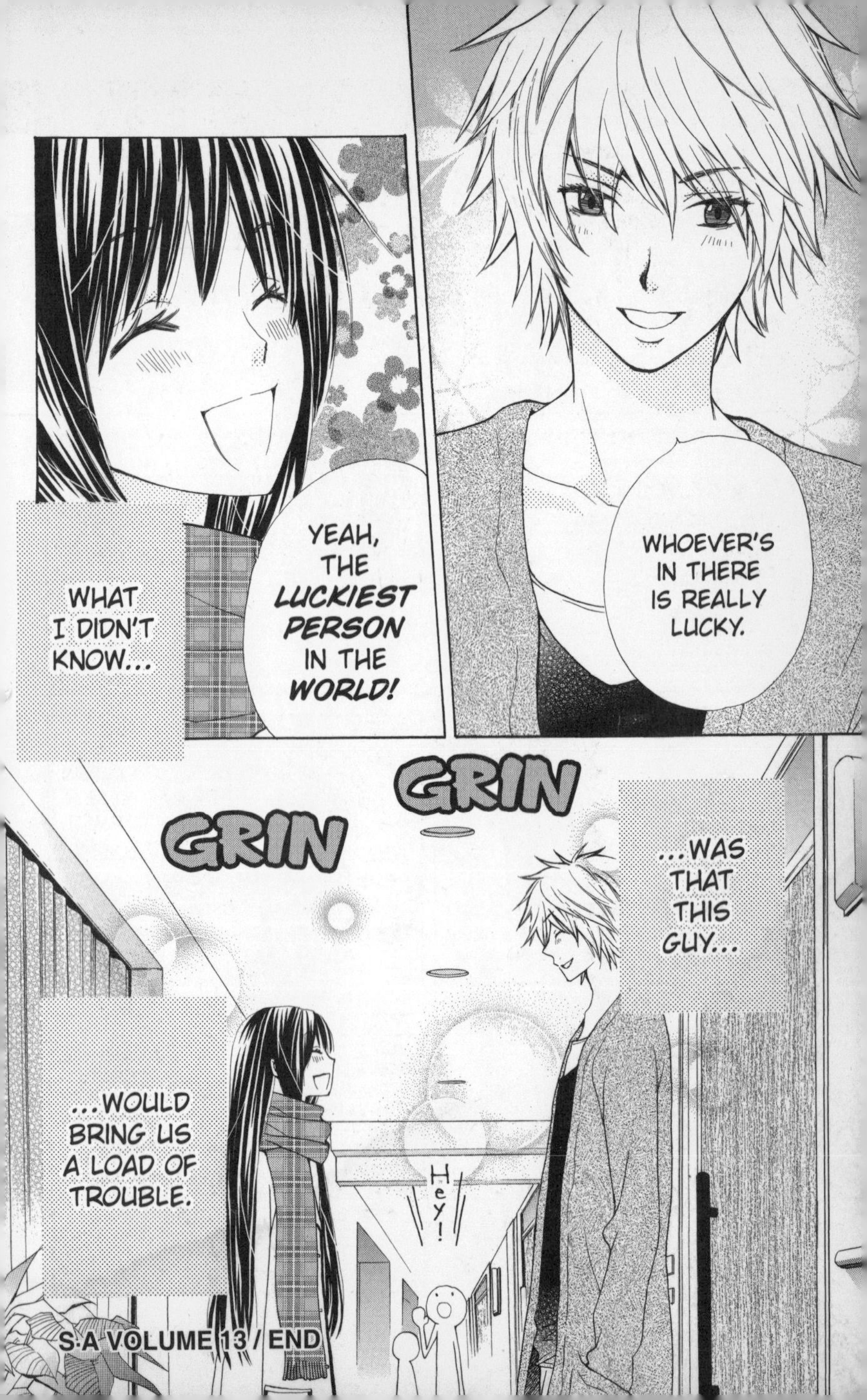
WHOEVER'S IN THERE IS REALLY LUCKY.
YEAH, THE LUCKIEST PERSON IN THE WORLD!
WHAT I DIDN'T KNOW...
GRIN
GRIN
...WAS THAT THIS GUY...
Hey!
...WOULD BRING US A LOAD OF TROUBLE.
S·A VOLUME 13 / END